UNIVERSITY
GLOUCESTERSHIRE

THE NEW
HIGHER EDUCATION

ISSUES AND DIRECTIONS
FOR THE
POST-DEARING UNIVERSITY

edited by

DAVID JARY & MARTIN PARKER

Staffordshire University Press

Published by
Staffordshire University Press
College Road, Stoke-on-Trent
Staffordshire ST4 2DE (UK)

First published 1998

ISBN 1 897898 34 7

Design, layout and setting
by Myrene L. McFee

Printed in Great Britain
by Staffordshire University Press

Preface

The chapters in this volume are revised versions of papers originally presented at 'The Dilemmas of Mass Higher Education' conference held at Staffordshire University, at Stoke-on-Trent in April 1996. The conference organised by David Jary and Martin Parker contained over sixty papers — including contributions from Anthony Giddens, George Ritzer, Ronald Barnett, David Robertson, Oliver Fulton, Philip Brown and Richard Scase, whose papers have in some cases been published elsewhere. The papers included as chapters in this volume have been selected as making a valuable contribution to the post-Dearing debate on the structure, role and funding of British Universities in the next century. That being said, it is important to note that the papers in their original form were delivered before the Dearing report was published, although often the authors have chosen to update their chapters to take more specific account of the issues raised by Dearing.

Acknowledgements

The editors wish to thank Sheena Bateman and Jean Wrench for their excellent administration and invaluable assistance in connection with the conference and in assembling the material for this volume; Sheelagh Rowbottom, Staffordshire University Thompson Library, for invaluable bibliographical assistance; Malcolm Henson for the preparation of the index.

They would also like to thank all those contributors to the conference whose papers and verbal contributions are not included directly in this volume but who contributed so much to what was a highly stimulating and enjoyable event.

Dedication

To Katie Richardson, born in the week of the conference, in the hope that the 'New Higher Education' will serve her and her peers as well as the old HE has served us.

Table of Contents

Notes on the Contributors

PATRICK AINLEY is a writer and researcher on education and training who has published widely in the generalist and specialist press on the basis of extensive experience of teaching and research at all levels in schools, further and higher education. As well as the studies of further and higher education referred to in his chapter, he is co-author of what is still the only history of 'The rise and fall of the Manpower Services Commission', published as *Training for the Future* by Cassell in 1990, and has also written on Youth Training, apprenticeship and learning generally.

ELAINE BALDWIN is a Lecturer in Sociology at the University of Salford. She trained as a social anthropologist at the University of Manchester and her teaching and research has maintained an ethnographic focus.

JIM BARRY is a political sociologist and teaches in Organisation Studies. He spent many years studying part-time (at North East London Polytechnic and Birkbeck College) while working as an administrator in London's local government. He joined the University of East London in 1987 and is currently Co-director of the University's Organisation Studies Research Group in the East London Business School. He is involved in two long-term research projects: one into gender and urban governance in London and Mumbai (formerly Bombay); another into gender and organisations with particular reference to higher education. He has published articles on gender and politics, gender and organisation and gender and Business ethics, is author of *The New Women's Movement and Local Politics* (1991) and co-editor with Heather Clark and John Chandler of *Organisation and Identities* (1994).

LOUISE BROADBENT is a research student associated with the Institute of Access Studies at Staffordshire University researching young person's patterns of educational and career decision-making in urban and rural areas.

JOHN CHANDLER is a sociologist who has worked in the Business School of the University of East London since 1978. His current research interests are gender and managerialism in Higher Education and in personal social service organisations. He is currently co-director of the Organisation Studies Research Group in the East London Business School. He is co-editor with Heather Clark and Jim Barry of *Organisations and Identities* (1994).

HEATHER CLARK is a sociologist who spent a number of years working in industry before entering education, where she taught a wide variety of courses. She currently teaches in Organisation Studies and is involved in a long-term research project into gender and organisations with particular reference to Higher Education. She previously co-ordinated Business Studies at Queen Mary and Westfield College and is currently Co-director of the University of East London's Organisation Studies Research Group in the East London Business School. She has published articles on gender and organisations, and gender and Business Ethics and is co-editor with Jim Barry and John Chandler of *Organisation and Identities* (1994).

PAMELA COTTERILL is Senior Lecturer in Sociology and Women's Studies in the School of Social Sciences at Staffordshire University. Her teaching and research interests are in the areas of social policy and social care, feminist epistemologies and methodologies and relationships between family women. She is the author of *Friendly Relations?: Mothers and their Daughters-in-Law*, and has published articles on feminist perspectives on sociological research, support relationships between family women and humour and social control.

STEPHEN COURT is a research officer at the Association of University Teachers, where his interests include the regional role of higher education, the employment of part-time staff, and the use of time by academic and related staff. He has presented papers at conferences run by the Society for Research into Higher Education, and the Organisation for Economic Co-operation and Development, and has had articles on higher education published by the *Higher Education Quarterly*, The *Times Higher Education Supplement* and *The Guardian*. An article by him on higher education in the South-West of England is to be published in *Higher Education Management*. He has also written a *Dictionary of Higher Education*, published in 1996 by the AUT.

JUDE COURTNEY works outside higher education and has a BA from Sussex University and an MA from Oxford University. She has three children with Martin Parker.

MARGARET EDWARDS has been a Lecturer in Sociology within the school of Social Science at Liverpool John Moores University since 1991. Her research interests include knowledge production within universities, the role of reflective practice within higher education and graduate skills and employability.

TIM EDWARDS is currently working on his PhD at Aston University in the Business School's Strategic Management Group. His MSc investigated training links between small and medium sized enterprises (SMEs) and universities. He is now investigating the management of technological alliances between universities and SMEs through the Teaching Company Scheme Programme.

DAVID ALAN GATLEY holds a joint teaching and research appointment in the Division of Sociology at Staffordshire University. His PhD was on Social Class and Higher Education and he has continued to research on higher education as well as historical demography. He was an associate author of *Ethnic Minorities and the Graduate Labour Market* (1990). He is currently associated with the newly established Institute for Access Studies at Staffordshire University.

SANDRA HARLEY is a Principal Lecturer in Sociology at De Montfort University, Leicester. She has written a book on the history of trade unionism in higher education. Her current area of interest is in the growth of managerialism in the public sector.

DAVID JARY is Professor of Sociology and Dean of the Graduate School at Staffordshire University. He is also associated with the newly founded Institute for Access Studies at Staffordshire University. He has long had research interests in the

Sociology of Higher Education and has published a number of articles in this area. His other interests include sociological theory and the sociology of sport and leisure. His published volumes include: *The Middle Class in Politics* (1978 with J. Garrard, et al.); *Sport, Leisure and Social Relations* (1988, with J. Horne and A. Tomlinson), *Giddens' Theory of Structuration: a Critical Appreciation* (1990, with C. Bryant); *Collins Dictionary of Sociology* (1991 and 1995 with J. Jary, Harper Collins); *The Sociology of Sports and Leisure* (1996 with J. Horne, M. Seino and B. Yamashita [in Japanese]); and *Anthony Giddens — Critical Assessments* (4 vols., Routledge 1997, with C. Bryant).

ANDREW LAWSON is Lecturer in American Studies and Cultural Studies at Staffordshire University. He has published articles on Anglo-American Modernism and Postmodernism and is currently writing a monograph on higher education and the public sphere.

FREDERIC S. LEE is a Reader in Economics at De Montfort University, Leicester. He has written books and articles on Post Keynesian economics and economics at Oxford University. His current areas of interest include the institutional history of 20th century economics.

SIMON LILLEY is Lecturer in management information and organisation at Keele University, where he is an active member of the Centre for Social Theory and Technology. His key research interests centre on post-structural responses to the supposed explosion in managerial information. He is not related to any former cabinet ministers.

LISA LUCAS is currently doing postgraduate research at Warwick University under the supervision of Professor Robert Burgess. She was previously Research Assistant, Oxford Centre for Staff Development, Oxford Brookes University, where she worked with Professor Graham Gibbs.

HENRY MILLER is a Lecturer in Sociology of Education in the Organisation Group of the Business School at Aston University. He has published on Professionalism and on The Management of Change in Universities and is currently researching changes in the management of universities in Australia, Canada and the United Kingdom.

JOHN O'NEILL currently Visiting Professor of Sociology at Staffordshire University, and is also Distinguished Research Professor of Sociology at York University, Toronto, and a Fellow of the Royal Society of Canada. He is the author of *Sociology as a Skin Trade* (1972); and *Five Bodies: The Human Shape of Modern Society* (1985). His more recent books are *The Communicative Body: Studies in Communicative Philosophy, Politics and Psychology* (1989); *Plato's Cave: Desire, Power and the Specular Functions of the Media* (1991); *Critical Conventions: Interpretation in the Literary Arts and Sciences* (1992); *The Missing Child in Liberal Theory* (1994); and *The Poverty of Postmodernism* (1995). He is Co-Editor of the International Quarterly, *Philosophy of the Social Sciences*. Currently, he is working on the political economy of child suffering, welfare state theory and civic practice.

MARTIN PARKER is Senior Lecturer in social and organisational theory at the University of Keele. Until 1995 he taught Sociology at Staffordshire University. His research and writing is on social theory, organisations, the sociology of culture and any other topics that interest him at the time. He has edited or co-edited three other books: *Postmodernism and Organisations* (1993), *Towards a New Theory of Organisations* (1994), *Ethics and Organisation* (1998) and is author of many journal articles. He has three children with Jude Courtney — Ben, Max, and Zoe who was the inspiration for the concluding chapter.

MIKE RUSTIN is Professor of Sociology and Dean of the faculty of Social Sciences at the University of East London. He is well-known for his writing on social theory and on contemporary politics and has previously written on higher education in *For a Pluralist Socialism* (Verso, 1985) and *A Degree of Choice: Post-School Education for All* (Penguin, 1986). His most recent article on higher education is 'Flexibility in Higher Education' in R. Burrows and B. Loader (eds) *Post-Fordism and the Welfare State* (Routledge, 1994).

PETER SCOTT has recently become Vice-Chancellor of Kingston University. Previously editor of the Times Higher Education Supplement and Professor of Education and Director of the Centre for Policy Studies in Education at the University of Leeds, he has written widely on higher education. His best known volumes are *The Crisis in the Universities* (1984) and *The Meanings of Mass Higher Education* (1995). He is also a member of the Board of the Further Education Agency.

TOM SELWYN is Professor of Social Anthropology at the University of North London. He convenes the post-graduate programme in the anthropology of tourism and directs a programme of work for the European Union on tourism and regional development in the Eastern Mediterranean.

CRIS SHORE is Lecturer in Social Anthropology at Goldsmiths College, University of London. He is author of several articles on higher education and anthropology. Recent publications include: with V. Goddard and J. Llobera, eds *The Anthropology of Europe* (Oxford: Berg, 1994); with A.S. Ahmed, eds *The Future of Anthropology: Its Relevance to the Contemporary World* (London: The Athlone Press, 1995); and with S. Wright, eds, *Anthropology of Policy: Critical Perspectives on Governance and Power* (London: Routledge, 1997).

GRAHAME THOMPSON is Senior Lecturer in Economics at the Open University. He is the managing editor of Economy and Society. With Paul Hirst he published *Globalisation in Question: The International Economy and Possibilities for Governance* (Polity Press) in 1996. In 1998 he will publish *Between Markets and Hierarchies: The History and Significance of Network Forms or Organization* (Oxford University Press).

PATRICIA WALTERS is a Senior Lecturer in Sociology at the University of Salford. Since the late 1970s her work has concentrated on employment, for instance in the British Civil Service (*Women and Top Jobs*, 1981) and comparatively between France and Britain (*French and British Mothers at Work*, 1993, with Shirley Dex).

RUTH WATERHOUSE is Senior Lecturer in Sociology and Women's Studies at Staffordshire University. Her teaching and research interests are in the areas of counselling, lesbian culture and sexuality. She has published articles on feminist counselling, lesbianism and women's humour. She has been involved in women's support groups in Stoke-on-Trent and worked as review co-editor for Lesbian, Gay, Socialist.

DAVID WATSON is Professor and Director of the University of Brighton. He was chair of the Higher Education Quality Council and served as a member of the Dearing Committee. He has written extensively on higher education issues and has a forthcoming book (with Richard Taylor) on *Lifelong Learning and the University*.

FRANK WEBSTER is Professor of Sociology, Oxford Brookes University. He is author of several books, including *The New Photography: Responsibility in Visual Communication* (Calder, 1980), *Information Technology: A Luddite Analysis*, with Kevin Robins (Ablex, New Jersey, 1986); *The Technical Fix: Education, Computers and Industry*, with Kevin Robins (Macmillan, 1989); *Theories of the Information Society* (Routledge, 1995); and *The Postmodern University? Contested Visions of Higher Education in Society*, edited with Anthony Smith (Open University Press, 1997).

I

INTRODUCTION

The New Higher Education — Dilemmas and Directions for the Post-Dearing University

David Jary and Martin Parker

From Robbins to Dearing — issues and dilemmas in the transition from elite to mass higher education

This introductory chapter begins by outlining the broad terrain of the 'new higher education', and follows this by introducing the nineteen contributions that follow. It seems fair to say that the changes in higher education that have taken place in the UK in the third of a century between the Robbins and Dearing Reports have been profound. They have resulted in a transition of UK higher education from an 'elite' to a 'mass' form which must be seen as irreversible. This transformation is part of a world-wide, vastly expanded 'social demand' for higher education. It seems to be what the users of higher education generally want. However, the actual institutional forms taken by the 'new higher education' have many critics as well as supporters, as this volume clearly illustrates.

As the editors of this volume — and contrary to elitist and culturally conservative critics of contemporary HE — our own view of the general shift from elite to mass forms of HE is that they should be welcomed as an important part of the continuation of a 'democratising' and 'emancipatory' project which began with the Enlightenment. We say this well aware of the assaults of 'postmodernism' on the 'project of modernity'. Plainly these assaults — which at times almost seem to undermine all basis for rationality — greatly complicate and inflect any case for 'democracy' and 'emancipation'. Yet we believe that a strong case can be still be made for higher education, as part of education in general. As the influential sociologist Jurgen Habermas suggests, it is through a democracy of access to knowledge institutions that the 'rational project' and the conditions for 'truth' can be continuously realised as a practice, and not merely an abstract ideal.

Contrary to both conservative critics and post-modernists, it is *not* the general goal of democratic access to knowledge and power which is most problematic. What has to be acknowledged, however, is that many of the transformations of UK HE that have *actually* taken place in UK HE in the last four decades *are* problematic — not least to many of the long-term denizens of higher education, its academic staff. Whether they be conservative or radical, modernist or post-modernist in disposition, many of the latter are dissatisfied, and currently manifest anxiety and low morale. Doubtless part of the reason is that this is the usual reaction of a 'producer group' whose own interests and previous life-style have been under threat. But this is not the only, or even the most important, reason. A significant further reason is that many of the changes actually occurring in HE are bound-up with a wider economic and cultural transformation of UK and world society, not least the 'marketisation' and more strident forms of 'managerialism' associated with the current phase of global capitalism. These are widely seen as having significant negative effects on HE or else are viewed ambivalently by many who would otherwise support the general principle of expansion of HE. Apart from this there also exist a number of more perennial dilemmas arising from the alternative forms which a genuinely democratic and functionally effective emancipatory mass HE might take.

What is plain — and the chapters in this volume reflect this — is that there exist many issues and dilemmas in the expansion of HE that have to be confronted critically and 'resolved' (see Figure 1.1) if the democratic and emancipatory potential of the 'new higher education' — which must include the widest possible sustainable economic and social impact — is to be fully realised.

1. Tradition *versus* Change
2. Quality *versus* Quantity
3. Excellence *versus* Equity
4. Exclusion *versus* Inclusion and Access
5. Research *versus* Teaching and Learning
6. Pure knowledge (and 'cultural capital') *versus* 'Performativity' (and 'human capital')
7. Professional control of the curriculum *versus* Student-led provision
8. 'Donnish dominion' *versus* Managerialism
9. Academic autonomy *versus* Accountability
10. Objectivity and Critical knowledge *versus* Relativism

Figure 1.1   Dilemmas of mass higher education[1]

Developmental models of higher educational change

The central issue in the realisation of a genuinely democratic and emancipatory expansion of HE is to identify what is *necessary* or inevitable and what is merely *contingent* in the present transformations of HE. Developmental models are unfashionable, but in our view the articulation of such models continues to possess a strong heuristic value in obtaining an analytical and critical 'fix' on social change. It would appear, for example, that some of those who ostensibly support an expansion of HE have not yet accepted what may be necessary changes in HE that must accompany this expansion: for example, that these changes seem bound to include some reduction in unit costs, which in turn will inevitably mean that some of the hallowed features of traditional forms of HE cannot be retained, even if it were desirable to do so. On the other hand, it seems equally apparent that a good deal of the drive to model the new HE 'managerially', in narrowly 'economistic' and 'consumerist' terms, may be better seen as other than essential, as perhaps simply 'contingent'. General developmental models can be helpful where they confront in the fullest possible general terms the alternatives and the dilemmas presented by the new HE.

UK higher education in global-historical developmental context

Seen in developmental terms, what is notable is that universities date back to mediaeval times. Like churches and states, they are among the longest surviving and the most adaptable of social organisations. Yet the longevity of universities as institutions might be explained by their adaptability. Despite some recent statements to the contrary (e.g. Hague, 1991), universities have rarely been dinosaurs.

However, in many countries, at least until recently, universities have displayed a greater willingness to embrace modernity and to adapt than in the UK. Writing in the 1960s and '70s two leading sociological exponents of the developmental modelling of mass HE, Martin Trow (1970) and Burton Clark (1983), referred to what they regarded as the 'exceptionalism' and 'backwardness' of HE in the UK compared with systems of HE elsewhere. The models of the development of 'mass' HE advanced by both Trow and Clark identify the crucial threshold of 'mass higher education' as having been crossed when the age participation rate in HE exceeds 15% of the relevant age group. 'Universal' mass higher education' is achieved when access to HE becomes a generally realisable aspiration. In these terms, the USA can be seen as having entered the era of 'mass' and then 'universal' higher education' in the 1950s and '60s. Other advanced nations that also achieved 'mass HE' in advance of the UK include Canada and Japan.

It is a *necessary* feature of mass HE systems according to both Clark and Trow that previous elite forms must change. It is generally characteristic of 'mass/universal' HE systems that they will tend to be associated with a far greater diversity of institutional mission, as well as with a more extended institutional hierarchy, than previously existed. Trow and Clark regard such diversity of mission and more extended hierarchy as 'functionally effective' for modern societies and as achieving the trick of maintaining a more expensive elite provision for the few, while also providing the expansion of cheaper mass provision and new kinds of course required by both the economy and an expanded 'social demand'. Compared with previous 'elite' forms of HE, both Trow and Clark present their model of mass/universal HE as one that can satisfy the requirement that it be both democratic and egalitarian. For them, the only achievable sense of these terms is that it can be an open 'meritocratic' system and allow the upward — as well as the downward — social mobility of both individuals and institutions.

In contrast with the requirements for such a system, the gradually expanding UK HE system, as it emerged after Robbins, attempted to retain too much of the earlier elite system (see Lawson's chapter for amplification of this point) and thus restricted its capacity to fully meet the new requirements of mass HE. It was not that post-Robbins HE provided *no* meritocractic access, but that this meritocractic access remained too narrow, and would remain so while UK HE clung on to its inappropriate elite form.

Recent changes in UK higher education

After years of being regarded as tardy and highly conservative by commentators such as Trow and Clark, the recent transition of the UK to mass HE — especially with the collapse of the 'binary' system and the adoption of modular courses — has been exceptionally rapid. Indeed, the rapidity of this transition may well have been a source of some of the particular problems — including academic staff unrest — experienced in the UK (Trow, 1993).

Trow and Clark must be regarded as among the most perceptive of sociological commentators on the transformations of HE. The generality and perceptiveness of their work stands in sharp contrast to the more parochial, abstractedly empiricist and narrowly policy-oriented character of much British academic study of HE. However, while their developmental model of HE provides a useful first bench mark from which begin to distinguish between what might be developmentally necessary — rather than merely contingent — there would appear to be a lot more going on in the transformation of HE than their general model allows.

Indeed, Trow himself accepts that a number of the specific problems of UK mass HE are problems *unnecessarily* created by particular policies: for example, over-zealous state-led drives to impose modish forms of managerialism and accountability rather than the use of 'softer' forms of the kind employed to better effect elsewhere. A more general reason why the Trow-Clark model of the expansion of HE must be seen as too simple is that it is obvious that some European HE systems — including the German and UK university systems — have succeeded, at least to some degree, in expanding their systems while avoiding some of the extremes of institutional differentiation and stratification associated with expansion elsewhere (see Teichler, 1988). The reluctance in the UK, for example, to give-up on an unitary notion of 'graduateness' — protected through the London external degree, the system of external examiners, the CNAA, and most recently in the work of the Quality Council (see Court's chapter) — may have placed some brake on expansion. From the perspective of his hierarchical and differentiated model of mass HE, Trow (1997) regards 'diversity' of provision and the end of a degree 'gold standard' as an issue not yet fully confronted by UK HE — even by Dearing — but one that must yet be faced. On the other hand, against Trow, a notional preservation of the gold standard — even if in part rhetorical — has been associated with a protection of the common currency in the educational credentials and experience available in non-elite institutions, which should perhaps not be discarded too lightly.

There are many other examples such as this where a careful appraisal of what should be retained and what should be changed must take place. The forms of debate and analysis required are represented in this volume, but let us also indicate some of the issues simply by listing the many changes that require consideration.

Increased 'social demand' for HE, expanded access, new kinds of students
- rapid expansion of student numbers (7% per annum over the period)
- increased 'access' to previously under-represented groups, including women, ethnic minorities, and mature students
- challenges to 'graduate' standards and a unitary conception of 'graduateness'

Changes in funding sources, new relationships with students and end-users
- general pressures on state expenditure — 'fiscal crisis in the tax state' (O'Connor, 1973)
- reduction of per capita student funding
- increased funding of higher education by student fees
- replacement of student grants by loans or graduate tax
- possible privatisation of some sectors of HE
- rising student-staff ratios, loss of 'intimacy' in staff-student relations
- increasing marketisation of the academy — the new 'service' academy

Organisational change, including new forms of audit, and accountability which reduce the autonomy of the academy
- change from 'collegial' self-governance to a more top-down managerial control (Becker and Kogan, 1982)
- increase in external and internal regulatory financial, 'quality' controls and accountability — the 'audit revolution' (Power, 1994; 1997)
- the deprofessionalisation of the academic

Changes in the curriculum and teaching, learning and assessment
- challenges to traditional academic disciplines and the spread of inter-disciplinarity

- modularization and semesterization — 'McDonaldization' of the curriculum (see Ritzer, 1993, 1996; Parker and Jary, 1995)
- emphasis on 'performativity' (Lyotard, 1984) and work-related knowledge
- new 'student centred' and IT-based approaches to teaching and learning
- the rise of coursework-based assessment along with 'grade domination' and 'grade inflation'

New forms of institutional competition and institutional stratification
- increasing inter-institutional competition and increasing hierarchisation of institutions — the advent of 'league tables'
- the sharpening of divisions between 'research' and 'mainly teaching' institutions

Changes in the individual 'economic' and 'cultural' returns from HE
- an inflationary spiral in qualificatory requirements — 'credentialism' or the 'diploma disease' (Dore, 1976; Berg, 1970)
- changing conceptions of graduate labour and a 'segmentation' of the graduate labour market, including graduate 'underemployment' and unemployment — the ending of a 'graduate elite'
- accentuation of the cultural advantage associated with elite forms 'cultural capital' — offsetting an emphasis on performativity (Bourdieu and Passeron, 1964; Brown and Scase, 1994)

Changes in the critical, cultural and research role of the universities compared with other institutions
- the consolidation of a 'knowledge' and a 'learning' society — the rise in importance of 'intellectual capital' and 'symbolic goods'
- increasing emphasis on market-orientation and wealth-creation in research at the expense of blue skies research or traditional intellectual scholarship
- changing balance of importance of universities compared with other knowledge-based and research organisations — the increasing importance of 'mode 2 knowledge' (Gibbons *et al.*, 1994) created in the context of application
- the 'multiplier effect' of universities on their regions and the increasing potential local and regional 'nodal' economic significance of the university (Castells, 1989, 1996)

Wider economic, social and intellectual changes associated with a globalising, information-based, and arguably 'post-modern' era
- the ending of the dominance of traditional epistemologies and 'grand narratives' (Lyotard, 1984)
- a new awareness of the implication of 'scientific' disciplines in the societal 'discourses' of 'power/knowledge' (Foucault, 1976), and a retreat from over-simplified conceptions of the academy as the site of 'objectivity'

- an 'implosion' of elite and mass forms of culture and the onset of a new cultural pluralism and an 'opening-up' as well as new closings of cultural discourse (including controversies over 'political correctness', feminism and the alleged 'closing of the American mind' — Bloom, 1987)
- the new global 'economy' of 'signs' and 'spaces' (Baudrillard, 1983) associated with a new 'post-Fordist' phase of capitalism and an expansion of consumer and cultural choice (Lash and Urry, 1987; 1994)
- 'reflexive modernity' and 'risk society' (Beck, 1992; Giddens, 1990, 1991) — increasing knowledge-based capacity for physical and social intervention, but new risks and uncertainties arising from this

Possible bases for a new compact between HE and society
- new 'non-foundationist', 'consensual' bases of truth and falsity and politics 'beyond objectivity or relativism' (Habermas, 1991; Bernstein, 1983; Barnett, 1990)
- 'utopian' possibility of reform of the labour market to reflect the increased availability of graduate labour (Teichler *et al.*, 1980)
- new openness and accountability in HE (Power, 1997) as the basis of a possible new compact between HE and civil society — a possible 'third way' in HE.

One model or alternative models of mass HE?

On the basis of the complexity of the issues above, our view of the transformations being undergone by UK HE is that many of the current formulations of the choices facing the system are vastly oversimplified. Undoubtedly there are dilemmas of mass HE systems of the kind indicated by Trow or by Clark that must be confronted As far as funding is concerned, there is probably no escape — certainly no immediate escape — from the formula that 'more students will mean less per student', at least for the majority of students.

However, as argued by Peter Scott (1995), no assumption can be made that any simple general model of mass/universal HE systems will apply trans-nationally. Historical and cultural differences between nations and the different timing of their transition to 'mass HE' might be expected to result in the *persistence* of markedly different patterns. Very importantly, it may also be that nations undergoing later transitions to mass HE have the opportunity to learn from, rather than simply follow, the pattern of other transitions. Although Trow and Clark regard their model of mass/universal HE as democratic and egalitarian as well as 'functionally effective' compared with previous elitist patterns, there may be other models of mass HE which can be realised that achieve these goals in different terms.

But just how different might these alternatives be? In what areas might functionally effective patterns of mass HE be forthcoming that might prove superior to those of the first wave? Notwithstanding the likelihood of variation, are there nevertheless functional limits to variation in HE systems within advanced societies? It is here that we come against the political and theoretical limits of this kind of structural analysis. The picture of the 'one best way' is one that downgrades the importance of a variety of agents and interest groups in formulating their own versions of desired futures. The role of books like this one is precisely to intervene, in a small way, in the constitution of the future. This is an issue that must be borne in mind when we consider the many different views expressed in this volume.

Beyond Dearing's analysis

We mentioned above that research on HE in Britain has tended, with some notable exceptions, to favour empiricism. In taking a wide-ranging, and generally humanist and progressive, view of the benefits of a further expansion of UK HE, the Dearing Report is to be very much commended. Unfortunately, given the magnitude of the issues raised by the new HE, for the most part the research commissioned by Dearing is still mainly narrowly 'empiricist'. It leaves most of Dearing's more expansive proposals inadequately grounded — not least with respect to the dilemmas and the alternatives facing UK HE. Since many of the more detailed proposals in the Report must be seen as a mish-mash of relatively mundane technical and administrative points, this means that a great deal is left for analysis if a compelling radical agenda for the new HE is to be created (see also Rustin's chapter). In these respects the totality of the Report and its appendices compares largely unfavourably with Robbins and with the far more penetrating Carnegie Reports on US HE carried out in the 1960s.

In contrast with Dearing, the chapters in this volume seek to explore tendencies in the new HE in more open-ended and critical ways, dealing with many issues facing HE that Dearing largely ignores. One important reason why they do so is that they reflect very directly, as Dearing on the whole does not, a practitioner's analysis of the 'new higher education'. As Trow (1997) has recently remarked, one especially crucial deficiency in the Dearing Report is that, because it largely fails to tap the staff view, it:

> ...simply does not know what is going on inside the colleges and universities while still pronounc[ing] ... about what should be happening. (Trow, 1997: 24)

For Trow , Dearing simply neglects the considerable authority over teaching and research which still inheres in the academic staff (1997: 24):

> If anything good is to happen in a university it must depend on the willing involvement or at least the assent of the teaching staff.

Thus, it can also be argued that an adequate analysis of change in HE and the creation of a new agenda must depend on taking fully into account the viewpoints of academic staff, though of course not uncritically. The chapters that follow show just how varied such viewpoints are.

The general context of HE change

The first of our chapters is not the least in living up to this billing of moving beyond Dearing. Noting but exposing the misplaced nostalgia associated with the 'intimacy' that has characterised UK HE, Peter Scott answers the question 'Do we have a mass higher education system?' with a resounding 'yes'. Both quantitatively, but more important qualitatively, the UK HE system has been 'profoundly transformed'. It is now a 'new' system. What diverts us from immediately accepting this is partly a nostalgic reluctance to embrace change, but also because this new system is *not* simply a replication of the American model. Where Scott's chapter excels is in providing an overview of the ways in which HE is changing and is likely to change further in response to the requirements arising from a shift from industrialism to post industrialism, 'post modernism' and 'Post-Fordism'. Seeing the new HE as a not insignificant element in the larger transformation of late-modern society, it is the reflexivity and flexibility of modern institutions and modern culture that Scott emphasises above all. 'Reflexivity' and flexibility are central to new methods of production and marketing, are a source of new knowledge-derived risks and uncertainties, and are manifest again in new requirements for organisational accountability, as well as in new reflexive forms of 'self identity' which are undermining the previous determination of 'life chances' by structural factors. Insisting that HE must respond fully to such tendencies and noting that the new HE is now a part of a wider 'entertainment-leisure-learning-heritage complex', Scott sees as essential the increasing access to the 'distributed university' using all forms of appropriate new technology.

The chapter by Tim Edwards and Henry Miller also provides a *general* location of UK HE. It complements Scott's in providing a comprehensive location of state-education relations within the UK in the broader context of global economic and political change, but emphasises the role of capitalist relations more fully. Three models of state-HE relations are identified by Edwards and Miller — regulative, compensatory and minimalist. Documenting the terms of the Thatcherite shift to a 'minimalist' economic ideology in the UK, they also note the marked change in language and discourse within HE which has accompanied this change. The complexity of 'old' and 'new' discourses that has resulted seems to provide grounds for a limited optimism. Although economic and managerialist rhetorics may have of late been in the ascendancy, the tensions between different discourses remain — for example within conceptions of life-long learning — and offer some hope for a different future.

Diversity and stratification in UK higher education

While the broad parameters of change are usefully documented by Scott's and Edwards and Miller's chapters, they deal relatively little with the implication of HE change for institutional hierarchy. The next of our chapters, by David Watson, deals precisely with this issue, mapping the changing institutional spectrum of UK HE and posing with great clarity a number a of key general questions that arise. Although he makes only oblique reference to general models, Watson's concern is with what we have argued is a central to the Clark-Trow model of mass HE, the issue of diversity of mission. Or, to put it another way, the question of how much institutional stratification is appropriate. In Clark-Trow terms, the issue is what is necessary if *both* the needs for minority elite provision and expanded access are to be adequately met.

The method by which such general issues are explored by Watson is to identify the existing identifiable 'reputational range' within the post-binary UK system and ask, how much can and should be retained? Watson is critical of those — Trow included — who underestimate the adaptability and flexibility of HE. There are differences of mission and function between 'ancient' and 'modern' universities but his argument is that the adaptability and expansion of the system that has been achieved by this means has not been at the expense of the maintenance of both the epistemological and the applied 'essence' of a truly higher education. In the UK this essence has been preserved by the operation of a unique system wide peer-review based means of standard setting. Watson notes the high levels of student satisfaction within UK HE. A virtue of Watson's chapter is that it offers both a way between the nostalgic and over-romanticised defence of 'traditional' forms of HE on the one hand, and a case for a new polarisation of 'elite' and 'mass' forms of HE as required by Clark and Trow on the other.

David Watson was in fact a member of the Dearing Committee. He has asked it to be made clear that the chapter represents his viewpoint *prior to* his appointment and participation in the work of the Committee. Nevertheless it is possible to see his influence in some, at the least, of Dearing's proposals. Watson's assumption, and that of Dearing, would also seem to be that the main barrier to the maintenance of a common essence is funding. Sufficient funding would enable a responsive and modernising HE, but within a controlled 'reputational range' rather than simply following the competitive free-for-all characteristic of US HE.

Chapter 5, by Jary, Gatley and Broadbent on the lessons of US Community Colleges, can be viewed as a pointed footnote to both Watson's chapter and to the aspirations of Dearing. It is also intended as a response to the Clark-Trow thesis more generally. Though the USA is often seen as image of the future, 'Americanisation' is a potent force and not an overwhelming one. Undoubtedly US mass HE provides one possible model of HE expansion. The rhetoric at times associated with US Community Colleges — not unlike some of the rhetoric surrounding the Dearing Report and the new Labour government's vision for further and higher education — is access, democracy and open opportunity. Whether the rhetoric was supportive or cynical, the reality of community colleges is somewhat different from the rhetoric and provides a timely warning to those who might buy into higher education expansion while failing to think through the many structural barriers to openness of opportunity and outcome. Community colleges have been much researched by educationalists and social scientists — far more so than our own HE changes. What this research shows is that the dilemmas of mass HE as exhibited by US Community Colleges are stark. These institutions are more often associated with increasing institutional and class *polarisation* than the reverse. A consideration of US community colleges underlines the importance of Watson's attempt to restrict 'reputational range' within UK HE.

A different angle on the issue of diversity is provided in the chapter by Lisa Lucas and Frank Webster, who examine the vexed issue of changing standards over time: an issue which also has serious implications for comparisons between institutions. Lucas and Webster suggest that it is the rise of coursework that explains the 'grade inflation' — the upward drift in the percentage of upper second degrees that is visible across the UK system — despite the expansion of student numbers. This is an issue that is now regularly remarked on in the UK media in the context of both GCSE and A level grades. The authors examine these apparent changes in marking standards over time by undertaking an empirical test, a remarking of archived earlier student work by modern examiners. However, their evidence suggests that standards have not dramatically changed. For Lucas and Webster it is vital that we continue to seek such empirical evidence in relation to all such issues of 'standards'. Not to do so will 'result in the promotion of crude reputational models of higher education which wholly favour the elite and the advantaged'. They also support a continuation of the external examiner system as an important protection of the reputation of the credentials of institutions outside the elite sphere.

The tendency to institutional hierarchy at work in the UK HE system as part of the pressures to intensifying competition is also seen in Stephen Court's chapter. Court explores the implications of various attempts at surveillance over the last ten years, including the research assessment exercise (RAE) and the Teaching Quality Audit (TQA). As Research Officer at the Association of University Teachers, he can attest to the importance of this 'audit explosion' on structuring the personal, organisational and sectoral responses to change in UK HE. After providing a history of the concept of a 'gold standard' of output, he goes on to show just how the new measures can be used to illustrate diversity, not unity. Indeed, a comparison of RAE and TQA scores, together with some other measures, very neatly illustrates the strength of the threat to reputational range. As Court's figures show, the 100 or so UK degree awarding bodies are broadly divisible into five strata — from elite old university to Higher Education College — which stretch the very meaning of 'Higher Education' to its limit. In terms of RAE scores, research income, TQA scores, and staff-student ratios there is a clear hierarchy evident. Any notion of a common standard of comparability must therefore be treated with great caution. As he concludes, there may be several standards, and there is little evidence of convergence.

Chapter 8, by Patrick Ainley, is one of the most hard hitting of those in this book concerned with the stratification of HE. He begins by recalling the previous reports with which Dearing was associated — Dearing I, II and III on the national curriculum, and on 16–19 qualifications. Ainley accepts the reality of the new HE, but *not* the rhetoric surrounding it in reports such as Dearing's. His conception of the new HE is as "a more differentiated Further and Higher Continuing Education (F&HCE) system". Whereas F&HCE posits the possibility of the "professional-isation' of occupations, in reality it is associated with the reverse process, "the proletarianisation of the professions". As well as describing the future occupations of students, proletarianisation is also affecting the current roles of teachers in HE. Ainley illustrates this latter point in his reports on a series of interviews with academic staff at both a pre-1992 and a post-1992 university. He identifies among these lecturers two ideal-typical categories of response to the new HE — 'hard' and 'soft'. The first response is typical of Oxbridge educated humanities and social science lecturers. The second corresponds to the 'original notion of polytechnic education'. Ainley finds neither the hard or the soft response satisfactory. Indeed, he suggests that:

> In order to recover and go beyond polytechnicism towards a new polyconceptualism that combines the best of both institutional positions, the ideal typical polarities of 'hard' and 'soft' self-conceptions among academic staff and students will have to be overcome.

Beyond the academy, one of the major wider problems seen by Ainley to be arising from the new F&HCE is the ever worsening situation of a new class with no qualifications, combined with the general insecurities of flexible labour markets even for those with credentials. Dearing I and II are accused in practice of seeking to resuscitate old divisions under the rhetorical guise of a new diversity.

> To contribute to a real learning society, rather than to what in reality is as yet only a *certified* one, [...] teachers at all levels of the new system of F&HCE must abandon the defensive ideology of professionalism and transcend the polarised reactions to reform illustrated in the interviews with HE teachers.

As a critique, Ainley's chapter is something of *tour de force*. But in pointing the way forward his chapter is less satisfactory. For him, the hope for HE lies in the frustration of students and the multiple discontents of staff. However, Ainley's proposed resolution is far from fully worked out. He says little, for example, of the way in which a less-divided, more comprehensive HE system might be brought about or the problems that such a system might engender. But then accepting a broadly neo-Marxist diagnosis of capitalism, and the various forms of labour that it requires, might leave us with little faith in grand policy solutions.

Organisational change in the new higher education

The following six chapters illustrate that an analysis of recent changes in UK HE must also be an institutional and an organisational one. That is to say that local problems must be given as much consideration as the wider observations characteristic of the previous chapters. Some of these papers may also help to counter the assumption that the massification of HE necessarily follows a developmental path. In other words, there may be alternatives.

Tom Selwyn and Cris Shore's 'Marketisation of Higher Education' places the 'neo-liberal cultural revolution' of the last few years in its organisational context by illustrating how contemporary management language is used in practice. They describe their chapter as an essay in political anthropology, and many of its observations about the way in which HE is being re-imagined are both entertaining and frightening. Formulations of 'performance', 'learning compact', 'communication', 'quality' and so on, provide a deceptively firm foundation for much HE management practice. However, as Shore and Selwyn show — applying Foucault — by attending to the discursive implications of the terms their practical application contains many paradoxes, and can eventually lead to a triumph of form over content. The 'culture of compliance and conformist consumerism' that they describe may not be universal, but its 'newspeak' is difficult to resist. Language, after all, is one of the most potent instruments of change and control.

Chapter 10, by Simon Lilley, continues this theme with a personal account of teaching on a massified scale. The term 'McDonaldisation' has entered the academic and popular vocabulary as a way of describing the Weberian 'iron cage' of rationalisation in which means become more important than ends. Teaching very large numbers of students, with texts and their attached teaching packs, can be a very alienating experience — one in which Selwyn and Shore's 'form' comes to inhabit the very body of the lecturer. Lilley describes such an experience in a way that recognises the benefits that 'bite sized' modules and programmed teaching have for students, whilst also attempting to re-frame the consequent encounter between staff and student as a form of 'kitsch'. The routinisation of the teaching and learning experience is one that can easily be responded to with an elitist disdain on the part of the lecturer. Yet, this does not mean that a romantic and nostalgic return to a more liberal age is possible, or indeed that the viewpoint of the lecturer is somehow more enlightened than that of the student as consumer. Both are effectively enrolled in the McDonaldising process. Whether managerialist kitsch can, or should, be resisted is hence a debateable point. Clearly, Lilley is unhappy with the situation, but he also acknowledges that his critique is located within another set of taken-for-granted assumptions. Academic resistance is not a simple matter, and we need to be clear what is being resisted and what other interests such resistance might serve.

The following chapter, 'Economics Divided' by Frederic Lee and Sandra Harley, illustrates some of the consequences of McDonaldised audit systems on research and publication patterns. Lee and Harley begin with a brief account of the RAE which amplifies some of the points made in Court's chapter in the previous section. Notions of research selectivity are certainly complicit in extending reputational range of institutions but, as this chapter neatly shows, such notions can also function to narrow what counts as 'proper science' within particular disciplines. Using the example of economics, the chapter shows how decisions about recruitment, peer assessment and journal reputation tended to marginalise non-mainstream publications. The financial and organisational pressures consequent on the RAE solidified a particular core for economics — one that simply reflected the views of those who were already in a position to decide what counted within the discipline. Harley and Lee describe this as a gradual 'cleansing process', one in which a dominant hegemony was provided with the tools to further silence opposition. Whilst, in principle, it might be possible to democratise the RAE system in order to allow for dissident voices to be heard, it does seem that managerialist audit procedures are always likely to produce these convergence effects. If careers and institutional funding depend on attending to some kind of surveillance system, then academics will tend to orient their practices to these ends.

The following two chapters address the managerialisation of UK HE from more inter-personal perspectives, particularly the complicity of certain conceptions of masculinity and management. In Chapter 12, Clark, Chandler and Barry address the costs and benefits of managerialism with reference to the role of women in higher education. As with most areas of economic life, women are under-represented in HE, particularly at higher levels. Managerialist control systems might result in organisational strategies that are less discriminatory because of their reliance on formal policies. However, as Clark et al. argue, their emergence in the UK was very much tied to a right wing marketising agenda. The legitimisation of an aggressively masculine form of management hence downplayed ways of working which were often favoured by women. Whilst this is no reason to be hostile to management per se, it does suggest that the particular configurations of managerialism we find in UK HE are still patriarchal in their practical operation. Clark, Chandler and Barry then go on to discuss the possibilities for resistance, whether individual or collective, and suggest that it is unlikely that a simple pattern will emerge. Different patterns are going to be found in old and new universities, and will depend on the role of men as will as the collectivism of women. As in Lilley's chapter, this becomes a question of who is resisting what, and why. Hence the question posed for academic managers in the title, is it better to be loved or feared? Or, is there another way of managing that might be more sensitive to issues of gender and power?

Issues of power, gender and management also form the subtext of Chapter 13 — 'Speaking confidentially or how long have I got?'. In this chapter Pamela Cotterill and Ruth Waterhouse discuss the role of the personal tutorial system within mass HE. 'Modularisation' and 'semesterisation' are strategies that have increasingly commodified the student experience as their contact with teaching staff has become more fleeting and limited. Added to that, the various pressures on academics to perform in terms of research and administration can lead to downplaying contact with students. More must be done with less, and the development of meaningful relationships with undergraduate students is simply disappearing. As Cotterill and Waterhouse note, this is sadly ironic when much of the language of access and opportunity is regularly used to legitimate HE expansion. Supporting non-standard students through their degrees is being replaced with warm rhetoric about learning communities and technologically assisted student empowerment. Yet, in practice, this can often result in no more than the insistence that students should no longer bother their lecturers, since they are too busy doing other things to deal with the detail of student problems. Even those matters that do get dealt with are increasingly bureaucratised as they enter the sphere of rational management. Spending time time on relationships becomes a matter that no longer make any sense for the career academic. As so many of the other chapters show, the power of the new HE is that it makes alternative, and perhaps older, practices, effectively unthinkable. Mass HE and personal relationships become antithetical, when perhaps 'education for life' should suggest that we struggle to make them complementary.

The final chapter in this section, by Patricia Walters and Elaine Baldwin, considers another neglected topic in studies of HE — the coping strategies of students faced with mounting debts. The 'more for less' mentioned by Cotterill and Waterhouse also impacts on students as less money available to fund their studies. Student loans, and the recent introduction of contributions for tuition fees, mean that virtually all students face mounting debts during the course of their degrees. However, the management of these debts is a complex matter. Some students will work — often for very low pay — during their studies; others will receive generous parental contributions or family gifts. Walters and Baldwin suggest that these strategies need to be seen as elements of family reproduction strategies and hence as very much related to issues of class, age and gender. Discovering how money moves around in the family economy should be regarded as an anthropological matter since it involves definitions of identity, of what counts as kinship reciprocity or economic exchange. Students are not simple economic ciphers, but agents in a series of complex transactions that involve a variety of others at different times and in different ways. Understanding how students might be better served by the new HE thus involves attending to local cultural values as much as it does to the more general issues of funding that are important at the organisational and sectoral level.

Higher education: a new compact

The chapters in this final section all share an interest in re-framing the dilemmas of mass HE in more general ways. Drawing on a variety of social theoretical perspectives, the authors investigate the broad issues that have shaped contemporary UK HE and suggest some alternative outlines for its future.

The section begins with Margaret Edward's 'Commodification and Control in Mass Higher Education', a chapter which considers the role of knowledge in late capitalist economies. Postmodern and postindustrial formulations of the knowledge economy suggest that the legitimation of knowledge production and generation is increasingly, as J-F Lyotard puts it, 'performative'. That is to say that information becomes commodified and knowledge something that can be bought and sold for economic gain. Universities are merely one of the players in this new game, and they can no longer rely on any assumed centrality to the process. When the student becomes a consumer, then modularised and market sensitive degree programmes have utility only insofar as they are effective. If they recruit, if graduates get jobs, then universities are performing. There are no other criteria suggested within this logic. However, Edwards resists the suggestion that this kind of description exhausts what can be said about HE change. Instead she describes a complex history of four interest groups — the 'quadrilateral' of the academic community, the state, the market, and society at large (see also Clark, 1983 and Premfors, 1978). Using Foucault and Gramsci, she concludes by suggesting that the 'regime of truth' which constitutes contemporary HE is a *contested* one. Resistance to, or re-articulation of, the consumerist model is actual and possible, as many of the chapters in this book suggest, but further sponsoring it requires that academics recognise the often conservative role they have played in the past. The new HE cannot afford to ignore either the role of the market or the importance of performativity within late capitalist society, but it can attempt to re-articulate its pedagogy and curriculum in ways that encourage more radical forms of reflexivity amongst the consumers of its knowledges.

Chapter 16, by Andrew Lawson, takes a similarly broad approach which also begins with reference to Lyotard. In historical terms Lawson argues that UK HE is in the latest phase of a long running dispute between cultural and utilitarian legitimations for education. Importantly however, this is a dispute which can never be settled, which relies for its energy on the existence of two irreconcilable language games. Its earliest manifestation as Oxbridge versus London, and the mutations of this dichotomy through the creation of redbrick, plateglass and polytechnics, all reflect the endurance of very different assumptions about why universities exist at all. Whether they transmit knowledge, the best that has been thought and said, or educate for various forms of profession and commerce is not a new problem. This anti-industrial bias amongst the elite is a curiously English phenomenon, but it begins to explain why academics are often the most conservative when HE change is discussed. As Lawson neatly shows, even the Robbins report dealt with the dispute, which has clear social class connotations, by enshrining elite cultural justifications at its centre. That Thatcherism then returned as a 'militant utilitarianism', which turned the HE sector into the battleground we currently inhabit, should hardly be surprising. As in the previous chapter, Lawson does conclude with a limited optimism. He suggests that the university could form part of a new public sphere, one in which a 'critical citizenship' is encouraged. However, to solve the dispute in this way also requires that we interrogate the dissensus in words like 'democracy' with more rigour than we usually do at present. The radicalisation of the university would then not be mere empty rhetoric, but a form of institution which practises what it has so often preached.

The following chapter, by Grahame Thompson, offers a sustained indictment of the mass mediocrity of mass HE. The commercialisation and managerialisation of HE teaching and research have been remarked on in previous chapters, but Thompson's chapter suggests that the outcome of these processes is to produce a 'kakistocracy' — a form of government by the least able. Creative and critical intellectuals are increasingly replaced by bureaucrats who are too busy administering the means to concentrate on ends. In other words, 'higher' is not necessarily 'better'. Responses to this increasing mediocrity might be simple despair, or attempts to expose the ideas that underpin such changes; but Thompson suggests these are largely defensive reactions, and that we would do better to focus instead on two other responses which are more 'positive' — a nostalgic concern with emancipation, and/or an attempt to use 'philosophical realist' arguments to assert that critical thinking should be taught within universities. In order to develop these positions, Thompson develops an economic argument that university education should be seen as a consumer-good and not a producer-good. Its value lies in what it does for people, not economies, states and corporations. Yet, this does not necessarily mean that HE should be treated in the same way as other consumer goods because its value is in producing citizens who can be fully engaged with the public domain. The humanities and social sciences are therefore strongly defensible as ways to encourage the 'plurality of voices' which are needed in a democratic pluralist society. Against the kakistocracy, Thompson promotes an 'intellectual elitism'. This is an 'offensive' argument, one that attempts to reverse the drive to mediocrity, but an argument that needs careful articulation in order that it does not become a justification for any form of 'social elitism'. Whether intellectual and social elitism are separable depends largely on whether the Dearing reforms increase the drive to bureaucratisation, or begin a more general debate around the ends of university education.

Chapter 18, John O'Neill's 'Civic Capital', is also engaged with notions of the public sphere and modes of governmentality. Using Theodore Schultz's formulation of 'human capital' in rather a subversive way, he proposes that this provides an important argument against the conception that HE should be only or primarily concerned with the effective generation of material capital for particular nation states. O'Neill's argument is one that depends on weakening the ties between corporations and the state, on insisting that educational institutions are not merely outsourced 'labour camps' for the economy. This does involve recognising the different interests of various parties in the formation of civic capital, but it is not a simple contradiction. As O'Neill puts it, "an uneducated economy will not absorb educated labour", but the reverse is also true — that a knowledge economy requires educated workers. Late capitalism and the civic society are in tension, but they also need each other. So, a 'civic covenant' is needed for both principled and economic reasons. Yet, echoing Thompson, O'Neill argues that this does not mean 'massification'. It must instead mean open access to all citizens who feel they might benefit from HE in order to prevent the waste, on a massive scale, of human potential. This form of life-long learning is underpinned by a largely spiritual sense of the 'civic mind' as being that which allows us to make some sense of all our other projects. Enabling access while at the same time defending education against the colonisation of economic interests is the most important task facing modern HE.

Michael Rustin's chapter is an especially forceful plea for a new radicalism in thinking about HE. In many ways taking up the baton from John O'Neill and others in the volume, his chapter focuses on what he terms the 'perverse modernisation' of British Universities, placing Dearing squarely in this context. Rustin locates much of the recent transformation of UK HE firmly in the context of Thatcherism and its overall drive to control the public sector, including primary and secondary education, health provision, the social services and the BBC. The polytechnics/new universities sector was used as a university-wide lever to drive down unit costs in HE as a whole. A populist Thatcherism found a ready target in a 'self-serving' professionalism in public institutions, and continues today as an often ideologically driven external audit — a 'posthumous Thatcherism'. In principle, Rustin sees much to be said for the enhanced 'customer voice' that the new accountability claims to offer. In practice, however, the outcome of accountability has often been to visibility denigrate and to stratify. In this overall context, Rustin sees Dearing as explicitly devised as a vehicle for reconciling the competing demands on public funds. But like others in this volume he is unconvinced that the 'softly, softly' approach of Dearing will provide sufficient defence for the unique qualities of UK HE. If Dearing is the only vision, then:

> ... equality of aspiration will be abandoned in the ostensible name of more opportunity, and not less. What will be constructed is a system

which ostensibly offers more consumer choice, higher standards ('guaranteed' by audit), and greater flexibility. It will however be more competitive, provide less support, have higher rates of failure, and become more steeply stratified. It will become more of a mirror of the market society.

Rustin concludes that the "approach of Dearing is unlikely to be enough to defend the university system we still have, let alone the one we might like to have".

An 'heretical postscript' to the main chapters

The final chapter, by Martin Parker and Jude Courtney, attempts to think against many of the arguments put forward in the bulk of the book. In a way, this chapter is intended to make readers — particularly if they have something invested in HE — examine some of their core assumptions about what universities are for in the first place. The Dearing report certainly didn't attempt to do this. Rather it took it as given that HE has certain benefits for individuals, nations, economies and so on. Yet many of these assumptions are untested: they form a kind of backdrop which is all too rarely questioned. So, what happens if we try to think 'heretically' in this context?

The argument of the chapter essentially proceeds from the assumption that, in late modern Welfare democracies, there will never be enough tax revenue to go around. In education, this means that various sectors — nursery, infants school, secondary school, sixth form, further education, adult education and, of course, higher education will inevitably be fighting over limited resources. What claim should HE have over this money? And how do its claims compare with those of other sectors — particularly those of nurseries? In a way that proceeds through the suspicion of various academic sacred cows, Parker and Courtney conclude by suggesting that tax revenue is perhaps better spent on providing good nursery education for all three and four year olds than on expanding an HE sector which is of questionable merit and efficacy. This certainly an argument with which few of the authors above, however critical, are likely to agree. However, if the case for mass HE is to be won, then it is an argument that must be acknowledged. Universities can no longer assume legitimacy, they have to earn it, and for Parker and Courtney, they sometimes seem to currently be doing little more than expanding for expansions sake.

A way forward for higher education

Concentrating on the tendencies of global capitalism, commodification, loss of HE autonomy, on the one hand, or on the more pessimistic, ironic, fragmentary tendencies of deconstruction and postmodernism on the other, it is easy at times to despair at the future of HE. In providing a way forward, the model of competing interests that figures especially in Margaret Edward's chapter is perhaps the most important of the general models of HE provided in this book, since it points both to the nature of the forces and the positive possible outcome of a working-out of competing interests in the contest over the future of HE. There can be optimism, not least because historically HE, and education in general, has usually found ways of adapting, responding to new elements of social demand, creating benefits for new groups. However, it will only do so in the future if debates about it continue to be open to all voices and if access to new groups and to non-degraded forms of HE is retained. In one important respect, Dearing was exactly right: what *is* needed now in HE is a new compact. But it is a wider compact than Dearing envisages that should be sought — replacing both the previous 'traditional' and the current narrowly based managerial and state driven compact — a compact that will mobilise academic staff as a whole, and engage more fully with the diverse external constituencies of HE, as well as with the state. As Michael Rustin suggests in his chapter:

> If the system is to become more universalist in its scope, then the advocates of a more democratic university system need to become bolder and more visionary about it. If fragmentation and stratification through market forces is to be avoided, then greater emphasis has to be placed on 'voice', on finding ways in which the various stakeholders in universities can make themselves heard.

This must mean, as Parker and Courtney insist, that universities do not merely *assume* their place in the sun. In terms of the 'quadrilateral of interests' in HE seen earlier (summarised in **Figure 1.2** opposite), hitherto the pressures to transform HE have mainly arisen from the triadic constellation: state—economy—academic oligarchy. What must come more into play is the wider range of interests that would be forthcoming from a fuller representation of the public sphere and a wider response to the 'social demand' for HE. As Rustin again suggests:

> Only if universities can demonstrate a commitment to being open, accountable and democratic institutions in the public domain, with a variety of forms of partnership with other institutions, will they succeed in making the claims on resources on the scale that they need. Holding actions are not enough. A democratic and universalist public sector will only survive in Britain if it finds some radical advocates who have not been cowed by the supposedly 'modernising', but actually marketising, revolution of the past two decades.

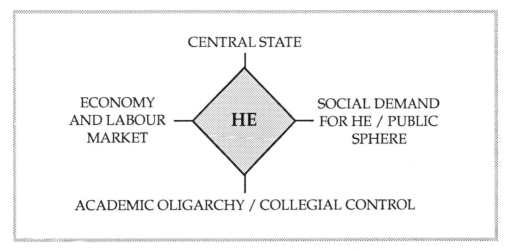

CENTRAL STATE

ECONOMY
AND LABOUR — HE — SOCIAL DEMAND
MARKET   FOR HE / PUBLIC
                                SPHERE

ACADEMIC OLIGARCHY / COLLEGIAL CONTROL

Figure 1.2   Quadrilateral of interests in higher education

Resolving the dilemmas?

The expansion of HE has been a necessary and entirely appropriate response to an increased 'social demand' for education of all kinds. As Scott suggests, we must accept that we do now have a 'mass' HE system. But can the 'new HE' still be seen as possessing an 'emancipatory potential'? Although we cannot presume to speak for all our contributors, we have already suggested that answer can be 'Yes". However, to achieve this — and to carry academic staff along with the change — rather than the terms of the sharp polarities shown in Figure 1.1 or Clark-Trow's 'elite-mass' resolution of the dilemmas, something different is required. Following from our contributors, an appropriate 'rhetoric', we suggest, may be that the pursuit of a resolution of the dilemmas should be couched in terms of seeking a 'third way'. Certainly this would seem to be what is required in relation to dilemmas 1-9 (Figure 1.1). Dilemma 10 may seem a different matter, but even here a 'third way' may be the way forward — rather than objectivity or relativism, a non-traditional 'discursive/dialogic' approach to the 'truth' is required which reflects the multiplicity of perspectives under apparently 'post-modern' conditions. As Anthony Giddens opined at the Staffordshire Conference, given their longevity and the competition from other institutions, there *is* a real danger that universities will become 'zombie institutions' — alive on the surface but decaying within. 'Reflexivity' and flexibility — as well-expressed by Scott — must be central in the new HE if its emancipatory role is to continue as we believe it can if the right steps are taken.

Note

[1] While most of the terms in this table are self-explanatory, the terms 'performativity' and 'donnish dominion' are less so. 'Performativity' is Lyotard's (1984) term for the increased emphasis on practical and vocational knowledge, and the situated source, of such knowledge; 'donnish dominion' is Halsey's (1992) term for the previous self-determining and collegial basis of HE.

References

Barnett, R. (1990) *The Idea of Higher Education*. Buckingham: Society for Research in Higher Education/Open University Press.

Baudrillard, J. (1983) *Simulations*. New York: Semiotext(e).

Becher, T., and Kogan, M. 1992) *Process and Structure in Higher Education*. London: Routledge.

Beck, U. (1992) *Risk Society: Towards a New Modernity*. London: Sage.

Berg, I. (1970) *Education and Jobs: the Great Training Robbery*. Harmondsworth: Penguin.

Bernstein, R. (1983) *Beyond Objectivism and Relativism*. London: Macmillan.

Bloom, T. (1987) *The Closing of the American Mind: How Higher Education Has Failed Democracy and Impoverished the Souls of Today's Students*. New York: Simon & Shuster.

Bourdieu, P. and Passeron, J-C. (1964) *The Inheritors: French Students and Their Relation to Culture*. Chicago: University of Chicago Press.

Brown, P. and Scase, R. (1994) *Higher Education and Corporate Realities: Class, Culture and the Decline of Graduate Careers*. London: UCL Press.

Castells, M. (1989) *The Informal City: Information Technology, Economic Restructuring, and the Urban-Regional Process*. London: Blackwell.

───── (1996) *The Rise of the Network Society*. London: Blackwell.

Clark, B. (1983) *The Higher Education System: Academic Organisation in Crossnational Perspective*, Berkeley: U of California Press.

Coffield, F. and Williamson, B. (1997) *Repositioning Higher Education*, Buckingham: Society for Research in Higher Education/Open University Press.

Dore, R. (1976) *The Diploma Disease: Education, Qualification and Development*. London: Allen & Unwin.

Foucault, M. (1976) *Discipline and Punish*. London: Penguin.

Gibbons, M. *et al.* (1994) *The New Production of Knowledge: The Dynamics of Science and Research in Contemporary Societies*. London: Sage.

Giddens, A. (1990) *The Consequences of Modernity*. Cambridge: Polity Press.

───── (1991) *Modernity and Self-Identity*. Cambridge: Polity Press.

───── (1994) *Beyond Left and Right*. Cambridge: Polity Press.

Habermas, J. (1991) *The Theory of Communicative Action, Vol. 1* Cambridge: Polity Press.

Halsey, A. (1992) *The Decline of Donnish Dominion: The British Academic Professions in the Twentieth Century.* Oxford: Clarendon Press..

Hague, D. (1991) *Beyond Universities: A New Republic of the Intellect.* London: Institute of Economic Affairs.

Kerr, C. (1993) *The Uses of the University.* Cambridge, MA: Harvard University Press.

Lash, S. and Urry, J. (1987) *The End of Organized Capitalism.* Cambridge: Polity Press.

———— (1994) *Economies of Signs and Spaces.* London: Sage.

Lyotard, J-F. (1984) *The Postmodern Condition: a Report on Knowledge.* Manchester: Manchester University Press.

National Committee of Inquiry into Higher Education (1997) *Higher Education in a Learning Society* [The Dearing Report]. London.

O'Connor, J. (1973) *The Fiscal Crisis of the State.* New York: St. Martin's Press.

Parker, M. and Jary, D. (1995) 'The McUniversity: organisation, management and academic subjectivity', *Organization,* 2(2): 319-338.

Power, M. (1994) *The Audit Explosion.* London: Demos.

———— (1997) *The Audit Society: Rituals of Verification.* Oxford: Oxford University Press.

Premfors, R. (1980) *The Politics of Higher education in a Comparative Perspective, France, Sweden and the UK.* Stockholm: University of Stockholm.

Robbins Report (1963) *Higher Education.* Committee on Higher Education [Cmnd. 2154].

Ritzer, G. (1993) *The McDonaldization of Society.* Newbury Park, CA: Pine Forge.

———— (1996) 'McUniversity in the Postmodern Consumer Society'. Paper presented at the *Dilemmas of Mass Higher Education Conference,* Staffordshire University, April. (This paper was subsequently published in *Quality in Higher Education.*)

Scott, P. (1984) *The Crisis of the University.* London: Croom Helm.

———— (1995) *The Meanings of Mass Higher Education.* Buckingham: Society for Research in Higher Education/Open University Press.

Smith, A. and Webster, F. (eds) (1997) *The Postmodern University? Contested Visions of Higher Education in Society.* Buckingham: Society for Research in Higher Education/Open University Press.

Teichler, U. (1988) *Changing Patterns of Higher Education Systems: The Experience of Three Decades.* London: Jessica Kingsley.

Teichler, U., Hartnung, D. and Nuthmann, R. (eds) (1980) *Higher Education and the Needs of Society.* Windsor: NFER.

Trow, M. (1970) 'Reflections on the transition from elite to mass higher education', *Daedalus: Journal of the American Academy of Arts and Sciences,* 90(1), 1-42.

———— (1973) *Problems in the Transition from Elite to Mass Higher Education.* Berkeley, Ca.: Carnegie Commission on Higher Education.

———— (1989) 'The Robbins trap: British attitudes and the limits to expansion', *Higher Education Quarterly,* 43(1): 55-75.

——— (1991) 'Comparative perspectives on policy', in Berdahl, R., Moodie, G. and Spitzberg, I. (eds.) *Quality and Access in Higher Education*. Buckingham: Society for Research in Higher Education/Open University Press.

——— (1989) The Robbins trap: British attitudes and the limits to expansion', *Higher Education Quarterly*, 43(1): 55-75.

——— (1993) *Managerialism and the Academic Profession: Quality and Control*. London: Quality Support Centre Higher Education Paper/Open University.

——— (1996) 'Trust, markets and accountability in Higher education: a comparative perspective', in *The Thirtieth Anniversary Seminars*. London: Society for Research in Higher Education/.

——— (1997) 'More trouble than it's worth'. *Times Higher Education Supplement*, 24 October, p. 26.

II

GENERAL CONTEXT
OF HIGHER EDUCATION CHANGE

Mass Higher Education: A New Civilisation?

2

Peter Scott

When I was invited to contribute to the Conference which led to this book, it was one of those invitations I could not possibly turn down. In Britain we have stumbled, absent-mindedly, into mass higher education. And, as usual, we are reluctant to analyse, or even reflect on, our present condition. So I congratulate David Jary and Martin Parker, and the Staffordshire University, for organising such a timely conference — and for persisting in it, despite 'consolidation' and budget cuts, because there are plenty of people in universities and colleges all too ready to believe that mass higher education has been called off. It's been and gone — or, for some, it never arrived. That is not a view I share. Rather I am convinced that British higher education is in the middle of a, probably irreversible and certainly fundamental, transition. There is no going back. So we had better get down to understanding where we are, and where we are heading, rather than indulging in wishful nostalgia.

There is one other thing I want to say by way of introduction, and that is to explain, or perhaps apologise, for my title — 'Mass Higher Education: A New Civilisation?'. Some of you may detect a reference, undeliberate I assure you, to the Webbs' book on Soviet Communism, now I guess pretty much a museum piece. After all, they got it spectacularly wrong. You could not have got it much more wrong than to describe Stalin's Russia on the brink of the purges and the Gulag as 'a new civilisation'. Well, a partial excuse is that I have included a question-mark at the end of my title. But, in general, it sums up my argument accurately. I do see mass higher education as, if not a new civilisation exactly, a new formation — for reasons I will try to explain in a moment; and I can only trust, and hope, that, unlike the Webbs, I have got it right.

My argument, in a nutshell, is this: mass higher education is not merely a bigger-and-better (or worse) version of élite higher education. The relationship between the two is as much dialectical as sequential, which is why I worry about talk of 'transition'. Rather I want to emphasise rupture, although it would be naive to deny the powerful continuities that link the two forms of higher education. The development of mass systems cannot be properly explained in terms of their 'inner' dynamics, whether academic (pertaining to disciplines) or organisational (pertaining to systems and institutions) forces similar to those that shaped élite systems. Instead, as open systems, they are defined as much in terms of 'external' dynamics, for example their role in shaping new social identities and novel divisions of labour and their broader affinities with post-Fordist change and those intellectual movements that are usually labelled post-modernism (although I want to emphasise equally significant changes in science, technology and innovation generally).

My chapter is divided into three main sections: First, I want to address the question — do we have a mass higher education system? (because, as I hinted a moment ago, I am aware there are still many doubters) and, if we do — what are its primary characteristics? Next, I want to discuss socio-economic change — post-Fordism and all that, if you like — and its impact on higher education. For me, the key word to describe that impact, or rather the relationship between socio-economic change and the development of mass systems, is reflexivity. And, third, I want to discuss the far-reaching shifts that are taking place in intellectual culture and innovation systems and, again, assess their influence on mass higher education. The key phrase here, for me, is the emergence of what I like to call open intellectual systems. Finally, I want to say just a few words in conclusion to summarise, and probably simplify, my argument.

Do we have a mass system — and what is it like?

Many of you (including David Watson, I suspect) remain to be convinced that Britain in 1996 has a mass system of higher education. I will attempt to convince you with two arguments. The first is simply quantitative, although you may already have gathered my interpretation of mass higher education is essentially quali-tative. The second is more subtle, in the sense that it is an explanation, or series of explanations, of the resistances we put up to the idea of mass higher education. I am interested in the question why we do not want to believe we have a mass system.

First, though, the quantitative case. It is fairly straightforward. According to Martin Trow (1970, 1973) [see also Ch. 1] higher education systems that enrol up to 15 per cent of the age group should be regarded as élite systems; those that enrol between 15 and 40 per cent as mass systems; and those enrolling more than 40 per cent as universal systems. If you accept this broad taxonomy, the British system ceased to be élite a decade ago, and with participation nudging 32 per cent is clearly a mass system, indeed more than half-way to becoming a universal system. Add in two further factors — that we have a rather 'tight' definition of higher education in Britain compared to many other countries which would probably include a fair chunk of further (and perhaps adult) education; and that wastage remains low despite expansion, with the result that Britain's output of graduates actually exceeds that of France and Germany — and the case for categorising British higher education as a mass system becomes even stronger.

Why the doubt then? One reason I suppose is that 'mass' does not seem the right word to describe a system that still excludes two out of every three (rather more, in fact: school-leaver participation is actually only 25 per cent). But that surely is merely a matter of terminology. I would be perfectly happy with the adjective 'extended' rather than 'mass'. No higher education system is truly 'mass' anywhere in the world, by this stern definition. A second reason is the Government's stop-go policy on higher education, although in this case it is go-stop. Expansion took off in the later 1980s as a result of an unknowable combination of financial incentives to institutions and deeper secular change. Now it has been choked off first by 'consolidation', apparently without an adverse impact on access opportunities, and now, of course, by the budget cuts of November 1995. That up-swelling of social demand for higher education, so pronounced and apparently irreversible in the late 1980s and early 1990s, seems for the moment — mysteriously — to have abated. But none of this, it seems to be, invalidates the categorisation of British higher education as a mass system. After all, in several other European countries, notably the Netherlands, university enrolments have declined — but this does not mean these systems have changed their character, or reverted to a long-discarded elitism.

More interesting, although for me still not persuasive, reasons for our strange reluctance to acknowledge that we have a mass system arise from the peculiar tradition of British higher education, especially of the 'old' universities and from the equally peculiar political culture that characterises Britain. The first can be summed up in the word 'intimacy', an idea (or ideal) that needs to be carefully unpacked but nevertheless profoundly influences our instincts about the best teaching styles, about the processes of academic and professional socialisation, about the management and scale of institutions. The distinctiveness of the English university tradition (the Scots tradition is subtly different) is very much bound up with this idea of intimacy, in both organisational and cognitive terms.

The second, the peculiarity of our political culture, is its obliqueness and pragmatism, its avoidance of principled argument, its neglect of systematic reflection. Again, this is reflected in both institutional and intellectual arenas. In the former there is an absence of truly 'modern' institutions; instead we have an unwritten constitution, the Common Law. Maurice Cowling once used the suggestive phrase 'public doctrine' which for me captures the vague religiosity of our political culture (Cowling, 1980). In the latter there is an absence of, in Perry Anderson's broad-brush meaning, a 'sociology'. As he once wrote: "The culture of British society is organised about an absent centre — an overall account of itself." (Anderson, 1968) One of the few positive things that can be said about

Thatcherism is that it broke open this inward, evasive, oblique and ideologically vacuous political culture. For higher education the result of the first, intimacy, is nostalgia, a reluctance to acknowledge the reality of a mass system that is antithetical to our secret instincts. Quite simply, we don't want to know. The result of the second, the incomplete adoption of modernity and the persistence of a primitive intellectual culture, is the absence of a suitable language, policy or theory in which to describe or capture the emergence of a mass system. Quite simply, we don't know how to know.

One final point on why we resist the idea of mass higher education.... The model of a mass system we carry around is based largely on the experience of the United States, complemented — or, rather, complicated — by inaccurate impressions of how other European systems work. This has led us into two traps. One is that all massification equals Americanisation. But the American system is exceptional, just as America is an atypical society — like all pioneers, I am tempted to add, in a double sense. First, America is a 'frontier' society mesmerised by its 'manifest destiny.' Second, the first revolutions, in any sphere, are, by definition, sui generis. The industrial revolution in 18th-century Britain was a unique event, not a template mechanically reproduced by Germany in the 19th or Japan in the 20th centuries. Moreover, period is important. The American mass system emerged in the 1960s, at the high noon of Keynesianism, the welfare state, the triumph of science and technology, the Cold War — the era, we should remind ourselves, of Robbins. The British system has emerged in a post-industrial age, disfigured by neo-conservatism, the death of theory and 'the end of history'. Of course, it is going to be, and feel, different.

The other trap is to look for regularity in mass systems. But with the collapse of faith in planning, the undermining of notions of community and collegiality, the vigorous belief in markets and niches, the erosion of the very idea of 'public' services, in short of all the values and practices that produce regularity, is this any longer a reasonable expectation? Surely we should expect irregularity, discontinuity, incoherence, complexity, difference — particularly as this corresponds more closely to the academic zeitgeist, the intellectual spirit-of-the-age. All totalising schemes, cognitive and organisational, are now treated with suspicion. The former are cons; the latter conspiracies. So my conclusion is this: I don't expect to recognise mass higher education. Rather, I expect it to be strange and inconsistent, characterised by regressions and recessions. I don't expect it to be like America. I, too, grieve for the loss of intimacy, or innocence — but not for the supercilious philistinism of the old political culture. I, too, feel that mass higher education has arrived rather suddenly, creeping up on me unawares. I, too, worry about applying the label 'mass' to a system that still excludes the majority. But none of this shakes my belief that British higher education has been profoundly transformed, that it has become, in a significant sense, a 'new' system. And it is this novelty I want to explore in the rest of my talk.

Post-Fordism and all that

The starting point has to be the nature of contemporary society and, in particular, of its change processes. I want to consider two main accounts. The first I will label, for convenience rather than accuracy, post-industrialism. It is strong on technological determinism. Innovation and productivity are the key to step-changes, or 'waves' (we are now, we are told, in the Fifth Wave). 'Knowledge', by which generally is meant information technology, is seen as the fundamental resource of late-20th century society, just as oil was in the mid-20th century and coal and steel in the Victorian age. Social change is subordinate. For example, in a recent article Christopher Freeman and Carlotta Perez (1988) argued that the Fifth Wave, the triumph of micro-electronics, demanded "a full-scale re-accommodation of social behaviour and institutions" (p. 59). Also, change is essentially linear. The teleological ghost is still in the machine.

The second account I will label post-Fordism. This is much more than a shift in the dominant mode of production, the result of a quantum leap in innovation-induced productivity. Rather it is an accumulation of abandonments — of undifferentiated mass production, of linear careers (indeed of 'work'), of hierarchical (and deferential) social structures, even of personal identities. Or, to put it another way, changes in the regime of accumulation are subordinate to changes in the mode of political, social and cultural regulation. Post-Mao 'cultural revolutions' have a bad name, of course. But post-Fordism is as much a cultural phenomenon as an economic one. It lacks regularity; indeed is wide-open to regression. And, while the relationship between industrial and post-industrial society is essentially linear, that between Fordist and post-Fordist regimes is dialectical.

These are very broad and sweeping generalisations, abstractions perhaps, that may appear to have very little to do with the development of mass higher education. But the essential question, I believe, is continuity — or, at any rate, a linear sequence of 'waves' — or rupture, dislocation, non-sequential novelty (whether we are talking of society at its most abstract or mass higher education systems which, after all, are among its most remarkable components). But let me try to be a little — only a little, I am afraid — more concrete. Here are five attributes of contemporary society which, I suspect, tend to support those who favour rupture — post-Fordism rather than post-industrialism in my short-hand:

- First, **acceleration**: not simply the exponential growth of almost everything — goods and services, data and images, which apparently only the most powerful computers can regulate; but, alongside velocity, volatility. Nothing, it seems, is for ever — or for very long. Lyotard (1984: 66) has written, revealingly, of "the temporary contract supplanting permanent institutions" — in politics, culture, the economy, intellectual life, social affairs, even the most intimate personal relationships.

- Second, radical new **compressions** (and conceptions) of time-space, what Helga Nowotny has labelled 'simultaneity', or 'u-chronia' now that utopias are no longer available. This is revealed by ungainly new coinages such as 'glocal- isation'. One effect is the intensification of time, whether in the labour process or in consumption patterns. Another is the urge to resist this intensification, by formulating a new 'ecology' of time-space.
- Third is **risk**. The gain in power produced by technological (and, for 'wave' enthusiasts, economic) progress is increasingly undermined by the accumulation of risks. Ask the British (or any other) nuclear industry, the Ministry of Health and/or Agriculture about BSE, RailTrack about safety on the railways. 'Risk' considerations can no longer be regarded as side-effects. Unintended 'risks' shape social action as decisively as intended outcomes, whether political reforms or technical innovations.
- Fourth, really a bundle of attributes — **complexity, non-linearity, circularity**. The first, complexity, is familiar enough — and, some argue, able to be contained and made comprehensible by refining ever more sophisticated models of chaos theory and building more powerful computational systems to handle mega- datasets. The second is mirrored in the popularity of more 'open' and fluid accounts of social, economic, technical change in preference to rationalistic, mechanistic, positivistic 'equilibrium' and similar models of human behaviour. Circularity, of course, is most apparent in the social sciences where 'social' knowledge 'grows' through interaction with its environments.
- The fifth, and for me decisive, attribute is **reflexivity**. This takes many forms. One is the democratisation (and marketisation) of knowledge production and innovation systems which I will discuss later, in the sense that 'subjects' and 'objects' of inquiry or action become jumbled up. Another is that, as expert and abstract systems take over from traditional structures, both values and institutions are freed from the fixities, or givens, of tradition. Instead they must be constructed, and frequently re-constructed, in the light of interaction between these expert systems and actual environments. A third is that, as traditional class, gender and other distinctions fall away, individuals are freer to write their biographies. In Ulrich Beck's (1992: 90) phrase, "the individual becomes the reproduction unit of the social" — not the same as Margaret Thatcher's celebrated denial of 'society'!.

It is against this background, I believe, that we must consider the more detailed socio-economic trends of our times — one of which, of course, is the growth of mass higher education. These trends include the 'death' of the welfare state (a premature announcement, I hope!); the rise of so-called 'audit society'; the accelerating shift from manufacturing to services (and the tendency for these services to be concerned with the high-velocity delivery of symbolic goods); the death of 'work' at least in the sense that bureaucratic careers are replaced by job 'portfolios';

the transformation of production through customisation, just-in-time and so on (and the parallel transformation of organisations as out-sourcing and right-sizing have their effect).

And these socio-economic changes have been accompanied by profound cultural effects. Two in particular I want to mention. First, where a generation ago people like Daniel Bell (1973; 1976) discerned a tension between global capitalism and mass culture, between the regulation of production and the recklessness of consumption, today we recognise their synergy. Manufacturing is the easy bit; marketing makes the profits. In a very real sense, images (and ideas) are commodities. Or, if you prefer, superstructure is now structural. Second, a far-reaching individualisation is under way. Life-styles, as realised through personal participation in consumption, are now more important than life-chances, as determined by one's place in the division of labour or conventional social hierarchy. Biographies have truly become reflexive, chosen as well as given.

What does this mean for mass higher education? I want to highlight three effects. The first, following on immediately from what I have just said, is that participation in higher education is now a key component in the manufacturing of social, and personal, identities — although I hesitate before going the whole way and arguing that being a graduate is now more decisive than being middle-class (instead the two categories have been elided). Traditional forms of occupational credentialisation have been complemented (superseded even) by new forms of cultural credentialisation. Higher education is no longer — so much — about sustaining, and modifying, the division of graduate labour or forming, and legitimising, social élites; it is now concerned with the wholesale construction of our social personalities. In a powerful sense, where élite systems merely followed the existing contours of society, mass system, mould them. But — an important 'but' — this does not make them more radical. Complex, if subtle, hierarchies of esteem develop within higher education. All graduates are no longer, even approximately, equal in the social market. Also mass systems are so firmly embedded in social practice that they cannot readily achieve critical 'distance'.

The second effect is linked to what I have just said about the development of hierarchies of esteem. Distinctively graduate careers, rooted in professional expertise (backed, of course, by social prestige and access to cultural capital), are in decline. Bureaucratic jobs, whether in the public or private sectors, are on the wane. Charisma is making a come-back, disguised as personal transferable skills which, despite their much more purposive articulation by 'new' universities, are seen, perhaps unsurprisingly, as axiomatically possessed by Oxbridge and other élite university graduates. But the wider effects are, first, to challenge the kind of specialised formation that universities in particular have traditionally provided; and, second, to weaken the links that bind higher education to the labour market. The relationship we once took for granted between the development of higher education and the formation of professional society has become problematical, because of massification and also, of course, because the bases of professional society are now contested.

The third effect is that mass higher education systems are elements within much larger continua, however they are labelled — grandly as the 'learning society' or pejoratively as the 'entertainment-learning-leisure-heritage complex'. As such they are vital economic sectors in their own right — not simply as producers of cultural capital or human resources; nor as key assets, and multipliers, for local, regional and national economies. The yoking together in the recent Technology Foresight exercise of leisure and learning as a single sector, generating 13 per cent of GNP, is not an outlandish association of commercial practice and academic ideals; rather it is an accurate account of the dynamics of post-Fordism. If there are no longer unified subjects protected from the transgressions of the market-place, no autonomous domains of culture and science, it is not only (or mainly) the result of 'external' aggression; it is also because culture and science are themselves now powerful cultural commodities, symbolic goods. On the whole this makes better sense than the characterisation of knowledge simply as an input, an economic resource.

The key, I argue, is reflexivity — reflexivity in organisational terms as accountability succeeds autonomy, shrinking the available critical spaces; reflexivity in terms of individual experience as higher education provides a key arena for the construction of personal biographies in place of inherited, and involuntary, identities; reflexivity because, in our intellectual culture, trust has been superseded by risk and, in our innovation systems, homogeneity and authority by heterogeneity and plurality. As a result, I believe, we are entitled to think of mass higher education as an entirely new formation, because élite systems were associated with their opposites — autonomy, trust, hierarchy and authority.

Culture and innovation

The third big topic I want to tackle in this talk is the transformation of our intellectual culture (how we conceptualise novelty) and innovation systems (how we put it into practice), and then try to relate both to the development of mass higher education. This is not the time, or place, to explore the postmodern condition. It is now a common-place to argue that a crucial frontier has been crossed from the modern system, organised (for all its restlessness, 'the institutionalisation of doubt', in the telling phrase of a speaker at the Staffordshire Conference Anthony Giddens, around universal values and 'unified subjects', to postmodernity, the trackless territory of deconstructed meanings, relative values, fleeting truths (or, to revert to my earlier comments, a *posthistoire* where the sociology of time has been transformed or, if you prefer, 'the end of history' because the dynamics of dialectical exchange are now exhausted).

On the whole I am sceptical of grand schemes, even (or especially) when disguised as anti-systems. I worry about the inevitable paradox, the need to exploit the techniques of modernism, of a critical rationality, to explode its intellectual claims. Also many of the characterisations we recognise as postmodern are in fact very old. Radical deconstructive scepticism began with Hume, or perhaps Bacon. What E. P. Thompson in his last book (on Blake) termed 'the non-rational affirmative' is part of a much older moral tradition, pre-modern in essence. The notion of intellectual progress being made through a complex set of negotiations between different 'languages' is not new either. Richard Rorty comes to mind. But I do not intend — nor do I have the necessary expertise — to go further into these questions. All I will say is that we need to be cautious about justifying the distinctiveness of the mass university in the context of this wider (but still contestable) intellectual transformation. Talk of a postmodern university must be treated with suspicion.

Having said that, I want to make two connections which I believe are significant in building up a picture of mass higher education. The first is the democratisation of academic discourses — both substantively and methodologically. The former, the substantive, presents few difficulties. New subjects are added because students are now drawn from much more diverse social constituencies (so black studies or women's writing), because the social world itself is being transformed (hence cultural studies, IT-with-everything), and because graduates now follow much more heterogeneous career paths (which explains the 'new vocationalism').

The latter, the methodological, is more problematic. The idea that academic knowledge can only be advanced by deploying appropriate conceptualisations and demonstrating adequate analytical skills — in short, that it demands discrimination between the cognitively worthy and un (or less) worthy — is hard to let go. Yet in the mass university we may have to accept the re-emergence of purely 'local knowledges'. For a long time it has been assumed that it was a one-way street. As expert systems (both technical and intellectual) became more sophisticated, 'common-sense' perspectives were inevitably attenuated. Knowledge and skills were sieved off from everyday life. Now there is a growing realisation that it is two-way street. 'Expert' knowledge is being reappropriated (and often challenged) by ordinary people who are now, because of much wider access, well represented within the mass university. There is also an intriguing rediscovery of notions such as 'social memory' — what Simon Schama (1995: 5) has called "the knowledge we already have, but knowledge which somehow eludes our recognition".

The second connection I want to make is summed up in the phrase 'the death of theory'. The cause, whether that death is the result of a kind of cosmic epistemological collapse or of the hundreds, thousands, of cuts inflicted by scientific reductionism, is secondary to the effect itself. It is, of course, a contested phenomenon. In purely descriptive terms, theories proliferate — promiscuously, it seems. In one of his better metaphors, George Steiner (1989: 21) referred in this context to "the interminability of the locust". But, in intellectual terms, they have often been transformed into archaeologies, systems of thought (or, rather, reference) in which we no longer truly believe but are reluctant to let go entirely. And, with the awesome advances in computer power, the gap between meaning, the ability to generalise in a moral (or hermeneutic) sense, and truth, or theory as the 'rules' of the positivistic game, has widened alarmingly.

The implications for higher education of these more open intellectual systems, a phrase I use to subsume the re-emergence of 'local knowledges' and the 'death of theory', are two-fold. First, in a cognitive context, the university's claim to deliver a special kind of knowledge, whether defined in terms of technical expertise or superior culture (probably with a capital 'C'), is undermined. Its distinctiveness now lies in its ability to construct for itself, and orchestrate for others, learning systems, rather than its 'ownership' of unique cognitive values. Second, in organisational terms, its claim to occupy a defined, and necessarily autonomous, space in society is also compromised. For, if universities neither deliver a special kind of knowledge nor are themselves special institutions, they are exposed to much more open environments. On the one hand this means that, stripped of their residual monopolies, universities must compete with rival institutions which may be only loosely, if at all, attached to the higher education system; on the other that they are able to transgress the traditional boundaries of the academic domain — to their own institutional advantage.

This picture fits in well with equally far-reaching changes in the knowledge production, or innovation, system. These have been described in terms of a shift from 'mode 1', or traditional scientific research, to 'mode 2', a kind of socially distributed knowledge production system (Gibbons *et al.*, 1994). Mode 1 is (was) dominated by closed scientific communities; mode 2 is an open system in terms of its social organisation where 'producers', 'users', 'brokers' (I even came across the term 'policy hustlers' in a recent American book) mingle promiscuously, none of them having a privileged role. Cognitively, mode 2 is eclectic. And it is inter-penetrated by 'markets' (political as well as commercial) rather than being an autonomous space.

Mode 2 knowledge production is seen as having five key attributes: First, it is generated within a context of application (this is not the same as applied science, because there may be no pre-existing 'science' to apply). Second, it is transdisciplinary (again, to be distinguished from multi- or inter-disciplinary practice where already constituted disciplines collaborate). Third, it is heterogeneous and diverse. Not only is knowledge produced on many sites, all Internet-ed together of course, there are also many new actors such as government (in all its labyrinthine complexity) think-tanks, consultancies, and small and medium-sized enterprises — all 'researching' as well as 'learning' organisations. Fourth, mode 2 is accountable, rather than autonomous, in the sense that it is highly reflexive. Fifth, it demands new definitions of quality. Peer review, after all, only makes sense in the context of autonomous institutions and discrete research communities, both of which are being eroded.

To claim that the transition from mode 1 to mode 2 represents a paradigm shift is going too far. Rather they are grinding up against, or sliding over each other rather like tectonic plates — and accompanied by equivalent seismic activity. We can all think of examples of mode 2-ish developments — Technology Foresight, the increasingly proactive and programmatic stance of the research councils, the growth of collaboration (especially across the academic-industrial divide), the proliferation of research sites. The key to this new innovation system, I believe, is that it is a distributed rather than a linear system. This brings me to the second key impact of this transformation of intellectual (and scientific) cultures and development of new innovation systems on higher education. The first, you will recall, was the growth of what I called 'open intellectual systems'. It can be summed up in a single word — de-institutionalisation. This is a profound change because we have always assumed a tight association between cognitive values and social organisation, which is why we have universities. We may have to get used to much looser relationships. The dispersed, distributed university perhaps?

Conclusion

Let me now try to draw the threads of my argument together. First, I do believe that we have a mass system of higher education in Britain, although it has become fashionable to doubt it. But, mass higher education, not least in Britain, cannot be regarded as a mere extension of the élite form. Their relationship is more dialectical than developmental. Nor can it be expected to be a regular or predictable formation, across time and cultures. Nor, yet again, is mass higher education immune from regression (not least because élite forms persist within it). Second, the growth of mass higher education must be seen as one element within a larger transformation of late-modern society. Radical shifts in social identifications, 'work' and organisational cultures have a direct impact on universities, both their positioning and their functions. At the same time higher education is swept up in the 'images' economy in which all kinds of symbols — cognitive, aesthetic, alluring — are vigorously traded. Third, the development of mass systems is tantalisingly aligned with the intellectual, and cultural, revolutions of our times; and more directly implicated in the growth of new innovation systems. To dismiss the former as coincidental, or the latter as peripheral, strikes me as mistaken. Mass higher education is a novel epistemological phenomenon as well as a new sociological formation.

I will end with two final words. The first is an apology for the parochialism of my presentation. Beneath my generalisations, buried in the shallowest of graves, is an account that is essentially derived from the, probably exceptional, experience of British higher education. It has not been tested against other experiences.

If it were, it would probably be found wanting. The second is also a kind of apology. What I have offered, largely to provoke debate and discussion but with serious and sincere intent, is a highly provisional statement about the nature of mass higher education. To be remotely satisfactory it requires much greater theoretical elaboration and also empirical underpinning than I can possibly offer. But this is a task which, I believe, is more urgent and important than even we imagine. I have a strong sense of a system cast adrift, both conceptually and in policy terms. It has drifted out of sight of well-known landmarks and familiar references. So far no substitutes have been found. Above all, therefore, we need a map — not only the kind of map that the Dearing committee has drawn upon but a mental map. It is in the spirit of that quest that I write.

References

Anderson, P. (1968) 'Components of the national culture', *New Left Review,* 50 May-June.

Beck, U. (1992) *Risk Society: Towards a New Modernity.* London: Sage.

Bell, D. (1966) *The Reforming of General Education: the Columbia College Experience in its National Setting.* New York: Columbia University Press.

―――― (1973) *The Coming of Post-Industrial Society.* London: Heinemann.

―――― (1976) *The Cultural Contradictions of Capitalism.* London: Heinemann.

Cowling, M. (1980) *Religion and Public Doctrine in Modern England.* Cambridge: Cambridge University Press.

Freeman, C. and Perez, C. (1988) 'Structural Crises of Adjustment, Business Cycles and Investment Behaviour', in G. Dosi *et al.* (eds) *Technical Change and Economic Theory.* London: Pinter.

Gibbons, M., Limoges, C., Nowotny, H., Schwartzman, S., Scott, P. and Trow, M. (1994) *The New Production of Knowledge: The Dynamics of Science and Research in Contemporary Societies.* London: Sage.

Giddens, A. (1990) *The Consequences of Modernity.* Cambridge: Polity Press.

―――― (1991) *Modernity and Self-Identity.* Cambridge: Polity Press.

Schama, S. (1995) *Landscape and Memory.* London: Harper Collins.

Steiner, G. (1989) *Real Presences.* London: Faber.

Thompson, E. P. (1993) *Witness Against the Beast: William Blake and the Moral Law.* Cambridge: Cambridge University Press.

Trow, M. (1970) 'Reflections on the transition from elite to mass higher education, *Daedalus: Journal of the American Academy of Arts and Sciences,* 90 (1): 1-42.

―――― (1973) *Problems in the Transition from Elite to Mass Higher Education.* Berkeley, CA.: Carnegie Commission on Higher Education.

Change in Mass Higher Education: University, State and Economy

3

Tim Edwards and Henry Miller

Introduction

The dilemmas of Mass Higher Education can be seen from the outside in terms of how universities relate to the needs of the state, economy or citizens. They can also be seen from the inside in terms of how academics, managers and students negotiate their tasks, how they understand the university and act within it.

One of the purposes of this chapter is to try to connect the external and internal understandings. This means paying attention to how dilemmas are conceptualised, what are the frames of reference and the nature of the discourses. The chapter draws on previous work done by both authors at Aston University which outlines ways in which the state pressures and frames university management to meet the needs of the economy and the ways in which academic managers in the United Kingdom conceptualise those pressures and their roles (Edwards, 1995; Miller, 1995a). This is followed by a discussion of the range and provenance of discourses at work within our universities and some thoughts about the likely future direction of the higher education system within the current political and economic context.

Economies, states and education

A fundamental question in any discussion of the relationship of states and universities to the economy is what is the nature and extent of the economy under consideration? Many writers from different standpoints (Wallerstein, 1974: 79; Giddens, 1985: 90; Kennedy, 1989: 93; Held, 1991) have noted, on the one hand, the increasing globalisation and interdependence of the world economy, where as Held (1991) puts it:

> The internationalization of production, finance and other economic resources is questionably eroding the capacity of an individual state to control its own economic future… (p.151) [and] …multinational corporations may have a clear national base, but their interest is above all in global profitability, country of origin is of little consequence for corporate strategy. (p. 152)

Some advocates of laissez-faire policies in the mid-1980s United Kingdom under the Thatcher Conservative government did not see this situation as a problem. They advocated the maximum reduction of the individual nation state's regulation of the economy with deregulation of monetary markets, to facilitate the free movement of capital as well as trade. They argued that trade always balances and that the decline of Britain's manufacturing base mattered little because the population could exist on service industries, finance and tourism. In contrast to its minimalist laissez-faire economic policies, the government pursued strong national policies in relation to foreign policy; the Falklands/Malvinas war, the European Community and the development of social policy informed by traditional moral codes. Given this, it is perhaps surprising the government did not allow individual universities to founder in bankruptcy as the result of cuts in state support in 1981, 1982, and 1983 — as might have been expected from an undiluted free market approach.

A more common position held by commentators such as Giddens (1985) and Kennedy (1989, 1992) and by politicians, policy makers and the majority of the population in the United Kingdom — as well as most other advanced industrialised powers — is that while in principle free trade and the free movement of capital and labour is desirable, this ought to be modified by government action in what is seen as the interests of the nation state's population. Such action may be protectionist, and in the past often was. More recently it has involved deregulation in significant areas. However, even if policies have been ineffective or counter productive they have had effects often involving universities. State policies were designed to increase the competitiveness of home-based companies or to attract multinationals to establish plants in their particular national territory rather than in some other. This often involved the state taking a proactive role to encourage universities to provide relevant, economically desirable research and an appropriately trained workforce.

Kennedy (1993) argues that with the ending of the cold war "military rivalries and arms races are being replaced by economic rivalries, technology races and various forms of commercial warfare" (p. 127). The language of economic rivalry has become increasingly military, industries 'under seige' and markets 'captured' or 'surrendered'. He continues, "The nation state is still at the centre of things engaged in a ceaseless jostling for advantages… A neomercantilist world order remains" (p. 127). Giddens (1985) emphasised the continuing importance of the nation state in the contemporary world. The balance of power and influence between individual states and corporations is affected and mediated by a range of material, organisational and knowledge resources, as well as alliances, regional groupings, cartels and the operation of the market.

However, the reality and rhetoric of globalisation has been taken on board not only by the free market right but also by New Labour as a constraint on government policy in monetary, financial, taxation and public policy areas (Hirst and Thompson, 1997).

It is within these configurations (state and corporate) of local, national and international interaction that universities, their staff, students and managers operate. Universities are at one and the same time international, national and local. The flows of knowledge and research, staff and students are in part international, partly because of changes in technology which make communication easier and faster, partly because of the international mission of most universities and partly because of the universal nature of much knowledge. However, all universities in the United Kingdom are public state institutions arising formally and legally by Royal Charter or Act of Parliament. Most funds come either directly or indirectly from national state taxes and the sources of funds means that the state is able to exercise predominant control over the broad parameters of student recruitment, academic salaries and, in more mediated ways, research policy.

Within the economic sphere, governments of nation states attempt to implement economic, monetary and fiscal policies which, in an uncynical view, are in the best interests of the population as a whole or at least those that elected them. A more critical view would be that governments' economic policies serve the interests of the dominant class or elite within which capital and corporate interests are usually predominant. However, whatever the rationale or provenance of economic policies, they are constrained by a number of forces.

To begin with, there is the power of the financial markets. The national currency of a state is often taken as a symbol of the state's legitimacy and worth and political and economic considerations are inextricably interwoven in the formation of monetary policy. This can be seen clearly in the history of sterling and the UK state and more particularly the leaving of the exchange rate mechanism (ERM) in September 1992. After World War II in 1947, the Bretton Woods Agreement, influenced by Keynes, provided semi-fixed exchange rates. The International Monetary Fund (IMF) was co-ordinating adjustments to the value of currencies, pegged to the US dollar, when justified by a fundamental disequilibrium in the balance of payments of a member country. Bretton Woods broke down in 1971, leaving exchange rates to fluctuate.

In 1979, with the election of the Conservative government headed by Mrs Thatcher, the United Kingdom abandoned the last vestiges of currency regulation, freeing capital movements and allowing a free hand to speculators. There had already been a turn to monetarist policies. From 1976, under the pressure from the International Monetary Fund, the control of money became the main means of regulating the economy under Labour Chancellor Healey. Thompson (1984) has made the point that, with respect to the influences of the state in economic policy in Britain in the 1980s, there was a constellation of differing perspectives, ranging from more or less full blown monetarism and supply side economics to the liberalism of Hayek's position. There were considerable differences in philosophical assumptions and policy implications. However, all these positions which have been influential on government in the United Kingdom shared a belief in the importance and superiority of markets over state planning. E. P. Thompson, the historian provides a striking account of the force of the idea of the market. He suspects that:

> The market economy, ... is often a metaphor (or mask) for capitalist process. It may even be employed as a myth. The most ideologically, compelling form of the myth lies in the notion of the market as some supposedly neutral but (by accident) beneficent entity; or, if not entity (since it can be formed in no space but the head) then an energising spirit — of differentiation, social mobility, individualism, innovation, growth, freedom. (Thompson, 1991: 305)

He continues:

> This 'market' may be projected as a benign consensual force which involuntarily maximises the best interests of the nation. It may be seen that it is the 'market system' which has 'produced' the nations wealth — Market is indeed a superb and mystifying metaphor for the energies released and the new needs (and choices) opened up by capitalist forms of exchange, with all conflict and contradictions withdrawn from view — Market is (when viewed from this aspect) a mask worn by particular interests, which are not coincident with those of 'the nation' or 'the community' but which are interested, above all in being mistaken to do so. (Thompson, 1991: 305)

Thompson was concerned that historians should show how such markets actually existed, and in his account of 'moral economy' and the effectiveness of riot in controlling food price fixing in the eighteenth century showed that they were then much modified. In the 1980s and 1990s, one may recognise the power of the market rhetoric of the World Bank, national politicians and policy makers, corporate apologists or academic managers but question how markets really work for lecturers, students or researchers. How are these markets managed, and are their effects wholly beneficial? Indeed, assessing benefit and loss is precisely what admission tutors or research administrators actually do when faced with the reality of managed markets whether students seeking places or funding bodies seeking research results.

Gray argues that:

> The market itself is politically and culturally constructed and may, even with capitalism, be constructed in different ways distributing advantages differently. On the other hand markets do have a real existence, resist attempts to mould them in certain directions and even have a disconcerting habit of re-emerging in spheres where they are supposed to have been abolished. The task for a critical social theory is to grasp these realities — the way that economics appear to behave autonomously, and to confront states and governments even 'capitalist' governments, as awkward and intractable givens — while avoiding their reification. (1990: 174)

In practice in the late 1970s, Thompson argues that it was the:

> ...actual circumstances and constraints in the economy combined with the onset of recession which was of crucial importance rather than the changes in ideological outlook on the part of policy makers. It was this matrix of events that provided the conditions for a different ideological explanation to be given for the economy's decline and for a different set of remedies to be thrown up that would solve these problems. During this period the whole era of 'public expenditure' came under increasing scrutiny and was considered as the major problem of the economy. (1984: 287-8)

Free market monetarism took a full blown form in the early period of Thatcherism from 1979 to the mid 1980s. The value of the pound fluctuated widely — at one time nearly equivalent to the United States dollar. Deregulation and the availability of credit, particularly in relation to the housing market, led to the boom of 1986 to 1989, but the British manufacturing industry was severely reduced in the 1980s and imports of manufactured goods grew faster than exports. The Conservative government seemed at times to think the British economy could be sustained primarily on the sale of services and investments overseas. Increasing Japanese investment in United Kingdom; while strengthening manufacturing industry in areas like automobiles and electronics meant that profits were exported and there was little concomitant growth in research and development.

Since Thatcher, events such as 'Black Monday' and the controversy surrounding the United Kingdom's membership of the European exchange rate mechanism (ERM) signal the ongoing debate within and beyond the Conservative party about fiscal and monetary policy and entry into monetary union. This debate illustrates the complexity and tensions on government policy which on the one hand espouses in free market rhetoric but, on the other, celebrates national interest and is not averse to state intervention in the economy or even universities in the interest of 'UK plc'.

The 'state' in state-market education relations

The mapping of state–education relations within the markets of liberal democratic capitalist societies requires an understanding of what is meant when we refer to the 'state'. There is a tendency to anthropomorphise, homogenise and rationalise the state and state action, particularly where the state is defined as nothing more than the government. However, the state is more than just the government: it is heterogenous, consisting of different organs which are not necessarily in line or in harmony with what is perceived as government policy. These characteristics of the state will affect the way we interpret state–education relations. This is indicated by Salter and Tapper, who recognise the inherent difficulties associated with co-ordinating the actions of the 'outer' state apparatus with the central organs of the state, and argue that they are implicit in the relationship between state and higher education and the development of an economic ideology of education:

> The modern economy, first of all, is fuelled by an ever-evolving mix of manpower and scientific knowledge and, ideally, would require the education system to train and research the appropriate educational products necessary for optimum economic advance. However, intervening between the economic dynamic and its potential impact upon education is the central bureaucracy of the state and the political institutions and interests, each with its own identity and concerns. To the best of its ability, each interprets and channels the demands from the economy in a way which suits the dynamic inherent in its own interests and policy preferences. (Salter and Tapper, 1994: 3)

The existence of quasi-state institutions such as funding councils and other bodies such as committees of vice-chancellors and principles shows the need for a broader analysis of the state and gives an indication of how the purposes of the state are connected with the practices of those working in higher education.

An appreciation of this conceptualisation of state education relations is aided by using three of Smith's (1990) models of the state — regulatory, compensatory and minimalist. The regulatory model assumes that government should utilise "expert knowledge in order to minimise social tension and optimise economic growth" (Smith, 1990: 192). This is reflected in, for instance, the White Paper *Realising Our Potential: A Strategy for Science, Engineering and Technology* (DoE, 1993), which refers to the importance of using research into science, engineering and technology to generate national prosperity and improve the quality of life in the United Kingdom. Moreover, the use of 'expert knowledge' to improve the nation's economic performance is not restricted to research; it has come to mean the promotion of lifelong learning through training and upskilling.

The compensatory model leads on from the regulatory model in what can be described as a welfare state direction. The university is seen as a means to reduce the relative degree of advantage enjoyed by the minority benefiting most from the unequal distribution of private property (Smith, 1990). For instance, the emphasis on using universities to improve the competencies of the nation's workforce and to encourage mature adults to return to education shows a 'welfare' element to the university portfolio, as well as an economic objective. Government, at times simplistically and/or ideologically, associates welfare of the individual with the economic well being of the nation.

Finally, the 1980s and 1990s have been dominated in the United Kingdom by the market and market philosophy. This characteristic of Conservative government rests on the belief that individuals will be better served by the market rather than by state action or the activities of public bodies. Instead, the law as enforced by the state will secure minimum social tension and optimum growth. The small state typifies the minimalist model. In its crude form, it assumes that practically all state action and activity by public bodies will be less efficient, effective or just than private individuals relating through the market — its foremost political champion being Margaret Thatcher. John Major did not substantially modify that stance while the new Premier, Tony Blair, and New Labour have adopted significant parts of the market rhetoric.

The framing of state actions in terms of particular dominant discourses is significant because it is the influence of such discourses which informs the debate on state–education relations. These discourses are evident throughout state action, within and between government bodies and ministries, and can be the cause of intra-state conflict. What is more, they epitomise the nature of state encroachment on different aspects of society. Institutions such as universities, although primarily located within civil society, are a terrain on which different forces operate, on which specific hegemonies and settlements are established reflecting the dominant power and discourses within state, society and economy.

Market–state–university relations: an economic liberal perspective

The market philosophy is most readily associated with economic liberalism. This tradition goes some way to explain contemporary economy and society and one framework for understanding the nature of state university relations. Economic liberalism remains a major form of analysis. It is significant as a way of analysing and understanding economics and society and the way in which universities work. But more importantly it has provided a major, in many cases, predominant ideology for key political decision makers concerned with the formation and implementation of public policy for universities as well as for education in general, health care, social services and housing. It remains powerful not least because of the robustness and resilience of market forms of economic organisation. As an ideology it has, however, been open to criticism:

> ... the urge to marketise every aspect of the way we live in the name of efficiency has eroded the fabric of our social life, which in its turn has weakened the economy. (Hutton, 1995: 192)

Alternatives to this ideology have been offered, including Hutton's (1997) proposed 'stakeholder society' — a Keynesian political economy emphasising welfare, social equality, and even corporatist governance. Nevertheless, economic liberalism and the associated notion of economic rationalism pervade current state university relations.

The incursion of economic rationalism with its emphasis on performance measures continues to affect university management. For instance, the recent massive expansion in student numbers from 1988 to 1998 compares with the Robbins Committee in the early 1960s, but has occurred without an equivalent increase in resources. Instead, it has been accompanied by a call for increased value for money and accountability (Prichard and Willmott, 1995).

This rationale is articulated in the White Paper, *Competitiveness: Helping Business To Win* (DTI, 1994), which states that the government can help firms improve their competitiveness by, amongst other measures, "improving value for money in those services which are best provided by the public sector" (Cm 2563, 1994: 15). The hard market economic emphasis (Pusey, 1991) is also characterised by the way government has worked to "establish a quasi market economy and the accompanying framework of industrial values in academic life" (Tasker and Packham, 1994: 183). Not only is there a growing expectation that industry should become an important customer of universities, but also that universities themselves should become competitors in the 'higher education industry' (Halsey, 1992). This industry has a dual role, both social and economic, connecting personal development with economic performance.

The purity of the *free* market ideology and practice is questionable. There has been a tendency in the 1980s and 1990s for the state to intervene and regulate university activities. The managed market suitably describes the current situation with individual, departmental and institutional competition in a range of inter-linked markets for student funds, research and even research productive academics. Moreover, the parameters of these markets are set directly by the state and its agencies.

Recent developments have intensified the debate regarding the control and role of universities. The predominance of a market discourse is most readily associated with the policies of recent Conservative governments' while the notion that higher education has economic responsibilities appears to be accepted by all the main political parties. At the same time, questions about the accountability and probity of senior academic management have become an issue with, for example, the establishment of the Amman committee to examine the governance of universities as well as other public bodies in the wake of concern about 'sleaze' in government.

The economic and political strategies of this period are mutually dependent and interrelated. The economic strategies which have evolved in the United Kingdom since the mid-1970s are based on fiscal and monetary policies which try to maintain a stable macroeconomic framework by keeping inflation and interest rates low. These strategies also include keeping a tight reign on public finances and making efforts to improve the supply side of the economy, i.e. improve the competitiveness of UK industry. The emergence of monetarism and anti-statism has been paramount in the attempt to address the fiscal crisis and the promotion of sustained economic growth. Such economic projects are associated with Thatcherism and largely continued under the subsequent Major government.

The gap between these policies and those of, for instance, New Labour appears to be relatively insignificant. Certainly at the macroeconomic level the policy statements made by New Labour during the run-up to the 1997 general election illustrate a similar concern with controlling public expenditure, maintaining stable economic growth with low inflation, and making efforts to ensure the competitiveness of the economy (New Labour, 1997). 'Blairism' in these instances is not that dissimilar from 'Majorism'; with the economy and the role of higher education closely tied .

The Conservative project has had widespread implications, not least in the way it has forced Labour towards 'new' political ground. According to Hutton (1995: 32), not since the advent of universal suffrage has the machinery of the British state been so determinedly used "to prosecute a particular party programme as that undertaken by the modern Conservative Party'. This strategy is most readily associated with a Thatcherite economic project based on a neo-liberal accumulation strategy, with the "deregulation of private capital, the privatisation of significant parts of the public sector, and the introduction of commercial criteria into the residual activities of the state sector', and a political strategy which has tried to "restructure the state system and its relations with civil society and the economy in the sphere of the politics of state power" (Jessop et al, 1984: 97-98).

Universities can be seen as contributors to the economy and social change; this is because higher education and, by implication, universities wield 'educational power'. This is "a unique blend of two resources essential for economic and social development: knowledge and status" (Salter and Tapper, 1994: 4). In the post-war period the state, through its various departments and bodies, has been attempting to gain greater control over higher education. This period of change in higher education has been interpreted as the "elite-mass paradigm shift" (Scott, 1995). However, such a transition, for Scott (1995) at least, cannot be explained through state action alone. Scott suggests that the emergence of a mass higher education system has resulted from "a series of multiple modernizations — of society, economy, culture and science as well as academy" (Scott, 1995: 168). It is within such complex modernizations that state action is located and where universities have become, Scott argues, more reflexive in respect of their political and socio-economic contexts.

However, there does appear to be an affinity between the apparent reflexivity of universities and the state's attempt to instigate an ideological shift away from the traditional liberal ideal of higher education towards what Tapper and Salter (1994) term the economic ideology of education:

> Its basic principle is that education is an economic resource which should be organised in a way that maximises its contribution to Britain's industrial development. From this premise it follows that socially relevant, or applied knowledge is more important than pure knowledge, that higher education institutions should be responsive to economic needs, and that it is the responsibility of the state to ensure that these institutions are held accountable for carrying out their economic role correctly. (Tapper and Salter, 1994: 12)

The use of educational power and the introduction of an economic ideology of education has taken on a new intensity since 1979. Consecutive Conservative governments have, it can be argued, been "intent to change the ethos of Universities as knowledge-based organisations and, more specifically, to harness the activities of academics more directly and explicitly to market forces as a means of raising their contribution to national economic performance" (Prichard and Willmott, 1995: 17-18).

However, such a philosophy has been resisted. The capitulation of the professions to this ideology, whether in health or education, has not been by any means complete: there continues to be resistance and constraint on the government's ability to restructure the economy and civil society (see Jessop et al,, 1984). Pritchard and Willmott (1995) have suggested that academics are able to resist the rigors of the new managerialism. Nevertheless, the dominance of an economic ideology in university state relations is real even if it is not guaranteed. For instance, reduced funding combined with the demands of rising student numbers is increasingly driving universities to find means in the market to support their activities, whether teaching or research: for example, the charging of high fees for MBAs. These practices reinforce a market discourse within the university. The growing use of such terms as 'efficiency', 'value for money', and 'accountability' in the day to day execution of academic activity such as teaching is an indication of its influence, as is the growing 'industrial ethic' associated with academic activity (Tasker and Packham, 1994).

Some would argue that these developments are "incommensurable with traditional values of the university" (Tasker and Packham, 1994: 183). However, this depends on whether you take a predominantly 'Oxbridge' interpretation of the university (Salter and Tapper, 1992, 1994; Halsey, 1992) or whether you accept that there is more than one university tradition which includes a tradition of close association with industry. Scott (1995) has argued that it is now no longer appropriate to talk of Cardinal Newman's 'idea of a University' (1910), or Clark Kerr's 'uses of the university' (1966), instead, much of what is apparent points to a mass higher education system biased towards 'UK plc'.

Discourses

The range of external and internal discourses, their connections, contradictions and complementarities is wide and complex.

Externally, but penetrating increasingly within the symbolic order of the university, there are a number of dominant discourses. Well documented (and not only in this paper) is what in broad terms might be termed 'the economic' as compared to, for example, 'the cultural'. This has a number of facets. One dominant feature is the discussion of the university, its purposes and practices in terms of meeting 'economic' needs. As we have noted, this can be defined as the need to improve the competitiveness of British Industry in the world market, and can be articulated in terms of guiding research efforts or encouraging universities to provide curricula, pedagogy and students who will meet the various workforce needs of corporate capital. This is usually defined as scientific, technical, entrepreneurial or managerial but it may also include the development of appropriate 'responsible' attitudes.

The 'economic' discourse also frames the discussions of the benefits to individual graduates of university education; this may then be articulated to a 'fairness' political discourse to justify reform of funding arrangements, graduate tax, loan schemes, access and equity. However, within the overall economic 'discourse' ('ideology is Tapper and Salter's term) there are a number of strands which can be wound together or fray apart.

Among these are the apparently contradictory emphases on the benefits, supremacy — indeed, inevitability — of the market as against the need for planning, co-ordination and direction. Tensions between these strands are apparent within our account of the United Kingdom state's attempts to improve the competitiveness of industry through university-industry links.

Internally, within the university similar tensions between central planning and the establishment of quasi-markets with cost centres, contracts and trading company models parallel and reflect conflicting pressures on the university.

A range of other discourses emerging, residual and resistant are at play outside and inside the university. Amongst these 'managerialism' seems to be emerging into a dominant position. However, its articulation with other discourses and practices — 'professional', 'collegial', 'vocationalism', 'democratic', even the 'intellectual' — remains open to interpretation and even intervention in a far from static situation.

Governmental and non-governmental policies and statements

The increasing importance given to the role of universities in the economy is perhaps best illustrated by reference to recent government and non-government policy documents and recommendations. The grounding of such an economic biased strategy lies in the assertion that:

> Changes in the international economy has gradually shifted the basis of a firm's competitive edge from static price competition towards dynamic improvements and are favouring firms that are able to create knowledge a little faster than their competitors. (Maskell and Malmberg, 1995: 3)

This clearly implies that not only should firms work to create their own new knowledge but that they should also utilise, where appropriate, existing knowledge to make themselves more competitive. To neglect these would, it is argued, affect their long-run performance. The UK government's response to wealth creation and competitiveness would appear to rest on a similar interpretation of the international economy. Part of government strategy to address this situation has been to encourage greater collaboration between higher education, government and industry. The utilisation of knowledge is central to a 'partnership' concerned more and more with diversifying the higher education system so that it is capable of providing more industrially relevant knowledge to a broader and larger number of users.

One aspect of this has been the theme of 'Lifelong Learning' and in particular the provision of continuing vocational education for employees in industry. The expansion of the higher education system is dependent in part on the inclusion of mature students who are currently in work. The significance of this policy is apparent in the recent government training targets:

> … on universities and colleges to help achieve the higher level national educational and training targets…[where]…at least 30 per cent of the workforce [is] to have an academic, vocational, professional or management qualification at National Vocational Qualification level 4 (broadly equivalent to a degree) or above by the year 2000. (*The Times Higher*, May 26: 1995)

The theme of education through life has grown in significance not only in this country but throughout Europe. However, the whole concept of education through life runs counter to what has traditionally been recognised as the time and place for education and training. For instance, Pearson (1983: 21-22) states:

Together with employers we have too readily accepted the notion
that education ends with a degree, and training with a few apprentice-
ships in different employment. Instead, we should be concerned to
play our part in the integration of education within work — with
'formation' to use the French word — which implies an element of
continuity and an element of cooperation. It is the continuity of
education through life-long 'formation' that has to be stressed, and
the need for cooperation based on mutual understanding between
educator and employer.

The need to integrate education within work expressed through life-long 'formation'
coincides with the views of The Round Table of European Industrialists (ERT,
1989: 170):

Work procedures and work itself are facing restructuring...The
contents and structure of jobs are changing. Ever higher competence
is expected in all occupations...more and more individuals are being
confronted with the stark reality that their education, completed
decades ago, no longer gives them the competence they need; indeed,
the very occupation for which that education prepared them is receding
below the horizon of history....

The ethos of linking work with education, i.e., the creation of a learning society,
is believed by many to be a key mechanism to help ensure the "future competitiveness of the European economic system" (ERT, 1989: 78). In the United Kingdom
the establishment of Training and Enterprise Councils (TECs), Local Enterprise
Companies (LECs) in Scotland, and Business Links epitomise some of the recent
efforts by government to respond to these concerns.

Contacts between industry and higher education are not new. The development
of 'University Extension' in the nineteenth century offering courses to working
men in mining, dairy, manures and soils is perhaps the earliest example of
collaboration between higher education and employees (Kelly, 1962). More recently,
programmes like the Teaching Company Scheme, established in 1975, bring firms
and academia together to solve business problems and generate better understanding between them. The Employment Department Group (1990a, b) has recently,
for instance, embarked on creating a framework with different methods of access,
delivery and assessment of training and upskilling provision. The development
of Work-based Learning techniques, Credit Accumulation and Transfer Schemes
(CATS) and the Accreditation of Prior Learning (APL) clearly illustrate this new
direction. The widening of access to higher education is intended to result in greater
flexibility of delivery and assessment and improved responsiveness to the needs
of employers. However, the concept of partnership is problematic. The assertion,
for example, that universities should provide employee training courses with

small and medium enterprises (SMEs) has been shown to be incredibly difficult for both partners with only a very limited number of successes (Edwards, 1995).

Nonetheless, 'partnership' remains a fundamental concept. Take for example, The Council for *Industry and Higher Education* (CIHE), an independent body made up of heads of large companies, universities and colleges. This body has attempted to encourage such collaboration and has represented such views to government, higher education and employers (CIHE, 1992). Although the CIHE is not responsible for government policy decisions, many of its proposals match subsequent government legislation. In particular, it sees government, higher education and industry needing to become partners in developing a different kind of higher education system (CIHE, 1987).

This new higher education system, according to the CIHE, would depend on a government strategy which was committed to expand higher education and on the "development of shared aims between companies and higher education through many levels of working contact" (CIHE, 1987: 1). The success of this 'new' system would be measured by its relevance to the needs of industry. The system would include new types of provision and methods of achievement with a more open system of higher education rebalanced towards mathematics, science and technology; providing appropriate courses for mature students still at work; achieved by collaboration with customers contributing to both the cost and character of provision and the introduction of improved cost-effectiveness and management (CIHE, 1987).

This strategy is reflected in recent government policy statements. For example:

- *Higher Education: Meeting the Challenge* (DoE, 1987) followed the CIHE's proposal for increasing student intake over the following ten years.

- *Realising Our Potential: A Strategy for Science, Engineering and Technology* (DoE, 1993), *Competitiveness: Helping Business To Win* (DTI, 1994), and *Competitiveness: Forging Ahead* (DTI, 1995) propose full governmental involvement in improving opportunities for wealth creation with specific emphasis given to research, education and training.

- *Realising Our Potential: A Strategy for Science, Engineering and Technology* (DoE, 1993), concentrates on developing a strategy for science, engineering and technology-based research through the Technology Foresight Programme. Its main objectives have been to build on the excellence of the work done by the science and engineering base (including universities) by establishing tighter relations with those experts from the commercial and industrial communities and reinventing the Research Councils and other research establishments in order to be able to deal more systematically with the 'global challenge' confronting the country.

The impact on universities of these White Papers and other government policy documents has been considerable. An idea of the purpose and nature of the impact can be gleaned from the titles of the most recent Paper's to affect universities. If one looks back to the White Paper *Working Together — Education and Training* (Department of Employment, 1986), and then more recently to *Higher Education, Meeting the Challenge* (1987) and *Higher Education: A New Framework* (1991), it is possible to discern the intention of government. This has been to re-mold the higher education system into a new *framework* which *working together* with industry would better equip universities in *meeting the challenge* of creating a competitive economy. This model of state university relations is one in which university activities conceived as outputs — such as research and teaching, including continuing education — have become more sensitised to the needs of the economy and seem to coincide with the notion of an overt economic ideology of education.

The effect of this model of state university relations is apparent in the 1991 Higher Education White Paper, the most significant aspect of which was the abolition of the binary divide between universities and polytechnics which allowed polytechnics to award their own degrees and to take on the title 'university'. The implication of this policy was the creation of an internal market where universities now had to compete more and more for funds in research and students and were to be encouraged to look (compete!) for increased levels of funding from private sources such as industry and commerce. These market rationales were based on the rationalisation of the higher education system and on improved management systems resulting in cost-effectiveness driven by quality, accountability, competition and selectivity.

The United Kingdom government has also attempted to set overall policy on student recruitment. By limiting overall funding and influencing the market of student demand and supply, government did influence the overall pattern. While overall direction was largely imposed, the impact on individual universities or colleges was often arbitrary not only because of changes to state funding policy exercised by the funding councils but also because of changes in student demand. Following the 1992 Higher Education Act and the establishment of a unified system and new funding regime, government control became more exact and the degree of autonomy and discretion of the funding councils severely limited.

As a result, individual university managements are often faced with difficult decisions in working out a strategy which will ensure financial and academic integrity because of the vagaries of government policy. In the United Kingdom's case, government policies have lacked long-term consistency — a situation exacerbated by the existence of a market-like situation in terms of student demand for particular courses or institutions. While there are some long-term trends and patterns, over a short period student demand for particular courses is subject to changes in fashion, unemployment rates and perceived job prospects. Thus university management in the specific area of student recruitment in the United Kingdom struggles to develop at least short-term plans. However, it is constrained by government policy, particularly changes in funding policy. At the same time, each university is in competition with other institutions in the market of student choice of universities and degrees.

Critics and advocates of markets may not recognise that markets are all to some degree regulated, if only in terms of basic legal framework guaranteeing rules of contract and the protection of private property. It has been recognised that the state may intervene to maintain a free market against the tendency for producers to organise into cartels. In the case of universities with the production of complex services involving teaching, learning, the acquisition of diplomas and degrees and the provision of research facilities and outcomes, it can and has been argued that a degree of state regulation may be necessary for the accreditation of universities, their courses and even research. The nature of the product or service makes it difficult for the operation of the market to protect consumer interests and some argue that this cannot be left to the professional competence or morality of the academics.

The effectiveness of state policy

We have reviewed some aspects of the United Kingdom state where governments in the 1980s and 1990s committed to free market competitive economic policies have developed policies intended to shape universities' education activities to increase the competitiveness of British industry and commerce. We have attempted to contextualise this both theoretically and substantively in terms of the relationship of the state to corporations within the world economy. A number of problems and paradoxes arise. It is not at all clear that the United Kingdom state under successive Conservative governments with its espousal of materialist and free market doctrines had either the ideology or the coherence to develop effective economic or higher education policies which would improve competitiveness. Alternative explanations of the problems of the United Kingdom economy (Hutton, 1995) which explains the United Kingdom's combination of high consumption and weak production in terms of market failure (the credit boom and sterling overvaluation) and archaic constitutional and institutional structures seem at least as convincing.

Furthermore, the specific policy proposals relating to universities with regard to influencing student recruitment, training and links with industry as well as research display a contradiction between allowing the market to function and the espousal of partnerships between industry and universities which has involved a good deal of state direction. There remains the general question of how far universities' activities in research, education and training can contribute (Sorge, 1994) to the development of a competitive economy.

More specifically, the nature of the partnerships proposed between universities and industry is problematic partly because the legitimacy and power of the respective partners can be ambiguous and contradictory and is confused by the broader espousal of a market ideology.

Important in the management of change on and in the universities has been the shift to an economic ideology with the celebration of the market and competition. Again this has not been simple and while some factors support and amplify each other in their effects, others remain ambiguous, paradoxical or even contradictory. Thus, at the same time as we have shown that there has been an increase in central direction and planning both from the state and in the university, there has been a greater ideological commitment to the operation of the market and to the virtues of competition. The institutional arrangements reflect and are framed by a changed language and discourse where references to managers, executives, quality, market and customers have come to dominate over language which refers to knowledge, scholarship, teachers and students.

While it is not always clear that university managements are effectively managing changes, the explicit reference to 'managers' in universities, their self reference (even self-consciousness) is a relatively new phenomenon which developed at different paces in different institutions in the 1980s. That is not to say that universities have not always in some sense been managed, but the notion of a separate managerial function, the dilution of collegial and professional authority and the explicit need to develop policy strategy and tactics to husband resources is relatively recent. This in part arises from two other common and interlinked features. These are firstly, the increased intervention of the state in the governance, control and even management of universities and secondly, the perceived increasing importance to the economy of the activities of the university in the provision of an educated and skilled workforce and the undertaking of useful and profitable research. These are linked by the assumption by the state, its politicians and functionaries that they have a role in bending the purposes of the university to meet the needs of competitive capitalist enterprise.

This produces some paradoxes: laissez-faire, market-orientated, monetarists in principle committed to the reduction of the powers of the state finding themselves involved in ever more intrusive expansions of state power into the domain of civil society in the name of improving the competitiveness of United Kingdom industry. Underlying these features of structure and political programme lie yet more basic unresolved questions of what should be the relationship of the universities to state and economy. These questions in turn are reflected in the continuing debates within the university about the nature and purposes of teaching and research. This in turn is related to the question of how the university should be governed and financed.

Conclusion — the future state-market dynamic

The recommendations of the National Committee of Inquiry into Higher Education (Dearing) are unlikely to reverse the general trends currently affecting the higher education system in the United kingdom. Taking a view of universities in terms of 'economic power', and as meeting the needs of the national economy, characterises much of the evidence to this committee. Leading politicians and business people continue to emphasise an economic ideology of education.

Any fundamental change in the direction of both major parties in policy towards the character of the higher education system following the change of government in May 1997 seems unlikely. The New Labour manifesto indicates that the Labour government will continue to encourage links between industry and universities; establishing for example, the 'University for Industry'. Indeed, the Labour manifesto openly supported the work of the Dearing Committee as a vehicle to "promote high-quality standards in science teaching and research throughout UK higher education" and a "collaborative approach between researchers and business" (New Labour, 1997: 16).

The continuing power of a market discourse in the higher education system is beyond doubt, as seen in the submissions to Dearing by influential bodies such as CIHE. The key recommendations of the CIHE (1996a) focused on themes such as 'partnership', 'accountability', 'applied learning', 'rationalisation', 'competitiveness', and 'efficiency'. It is taken as given that universities, colleges and business should work closely together, linking the general needs of society with the practical requirements of the world of work. This is articulated most clearly by the demand for both high quality discipline-based courses and applied learning courses which takes the 'world of work' as its context (CIHE, 1996a).

The type of higher education system advocated by the CIHE is one which is market orientated. Institutions are recommended to show more explicitly how 'their' graduates (customers) would be "better equipped to meet a more uncertain and constantly changing future". The emphasis is on customer choice and the university meeting that demand. Greater emphasis is given to partnerships between further and higher education institutions — regionalisation. This would allow institutions to rationalise their operations, buying-in courses and closing down 'weak' departments. Notions of efficiency and out-sourcing are clearly implied. However, as mentioned earlier, this illustrates a paradox between the notion of a free market and the realities of a managed market directed by the state. Regionalisation would demand a degree of planning and collaboration rather than competition between institutions.

Regionalisation equates with rationalisation. As admitted by the CIHE, there has been a decrease in revenue for higher education which makes it ever more difficult to meet the demands placed on the system. However, the CIHE does not advocate increases in public expenditure. Like the Labour party (see New

Labour, 1997), the CIHE advocates that students contribute to the costs of their education. Regionalisation is equated with savings in expenditure, cutting-out those elements that do not contribute 'efficiently' to the running of the system. Associated with this ethos are managerial notions of 'benchmarking' and 'cost-benefit analysis'. Such discourses are seen to enable institutions to compete more effectively and to quantify their value-added. In other words, "threshold standards, greater explicitness plus a greater readiness to accept independent, external assessment would reassure employers on relative standards" (CIHE, 1996b: 9).

To conclude, the market-dynamic continues to influence and reflect the social practices which constitute the activities of higher education institutions. This is likely to continue even with the recent change of government, because those discourses have been largely adopted by Prime Minister Blair and much of his New Labour government, if not necessarily the party or most Labour voters. The continuing constraints on public funding mean that universities will increase their market orientated behaviour and the search for additional non-governmental funding. The language and practice of governance in mass universities has become overtly managerial and market orientated.

References

Council for Industry and Higher Education (CIHE) (1987) *Towards a Partnership: Higher Education-Government-Industry*. London: CIHE.

———— (1992) *Investing in Diversity: An Assessment of Higher Education Policy*. London: CIHE.

———— (1996a) *A Learning Nation*. London: CIHE.

———— (1996b) *Annual Report and Accounts*. London: CIHE.

Department of Education and Science (1986) *City Technology Colleges. A New Choice of School*. London: DES.

Department of Education (1987) *Higher Education: Meeting the Challenge*. London: HMSO.

———— (1991) *Higher Education: A New Framework*. Cmnd 1541, London: HMSO.

———— (1993) *Realising our Potential: A Strategy for Science, Engineering and Technology*. Cmnd 2259, London: HMSO

Department of Employment (1986) *Working Together — Education and Training*. Cmnd 9823, London: HMSO.

Department of Trade and Industry (DTI) (1994) *Competitiveness: Helping Business to Win*. Cmnd 2563, London: HMSO.

———— (1995) *Competitiveness: Forging Ahead*. Cmnd 2867, London: HMSO.

Edwards, T.J. (1995) *Universities and the User Community: Marriage or Mismatch?* Unpublished MSc thesis, Aston University.

Employment Department Group (1990) *Higher Education Developments — The Skills Link*. Sheffield: EDG.

Employment Department Group (1990) *Higher Education Developments — The Skills Link 2*. Sheffield: EDG.

Giddens, A. (1985) *The Nation State and Violence*. Cambridge: Polity Press.

———— (1990) *The Consequences of Modernity*. Stanford: Stanford University Press.

Gray, R. (1990) 'History, marxism and theory', in H.J. Kay and K. McLelland (eds) *E.P. Thompson: Critical Perspectives*. Cambridge: Polity Press.

Halsey, A. (1992) *The Decline of Donnish Dominion*. Oxford: Claredon Press.

Harrison, M. (1991) 'Crisis Deepens on Britain's Campuses', *Observer*, 10 November 1991.

Held, D (1991) 'Democracy, the Nation-State and the Global System', in Held, D. (ed.) *Political Theory Today*, Cambridge: Polity Press.

Hirst, P. and Thompson, G. (1997) 'Globalisation: Ten Frequently Asked Questions and Some Surprising Answers', *Soundings*.

Hutton, W. (1995) *The State We're In*. London: Random House.

———— (1997) *The State to Come*. London: Random House.

Jessop, B. *et al* (1984) 'Authoritarian populism, two nations and Thatcherism', *New Left Review*, 147: pp.32-60.

Kelly, T. (1962) *A History of Adult Education in Great Britain*. Liverpool: University Press.

Kennedy, P.M. (1989) *The Rise and Fall of the Great Powers*. London: Unwin/Hyman.

———— (1993) *Preparing for the Twentieth Century*. London: Harper/Collins.

Laurens, R. (1990) 'University management: Tensions in a Changing Environment', *Journal of Tertiary Educational Administration*, 12 (1): May.

Marginson, S. (1996) '1983-1996 Labor in Review: higher education revolutionaries', *Campus Review*, March 14-20: 8-9.

Maskell, P. and Malmberg, A. (1995) Localised Learning and Industrial Competitiveness. Paper presented at the Regional Studies Association European Conference on *Regional Futures*.

Maslen, G. (1994) 'Universities hit technical hitch', *The Times Higher Educational Supplement*, January: 6.

Miller, H. (1995a) *The Management of Change in Universities*. Buckingham: Open University Press.

———— (1995b) 'Dons, domination and the state', Review essay in *British Journal of Sociology of Education*, 16(2).

Miller, H. and Wheeler, S. (1989) *Changing Patterns of Power in Higher education: A Case Study*. Paper to Ethnography and educational Reform Conference, Warwick University. September.

New Labour (1997) *Election Manifesto* for the 2nd May, 1997 general election.

Pearson, R. (1983) *Industry and Higher Education: Future Collaboration — The Training Dimension*. Institute of Manpower Studies.

Pritchard, C. and Willmott, H. (1995) Knowing Change in Changing Knowledge-based Organisations — an Education for Senior Academics in UK Universities. Paper for 'Change in Knowledge Based Organisations' Conference, University of Alberta, Canada (May).

Pusey, M. (1991) *Economic Rationalism in Canberra*. Cambridge: Cambridge University Press.

Robson, M. and Walford, G. (1989) 'Independent Schools and Tax Policy Under Mrs Thatcher', *Journal of Education Policy*, 4 (2): 49-162.

Salter, B. and Tapper, T. (1994) *The State and Higher Education*. Essex: Woburn Press.

Scott, P. (1995) *The Meanings of Mass Higher Education*. Buckingham: Open University Press.

Smith, D. (1990) *Capitalist Democracy on Trial: The Transatlantic Debate from Toqueville to the Present*. London: Routledge.

Smyth, J. (1995) *Academic Work*. Buckingham: Open University Press.

Sorge, A. (1994) 'The reform of technical education and training in Great Britain: A comparison of institutional learning in Europe', *Vocational Training European Journal*, 3: 59-68.

Tasker, M. and Packham, D. (1994) 'Government, higher education and the industrial ethic', *Higher Education Quarterly*, 48 (3).

The Round Table of European Industrialists (ERT) (1989) *Education for Life — A European Strategy*. Butterworth.

Thompson, E.P. (1991) *Customs in Commons*. London: Routledge/Kegan Paul.

Thompson, G.I. (1984) 'Rolling back the state? Economic intervention 1975-82', in Mclennan, G. Held, D. and Hall, S. (eds) *State and Society in Contemporary Britain*. Cambridge: Polity Press.

Wallerstein, I. (1974) *The Modern World System*. New York: Academic Press.

———— (1979) *The Capitalist World Economy*. Cambridge: Cambridge University Press.

III

DIVERSITY AND STRATIFICATION
IN UK HIGHER EDUCATION

The Limits to Diversity

4

David Watson

Introduction

In many ways what I have to say begins where Peter Scott (1995) has finished. I would like to break with all of my academic instincts and offer an argument which is as much advocacy and policy-oriented as reflective and analytical. I want to try to answer the question of how we resolve at least some of the dilemmas of mass higher education as they impact upon the United Kingdom. To show my hand early, I believe that the answer lies in being disciplined and open about the limits of diversity.

In making this case I want to challenge some received wisdom, and some stultifying cultural commitments made both by opponents and champions of 'massification'. Scott has done some of this already, by exposing some comfortable myths: about the antiquity, unity and autonomy of English universities in particular, and about their claimed centrality within both scientific research and national developments in intellectual life more generally. He has also undermined the popular interpretation that expansion has somehow meant 'privatisation', along the lines of water, electricity or telecommunications.

Scott is an effective, informed and sober guide to how we have arrived where we are. However, he is less assertive about where we can, or should go from here, which I take it to be at least a part of the agenda for this important conference. I intend to be less 'responsible'.

'Diversity' as code

How adequate is the term 'diversity' as a description of the UK higher educational scene? The answer is 'not very', especially if you believe what the colleges and universities say about themselves.

Mission analysis

I base the above assertion on the several analyses that are now available of institutional mission statements. For the most part these are mixtures of open-ended (emphatically not 'niche') marketing statements and the efforts of institutional leaders to keep all of their options open.

In 1991 John Earwaker read all of the statements published in the PCFC 'Profiles' and separated the 'hurrah' from the 'boo' words. The former included "international, technology, market-orientated...cost-effective.... high quality, enterprise, innovative, flexible, responsive, value-added.... vocationally relevant.... regional, employment-orientated, staff development.... competitive, accountable". The latter (sometimes grudgingly creeping in) included "academic community, cultural, free inquiry.... support services, scholarship, student welfare, learning" (Earwaker, 1991: 4). A crude summary might be to say that everybody wanted access, excellence, the region, Europe and staff loyalty.

There is not a lot of evidence that we (former UFC and PCFC institutions) have learned much since then. Mackay, Scott and Smith have analysed 168 mission statements and concluded that the key characteristic is the hedging of bets. Their overall conclusion is that "the intentions of the mission statements .... may be more defensive than offensive, to express group identity and conformity rather than reflect individuality and distinctiveness" (Mackay et al., 1995: 203).

Even in their most aggressively promotional behaviour the institutions tell the market the same things. For the last two years universities and colleges have been taking advantage of their charitable status to avoid VAT on advertising, through the use of tag-lines. These, again, are extraordinarily undifferentiated. Most (like Birkbeck) stress 'access and excellence,' or (like Portsmouth) excellence in 'teaching and research'. Very few seek further differentiation, although Lancaster describes itself as a 'campus university', Kent as 'Britain's European University', Nottingham as 'research-led', Sheffield Hallam as concerned with 'education for business and the professions' and Oxford Brookes as 'working with students to achieve excellence'. **Table 4.1** (opposite) shows the distribution of the most commonly claimed characteristics. Will 'research' still be top after the 1996 RAe?

The beleaguered Vice-Chancellor's trump card

This reluctance to be specific undermines one element of what might be called the 'vice-cancellarian complaint' about what is happening to the system. Put simply, this claims that any external criticism (of quality, or of strategy) is a failure to 'understand diversity'. Moreover, the failure to address mission specificity — or singularity of mission — fuels a public suspicion that rapid expansion plus diversity has come to mean that 'anything goes'. In other words, we are in danger of having 'diversity as excuse' rather than disciplined pluralism.

Table 4.1   Analysis of 'charity tag-lines'

	'Old' universities (39)	'New' universities (28)	Colleges of HE (8)	Total (75)
Research	30	12	4	46
Excellence	21	12	2	35
Teaching	20	6	3	29
Education	9	14	2	25
Learning	12	3	2	17
Quality	3	1	2	6
Vocational/Careers	0	4	1	5
Access	1	3	0	4
Knowledge	4	0	0	4
Lifelong learning	1	2	0	3
Training	0	0	2	2
International	2	0	0	2

John Patten (September 1993) on diversity and quality

Government and the DfEE have not been much help either. While piously expressing concern about an incipient public and journalistic outrage (see, for example, leaders in the *Daily Telegraph* (1995) as well as the summer of 1995's silly season stories about entry qualifications), they simultaneously try to imply to the institutions that they can have it all (Clare, 1995; Woodrow, 1995). The code for their concern is the demand for evidence about the maintenance of *standards*. The frequent assertion is that we can have both diversification and *quality*. John Patten's now notorious address to the CVCP conference of September 1993 gives a classic example of this juxtaposition:

> Diversity, and flexibility, will continue to be the watchwords as the student body continues to evolve. Higher Education needs to respond to the growing diversity of students — diversity of age, diversity of experience and diversity of patterns of study...That will mean increasingly flexible institutions, ready to adjust course patterns and modes of learning as well as traditional academic qualifications to meet the changing needs. The breaking down of the old divide has already unleashed institutional creativity on both sides of the divide. I expect much more to come...

But, he continued:

> [t]he government wants to maintain the high standards and reputation of British higher education. We do not want a system in which some British degrees or universities are seen as second or third rate. All students should have high quality higher education wherever they are and whatever course they are on.

To see a government that has specifically nourished competition at the expense of collaboration (which as a process has relied historically upon sector-wide patterns of self-regulation) suddenly express concern about possible failures collectively to guarantee standards is deeply ironic.

Funding: the 'convergence/compliance' argument

It is not just quality that the vice-chancellors accuse of bringing about a compliance culture, but also the systems used to distribute funding. Again the story is rather more complicated than they would generally like to admit. Look at the apparent winners and losers from the HEFCE's arrangements for teaching funding (see **Table 4.2**). Both groups look satisfactorily 'diverse' to me.

Historically, of course, it was research funding which marked the difference between the two former sectors, preserved until the settlement of 1995-96 in the relative protection it was afforded from so-called 'efficiency gains'. Opening up the competition for Funding Council research funds has created its own tensions, as is shown by resulting league table (see **Table 4.3**) of the 'R' element in funding. This not only underlines the difficulty of achieving promotion (as opposed to relegation), but also a serious question about the sensible limits of selectivity. I would urge that the funding problem is more about the total sum made available from public sources than about its distribution, and that again 'diversity' has been unhelpful in clarifying the issue. This is one story behind the fate of the famous 'unit of resource' (see **Table 4.4**) (another is, of course, the willingness of the PCFC sector to expand student numbers in the late 1980s as the UFC effectively, but probably shortsightedly, cartelised against such expansion).

We now face a potentially very immediate resourcing dilemma, from which the Dearing Committee of Inquiry (welcome though it is) is potentially a serious distraction. The system, in fact, finally faces a general crisis (not just the potentially isolable failure of a small number of institutions), as data from institutions collected before the cuts in the 1995 budget makes clear.

The stark question is whether or not we have reached what John Beavan used to call the 'impending precipice'. The advocates of retrenchment would clearly have preferred a quality crisis to prove the merits of their case. This the sector has resolutely refused to deliver. Instead of which we may have a financial crisis (which I would define as a significant minority of institutions being unable to meet the terms of the financial memorandum) in advance of the quality crisis.

Table 4.2   **1994/95 'T' funding per student above or below average funding**

FULL-TIME/SANDWICH		PART-TIME	
Oxford Brookes	+468	Oxford	+2,559
Leeds Met	+424	Cambridge	+731
Sheffield Hallam	+378	UMIST	+678
Oxford	+313	North London	+493
Liverpool JM	+300	East London	+448
Brighton	+299	Birkbeck	+376
Kingston	+266	Oxford Brookes	+350
Northumbria	+263	Newcastle	+268
Imperial	+258	Manchester Met	+261
Aston	+238	Brighton	+222
SOAS	-268	Middlesex	-446
Anglia	-308	Leicester	-463
Warwick	-311	Luton	-465
Humberside	-313	Liverpool	-499
Brunel	-313	Sheffield	-499
City	-417	Southampton	-546
Surrey	-429	Lancaster	-587
Birkbeck	-465	Bristol	-617
Derby	-471	Exeter	-712
Luton	-484	Bath	-932

Source: Peter Knight, *THES* 16 February 1996.

Table 4.3   HEFCE research funding as a % of total grant 1995–1996

% of Total Grant 1995-96	No.	Institution
0.01 — 0.12	2	Luton, Central England
1.20 — 2.75	8	Humberside, Anglia Polytechnic, Thames Valley, Bournemouth, London Guildhall, Derby, Central Lancashire, Wolverhampton
3.22 — 4.59	15	Leeds Metropolitan, Greenwich, Teesside, Nottingham Trent, North London, Staffordshire, Liverpool John Moores, East London, South Bank, Huddersfield, West of England, Kingston, Open, Hertfordshire, Westminster
5.10 — 5.94	5	De Montfort, Northumbria, Manchester Metropolitan, Sheffield Hallam, Sunderland
6.83 — 9.80	6	Middlesex, Plymouth, Coventry, Brighton, Oxford Brookes, Portsmouth
16.14 — 16.27	2	Brunel, Goldsmiths
19.88 — 25.23	8	Salford, Aston, Royal Holloway, City, Cranfield, Birkbeck, Bradford, Hull
28.42 — 34.63	15	Kent, Queen Mary & Westfield, London, Keele, Loughborough, Liverpool, Durham, Leeds, Leicester, Exeter, Sheffield, Newcastle-upon-Tyne, Essex, Bristol, Surrey
35.76 — 38.45	11	Lancaster, Birmingham, Nottingham, Sussex, East Anglia, Manchester, Reading, Southampton, Bath, King's College, York
41.51 — 43.29	3	UMIST, Warwick, University College
45.16 — 46.87	2	Imperial, LSE
57.36 — 59.62	2	London Business School, Cambridge
61.07	1	Oxford

Table 4.4   Unit public funding

Year	INDEX		
	Universities	HEFCE	Polytechnics
1979-80	100		100
1980-81	106		99
1981-82	103		94
1982-83	106		89
1983-84	107		82
1984-85	106		79
1985-86	103		78
1986-87	102		79
1987-88	105		76
1988-89	103		75
1989-90	100	100	100
1990-91		92	
1991-92		86	
1992-93		79	
1993-94		77	
1994-95		75	
1995-96		73	
1996-97		71	
1997-98		69	

Public funding per FTE in HE in real terms (using Nov 1993 GDP) index on differing base years at 100.

Sources: 1979-80 to 1988-89: PQ Written answers 3 Dec 91 for both University and Polytechnic data. 1989-90 to 1996-97: DFE Departmental Report 1994 and 1995.

Table 4.5   1995 financial forecasts HEFCE sector summary income and expenditure account

	1993-94 £000	1994-95 £000	1995-96 £000	1996-97 £000	1997-98 £000	1998-99 £000
Total Income	7,591,000	8,005,146	8,373,288	8,604,632	8,858,375	9,106,410
Total Expenditure	7,344,642	7,846,711	8,306,829	8,578,887	8,835,984	9,090,723
Surplus/(Deficit) after Depreciation of Assets at Valuation and Tax	245,192	157,616	65,683	24,839	21,347	14,631
Historical Cost Surplus/(Deficit) after Tax	285,015	204,038	110,925	68,544	64,578	57,670

Source: HEFCE Circular 28/95

Table 4.6   Analyses of sensitivity of financial forecasts to changes in key assumptions

	1995-96 £M	1996-97 £M	1997-98 £M	1998-99 £M
1 per cent increase in pay inflation	-32	-65	-101	-140
1 per cent increase in non-pay inflation	-21	-40	-60	-82
0.5% increase in efficiency gain on Council funding	-11	-26	-41	-57
5 per cent shortfall in research contract income	-14	-25	-37	-51
1 per cent shortfall in Home and EC full-time student recruitment	-12	-21	-30	-39
3 per cent shortfall in part-time recruitment	-7	-12	-16	-23
2 per cent shortfall in recovery rates on research contracts	-7	-11	-15	-20
1 per cent increase in interest payable	-5	-10	-14	-19
1 per cent shortfall in overseas student recruitment	-4	-6	-10	-13

Source: HEFCE Circular 28/95

Table 4.7   Aggregated strategic plan highlights

1993-99
Full-time and Sandwich (FTE) overseas students up 27% (all institutions)
Part-time overseas students up 32% (all institutions)
80% of institutions increasing p.g. provision
66% of institutions increasing part-time provision
33% of institutions increasing employer links in CVE
Home and EC part-time numbers up 40% (all institutions)
100% replacement of TTA-related reductions
Overall improvement in RAE ratings

Source: HEFCE Circular 28/95

HEFCE Circular 28/95 aggregates information about institutions' financial forecasts and strategic plans. It reveals that relentless efficiency gains have not simply sweated out a very few poorly managed institutions, but have instead reduced the sector as a whole to margins which are wafer-thin (see **Table 4.5**) (HEFCE, 1995).

Even before the latest rounds of cuts it was clear that these tiny relative surpluses were immediately vulnerable to quite modest shifts in sensitivity. The same circular showed the effect of several of these (**Table 4.6**). For example, it would only take an increase in pay of 1% above that forecast or a 5% shortfall in research contract income to pitch the sector as a whole into deficit in the next financial year.

The other main lesson of Circular 28/95 lies in the aggregated strategic plans (**Table 4.7**). Plainly all of the institutions think that they can win in all of the markets all of the time.

Against this background I would like to open up a discussion about possible futures, which I propose to do in three stages. I will offer a model for possible futures of the system as a whole, and then of individual institutions. Finally, I shall try to unpack what I believe to be the key dilemmas of my preferred option.

HE futures

Where does a 'mass UK system' go? Looking in summary at the experience on the one hand of the rest of Europe and on another the features of higher education in North America gives us two alternative visions of the future. These can then be compared with a third, even more hypothetical future: the elements to be retained by the UK system if it is able to expand without abandoning a range of historical commitments (**Table 4.8**).

The modern 'European' university is large (at least 20,000 undergraduate students) and fairly uniform (in the sense that its mission and style would be readily recognised by its peers). Its students normally have an extensive entitlement to free, or almost free, tuition, but very little by way of maintenance or other support. Partly as a result, the vast majority study in their home city or one to which they can travel to study from home. While they are enrolled their access to facilities (including often libraries) is fairly restricted, and the range of 'Student Service' or 'Student Union'-style facilities common to UK higher education institutions is conspicuously absent. The course leading to an undergraduate degree is a long

Table 4.8   HE futures

FEATURES	MODELS		
	EUROPE	N. AMERICA	'EXPANDED UK'
Institutional characteristics	large uniform	variable size highly stratified	relatively small guaranteed standards
Student experience	free tuition study-from-home rationed facilities	variable costs work-study variable facilities	state support away from home controlled range of facilities
Curriculum	long courses qualification filters	varied pace of study general u.g. 'professional' p.g.	intensive courses general and 'professional' u.g.
Outcomes	low completion	delayed completion	high completion

one (a minimum of four years, often extended to seven or more by tacit agreement between student, sponsors and institutions). Progression filters (for example at the end of the first year) operate ruthlessly and constitute the most important element of quality control; however, this rarely prevents students from being able to repeat, leading to a dramatic skewing of cohort and hence class size towards the early years of courses. As a result, one of the most striking outcomes is the low graduation rate.

Compared to this no-doubt exaggerated picture, the North American system demonstrates a dramatic diversity. Institutions not only vary enormously in size but also in mission and orientation, with a resulting wide reputational range (converted into a mathematical scale for such purposes as postgraduate admissions). The student experience varies accordingly, with costs and facilities moving together and a widespread acceptance that participation by relatively poor students in relatively expensive institutions is only possible through a complex and individualised system of financial aid, often involving work-study. In curriculum terms, almost universal modularisation (including the ubiquitous availability of summer schools) and a commitment to credit exchange results in significantly varied pace of study as well as the phenomenon of a high proportion of graduates earning their degrees from institutions other than those with which they started. (This latter feature is not always absorbed by the British 'access through CATS' vanguard; most would be reluctant to see their institutions passing on their ablest students, once securely launched in higher education, to more prestigious neighbours.)

Two further features are worthy of note. In North America (Canada as well as the United States), the first degree, built centrally on student choice often with the delayed choice of a disciplinary 'major', is rarely if ever the key professional qualification and licence to practice. In most professional areas (despite the distortions caused by 'pre-law' and 'pre-medicine' streams), the prerequisite for employment is at least the specialised masters degree. Secondly, the price for all of this flexibility, reputational spread, and (indirectly) a world-leading age participation rate (APR) is a pattern of elongated involvement and frequently delayed completion.

The contrast between these two models and what we know (and love?) about the British scene is occasionally stark and almost always clear. British universities (with the possible exceptions of Manchester Metropolitan, the De Montfort diaspora, and the federal fictions of London and Wales) are small in comparison with Europe. Unlike the North American case, all degree-awarding bodies are locked into a common framework of standards and quality assurance, based upon external examination, 'audit' by the Higher Education Quality Council (HEQC) and 'assessment' by the Funding Councils; in this sense a 'universal' and internationally envied system of self-regulation applies.

Students in the UK system receive a significant amount of state support, to cover all fees, and a means-tested contribution to maintenance (around £2b of a total of £7b of the public funds spent on higher education in 1995-96). The fact that the principles underlying this contribution have broken down (and pose the most immediate political question facing higher education and its funders) does not reduce its macro-economic significance. Also, and at least partly as a result of sector-wide quality assurance (as well as the growing movement for student charters), they can expect to enjoy student facilities (including pastoral care and academic-tutorial support) within a controlled range. Their courses are more intensive than in either of the other two cases, mixing both general and 'professional' objectives at the undergraduate stage, and their chief merit on the international scale of performance indicators is a high completion (or 'graduation-per-cohort') rate.

My assertion is that much of this can and should be preserved in a larger and more democratic system, that the British system of mass higher education can build on what was perceived to be of value in its past and which contributes to much of its attraction to students, including from overseas. To do so requires proper funding (for students and for institutions), the acceptance (through quality assurance) of a controlled reputational range, and shared understanding of a pluralist and a post-modular curricular world.

Institutional futures: universities ancient and modern

The key challenge to individual institutions is how to find their own effective roles within such a system. The task is daunting, with 190 separate institutions (123 of them entitled to include 'university' somewhere in their titles) graduating approximately 160,000 students each year. Using some Weberian techniques, let us try to identify in 'ideal' terms the two ends of the available spectrum (see **Table 4.9**).

The image of the ancient university is of an elite institution to which 'admission' is on a highly competitive basis. Its courses are all full-time and highly structured, usually around the single subject honours degree. Its postgraduate students are all doing research, and its research mission is to investigate 'basic' or 'fundamental' questions, removed from applications. As a result it is organised around traditional disciplines or subjects, and its teaching and learning styles follow suit. A high proportion of its students aspire to go on to be researchers themselves. From outside the ancient university fits the stereotype of the 'ivory tower'. Its main concern is with its international reputation, which is used to justify its relatively high costs.

The modern university presents a mirror image of these features. Its openness and accessibility is reflected in the fact that it 'enrols' rather than admits students. They can be on a variety of modes of study (full-time, part-time, mixed), and the awards they achieve are similarly flexible (certificates, diplomas and degrees,

Table 4.9   Universities: ancient and modern

ANCIENT	MODERN
Elite	Open
Competitive 'admission'	Accessible 'enrolment'
Full-time	Full-time, part-time, mixed mode
Highly structured	Flexible, modular
Single honours	Many levels, intermediate awards, CATS
Postgraduate research	Postgraduate and post-experience, CPD
Traditional teaching	Innovative learning styles
Subjects and disciplines	Interdisciplinarity Professional and vocational applications
Pure/basic research	Applied research, consultancy, 'technology transfer'
Graduates to research and further study	High graduate employment
The 'ivory tower'	Many partnerships
National/international reputation	Local/regional role
High costs	High VFM

usually on a modular or credit accumulation basis). Teaching and learning methods are innovative and imaginative; interdisciplinarity is important, as are the professional and vocational aspects of knowledge, including core or 'transferable skills'. Preparation for employment across a wide range is important (in other public services and the voluntary sector as well as industry and commerce) and the university is intensively used by 'post-experience' students as part of their career and professional development. The same priorities structure its research mission, with strong emphasis on applied knowledge, on high level consultancy, and on knowledge and technology transfer. Externally, the modern university thrives through partnerships and synergy with other regional players. Its community profile is high, and its financial strategy is to deliver the best possible value for money.

These ideal-types represent the outer boundaries within which institutional diversity can be fixed.

Limiting reputational range

After funding, controlling the reputational range is arguably the toughest question we face collectively. How could and should we get a grip on diversity in the interests of effective pluralism?

Philosophical issues

A first set of issues is philosophical. If we are committed to equal opportunities in higher education, there must be structures which will allow us to deliver a recognisable student experience of it. This in turn raises definitional questions; as Ron Barnett and others have eloquently argued, there may be an irreducible 'essence' of higher education without which it would not deserve the name (Barnett, 1990). The question of responsibility is ultimately a philosophical one too — does it belong to the higher education community as a whole (the sectoral view), or does this very idea fatally undermine institutional autonomy?

Another way of articulating these dilemmas is in terms of the regulating 'conscience' of the system. Is it primarily internal, and concerned with the protection and development of a tradition? If so, what are its key points of reference: the system, the institution, or the subject? Or does it allow for modification in response to legitimate external requirements, including the changing needs of students?

To nail my colours to the mast, I am also at heart an essentialist. Students are not simply 'customers' or 'consumers', but ideally 'members' of academic communities. As such, however, they should be entitled to some formative influence over the development of those communities. Equally, I do believe that there is something both epistemological and applied in the 'higher' part of higher education. I do, however, resent attempts to ration access to this good on the basis of what are regarded as fixed historical costs, and I want the 'essence' broadened in the service of a wider range of purposes. 'Higher educational' criteria are at least as applicable to physiotherapy as they are to chemistry.

Cultural issues

Such philosophical questions lead more directly than is comfortable for many of us into questions of everyday values and cultural commitments. There is, for example, a well-established critique of developments within the academy that conveniently and powerfully merges anxieties and resentments of both the left and the right (the former being better represented at this conference). This focuses strongly upon the immiseration of the academic estate, and is curiously dismissive of the changing needs of students and other clients of a 'modern' university system.

The target, of both left and right, is conveniently new or 'hard' management, thereby eliding resentments of a variety of types: at under-resourcing; at loss of exclusive control over the curriculum; and at new forms of accountability. The attack has some powerful champions. An exemplar is Martin Trow, as represented by his evocative thesis of the 'Robbins Trap' (Trow, 1989).

Trow and his willing followers are not only victims of misplaced nostalgia (as I believe Scott to have conclusively established) but have also failed to understand the true significance of the expansion of the 1980s, as opposed to that of the 1960s. It was the achievement of the 'polytechnic' tradition not just to establish higher education in a number of vocational fields, but in doing so to bind together both academic and professional values (Bines and Watson, 1992). In this sense its agents did anything but fall into the 'Robbins trap'. What is more, especially through the work of the Council for National Academic Awards, this transformation was achieved through a disciplined series of additions to the field of acceptable diversity within UK higher education (Watson, 1997). This record must not be allowed to be confused by what is, at root, a defensively elitist rearguard action associating falling unit costs, assumed changes in management practices, and a lack of respect for changing student priorities, with strikingly anti-empirical claims about loss of professional autonomy.

Organisational issues

It is not hard to turn all of these problems into practical issues of implementation. However flawed the 'market' metaphor may be for educational systems (including higher education) some form of understood currency is necessary for managing it (whether it is the concept of the honours degree or a fully fledged Robertsonian CATS scheme) (Robertson, 1994). Simultaneously, the various stakeholders — students and their sponsors, government and other funders, industry and other partners, and not least the staff who have invested their careers — will want and need measures of accountability.

This leads directly back to the issues of mutual respect, understanding of outer boundaries (even if peer responsibility means that these are initially conservatively defined), and practical expressions of inter-institutional reciprocity: external examination, quality assurance, professional accreditation and the like. My sense is that we are painfully moving past a period of modular and CATs fetishism, to a genuinely post-modular world. This future world will be characterised by units of study, potentially portable credit, intermediate as well as major awards, individualised as well as group-customised programmes of study, personal as well as professional development; in other words lifelong learning or continuing education. With good will, and an effective restoration of collaborative as opposed to competitive drives within the system, we can make the best of this world within a genuinely pluralist system.

Conclusion

We could pursue all of these issues at much greater length. None the less I feel that an expanded UK system with an appropriate range of diverse missions fairly clearly needs to make rapid progress in at least three areas. They frame the real agenda for Dearing.

First, there is the challenge of funding the institutions (from a variety of sources, including private) to do an effective job in an appropriate environment (i.e. capital as well as revenue). Secondly, we must make the right arrangements for access and the flexible curriculum (including student support and tidying up the jungle of current post-compulsory qualifying systems; both have been recommended firmly by the National Commission on Education) (NCE, 1995). Finally, we must sort out both standards and quality assurance.

Significantly it is this last arena where most of the acceptable solutions lie in our own hands, and, unless we are careful, we (as now represented by the Joint Planning Group of the Funding Councils and CVCP) may drop them. Above all we need to retain and develop rigorous peer review through both external examination and a sensibly merged system of subject assessment and audit. The systems we need to develop depend on external peers and are thus inescapably messy. They are, however, the best we have got and infinitely preferable to the roads not taken (including 'inspection', reliance on simplistic performance indicators, or a Canute-like insistence that purely internal processes will suffice). The real danger in the present climate, as I have argued throughout this paper, is a breakdown of the principles of institutional reciprocity and mutual esteem. We have already seen this on funding, with the advocates of 'top-up' fees and the like aiming at a system where the 'market will decide'; on standards and quality this could be fatal (Watson, 1997).

I am aware, in bringing this chapter to a close, how generally critical the tone must appear of current attitudes and practices within and outside the academy Much of the chapter has in fact been an analysis of deficit: in funding, adaptability, and responsibility for quality and standards. The impression could be gained of a case for shoring-up a rickety structure, hopelessly ill-adapted for the next century. This is not the impression I intend to give. In a genuinely historical perspective, such as that provided by Peter Scott, the story of the last two decades has much to commend it, especially in terms of access, of equity, and of relevance. What is more, much of this success has been achieved against the odds. It is remarkable how much the system has held together, after the roller-coaster of government policy has taken its toll, and given the systematic elevation of the competitive over the collaborative gene. Throughout this process, those of us who have been engaged on the inside have had to accept some hard things: lower unit funding, a challenging growth of student entitlement, pressures to be specific about 'professional' commitments, a disturbing move to politicise traditional responsibilities for quality and standards (even if this has been much more successfully resisted than we would like to admit). But amidst all of these constraints we have retained the core of a higher education culture and practice for the next century. To deliver it successfully will now need some steady nerves and some cool thinking.

References

Barnett, R. (1990) *The Idea of Higher Education*. Milton Keynes: Society for Research into Higher Education/Open University Press.

Bines, H. and Watson, D. (1992) *Developing Professional Education*. Buckingham: Society for Research into Higher Education/Open University Press.

Clare, J. (1995) 'Universities fail to make the grade', *Daily Telegraph*, 22 March, p. 19.

Daily Telegraph (1995) Leader: 'University Failures', *Daily Telegraph*, 22 March, p. 22.

Earwaker, J. (1991) 'Boo to the Barbarians', *Times Higher Education Supplement*, 29 March, p. 4.

Higher Education Funding Council for England (1995) *Recurrent Grant for the Academic Year 1995-96: Final Allocation* Circular 25/95 October 1995. Bristol: HEFCE.

Higher Education Funding Council for England (1995) *Analysis of 1995 Strategic Plans and Financial Forecasts* Circular 28/95 November 1995. Bristol, HEFCE.

Knight, P. (1996) 'New currency proves worth', *Times Higher Education Supplement*, 16 February, p. 6.

Mackay, L., Scott, P. and Smith, D. (1995) 'Restructured and Differentiated? Institutional Responses to the Changing Environment of UK Higher Education', *Higher Education Management* 7 (2): 193-205.

National Commission on Education (1995) *Learning to Succeed. The Way Ahead. A Report from the Paul Hamlyn Foundation National Commission on Education*. London: NCE.

Patten, J. (1993) Speech to CVCP Conference, University of Leicester, September.

Robertson, D. (1994) *Choosing to Change; Extending Access, Choice and Mobility in Higher Education*. The report of the HEQC CAT Development Project. London: HEQC.

Scott, P. (1995) *The Meanings of Mass Higher Education*. Milton Keynes: Society for Research into Higher Education and Open University Press.

Trow, M. (1989) 'The Robbins Trap: British Attitudes and the Limits of Expansion', *Higher Education Quarterly* 43 (1): 55-75.

Watson, D. (1997) 'Quality, standards and institutional reciprocity', in J. Brennan *et al.* (eds) *Standards and Quality in Higher Education*. London: Jessica Kingsley.

Woodrow, M. (1995) 'The Foundation Smokescreen', *Times Higher Education Supplement* 8 September, p. 13.

The US Community College: a Positive or Negative Model for UK Higher Education?

5

David Jary, David Alan Gatley and Louise Broadbent

Introduction

In *Higher Education for the 21st Century* (1998), its response to the Dearing Report, the UK Government declares that its "priority is to reach out and include those under-represented in higher education..." (p. 11). However it goes on to suggest that growth is to be "at sub-degree level, mainly in further education colleges". Money for extra places is to go to "institutions that can demonstrate a commitment to widening access".

In the UK, access to HE from previously under-represented groups has increased in the last decade, but significantly it has increased far more in the former polytechnic and college sector/'new' universities than in older pre-1992 universities.

The question addressed in this chapter is: *'Access to what?'*.

Patterns of recruitment to HE institutions in higher education systems further down the track of mass higher education than the UK suggest a possible general tendency to an increasing institutional and social stratification in mass HE systems as access expands (Scott, 1995). In this chapter we consider the direction and implications of changing patterns of participation in UK higher education for equality of opportunity and equality more generally. Comparisons, in particular with US higher education, are drawn which will help to raise questions about the direction now being proposed for UK higher education and whether international tendencies to greater institutional stratification can (or should) be resisted.

At a time when cost-effective and regional solutions to the problems of providing an expanded mass higher education are being suggested — not least the concentration of further expansion of higher education in FE colleges and on 'sub-degree' courses — an especially pertinent comparison is provided by the US Community College movement. Although there are some 'positive' features,

83

the lessons from these institutions are, to say the least, mixed. They are associated with more limited educational and occupational opportunities than universities. We will do well to note such warnings in taking higher education down the route of potentially even more stratified provision.

A developmental model of higher education systems

Figure 5.1 presents a comparative developmental model of HE advanced recently by Peter Scott (1995).

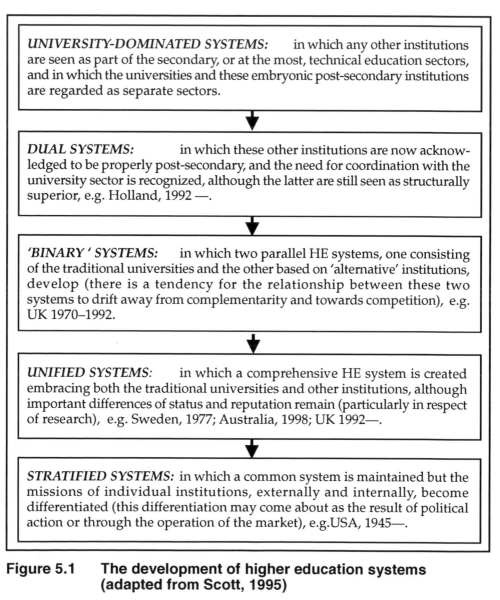

UNIVERSITY-DOMINATED SYSTEMS: in which any other institutions are seen as part of the secondary, or at the most, technical education sectors, and in which the universities and these embryonic post-secondary institutions are regarded as separate sectors.

DUAL SYSTEMS: in which these other institutions are now acknow-ledged to be properly post-secondary, and the need for coordination with the university sector is recognized, although the latter are still seen as structurally superior, e.g. Holland, 1992 —.

'BINARY' SYSTEMS: in which two parallel HE systems, one consisting of the traditional universities and the other based on 'alternative' institutions, develop (there is a tendency for the relationship between these two systems to drift away from complementarity and towards competition), e.g. UK 1970–1992.

UNIFIED SYSTEMS: in which a comprehensive HE system is created embracing both the traditional universities and other institutions, although important differences of status and reputation remain (particularly in respect of research), e.g. Sweden, 1977; Australia, 1998; UK 1992—.

STRATIFIED SYSTEMS: in which a common system is maintained but the missions of individual institutions, externally and internally, become differentiated (this differentiation may come about as the result of political action or through the operation of the market), e.g.USA, 1945—.

**Figure 5.1   The development of higher education systems
(adapted from Scott, 1995)**

The historical development of the US higher education system illustrates the general developmental pattern. Scott notes the continued importance of historical and cultural differences in HE patterns internationally, and as an historian he is rightly cautious in advancing too strongly any general proposition. Nevertheless, a tendency to increasing institutional stratification appears strongly evident internationally, the result both of 'market' competition between institutions and of government action to hold down or reduce the cost of provision — and also protect elite provision — by expanding non-elite mass provision.

In terms of Scott's developmental model, the move from a 'binary' to a 'unified' system undertaken by the UK can be seen as *paradoxical* because while the creation of a system embracing both traditional universities and previous non-universities has made university education more widely available, it also has had the effect of intensifying competitive pressures between institutions and making selective state funding to protect elite provision *more* likely — both of which increase the tendency to institutional hierarchy.

The 'lessons' of the USA

In their important study of US community colleges — *The Diverted Dream* (1989) — Steven Brint and Jerome Karabel indicate the effects of the extended hierarchy of institutions within the highly stratified US system[1]. Within the US, junior and community colleges stand at the base of the HE system, offering two-year courses which can, but do not necessarily, lead on to the completion of four-year bachelor courses in universities.

What Brint and Karabel suggest about these institutions is that they can be seen as having:

> ... faced two contradictory tasks: the *democratic* one of bringing new populations into higher education [but] the *exclusionary* one of channeling them away from the four-year institutions that they hoped to attend. (1989: 208, emphasis added)

They note how many commentators have been prepared to regard:

> ... the two-year college's task as the firm but gentle rechanneling of ... students toward middle-level jobs commensurate with their presumed abilities and past accomplishments. Seen through this prism, the educational and occupational aspirations of most junior college students were 'excessive' and therefore in need of 'adjustment'. (pp. 208-9)

The double stratification — *social* as well as *institutional* — that has resulted historically from the location of community/junior colleges within the hierarchical

US system is indicated in **Tables 5.1a–1d** (source: Brint and Karabel, *The Diverted Dream, 1989*). The historical tendency for students in community colleges to be drawn from lower class (**Tables 5.1a–1b**) and ethnic minority backgrounds (**Table 5.1c**) is clear, as is the more restricted entry to high status jobs associated with these institutions (**Table 5.1d**).

Table 5.1a–5.1b Historical patterns of social recruitment in community colleges (Brint and Karabel, 1989)

Table 5.1a Percentage distribution by occupational groups of fathers of students in public high schools and in different types of US college and university (1920s)

Parental Occupation	Public High School	Public Junior College	Public JCs Sophomores Only	Private	Sophomores in College and State University	Freshmen in large Eastern University
1 Proprietors	19.8	19.1	17.8	29.5	25.1	35.7
2 Professional service	9.4	14.0	15.3	15.3	20.8	30.3
3 Managerial service	16.5	16.3	17.8	9.4	7.8	5.4
4 Commercial service	9.5	9.3	9.6	6.9	8.7	8.6
5 Clerical service	5.8	3.8	2.8	1.1	3.5	2.4
6 Agricultural service	2.4	14.2	11.7	26.9	22.5	1.4
7 Artisan-proprietors	4.2	2.8	3.2	1.7	2.6	0.3
8 Manual labor	29.1	15.6	18.3	6.7	7.1	6.5
9 Unknown	3.3	4.9	3.6	2.4	2.0	9.4
Total:	100.0	100.0	100.1	99.9	100.1	100.0

Original source: Koos 1924: 138 (Brint and Karabel, 1989, p. 44)

Table 5.1b   Comparison of samples of male students at four California Colleges by occupation of student's father (percentages) , working and male population (over 14) of the city of San Jose, 1950s

College	Upper White - Collar	Lower White - Collar	Upper Blue- Collar	Lower Blue- Collar	Total
Stanford University	87	7	6	0	100 (N=55)
University of California	69	14	11	6	100 (N=52)
San Jose State College	38	17	29	16	100z (147)
San Jose Junior College	23	15	45	17	100 (N=95)
City of San Jose	26	17	38	19	100 (N=23,699)

Original source: Clarke 1960, p. 54 (Brint and Karabel, p. 74)

Table 5.1c   Percentage of college students in different types of institution, by ethnic group (USA, 1978)

	Universities	Other Four-Year Institutions	Two-Year Colleges
Public Institutions:			
Whites	19.7	24.8	33.2
Blacks	9.7	30.6	39.3
Hispanics	8.6	25.0	53.3
Native Americans	12.5	22.4	53.0
All students	18.4	25.2	34.5
Private Institutions:			
Whites	6.5	14.6	1.3
Blacks	4.3	13.5	2.7
Hispanics	4.1	7.9	1.1
Native Americans	2.9	7.1	2.1
All students	6.4	14.1	1.4

Source: Astin 1982: 130, adapted from Dearman and Plisko 1980: 110 (Brint and Karabel, p. 128)

Table 5.1d   *Occupation by first college entered and highest degree achieved, national longitudinal study, USA, early 1980s*

Occupation	First College entered		Highest DegreeAchieved	
	Community	Four-Year	2-year Associate Award	B.A.
Blue collar	21.4	10.4	20.2	5.8
White collar	55.3	46.8	58.6	38.7
Professional & managerial	23.3	42.9	21.2	55.4
Total	100.0 (N=318)	100.1 (N=870)	100.0 (N=104)	99.9 (N=720)

Source: Monk-Turner 1983, p. 398 (Brint and Karabel, p. 123)

The historical pattern documented by Brint and Karabel is a general picture repeated by numerous studies of community colleges through to the present day. Dougherty (1987) regards these colleges as having three distinct functions: (1) the function of transfer to universities; (2) more immediate career functions; and (3) more diffuse 'remedial' functions which by no means succeed in placing students back onto the main track. On balance, however, Dougherty sees these institutions as 'confirming' class location and contributing to 'class reproduction' rather than to social mobility. While more cautious in his judgement than Brint and Karabel (whom he sees as underestimating the importance of initial differences in the academic attainment of students in two-year compared with four-year colleges and universities), he nevertheless concludes that community college students achieve "significantly fewer bachelor degrees, fewer years of education, less prestigious jobs, and in the longer run poorer paying jobs than *comparable* students entering four-year colleges" (p. 100). He finds it regrettable that often the "community college has become the *main* point of entry for working class and minority students" (Dougherty, 1992: 206).

Dougherty is not alone in reaching such general conclusions about community colleges. While Rouse (1995), for example, accepts that they sometimes represent a 'democratisation' of HE for those who would not otherwise have attended HE and go on to universities, he nonetheless presents them as also often having a 'diversionary role' for those who might otherwise have gone on directly to 4 year colleges. Likewise, Valadez (1996) confirms the frequent 'cooling out' function of community colleges earlier identified by Clark (1961). He recognises some advantages of community colleges in easing the culture shock presented by entry to HE for students from backgrounds with a limited tradition of participation in higher education. Against this, he remarks on the *barriers* to further progress often presented by an 'unchallenging' collective culture within these institutions. Valadez, like many other commentators, also points to the lack of public awareness of the differential opportunity and more limited labour market outcomes provided by Community Colleges. It is not that qualifications from community colleges provide no labour market advantage of do not enhance earning power. However, this is true only selectively (Grubb, 1995), and is far less so than for attendance at four-year colleges and universities.

Widening HE participation in the UK

The increased participation of previously under-represented groups in UK higher education as part of the overall expansion of participation over the last two decades has been widely documented.

For example, as the ARP (Age Participation Rate) for HE increased from 7% in 1963 to 20% in 1990, male participation increased by 20% but female participation expanded by 30% so that in the present decade a parity between male and female participation has been achieved.

Although the share of HE places gained by entrants from manual Social Classes IIIm–V compared with non-manual Social Classes I–IIIn has widely been regarded as relatively resistant to improvement (see Halsey *et al.*, 1980), even here pleasing improvements have been recorded in recent decades. As Glennerster and Low (1990: cited in Halsey, 1992 and 1993) show using General Household Survey data, the proportion of those entering higher education from manual working families has increased relative to the proportion of those from professional and managerial backgrounds. In the 'pre-1992 universities' between 1985 and 1992, the index of class participation for classes I and II rose from 100 to 152.2, for classes IIIN and IIIM this increased to 218.6, and for classes IV and V to 284.4 (cf. Gatley, 1988). Participation by students from ethnic minority groups has shown similar above average increases to those for class.

Plainly, all these tendencies can be seen positively in relation to the goal of expanded participation. They also indicate a degree of responsiveness in the UK higher education system that is sometimes under recognised, especially so since a significant part of the expansion in numbers has come about from an increased entry of mature (i.e. over age students) and 'access students', entering HE with 'non-standard' qualifications. At one level, all of these tendencies can only be seen as representing a significant expansion of equality of opportunity in UK higher education.

The social and institutional stratification of existing UK higher education

Where the above picture must undoubtedly be tempered, however, is in the distribution of such changes in participation *across institutions*. It is apparent that the gains have been disproportionately in the 'post-1992 universities'/former polytechnic and college sector rather than in the older universities. This is shown in **Tables 5.2a–d** and **Figure 5.2** (following pages).

Tables 5.2a — 5.2d **Comparison of UK universities and then-public sector institutions 1993** (Source: PECAS Annual Report, UCCA Annual Report)

Table 5.2a *Social class by institutional types*

Social Class	Universities % (rounded)	Polytechnic & Colleges % (rounded)	
		Degree	HND
I	21	13	10
II	45	41	39
IIIN	12	13	14
IIIM	15	21	23
IV	6	9	11
V	1	2	3
Total	100 (N=120,054)	100 (N=81,933)	100 (N=20,403)

Table 5.2b *Age of entry by institutional type*

Age at entry	Universities % (rounded)	Polytechnic & Colleges % (rounded)
18 and under	59	39
18-19	20	24
19-20	5	9
21-24	7	13
25-39	8	12
40 and above	2	2
Total	100 (N=127,476)	100 (N=102,336)

Table 5.2c   *Type of secondary education by institutional type*

Secondary education	Universities % (rounded)	Polytechnic & Colleges % (rounded)
Grammar	8	5
6th form college	13	11
Comprehensive	33	32
Other secondary	0	1
(Total maintained)	*(55)*	*(49)*
Independent	21	7
FE/HE	24	44
Total	100 (N=95,385)	100 (N=65,877)

Table 5.2d   *Ethnic origins by institutional type*

Ethnic origins	Universities % (rounded)	Polytechnic & Colleges % (rounded)	
		Degree	HND
Bangladeshi	0.3	0.4	0.5
Chinese	0.8	0.7	0.9
Indian	2.5	3.9	5.4
Pakistani	1.1	1.7	2.3
Other Asian	1.2	1.0	1.0
(Total Asian)	*(6.0)*	*(7.7)*	*(10.2)*
African	0.7	1.7	1.7
Carribean	0.5	1.5	1.8
Other Black	0.2	0.5	0.4
(Total Black)	*(1.4)*	*(3.7)*	*(3.8)*
White	91.6	87.4	84.9
Other	1.1	1.2	1.1
Not known	—	—	—
Grand Total	100 (N=127,476)	100 (N=80,007)	100 (N=19,926)

Table 5.3   **Ethnic background of students by university sector, 1996** (Survey of 2,000 final year students in 15 HEIs)

University Sector	White (%)	Black (%)	Indian subcont. (%)	Other (%)	Not Known
'Old'	56	27	57	71	46
'New'	44	73	43	29	54
TOTAL	100	100	100	100	100

(Source: Dearing Report 1997, Report 5: *Widening Participation in Higher Education by Ethnic Minorities, Women and Alternative Students*, p. 6)

It is readily apparent from these tables that participation by students from Classes IIIm-V (**Table 5.2a**), by mature students (**Table 5.2b**), by students from FE (**Table 5.2c**), and from ethnic minority groups (**Table 5.2d**), especially black students (**Table 5.3**), tends to be in lower status institutions.

The increased participation of women has also been more rapid in the former polytechnic and college sector (see **Figure 5.2**). The degree of social and institutional stratification *already* present in existing UK higher education reflected in these statistics is plain. If, to the above picture, one adds data on differences in occupational destinations of various kinds (see **Figure 5.3**), then the picture of social and institutional inequalities is even more striking. [For accounts of the persistent general differences in labour market outcomes of students from pre-1992 and post-1992 universities, also see Boys and Kirkland, 1988; Brennan *et al.*, 1988, Brennan and McGovern, 1993.] Prior cultural capital possessed by students, supplemented by attendance at elite universities, is a potent factor in occupational selection (Brown and Scase, 1994). Whereas a first wave of expanded participation and access to higher education for students from lower social status and ethnic minority backgrounds were often able to achieve access to elite institutions, subsequent waves of expanded participation have increasingly been cut-off from such access. Expansion of HE primarily outside the universities — both old and new universities — would risk compounding this.

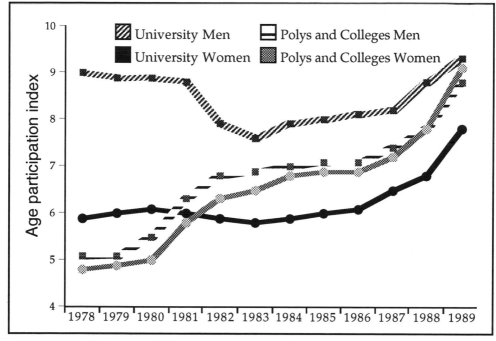

Figure 5.2   Age participation rates for men and women, by type of Institution

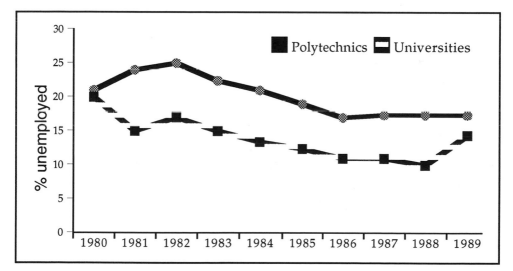

Figure 5.3   Graduate unemployment, 6 months after graduation

(Source Figures 5.2 and 5.3: Council for National Academic Awards Higher Education in Labour Market database)

Current tendencies toward institutional stratification in UK higher education

It is in the circumstances of *already existing* institutional and social stratification such as seen above that the exploration of possible parallels with the development of US higher education (and also expanded systems elsewhere) becomes especially pertinent to an exploration of the issues facing UK higher education.

Paradoxically in some respects — although not unexpected given Scott's model — the new formally 'unified' UK higher education system that has replaced the previous binary system, in opening up UK higher education to more intensified competition, also opens the way for *increased* institutional and social stratification to occur.

Currently there are a number of tendencies which already within the existing UK higher education system make it likely that the hierarchy of higher education institutions will become more extended. The most obvious of these include: an accentuation of the research hierarchy associated with the RAE (see also Chapter 7 in this volume); the possibility of 'top-up' fees for entry into to elite institutions; the phasing-out of maintenance grants; and a tendency to regional recruitment of students from less well-off backgrounds. An overall increase in the numbers of graduates and an increasing differentiation of the graduate labour market provide a further impetus to an increasing stratification of the HE system.

More specifically in the Dearing and also the Kennedy Report there is also now an explicit recommendation that further expansion of HE should take place largely outside the universities, not just outside the pre-1992 but also outside the post-1992 universities. As noted explicitly by Shattock (1998), taking the option of expanding HE within the existing FE sector would be effectively to create in the UK an equivalent to the US community college sector. Since, as we have seen, significant *social* stratification is already associated with the division between pre-1992 and post 1992 universities, the progressive enlargement of a third tier of HE obviously risks adding further to the existing inequalities of outcome.

Is there an alternative to increasing institutional stratification?

In the USA as many as 40-50% of students now begin (and often end) their HE in the community college sector. While some students do transfer to the university system most do not[2]. Leading theorists of mass HE systems such as Martin Trow and Burton Clark (as discussed in Chapter 1 in this volume) suggest that there is really no alternative to such a highly stratified, mass system which provides both elite institutions and institutions of mass participation. They see this as providing the *best* option for a modern society. Such a functionalist and meritocratic view as Clark's or Trow's, however, would appear to assume that the social inequalities generated by such an elite-mass system have no serious side-effects or are a price worth paying to achieve the required mix of elite and mass provision[3]. While an increased *purely* 'meritocratic' stratification of HE might find support, what is in fact associated with mass HE systems in the Clark-Trow mould is an increasing tendency to institutional stratification of higher education, which also brings with it an associated increase in stratification of institutions by *social origins* and *social background*.

But is there no alternative to the Clark-Trow model?

Limits to opportunity in US Community Colleges

Brint and Karabel document the reasons for the retreat in many community colleges from the goal of democracy and open opportunity to a 'limited cycle', often narrowly vocational conception of higher education. They locate the origins of this retreat in the US class structure and crucially in the institutional interests of colleges, but it is a retreat that they regret and do not see as inevitable.

Brint and Karabel's (1989) account of the community college movement contains some very mixed messages which typify the significant dilemmas which everywhere accompany the expansion of higher education. These colleges have been institutions that have had democracy and opportunity as a goal, yet the reality has been that more usually they have come to play an exclusionary role, 'cooling out' and 'managing' ambition. Among university administrators, the "proper function" of such institutions came to be seen as "shock absorbers", "sieves" and "bumpers" (p. 229). What Brint and Karabel also emphasise is how 'institutional interest' led the college leaders to collude in this diminution of role, in particular in a 'vocational' project, "the appeal of which":

> ...resided in its promise to provide 'latent terminal' students with at least short-range upward mobility at the same time that it would satisfy the junior college's organizational interests by capturing for them the best training markets still unoccupied by their four-year competitors. (pp. 208-209)

Brint and Karabel do not suggest that this vocational programme has been without some substance. But they challenge the desirability (and the inevitably) of settling for this as the main role of community colleges. As they see it, educational systems may either "tend to promote a sense that the boundaries between social groups are clearly defined and formidable" or "that they are fluid and easily traversed" (p. 233). The US educational system, they suggest, has often reaffirmed "the national belief that any individual, ... can rise as far as ability and hard work will take him; *even* the seemingly rigid boundary between student and nonstudent has been eroded by the fluidity of the American system" (p. 233). They stress that at *best* the community colleges have been the "quintessential open-door institutions" and have:

> ...yielded some impressive results: in opportunities provided, in horizons expanded, in academic deficiencies remedied, and, in a not inconsiderable number of cases, ambitions "heated up" rather than "cooled out".... (p. 233)

They accept that:

> [I]n the absence of community colleges, many highly motivated and able individuals — among them, workers, immigrants, minorities, and women — would never have entered, much less graduated from, an institution of higher education. (p. 233)

What Brint and Karabel insist, however, is that "the very real contribution that the community college has made to the expansion of opportunities for some individuals" has *not* meant that the *aggregate* effect has been positive. "On the contrary", in their view:

> ...the two-year institution has accentuated rather than reduced existing patterns of social inequality. Indeed, in both the social origins and the occupational destinations of its students, the community college clearly constitutes the bottom tier of a class-linked tracking system in higher education. (p. 226)

Too often these institutions have remained places "where students reach undesired destinations". US society can be said to remain a society:

> ...striving still to reconcile the democratic promise of upward mobility through education with the stubborn reality of a class structure with limited room at the top. (p. 213)

However, although constrained both by organizational interests and the logic of the larger society in which they are embedded, in Brint and Karabel's view the community colleges have a 'choice' and must continue to seek their wider goals (p. 232). There are problems that all developing HE systems must confront. But no inexorable logic of higher education development exists to rule out a more egalitarian outcome[4].

Can we place a limit on institutional stratification in UK higher education?

As Brint and Karabel suggest, "relatively undifferentiated university systems in Europe and elsewhere face the problems posed by mass higher education, [thus] the junior college — or something like it — may well become even more of a presence on the world scene" (p. 225). Greater stratification may be the outcome, intended or otherwise, of many widely proposed changes. Calls for diversification of mission, more regional recruitment etc., put the UK system in danger of taking the US stratified HE route unless careful account is taken of the risk of increased stratification.

It is widely acknowledged that the previous UK 'binary' HE system was *unusual* among emerging mass HE systems in retaining a number of crucial features of the previous unitary elite system (e.g. a common external examiner system and the retention of a system-wide conception of the undergraduate degree). The argument is that rapid expansion of modern HE means that these 'elite' characteristics cannot be sustained — but is this so?

As Trow sees it, the root problems of the UK higher education system are:

> ...strains arising from Britain's efforts to create a system of higher education that can serve an advanced or post-industrial society without surrendering the élite character and size of the existing system. (Trow, 1991:14-15, citing Halsey and Trow, 1971)

For Trow:

> The concept of high and uniform academic standards is in British academic life something of a fetish or totem, the object of unquestioned and almost religious veneration and not of analytical scrutiny. This has precluded a closer relationship between higher education and further education, a connection which surely is Britain's most feasible path to a system of mass higher education which combines access and excellence. (Trow, 1991: 20, citing Trow, 1987)

Somewhat surprisingly these extracts are cited by David Robertson (1995), leading advocate of a new credit revolution in HE and critic of what he sees as the non-responsiveness and general failings of UK higher education. Earlier critics of what they term 'academic drift' in polytechnics and colleges, Burgess and Pratt (1970) and Pratt and Burgess (1974) can also be seen as unwitting proponents of the Trow/Clark model of mass HE.

A counter to any such apparently straightforward acceptance of an elite-mass model as necessarily the way forward is however possible. Above all, it is important not to lose sight of the fact that the relative success of opening up the UK higher education system to worthwhile access has been a result of this system being in significant respects *less* stratified than many systems elsewhere. We would agree with David Watson (*contra* Pratt, and Burgess) that it is not the case that this feature of the UK higher education system has been a barrier to flexibility of response, and that the system has proved itself capable of 'high value added' *precisely* because of its *general* retention of features associated with the previous 'elite' system.

Formally Binary Systems	Formally Unitary Systems
1. Full separation of universities and second tier HE/FE institutions — e.g. Germany (Fachhochschulen), France (IUTs)	2. Paradoxical US 'unitary' system — competitive hierarchy and extended reputational range
3. Paradoxical, inherently unstable, UK 'binary' system — common standards for degrees, leading to convergence of systems	4. Existing UK 'unitary' system — competitive hierarchy with relatively restricted reputational range

Figure 5.4   Alternative binary and unitary models of HE

It is for this reason that the possibility of retention of a less hierarchical, more egalitarian, HE system than envisaged by Clark or Trow can be realistically proposed. The alternative scenario which we think worth advancing is to heed the warning signs already present of an increasing double — social and institutional — stratification of UK higher education and to seek to retain what Watson (Chapter 3, this volume) refers to as the 'limited reputational range' of UK higher education. Our argument is that having embarked on mass higher education at a different point in 'world time' and with different cultural traditions, there is no necessity for UK higher education to entirely repeat the pattern of the US (see Figure 5.4).[5]

Maintaining a limit on 'reputational range', including a common currency for HE credentials, will require, however, that we heed the obvious lessons of the US and the observable warning signs of the potential for an increased institutional and social stratification of UK higher education. This will occur only if there is a commitment to actively seeking a system that maintains, or even further controls, this 'reputational range'.

Actively seeking a limit to institutional stratification and 'reputational range'

If HMG's response to Dearing *Higher Education for the 21st Century* is to 'reach out and include those under-represented in higher education', and if growth is to be especially 'at sub-degree level, mainly in further education colleges', then what needs to be done to ensure that an expanded access produces a worthwhile outcome for students?

According to Smithers and Robinson (1995), 11% of HE students are already located in further education. Currently, three-quarters of students on sub-degree courses are in universities, mainly in new universities. Under some proposals, as many as 400,000 students may be redirected to further education. In the USA, depending on criteria employed, between 35 and 45 per cent of further education students are in Community Colleges: Townsend (1988) presents these as 'colleges of choice' for lower qualified candidates. The problem is how to avoid the worst extremes of the US route?

The pessimistic position in all of this is stated by Triesman (1996: 12):

> The 'American' answer is to give [previously under-represented groups], unlike their middle class predecessors, a pretend degree. Two years of study which nobody will believe is equivalent to current or past higher education will earn only a diploma.

Undoubtedly Triesman's view is too negative. But active steps must be taken for his worst fears not to be borne out and a more positive outcome achieved.

The evidence is that where community colleges have been successful in the US it has been because they have continued to provide a *comprehensive* learning environment, and have enhanced student self-esteem and aspirations. An undoubted virtue in the move to mass HE is not only the lower costs of community college provision but a capacity of these colleges — especially for mature students and women returners — to minimize the cultural barriers to entry to HE for under-represented groups (see Griffith and Connor, 1994).

However, the evidence also is that these 'advantages' will be exploited fully by students only where good connections and formal links with universities exist and access routes to universities are maintained.

If the expansion of college and sub-degree provision is to be effective — and not become a separate tier of higher education — the following can be suggested as essential:

- the preservation as far as possible of *one system*, with continued controls of 'reputational range' in HE
- the retention by all universities of key features of the previous 'elite' system, including an underpinning by research, and the provision of research degrees
- national conceptions of 'graduateness' and 'standards', including a national external examiner system (however the machinery for this must be relatively 'light touch', not bureaucratic and not alienating to academic staff)
- 'metrics' used in compiling 'league tables' that fairly reflect diversity but do not artificially accentuate difference
- recognition of the value of provision of new points of access — including new 'distributed' access available via IT — *outside* the traditional university but *only* in a context in which good links with universities are maintained and extended by the creation of regional networks and federations providing direct access to universities[6]
- a policy that recognises that local and regional access requires credible regional universities which offer worthwhile credentials

If it is thought that these proposals show too little concern for the needs of 'elite' institutions, then attention to the goal of a less divisive expansion of HE can be justified as follows:

- to head-off the growth of an HE underclass which suffers from low esteem and low aspirations that will counter the benefits of HE
- to maximise the gain from a nation-wide development of intellectual capital vital in a 'knowledge society'.

Arguably a better overall diversity of provision is likely to be achieved *within* a protected reputational range.

Conclusion: a realistic and a 'utopian realist' postscript

We are under no illusions that holding in check a global competitive tendency to increasing hierarchisation and polarisation of HE will be easy (for example, the likelihood that elite institutions will at some point find ways to charge top-up fees — Shattock, 1998). As Karabel (1977: 250) has remarked:

> If we are genuinely concerned about creating a more egalitarian society, it will be necessarily to change our economic institutions as well as education.

This makes it even more important, however, that steps to limit 'reputational range' are made wherever possible. Researchers of the relation between higher education and work such as Brown and Scase (1994) find an accentuation of elitist cultural advantage occurring as a result of the expansion of higher education. However, despite this, there is little justification for the extreme 'credentialist'/ 'positionalist' conception (Dore, 1976; Berg, 1973) of an inherently limited 'market' for, and an over-supply of, graduate labour (see Wilson, 1995). A steady expansion of the content of work in response to an increasing supply of graduates can be noted. Any narrowly credentialist view of HE expansion would also appear to wholly discount the extra-economic benefits of higher education in enhancing life experience in general terms. In a wider way, Ulrich Teichler (Teichler *et al.*, 1980; Teichler, 1988; Hermanns *et al.*, 1983) and Anthony Giddens (1990) also sketch a possible alternative — 'utopian realist'[7] — future involving the potential for a more equal allocation of work occurring within a society no longer so dominated by issues of 'scarcity'. Teichler is also among the most powerful advocates of a less hierarchical vision of a new HE (Teichler *et al.*, 1980; Teichler, 1988). The goal of a more egalitarian society need not be dead.

Acknowledgement: We are pleased to note the contribution to this chapter of Myrene McFee, who offered additional information and whose comments prompted us to clarify some aspects of the content of this final version.

Notes

1   For a comprehensive review of pre-1970s data on community colleges see Karabel and Halsey (1977).

2   The table below shows student transfers from community colleges to California universities in selected years over the period 1973 to 1994.

	1973-4	1979-80	1993-4
University of California	8,193	5,699	8,758
Californa State University	30,428	33,089	30,228

California has one of the more open systems, with 1.45 million total student enrollments in community colleges in Fall 1997, of whom 44% were white, and 75% part-time. Around 25% of University of California bachelor degrees and around 50% of California State University bachelor degrees are awarded annually to community college transfers (sources: Brint and Karabel, 1989 and 'CA Community College Statewide Enrollments', Management Information Services Statistical Library, http://www.cccco.edu/cccco/mis/statlib/stw/studF97.htm).

3   A continuity in HE theory and policy — not least an emphasis on meritocracy and the protection of the elite institutions — is traceable in the thinking of James Conant, President of Harvard from 1933 to 1953 and a leading spokesman on higher education policy; influential theorist-administrators such as Clark Kerr, President of the University of California in the 1960s; and in the thinking of both Burton Clark and Martin Trow.

4   This contrasts with the well-known marxist educational theorists Bowles and Gintis (1976), as well as with both Clark and Trow.

5   Interestingly in his recent book *The Polytechnic Experiment* (1997) Pratt now also appears to accept this. He points to the benefits of the previous UK 'binary' system compared with the relative exclusion of the German and the French second tier HE from formal comparability of status with universities, suggesting that these systems might have something to learn from the UK experience.

6   Here the US conception of the 'multiversity' (Kerr, 1973) and the German conception of the 'comprehensive university' (Hermanns *et al.*, 1983; Teichler, 1988) are potentially highly important ideas that cannot be explored fully in the present chapter. The attempted merger of the then North Staffordshire Polytechnic and Keele University in the 1980s (see Kolbert, 1998) provides an illustration of the context in which new federal structures might emerge. Kolbert suggests that had the two institutions merged in the 1980s it would have been a 'major innovation'. Arguably the educational, as well as the cultural and economic, prospects for the Potteries sub-region would be enhanced by an innovative and strengthened 'multiversity' and regional cooperation rather than competition between institutions.

7   'Utopian realism' involves the extrapolation from known tendencies to possible futures (see Giddens, 1990).

References

Astin, A. (1982) *Minorities in American Higher Education.* San Francisco: Jossey-Bass.

Berg, I. (1973) *Education and Jobs: The Great Training Robbery.* Harmondsworth: Penguin.

Bowles, S. and Gintis, H. (1976) *Schooling in Capitalist America.* New York: Basic Books.

Boys, C. and Kirkland, J. (1988) *Degrees of Success.* London: Jessica Kingsley.

Brennan, J. and McGeevor, P. (1988) *Graduates At Work: Degree Courses and the Labour Market.* London: Jessica Kingsley.

Brennan, J. and Lyon, S. *et al.* (1993) *Students, Courses and Jobs: The Relationship Between Higher Education and the Labour Market.* London: CNAA/Jessica Kingsley.

Brint, S. and Karabel, J. (1989) *The Diverted Dream: Community Colleges and the Promise of Educational Opportunity in America, 1900-1985.* New York: Oxford University Press.

Brown, P. and Scase, R., (1994) *Higher Education and Corporate Realities: Class, Culture and the Decline of Graduate Careers.* London: UCL Press.

Burgess, T. and Pratt, J. (1970) *Policy and Practice — The Colleges of Advanced Technology.* London: Allen Lane.

Clark, B. (1960) *The Open Door College: Case Study.* New York: McGraw Hill.

—— (1961) '"The Cooling Out" Function in Higher Education', in A. Halsey, J. Floud and C. Anderson (eds) *Economy, Education and Society.* New York: Free Press, pp. 513–26.

Dore, R. (1976) *The Diploma Disease: Education, Qualification and Development.* London: Unwin.

Dougherty, K. (1987) 'The effects of community colleges: aid or hindrance to socioeconomic attainment', *Sociology of Education,* 60: 86-103.

—— (1992) 'Community colleges and baccalaureate attainment', *Journal of Higher Education,* 63 (2): 188-214.

Gatley, D. (1988) The Influence of Social-Class Origins on the Choice of Course, Career Preferences, and Entry to Employment of CNAA Graduates. Unpublished PhD Thesis/Staffordshire: Polytechnic/CNAA.

Giddens. A. (1990) *The Consequences of Modernity.* Cambridge: Polity Press.

Glennerster, H. and Low, W. (1990) 'Education and the Welfare State: Does it Add Up?', in J. Hills (ed) *The State of Welfare.* Oxford: Clarendon Press, cited in Halsey (1992; 1993).

Griffith, M. and Connor, A. (1994) *Democracy's Open Door: The Community College in America's Future.* Portsmouth, NH: Heinemann.

Grubb, W. (1995) 'The varied economic returns to postsecondary education — new evidence from the class of 1972', *Journal of Human Resources,* 30(1): 222-28.

Halsey, A. H. (1992) *Opening Wide the Doors of Higher Education.* London: National Commission on Education, Briefing Paper No 6.

————(1993) 'Trends in access and equity in higher education: Britain in international perspective'. *Oxford Review of Education*, 19 (2): 129-140.

Halsey, A. H., Heath, A. and Ridge, J. (1980) *Origins and Destinations*. Oxford: Clarendon Press.

Halsey, A. H. and Trow, M. (1971) *The British Academics*. London: Faber.

Hermanns, H. and Teichler, U. (1983) 'Integration of Higher Education', in H. Hermanns *et al.* (eds) (1983), pp. 1-19.

Hermanns, H., Teichler, U. and Wasser. (eds) (1983) *The Compleat University: Break from Tradition in Germany, Sweden and the USA*. Cambridge, Mass.: Schenkman.

Karabel, J.(1977)'The community colleges and social stratification: submerged class conflict in American higher education', in J. Karabel and A. H. Halsey (eds) 1977, pp. 232-54.

Karabel, J. and Halsey, A. H. (eds) (1977) *Power and Ideology in Education*, New York: Oxford University Press.

Kerr, C. (1973) *The Uses of the University*. Cambridge, MA: Harvard University Press.

Kolbert, J. (1998, forthcoming) *The University of Keele: A History*. Keele: University of Keele Press.

Koos, L. (1924) *The Junior College*. Minneapolis: University of Minnesota Press.

Monk-Turner, E. (1983) 'Sex, educational differentiation and occupational status: analysing occupational differences for community and four-year college entrants', *Sociological Quarterly*, 24: 293-404.

National Committee of Inquiry into Higher Education (1997) *Higher Education in a Learning Society*. (The Dearing Report) London.

Pratt, J. (1997) *The Polytechnic Experiment 1965–92*. Milton Keynes: Open University Press.

Pratt, J. and Burgess, T. (1974) *Polytecnhics: a Report*. London: Pitman.

Robbins Report (1963) *Report of the Committee on Higher Education*. London: HMSO.

Robertson, D. (1995) 'The Reform of Higher Education for Social Equity, Individual Choice and Mobility', in F. Coffield (ed) *Higher Education in a Learning Society*. Durham: School of Education, Durham University, pp. 45-66.

Rouse, C. (1995) 'Democratization or diversion? The effect of community colleges on educational attainment'. *Journal of Business and Economic Statistics*, 13 (2): 217-224.

Scott, P. (1995) *The Meanings of Mass Higher Education*. Buckingham: Society for Research into Higher Education and Open University Press .

Shattock, M. (1998) 'The academic divide', *Guardian Higher*, March 10.

Smithers, A and Robinson, P. (1995) *Post 18 Education: Growth Change and Prospects*. London: CIHE.

Teichler, U. (1988) *Changing Patterns of the Higher Education System: The Experience of Three Decades*. London: Jessica Kingsley.

Teichler, U., Hartnung, D. and Nuthmann, R. (1980) *Higher Education and the Needs of Society*. Windsor: NFER.

Townsend, B. (1988) Review of Eaton, J. (1988) *Colleges of Choice — the Enabling Impact of the Community College'*, *Higher Education* 17 (4): 463-66.

Triesman, D (1996) 'Community challenges', *The Guardian Higher*, November 5.

Trow, M. (1970) 'Reflections on the Transition from Mass to Higher Education', *Daedalus*. 90 (1): 1-42.

—— (1987) 'The University at the End of the Twentieth Century and Trends Toward Continued Development', in Rohrs, H. (ed) *Tradition and Reform of the University under an International* Perspective. Frankfurt a.M: Lang.

—— (1991) 'Comparative Perspectives on Policy', in R. Berdahl, G. Moodie and I. Spitzberg (eds) *Quality and Access in Higher Education*. Buckingham: Society for Research into Higher Education / Open University Press.

Valadez, J. (1996) 'Educational access and social mobility in a rural community college', *The Review of Higher Education* 19 (4): 391-409.

Wilson, R. (1995) 'Prospects for the Labour Market for the Highly Qualified', in F. Coffield (ed) *Higher Education in a Learning Society*. Durham: School of Education, Durham University, pp. 111-139.

Maintaining Standards in Higher Education?: A Case Study

6

Lisa Lucas and Frank Webster

Introduction

The maintenance of standards through time and throughout the system is axiomatic to British education. If one were not confident in arguing that an Upper Second is the same in Aberdeen as it is in Plymouth, in Bangor as in Norwich, then what chaos might ensue. And if we cannot be assured that a First gained in 1996 is much the same as one achieved in 1966, then just where would this leave the mutual regard of junior and superior colleagues in the world of work? Postgraduate awards are made on the basis of the comparability of results, jobs are decided on the presumption that equality of grade represents equality of attainment, and even conceptions of self draw heavily on the presupposition that the degree classification awarded signals a reliable measure. It is to bolster confidence in the comparability of results that, in the UK, higher education employs an elaborate network of external examiners charged with assuring that standards remain constant across the system and over the years. It is indisputable that, were confidence in standards to be eroded, then serious consequences would have to be faced at the individual and societal levels.

Standards in doubt

Despite its pivotal importance, however, it is evident that confidence in the maintenance of standards and comparability of awards between institutions is weak and probably weakening. There has long been a rough and ready hierarchy of universities in the public mind, one which has readily translated into a presupposition that a Second from Oxford is superior to the same degree from Strathclyde (cf. Halsey 1992). While some of this might be dismissed as mere snobbishness, the concentration of academic talent — from students' entry qualifications to staffs' standing amongst peers — in a cluster of élite universities must raise concerns as to the extent of the comparability of their results with less prestigious institutions. Who cannot but anticipate candidates with nigh perfect A-levels, taught in generously endowed surroundings by leaders in their fields, doing very well indeed? (see Watson, and Court, this volume). Yet it is this expectation that is confounded, since the distribution of degree classifications, while variable between institutions, does not vary in close accord with the palpable differences of qualities and qualifications of those involved (Bee and Dolton 1985). In fact, when it comes to empirical analysis of the spread of degree awards, the *lack* of comparability between institutions is nothing less than striking (cf. Johnes and Taylor, 1987).

Moreover, it is commonplace in higher education nowadays to declare that the external examiner role has been undermined, that the days in which externals could ensure equality of standards have gone, driven away by the spread of course work assessment that is difficult to moderate and by the sheer complexity of the university. Perhaps not surprisingly, then, a recent Higher Education Quality Council (1996) review confirmed that academics admitted that degree standards varied widely between universities and even within a single institution.

Arguably, this reduction in confidence in standards has been most exacerbated by recent trends in British higher education. The shift from élite to mass higher education in double quick time, and with it the legacy of a distinctively Anglo-Saxon model of the university still much in the mind of participants and commentators, has brought about serious questioning of much that takes place in higher education (Smith and Webster, 1997), and even grief for a perceived loss of intimacy that once prevailed amongst university members (Scott, 1995). An age participation ratio that has jumped from between 10 and 12% to in excess of 30%, plus a rapid expansion of what are euphemistically termed 'non-traditional' students (i.e. those who, for the most part, are not equipped with good A-level passes), has led to a 70% increase in those attending university over the last decade while the collapse of the binary divide in 1992 has vastly increased the number of institutions with the word university in their titles. Accompanying this growth, to a total student body in higher education of around 1 million, has been the development of radically new degree programmes, each bringing with them attendant difficulties of establishing standards and achieving legitimacy — for instance, Cultural Studies, Tourism, Women's Studies, Information Technology courses of one sort or another, and, most dramatic of all, Business Studies. Alongside has been the steady diminution of the funding per student, a decline in real terms of 30% in the unit of resource (Scott and Watson, 1994).

Outcomes of this turmoil are easy enough to observe: many more students of course, but also a greater variety of students, radically different curricula and modes of study, larger classes, crowded corridors, less personal attention from tutors, poorer library facilities, a general deterioration of the fabric of institutions.

Moreover, the increased shift of the burden of funding from the state to the students (a bipartisan policy in British politics) has encouraged a great deal of part-time employment of students during their courses of study, in effect resulting in the transformation of full-time to part-time studying for a degree, although the undergraduate programme remains characteristically a three-year period.

Accordingly, it cannot be much of a surprise to come across those who interpret the rapid shift to mass higher education as one which has entailed a decline in the quality of educational attainment. It is certainly extraordinarily difficult, probably more difficult than ever, to gain entry to the most prestigious residential universities (most notably Oxbridge, but also Durham, Bristol, LSE, Imperial College and the like). But since pretty well anyone can enrol at least at one of the nation's new universities (and, increasingly, one near home since this reduces the burden of cost/debt to the student) where (so this kind of argument goes) they are likely to receive a cut-price education, there is widespread suspicion that the quality of a university degree is not what it once was. Anecdotes abound — and these surely permeate the wider culture in due course — of inadequately prepared students who require substantial remedial instruction in numeracy, literacy and study skills, of students with poor A-level results (and often without even these) gaining admission to university where more and more of them are forced to find part-time work to subsidise their period of study, and where increasingly harassed staff find the pressures of coping with large numbers while simultaneously developing and sustaining a research profile antipathetic to effective teaching. The conclusion that such students are not up to scratch, that they are not achieving what their forebears managed, is hard to avoid (Phillips, 1996). Similarly, it is difficult to maintain that there is a common standard of degree when entry to some universities requires high A-level scores while others allow access with Ds and Cs, though all appear to emerge with a roughly similar spread of degree results. The *Sunday Times* (3 September 1995: 7) captures what is a widespread perception when it editorialised that "relative exclusivity has now been sacrificed to the god of mass production, and the inevitable result is that quality has been sacrificed to quantity".

It is easy enough to appreciate the consequences of scepticism about, distrust of, and concern for degree standards. New graduates are regarded as less valuable as those that came before, there is a renewal of the late Sixties refrain that 'more means worse', and those students from the less prestigious institutions are seen as inferior to those of the more élite. There is reliable evidence that employers recruit graduates on the basis of a university hierarchy which, if it has some fuzziness in the middle ranks, relegates most universities, notably the newer ones, to the lowest positions (Brown and Scase, 1994) where candidates are awarded what the *Sunday Times* called 'dummy degrees' (3 September, 1995: 12-13). In these terms, since degree results cannot be trusted to be a reliable measure through time or between institutions, then recourse is towards the socially and academically

107

esteemed, most privileged universities and students of distinctively advantaged backgrounds.

It is scarcely necessary to spell out the implications such a collapse of confidence in standards has in terms of social justice. What may be termed the democratisation of higher education, a process led by the new universities especially, which has allowed large numbers of hitherto excluded groups the opportunity of studying for a degree, is being thwarted by the increased questioning of the genuine quality of the certification which those students attain. It is well known that there are considerable advantages gained from family circumstances in scoring well at A-level, and there is no doubt that the growing expense of attendance at a residential university favours the materially successful, in which case one may anticipate a growing bifurcation between students who are able to attend the most élite institutions and those ushered into the local ex-polytechnic or unfashionable former college of advanced technology. Since employers favour the élite universities, then much of the efforts of those in the less regarded institutions might appear to be wasted.

Despite such dispiriting reports, student performance, at least as measured by attainment of degree classifications, has actually improved across the university system as a whole. Resources might be continually reducing, but since degree results suggest improvement rather than any decline in quality, then it is not unexpected to come across the then Higher Education Minister Eric Forth proclaiming that he "do[es] not think there is a direct causal relationship between money spent and the quality of the output" (*Times Higher Education Supplement*, 22 March 1996: 1). How can those who insist that 'more means worse' respond to the evidence that the proportion of students getting a good degree (a first or upper second) has risen from about 30% in the 1970s to almost 50% today? Such a statistic turns on its head suggestions that things are getting worse in higher education. It is quite possible to argue quite the contrary, and indeed it is so argued, with proponents of improvement making assertions of better teaching, more diligent students (in contrast to those time-wasters of the Sixties!), and a more rigorous and real-world university experience leading to overall improvement (MacFarlane, 1992).

Of course, the easy (and cynical) reply is that standards in universities have fallen, that since students can enter higher education without an A-level, then we ought not to be surprised that getting a degree is easier than before. And with this we are into what seems an irresolvable debate, because it is one which hinges on differential *interpretations* of results rather than reliable evidence. Thus while no-one denies that degree classifications have registered an improvement, one side alleges that this is because courses have become easier, while the other insists that there are alternative, equally plausible, explanations for this improvement.

Oxford Brookes case study

We are eager to advance debate about the maintenance of standards beyond mutually contradictory interpretations that draw upon whatever evidence seems to suit their respective and oppositional positions. We cannot of course offer a definitive answer to all aspects of the debates about standards. We do not, for instance, comment here on the relative quality of Brookes' degrees vis-à-vis that pertaining at other universities. However, we can endeavour, through a close examination of what has happened at Oxford Brookes over the years between 1984 and 1994, to advance more robust evidence than is generally offered about the maintenance of academic standards, where opinion and prejudice appear to play a disproportionate role. In what follows we will not report at great length on quantitative data we have generated, since much of it has been published elsewhere. Instead we will focus on a few key pieces of information we have generated from analysis of Brookes' Modular Course records that relate to the question of standards and from a small re-marking experiment we commissioned on dissertations completed in 1984 and 1994.

Records from Oxford Brookes' Modular Degree programme allow us to examine performance at the local level. Sociology at Brookes has been part of the Modular Degree since 1978, and we have accumulated a substantial data base of that which readily lends itself to analysis. It was not difficult to extract data on Sociology students' performance by module registration, mode of assessment and method of teaching between the years 1984 and 1994. At Brookes all modules are of an equal size in terms of learning hours and module grades receive equal weighting for degree results, so making comparisons across the years is not easily bedevilled by accusations that one is not comparing like with like.

We decided to focus on two issues in particular. First the *relation between module size and student performance*, seeking to test the proposition that the larger the classes the less well students perform. Second, we looked at the *relationships between patterns of teaching and of assessment and student attainment*.

What we discovered was rather surprising. We did confirm the general finding that students do less well on big modules (for our purposes over seventy registrations) than they do on small ones (under twenty) . It would seem to follow, therefore, that as classes have generally increased in size as staff:student ratios have expanded from about 13:1 to 22:1, then students will do less well — and the common sense view that standards are declining will be confirmed. However, the records show that, in spite of a 70% increase in enrolment on modules, average performance of students has been maintained (at 58%) and has even marginally improved over the decade. Moreover, our students have always done relatively less well on large modules and, while we supposed that this deterioration of performance would be exacerbated as modules got bigger still, our records confounded this presumption. All this is counter-intuitive. Students do less well in bigger classes, and classes are getting bigger, but then why are their overall scores being maintained and, if anything, improving? The answer is to be found in the second issue that we examined: the connection between teaching and assessment and student performance.

Some might think that sterling efforts by teaching staff have been the key to stemming a decline during sustained cuts. The image is projected of the committed don putting in the extra hours to make up for the general deterioration of conditions that students must endure. Unfortunately for this supposition, our analysis of contact with teachers was revealing. We found that, on average, class contact has declined by half over the ten year period, yet there is no relationship between contact with the tutor and student marks on the module. This surely raises some questions about the presumption that lots of teaching raises standards: given appropriate circumstances, it is clear that students can and do do well with little access to lecturers.

However, what we did find was axiomatic to maintaining standards was the very significant change in methods of assessment introduced since 1984. Bluntly, course work as a proportion of total assessment has shifted from just 16% of assessment in 1984 to almost three-quarters in 1994. Furthermore, there is a very positive correlation between course work and student performance, marks being significantly better on course work than in examinations. This seems to be the key factor in accounting for poorer student performance in large modules. These are prohibitively expensive to run if course work is included, so the trend is towards having large modules assessed by examination, and it is with this means of assessment that students do particularly badly. Our suspicion is that, if a large module is assessed by course work, then standards will be maintained. As it is, however, it is smaller modules on which course work predominates, and where students do relatively well.

To be sure, some will argue that we may have even relaxed our marking standards on course work since the 1980s, so that it isn't just more of the latter that has kept things afloat. At Brookes we tried to test for this by taking ten undergraduate dissertations from 1984 and another ten from 1994 and having them blind marked by four assessors (two internal and two external to the institution). The experiment was less than perfect, not least because it is impractical to disguise entirely the date of production of the dissertations since topic and content are usually give-aways. Nonetheless, the exercise gave no support to the proposition that marking standards have eased over the years. Indeed, while the average mark given to 1984 dissertations in 1984 was 61.2%, the average mark given to the same dissertations in 1995 was 59.7%, suggesting little change in standards of marking. The re-marking exercise did demonstrate a rather alarming variance within the range of marks, something we ascribe to the lack of explicit marking criteria, but it did nothing to suggest that assessment itself had become more generous.

It seems to us that it is the prevalence of course work assessment that is the key to the maintenance of graduate standards over the past decade. Since our students have a similar socio-economic profile, and since they come with much the same A-level scores as before (there has been a small improvement in scores over the years, but scarcely one of significance), then it is hard to resist the view that course work is the primary reason for good performance. We may be more able teachers today, but we doubt that is central to the holding of the ground that has taken place. It is certainly a moot point whether degree standards would be the same in 1996 if we had retained the norm of three-hour unseen examination papers of the early 1980s.

This does not mean we now provide degrees of a lower standard. A good case can be made for the appropriateness of course work assessment over examinations. It motivates students learning much more effectively than end-of -erm tests, it is more akin to the world outside academe, and its superiority as a mechanism for assessment is probably accepted by most academics today. Nevertheless, course work is expensive on staff time and energy. As cuts inexorably continue, then there must be others who are tempted to return to examination-only assessment since it is so cheap to offer. Were that to happen, then our fear is that a real decline in student performance would be registered. And then Mr Forth, the ex-Minister of Higher Education whom we quoted earlier in this article, might just be forced to agree that there is a causal relation between money spent on higher education and the quality of output.

Limitations of quantitative data

Hard figures can facilitate hard thinking. Too often when it comes to discussion of academic standards, commentators draw on localised experience, memory, and 'feelings' about the subject. That is why we have drawn here on data from the Sociology Field at Oxford Brookes. Statistical analysis of the Modular Course data base provides useful information to set alongside the unreliability of a great deal of discussion of standards in higher education. It is salutary to be reminded that student achievement might not be straightforwardly associated, for instance, with time spent in class with teachers as, indeed, it is instructive to realise that the development of increased proportions of course work appears to be a critical factor in maintaining student performance in harder times.

However, we cannot invest too much trust in the statistical evidence. Marks awarded to students, which supply so much of the data examined, are always interpretive actions situated in time and place, and are thereby subject to the subjectivities of those involved. For example, it is quite easy to imagine that even a sudden reversion to all-examination assessment might not register declining student scores because markers may, in subtle ways, take this into account when grading, perhaps because they feel some guilt at spending less time with their students. Again, course work may increase, and it may even be a more appropriate way of encouraging student learning, but the marks achieved cannot be unproblematic measures of quality readily amenable to comparison with marks achieved under examination conditions because, while they may be assessed rigorously, there remains the major difficulty of overcoming the increased risks of plagiarism and ensuring that the work is the student's own. In addition, one cannot presume that marks remain trustworthy through time just because a mode of assessment is retained — the content of the curriculum may itself have changed, as might the manner of teaching within a given mode, either of which may impact on the final grades.

All of this is to warn against too ready a reliance on apparently hard data. When it comes to judgements of the maintenance of academic standards we are, willy nilly, involved in an interpretative exercise.

This is not to say, however, that any interpretation goes. Were we to adopt that position, then we deny any comparative measure of the quality of degrees through time and between institutions. We have already noted the consequence of such a position: it would result in the promotion of a crude reputational model of higher education which favours the élite and the already advantaged, and relegates to the bottom of the heap the less socially esteemed.

We must hold therefore to the project of defending and producing standards that may be maintained through time and across institutions. Analysis of the efficacy of this must accordingly take us back both to the network of external examiners and to colleagues with long experience of assessment within universities in the UK who are charged with ensuring some commonality and retention of standards. While there are signs that the system is under strain, nevertheless it seems to us that it is here, in the experiences and judgements of those most closely involved in the maintenance of academic standards, where we should look for most authoritative assessments of quality in the university system.

Notes

[1]   This is something which the Teaching Quality Assessment singularly avoids because, though it is a national system, it instructs assessors to evaluate degree courses in terms of the programme's *own* aims and objectives.

[2]   A-level grades have for a long period been regarded as a 'gold standard', something which adversely affects the perception of degree attainment of those with poor A-level grades; but even these are doubted in 1996, with the schools inspectorate Ofsted and the Schools Curriculum Assessment Authority reporting that there has been a relaxation of standards here over the last twenty years (*Guardian*, 29 July, 1996).

3　Data were analysed from 127 modules involving 5,779 student grades. This data set included all taught Stage 1 (normally corresponding to year one) and Stage 2 (normally corresponding to years two and three) modules for the years 1984-85 to 1993-94. Project, dissertation and other forms of modules which are normally individually supervised rather than taught in class were excluded from the study (except, of course, for the re-marking exercise). The data analysed included Stage (1 or 2), year, module enrolment, the number and proportion of students gaining grades A, B+, B, C and F (corresponding to a First, Upper Second, Lower Second, Third and a Fail), and average module mark, expressed as a percentage, for each module.

4　In the remarking exercise assessors were asked to identify and rate the criteria they used. From this it was evident that assessors valued significantly different qualities and characteristics in dissertations — for example, some emphasising disciplinary thought while others leaned towards more generalised transferable skills such as construction of argument. The conclusion we drew was that, in the name of consistency and fairness to candidates, the least assessors should do was agree explicit marking criteria.

References

Bee, M. and Dolton, P.J. (1985) 'Degree Class and Pass Rates: An inter-university comparison', *Higher Education Review*, (Spring): 45-52.

Brown, P. and Scase, R. (1994) *Higher Education and Corporate Realities: Class, Culture and the Decline of Graduate Careers*. UCL Press.

Halsey, A.H. (1992) *Decline of Donnish Dominion: The British Academic Professions in the Twentieth Century*. Oxford: Clarendon Press.

Higher Education Quality Council (1996) *Academic Standards in the Approval, Review and Classification of Degrees*. London: HEQC.

Johnes, J. and Taylor, J. (1987) 'Degree Quality — An Investigation into Differences Between UK Universities', *Higher Education*, 16 (5): 581 602.

MacFarlane, B. (1992) 'The "Thatcherite" Generation and University Degree Results', *Journal of Higher Education*, 16 (2): 60-70.

Phillips, M. (1996) *All Must have Prizes*. London: Little, Brown and Company.

Scott, P. (1995) *The Meanings of Mass Higher Education*. Buckingham: Open University Press/SRHE.

Scott, P. and Watson, D. (1994) 'Setting the Scene', in J. Bocock and D. Watson (eds) *Managing the University Curriculum: Making Common Cause*. Buckingham: Open University Press/SRHE.

Smith, A. and Webster, F. (1997) *The Postmodern University? Contested Visions of Higher Education in Society*. Buckingham: Open University Press/SRHE.

The Research Assessment Exercise: the Basis for a New Gold Standard in Higher Education?

7

Stephen Court

The aim of this chapter is to investigate whether the results of assessment and other available data can provide a guide to the academic standards of different types of institutions in a mass higher education system, and to consider the implications of this for research and teaching in the provision of higher education.

Academic standards in higher education in the UK

Standards in an elite higher education system

> The gold standard of the traditional honours degree has underpinned the growth of higher education in the United Kingdom in this century, and has itself rested on largely unspoken assumptions about undergraduate degree standards and about the reliability of the classification structure and process. (Silver *et al.*, 1995: 39)

In the early 1960s, the era of the Robbins Report, the UK had an elite higher education system. Only six per cent of people of the 18-21 age group went to university. There were 26 universities in the UK in 1961, with some 250,000 students (HEQC, 1995: 24). In general, each university had responsibility for guaranteeing the standard of the awards it made. Each university's internal examiners were assisted by external examiners — normally fellow academics at other universities — to moderate exam papers, sample exam scripts and attend examiners' meetings, in order to ensure the comparability of degrees. The system was generally homogeneous enough for academic staff to share a common sense of standards (HEQC, 1995: 25). And so, at least in theory, there was an academic gold standard which guaranteed the quality of a UK undergraduate degree.

I say in theory because even in the days when there were only a small number of degree-awarding institutions in the UK, universities — and departments within universities — had their own reputations, powerful or otherwise. The effect on degree results of the differing traditions and reputations of institutions, their departments and their academic staff, cannot be discounted, with the reputation attached to a particular institution perhaps having an unwarranted influence on the judgement of examiners. It was then, as it is now, probably impossible to guarantee the comparability of degrees. Sir John Wolfenden, addressing the Court of the University of Reading in 1956, said: "to talk of 'university standards' as if they represented something absolute, or even relatively permanent, is a misconception" (Silver and Silver, 1986: 17).

Despite these reservations, the universities generally felt confident (critics might say complacent) that there was comparability of degrees, and that the degrees they awarded conformed to a common high standard. In fact, in the early 1960s, standards hardly seemed to be an issue at all. The Robbins Report made little reference to standards, and where it did, there appeared to be an assumption that institutions had upheld academic standards, and that the honours standard was self-evident. Although Robbins said "we must demand of a system that it produces as much high excellence as possible" (Committee on Higher Education, 1963: 10), the nature of that high excellence was not spelled out. Likewise, Robbins said institutions could rightly claim to have maintained academic standards (pp. 87-88), but this was not substantiated. The report did not define academic standards or the honours degree standard, except in the sense that the latter was higher than a pass degree. The aim of the standards agency it proposed, the Council for National Academic Awards (CNAA), was to promote "uniformity of standards" (p. 254). With a sense of idealism, Robbins said the CNAA would help ensure that degrees in the non-university higher education sector "would meet the requirement that artificial differences of status among the institutions should be eliminated" (p. 266).

Standards in a period of transition

The expansion in the number of higher education institutions that coincided with and followed the Robbins Report began to shake assumptions about standards. By the 1980s, Moodie felt the increase in the number of subjects, staff and departments "have made the old 'grape-vine' monitoring of standards less reliable" (Moodie, 1986: 2). The external examiner system had developed out of the University of London external degree, "to guarantee equivalent, or at least comparable standards" (Silver and Silver, 1986: 15). But the increased numbers of students in the 1980s gave rise to questions about the ability of external examiners effectively to make overall judgements about the standards of candidates. Williams, in 1986, wrote: "The external examiner system operates in such a way as to buttress self-regulation rather than apply collectively agreed standards" (Williams, 1986: 37). In the same year, the Committee of Vice-Chancellors and Principals (CVCP) published *Academic Standards in Universities*.

The CVCP report said it was "evident that a first class in chemistry is measuring different things from a first class in history" (CVCP, 1986: 3). There was also a difference between assessment based on course work and on exams. The CVCP concluded that, in discussing standards, it was necessary to find a balance between complete freedom for institutions, and being prescriptive. "To make the statement 'This system is better than that one' requires an explicit and exclusive determination of the purposes of higher education and a universally-applied blueprint of entry criteria, of teaching and assessment procedures, and of classification procedures" — an "unwise and unacceptable" approach (CVCP, 1986: 3).

The CVCP decided to steer a middle course, aiming to "strengthen universities' procedures" by using the audit of institutions' quality assurance processes to upgrade the standards of teaching, courses, resources, assessment and staff appraisal and development. The report underlined the importance of staff: "Standards are affected more by the quality of the academic staff than by any advisory or monitoring procedures" (CVCP, 1986: 19). Although the report concluded that "exact congruence between one course and another and their respective assessments is neither possible nor desirable" (p. 5), it nevertheless saw relative degree comparability as achievable, and the external examiner system as the most important method of achieving it. In the report there were signs of growing emphasis being placed by the government and others on higher education proving its worth, particularly through producing the quantity and quality of graduates to meet the needs of employers. "Comparability is important partly because of the weight often given by employers to the class of degree that has been awarded..." (p. 5).

Academic standards in a mass higher education system

The pressures on the higher education system which were being felt in the mid-1980s, and the impetus towards assessment and management by quantification, were only a foretaste of what was to come in the following decade. The number of degree-awarding institutions in the UK increased sharply following the Further and Higher Education Acts 1992. The Acts brought about the official ending of the binary divide between universities and polytechnics, by enabling the latter to apply for university status. Under the Acts, the CNAA was abolished, and the polytechnics joined the 'old' universities in having the right to award their own degrees; by 1995, there were 104 universities and colleges with power to award first degrees, with a student enrolment of around 1.5 million. There were changes in the make-up of the student population, with greater variety in the qualifications of university entrants. In 1993, only 77 per cent of students had A-levels, compared with 93 per cent in 1978 (HEQC, 1995: 25) — an indication of the increasing use of vocational and other qualifications for university entrance. There has been widespread adoption of modular course structures, with traditional 'honours in depth' being superseded by 'honours in breadth'. In addition to the pressure of increasing numbers, the unit of resource per higher education student has been driven down through a series of 'efficiency gains' imposed by the government (AUT, 1996: 13-14). Despite rising student numbers and falling funding levels, there has been a statistical increase in the standard of graduates, as measured by degree class, with a general increase in the proportion of 'good' degrees, i.e. firsts and upper seconds; the upper second has become the modal degree, whereas in 1973 the lower second was the modal degree class (HEQC, 1995: 7). There is, however, substantial variation among institutions (pre-1992 universities only) in the proportion of firsts and upper seconds awarded, ranging from below 30 per cent to more than 70 per cent (pp. 7-8).

Given the scale and diversity of this system, is it still possible to talk in terms of comparable standards in higher education, whether from the point of view of government, institutions, students, staff or employers of graduates? There is a widespread view that a gold standard in higher education is no longer possible or desirable: "The notion of a single 'gold standard', applied to the first degree, is neither well-founded nor helpful when applied to the range, diversity and complexity of the teaching and learning offered in higher education institutions" (Webb, 1994: 47).

However, there is evidence that higher education institutions — especially among the universities established before 1992 — are rethinking degree standards in terms of an academic standard related to the degrees of particular institutions, set in the context of the institutions' tradition and reputation in teaching and research. For example, Professor Howard Newby, Vice-Chancellor of the University of Southampton, was reported by his university's Bulletin newsletter (23 October, 1995) to be "keen to establish a University of Southampton degree as a 'Gold Standard' — the University should be at the forefront of applying standards of excellence in teaching as well as in research".

Such a concept is a departure from the traditional, collegial nature of universities. In the days of the elite higher education system, the honours degree gold standard was inclusive, in that it was supposed to represent a standard across all universities. The institution-related gold standard is exclusive, in that it is based on institutions which have attained a certain standard, determined to some extent by the results of the assessment of research and teaching (see next section). Thus, in the era of mass higher education, the quest for comparable standards has not disappeared. This is particularly the case for institutions trying to uphold a long-standing research tradition, against the background of the growth in the number of institutions competing for approximately the same amount of recurrent research funding from the funding councils. Sir Ronald Oxburgh, the Rector of Imperial College, London — one of the UK's top research institutions, commented at the college's Commemoration Day in 1995 that:

> ...this very rapid expansion has meant that what is meant by words such as graduate, degree or even professor, is something very different and more diverse than a dozen years ago. It also means that institutions such as ours and a handful of others that have prided themselves on maintaining the highest standards are now a small minority, even an oddity, within a system of mass higher education that has its centre of gravity very far from where we stand.

His views find their reification in the formation, since the end of the binary divide, of unofficial interest groups of old universities, such as the Russell Group and the 94 Group, which aim to maintain the research strength and funding of their members.

The assessment of research and teaching, and quality audit

These changes have been accompanied by the development of the assessment of research and teaching, as well as institutional audit. In the 1980s, the Conservative government's aims of reducing public expenditure, and increasing accountability and efficiency in the use of funding for research, gave rise to the retrospective peer review — coordinated by the predecessors of the higher education funding councils — of the quality of research in higher education. The intention of the review was to promote selectivity in the allocation of research funding. This policy was expressed by the government, as follows: "... funding for research should be allocated selectively to encourage institutions to concentrate on their strengths" (DES, 1991: 18). In 1986, the first research assessment exercise (RAE) was carried out, and was followed by similar exercises in 1989, 1992 and 1996. The basis of the RAE is the 'norm-referenced' assessment of research (or other original work) against a standard ranging from international excellence to below national excellence. In 1992 a five-grade scale was used; in 1996, there were seven grades. The RAE also quantifies the number and proportion of research active staff, among other indicators, and is used directly to determine the bulk of recurrent research funding allocated by the higher education funding councils. Indirectly, a department's RAE rating is used in a number of ways, such as informing the decisions of research councils, charities, industry and other funders of university research. Ratings are increasingly used by university managements to determine how to allocate internal funding, make funding cuts, and which staff to appoint, promote or select for redundancy (see Lee and Harley, this volume).

The assessment by the higher education funding councils of the quality of the teaching — and other aspects of education — provided by universities and other higher education institutions in the UK began in 1993, on an approximately five-year cycle. While research assessment is intended to be made against a standard of international excellence, teaching quality assessment is 'criterion-referenced'; that is, judgement is made according to the goals the institution being assessed has set itself:

> The [Funding] Council's quality assessment method examines the quality of the student learning experience and student achievement within the context set by the particular institutional mission and the subject aims and objectives. It follows from this that there can be no 'gold standard' against which all provision can be measured. (HEFCE, 1994: 9)

Assessment is intended also to cover quantifiable performance indicators and calculations of the 'value added' element.

Initially, teaching quality assessment in England, Wales and Northern Ireland was made on a three-grade basis (unsatisfactory, satisfactory and excellent); now assessment is made on the basis of six core aspects of provision (such as teaching, resources, student support) which are each graded on a scale of 1-4, with 4 the highest point. An overall threshold judgement of 'quality approved' is made if all the scores are above grade 1. If any aspects are given grade 1, and on reassessment are still found to be unsatisfactory, then funding will be withdrawn whole or in part. In Scotland, a four-grade scale is used.

Quality audit is carried out at institutional level by the Higher Education Quality Council (HEQC), a company set up in 1992 by the universities to maintain quality and standards in UK higher education and protect academic autonomy. Quality audit is a means of checking that relevant systems and structures within an institution support its key teaching mission (DES, 1991: 26). As with quality assessment, audit is not intended to be carried out with a national or international standard in mind; rather, it is intended to be relative to each institution s "own aims and objectives, rather than a 'gold' standard against which to measure compliance" (HEQC, 1994: viii). Unlike in quality assessment, a final judgement is not made.

The current debate on standards

The development of higher education in the UK into a mass system in the late 1980s and early 1990s raised serious concerns about standards, not least among the members of the Conservative government which had set the goal of one in three 18-19 year-olds participating in higher education by the year 2000. In a speech in April 1994, the then Secretary of State for Education, John Patten, called on the HEQC, "to place more emphasis on broad comparability in the standards of degrees offered by different institutions". Mr Patten expressed the ironic concern of the government that, in the period of 'consolidation' of student numbers, and reduced funding, which followed expansion, "the academic reputation and standards in British higher education should be maintained at their high level". With his thoughts particularly focused on the overseas market for British university places, Mr Patten — a former university lecturer — voiced the allegation that "examiners have become less demanding recently".

Two months after this speech, the CVCP commissioned the HEQC to investigate academic standards. The CVCP reaffirmed that institutions were responsible for the standards of their awards, but said there was a need to create an overt standards assurance system. The CVCP stated that broad comparability of standards could "best be achieved in a diverse system through assurance of threshold standards [i.e. a minimum acceptable level of achievement]" (HEQC, 1995: 21). Among factors giving concern about standards were the increasing number of first and upper second honours degrees; the worries of professional and statutory bodies which give accreditation to university degrees about the variability of graduate output; and the strains on the external examiner system caused by increased student numbers and modularisation. As Mr Patten's speech indicated, standards were being increasingly viewed in an international context. The drive by the European Union towards harmonised qualifications emphasised the need for greater explicitness of what British academic awards signified. International student exchanges were leading to some unfavourable comparisons between British students and students from other higher education systems.

Later in 1994 the HEQC set up the Graduate Standards Programme (GSP) to consider the comparability of first degrees, and the development of threshold standards for them. The primary concern of the GSP was therefore output standards, rather than the inputs into, or process of higher education, which were being assessed through the research and teaching quality assessment programmes, as well as through institutional quality audit run by the HEQC. The GSP, in its Interim *Report* in 1995, rapidly concluded that it was no longer possible to rely on "collegial processes" to make judgements about academic standards, because of the growth and changes in the higher education system (HEQC, 1995: 5). It said "such changes create the need for more explicit descriptors and criteria to provide a framework within which judgements can be made" (p. 5). But there were limits to the extent of such a framework. The report said "uniformity in the standards of all degrees across all institutions (which might be achieved through national curricula or examinations) is neither regarded as desirable nor sensible" (HEQC, 1995: 8); such a move might stifle innovation and the responsiveness of institutions to their individual missions and the requirements of their 'consumers'. The report said it was at the level of the module that it was "feasible to define standards" (p. 15), rather than at the end of a course. Such developments, it said, were "tending to move the assessment process away from the traditional 'norm-referenced' assessment model towards one that is 'criterion-referenced'" (pp. 15-16). Credit accumulation and transfer schemes, which in theory allow for the transfer of credit from one institution to another (although in practice this has generally been limited to credit transfers within an institution), by nature call for comparability of standards.

The GSP has included investigation into the working of the external examiner system. There has also been a separate inquiry, commissioned in 1994 by the HEQC, into the future of the external examiner system. The report of evidence given to the inquiry was careful to avoid making over-arching claims for the role of externals. It said: "... it is important here to emphasise the strength with which comparability is urged in the evidence as relating primarily to standards within subjects ... Very few institutions claimed that comprehensive, cross-subject comparison is possible or valid" (Silver *et al.*, 1995: 37). The report concluded that although there was wide support for the external examining system, "a defence of external examining is not expressed as a defence of absolute standards or of a gold standard embodied in the honours classification system" (p. 37).

The draft report and recommendations of the GSP, published in November 1996, found there were difficulties with the concept of 'graduateness', i.e. "those features that make a programme of study or a level of student achievement degree-worthy" (HEQC, 1996: 10). It concluded that graduateness was not, at least for the time being "sufficiently robust to be used to define the nature of a UK first degree or to offer a threshold standard for all degrees" (p. 20). Nor did the external examiner system offer a great deal of help in upholding comparable academic standards: "The role of external examiner as guarantor of comparability of standards has been rendered increasingly unrealistic both by a lack of explicit benchmarks for standards at a time of growing diversity of educational mission, and increasing scepticism about the existence or value of general comparability" (p. 24). And the possibility of a common threshold standard for degrees did not appear practicable, despite being welcomed in principle during the GSP's consultation exercise.

Faced with this lack of consensus, the GSP was able to recommend only that higher education institutions should give greater attention to clarity in establishing, comparing and reviewing standards and to enhancing academics' skills in setting standards. The HEQC stressed that its aim was to strengthen the means of identifying, comparing and assuring standards — not the defining of standards per se. The development of a threshold standard was expressed as an option for institutions, not a recommendation. At the time of writing this chapter, the final report and recommendations of the GSP had not been published, but from the draft recommendations, it is evident that the current debate on standards is still far from resolved. This chapter was also written before the report of the Dearing inquiry into higher education — and its conclusions about academic standards — were published, and before the new Quality Assurance Agency for higher education (established in April 1997) — which is to have the dual role of monitoring teaching quality and academic standards — had become fully operational.

Towards an institution-related model of academic standards

The use of data

In the decade since the first RAE in 1986, the UK higher education system has developed a range of statistics in an attempt to measure its performance, account for the public funding it receives, inform management decisions, satisfy students, employers of graduates and other 'customers' of higher education, of the quality of the services it provides, and give assurance that academic standards are being maintained. Additional indicators, not officially provided in the publications of the CVCP, the Higher Education Statistics Agency (or its predecessor, the Universities' Statistical Record), or the funding councils, but based on the information they provide, can also be calculated.

There are important caveats about the use of performance indicators (Johnes and Taylor, 1990: 183; Cave *et al.*, 1997: passim). Much of what comprises higher education is a dynamic process of interaction between teachers and their students, which cannot be broken down into quantifiable components. It is doubtful whether indicators can give an accurate idea of the degree of 'value added' provided by an institution. The very existence and nature of the RAE, particularly because of its consequences for resource allocation, may be determining — rather than measuring — the way research is conducted in universities (Cave *et al.*, 1997: 163-164; Lee and Harley, this volume). Performance indicators tend to go hand-in-hand with 'managerialism' in the running of universities, and create a tension with the traditional collegial approach of academics to running their affairs, and with the tradition of institutional autonomy in the pre-1992 universities (Cave *et al.*, 1997: 226). Despite these and other reservations, there may be ways in which indicators can be used positively: "Indicators which can enable institutional leaders to identify, or at least raise questions about, strengths and weaknesses of comparable departments and programmes are welcomed" (p. 226).

Data analysis

I have looked at a number of variables which are relevant to different aspects of higher education in terms of input, process and output, to see if there are any patterns which support the concept of an institution-related model of standards (see **Table 7.1**). Analysis of variance indicated significant differences among higher education institutions, chiefly between the three categories of 'old' universities on the one hand, and the new universities and other HEIs on the other.

One key indicator which is missing is information about the qualifications of university entrants for each institution. The average A-level results of entrants were formerly published by the CVCP for the old universities in its annual

Table 7.1   Data for five groups of English higher education institutions (HEIs)

	Russell Group*	94 Group*	Other Old Universities	New universities	Other HEIs
1. Total income: average percentage derived from research funding 1994-95 (p<0.0005)*	35.7% SD*: 94 group, other old, new, other HEIs	29.1% SD: other old, new, other HEIs	21.7% SD: new, other HEIs	4.1%	1.2%
2. Average weighted* rating in 1992 RAE (p<0.0005)	4.0 SD: other old, new, other HEIs	3.9 SD: new, other HEIs	3.6 SD: new, other HEIs	1.9	1.8
3. Average weighted rating in 1996 RAE (p<0.0005)	4.5 SD: other old, new, other HEIs	4.3 SD: new, other HEIs	4.1 SD: new, other HEIs	2.5	2.4
4. Average rating in TQA 1993-95 (p<0.0005)	2.7 SD: other old, new, other HEIs	2.5 SD: new, other HEIs	2.3 SD: new, other HEIs	2.1	2.1
5. Average rating in TQA 1995-96 (p<0.05)	20.8 SD: new, other HEIs	20.3	20.1	19.3	19.0
6. Average full-time equivalent staff: student ratios 1994-95 (p<0.0005)	1:7.4 SD: other old, new, other HEIs	1:10.2 SD: new, other HEIs	1:10.8 SD: new, other HEIs	1:18.4	1:18.2
7. Average percentage of all degrees which were firsts & upper seconds 1994-95 (p<0.0005)*	59.7% SD*: other old, new, HEIs,	60.4% SD: other old, new, HEIs	54.2% SD: new, HEIs	44.7%	44.8%
Maximum number	15	9	28	35	40

*   See Table 7.1 Notes, facing page.

Sources: Universities Funding Council (1992); Higher Education Statistics Agency (1996a,b); HEFCE 'Subject Overview Reports'

performance indicators; however, since the ending of the binary divide, A-level results per institution are no longer publicly available. It is therefore not possible to use average A-level and degree results as an indicator of the academic value added by an institution. This matters less than it might previously have done, because of the decrease in the proportion of entrants with A-levels to higher education.

*   Table 7.1 Notes:

The table of indicators does not include the Open University (which has an abnormally large number of part-time students), and the medical schools (many do not have degree classifications).

The Russell Group of universities comprised Cambridge, Oxford, University College, London, Imperial College, Warwick, the LSE, Edinburgh, Birmingham, Manchester, Bristol, Glasgow, Leeds, Liverpool, Newcastle, Nottingham, Sheffield and Southampton.

The 94 Group of universities comprised East Anglia, Essex, Durham, York, Sussex, Lancaster, Reading, Exeter, Bath, and Birkbeck College, London. Warwick and the LSE were members of both groups; in the table, they are included in the 94 Group only. These two groups of old (i.e. existing pre-1992) universities are unofficial, and are intended to reflect the common interests, respective sizes and research traditions of their members. The membership of the groups was listed in a document sent by Dr Derek Roberts, the Provost of University College, London, to the Secretary of State for Education in March 1995. The presence of significant differences between the groups of institutions is indicated by the letters SD. The RAE ratings are weighted to indicate the number of research active staff.

The first variable, on funding, can be classified as an input variable, and shows the average percentage of total income derived from research funding in 1994-95. The research figure includes recurrent funding from the Higher Education Funding Council for England (HEFCE), and research grants and contracts (including funding from research councils and charities). This is expressed as a percentage of all funding, including recurrent funding for teaching, tuition fees and capital grants. This is a useful indicator of the research strength of an institution, and shows the gulf in terms of research funding between the old universities on one hand, and the new universities and other HEIs on the other. It also shows why the various unofficial interest groups within the old sector have developed, since there are significant differences in funding between the Russell Group and the 94 Group, and the 94 Group and the rest of the old universities. The overall relevance of this variable to standards is that it shows where the universities with a research-rich environment can be found.

The average RAE ratings, indicating the research strengths of different departments within institutions, have a close link to the funding variable. This is to be expected, since RAE ratings are used as a weighting in the allocation of recurrent research funding by the funding councils. Although the new universities and other HEIs have increased their research activity since the previous RAE in 1992, they still lag behind the old universities, and are unlikely to bridge the gap while the current policy of selectivity in research funding is still in place.

Analysis of unweighted average RAE ratings in 1992 indicated a range according to different academic subject categories (ASCs - the subject units used by the HEFCE for allocating teaching funding) from 2.4 for business and management, to 2.9 for art and design. When rounded, the averages indicate that it is easier to get a 3 rating in some subjects than others. This is important because of the funding implications (low-scoring departments in an institution may get less funding or be a target for job cuts), and because of the status attached within institutions to a department getting a higher RAE grade, even though higher grades were more frequent in some subjects than others. The range for the old universities was from 3.2 (medicine, dentistry and veterinary) to 3.8 (education). The range for new universities was from 1.0 (medicine, dentistry and veterinary - this was only for one institution) to 2.4 (art and design).

The two teaching quality variables tell an interesting story. Teaching quality assessment is intended to monitor the provision of education — such as teaching, resources and student support — at the subject level, according to the specific aims of the institution being assessed. It is therefore criterion-referenced, whereas the RAE is norm-referenced. Nevertheless, there is evidence of a trend in the assessments. In the first round of teaching assessment by the HEFCE, 15 subjects were assessed — a mixture of science, social science, engineering and arts subjects. Provision was assessed on a three-point scale of unsatisfactory (1), satisfactory (2) and excellent (3). The old universities received higher ratings than the new and the other HEIs. In the second round, the HEFCE used a different grading system, with six core aspects of provision each graded on a four-point scale, with a score of one indicating unsatisfactory, with a total of 24 points. Eight subjects were assessed, most of them languages. The level of significance was lower than in the previous round, and post hoc testing indicated the only significant difference was between the Russell Group, and new universities and other HEIs. One possible explanation for the comparative changes in results might be that the small number of subjects and their limited range are related to the narrowing of the scores. There might also have been a general improvement by the new universities and other HEIs in 'being assessed', although this looks unlikely because the former polytechnics have a longer tradition of assessment than the old universities. When TQA scores for the 1993-95 round were analysed according to academic subject category, there again were imbalances. For example, the average for maths and information technology (in the old universities) was 2.2 (i.e. satisfactory), and art and design was 2.7 (i.e. excellent).

The fifth input variable — staff:student ratios — also relates to the quality of student experience. The ratios are lower in the old sector than the new, with the implication that the greater the number of staff to students, the better will be the quality of education and service provided for those students. In the new universities, there were more than twice the number of students per member of staff than in the Russell Group.

In terms of degree 'output', the degree classes were better at the old universities, although there was a significant difference between the Russell and 94 groups on one hand, and the other old universities on the other. This evidence of a trend in graduate quality, or at least in the grading of undergraduates, linked to particular types of institutions, appears to support a model of institution-related degree standards. There may be a number of factors at work in this situation: the old universities are richer, they can afford more staff and better equipment, they provide learning within a strong research tradition. It may also be that examiners are in some way influenced by the reputation of a particular institution, to the benefit of candidates at the longer-established and more prestigious institutions. These results provide evidence of different standards at different types of institutions. As might be expected, degree results correlate highly with the variables used. Further analysis is needed to test whether these variables can be used to predict degree results. However, the lack of published data on university entrance qualifications is currently hindering such an analysis.

Conclusion

In conclusion I would like to look at the relationship between teaching and research in higher education, because of their probable impact on academic standards. The data in the previous section suggest that high ratings in teaching and research assessment are linked to high degree results. So should teaching be closely linked with research activity in the provision of higher education? Or is it possible to have high academic standards in institutions where there is a limited amount of research by academic staff? In general, staff at the pre-1992 universities would say yes to the former question, and staff at the post-1992 universities would say yes to the latter question. Further analysis of the link between research and teaching provides mixed results. There is a strong correlation between the 1992 RAE and TQA in 1993-95, accounting for 59 per cent of the variance. As the report in 1994 on teaching quality assessment by the Centre for Higher Education Studies concluded: "Implicit in any grading system is likely to be a common set of criteria and requirements even if they are not spelt out ... the legitimate need to employ criteria which are cross-institutional in character must cut across the wish to be mission sensitive. And, indeed, that most of the excellent ratings have so far been awarded to older universities suggests both that a cross-institutional set of criteria is in place and that it favours one sub-group of institutions" (CHES, 1994: 44-45). However, more recent data suggest a different pattern: the correlation between the 1996 RAE and TQA in 1995-96 is weak, only accounting for 17 per cent of the variance.

The British academic profession has "traditionally distinguished itself from its foreign counterparts by the strength of its conviction that research and teaching must be tightly linked in the pursuit of scholarship and science" (Halsey, 1992: 176). The Robbins Report in 1963 expressed total disagreement with the extreme view that would remove research altogether from the universities. The presence of research work "gives intellectual and spiritual vitality to work at all levels in institutions where it is pursued". Separation of the two activities was pointless: "There is no borderline between teaching and research; they are complementary and overlapping activities" (Committee on Higher Education, 1963: 181-182). Surveys by Halsey in 1976 and 1989 of the opinions of academic staff at universities and the former polytechnics indicated the great majority agreed that "An active research interest is essential if a person is to be a good university teacher"; a slightly lesser majority believed "An active research interest is essential if a person is to be a good polytechnic teacher" (Halsey, 1992: 316). A survey in 1996 of staff in the pre-1992 universities found that while 53 per cent of permanent staff said their interests lay primarily in research, only 33.5 per cent of fixed-term staff said this (AUT, 1997).

There is strong adherence among senior figures in the pre-1992 universities to the importance of research being linked to teaching in higher education. Sir John Kingman, Vice-Chancellor of the University of Bristol, believes there is no alternative to having teaching "in a university which offers learning in a research environment" (Kingman, 1993). Likewise, Professor Ivor Crewe, Vice-Chancellor of the University of Essex: "At this University, top-rank research and high-quality teaching go together" (*Wyvern, University of Essex* newsletter, 24 April 1996).

Against this, recent studies have argued against the need for teaching to be closely interlinked with research. The Royal Society's report, *Higher Education Futures*, concluded: "Given sufficient opportunity for scholarship, we believe that there is no absolute requirement that all higher education teachers must pursue both teaching and research" (Royal Society Study Group, 1993: 37). Instead, the report makes a vague recommendation that students in institutions with a primary emphasis on teaching "should have some exposure to an environment in which research or professional practice … is pursued" (Royal Society Study Group, 1993: 37-38). *Learning to Succeed*, the report of the National Commission on Education, emphasised the importance of diversity in higher education. "What undergraduates require is exposure to a significant number of teachers whose involvement in advanced work underpins their teaching" (National Commission on Education, 1993: 308). As with the Royal Society report, *Learning to Succeed* is not clear about how much exposure to research is necessary. It does not specify what "advanced work" entails; from the context, it would appear that "advanced work" falls somewhat short of basic research. Hughes and Tight question whether "the idea of linkage is being stretched too far" (Hughes and Tight, 1995: 57). Their concept of teaching and research linked in the university at departmental level, mediated through staff development, makes sense, although there is no reason to suppose that this precludes a direct link in research-active academics.

Some are more explicit in their opposition to the research-teaching link. Sir Christopher Ball, Director of Learning, Royal Society of Arts, has written: "Neither fundamental nor contract research necessarily enhance the quality of teaching - though they may do so - and it therefore follows that they are not a necessary condition for, or accompaniment to, higher education" (Ball, 1992: 134). He describes the "challenge of finally breaking 'the fundamental link' between teaching and research" (p. 136). His iconoclastic tone follows that of Ronald Barnett, at the University of London's Institute of Education: " …research is not an essential part of the process of higher education as such" (Barnett, 1990: 123). He maintains that "…in some respects, the research culture can have deleterious effects on the teaching process" (Barnett, 1990: 130), for example, in researchers who delve too deeply into a subject, or who develop tunnel vision (although in fairness, research active staff are not the only academics to suffer from such problems). For Barnett, "The relationship between research and higher education is such that someone, somewhere, should have engaged in research; but that does not mean that research is part of the meaning of higher education" (p. 129).

Roger Brown, former Chief Executive of the HEQC, maintains that "there is little empirical evidence to support the view that quality in research is necessary for quality in teaching" (Brown, 1995). But if the data in this paper concerning the RAE and quality assessment reflect the relationship between research and teaching in higher education, then Brown's conclusion may need to be reconsidered. Brown goes on to say there is growing evidence to suggest that research, "and in particular the funding of research on the basis of judgements reached through the research assessment exercise, is having a negative impact on teaching and learning and especially innovation in teaching" (Brown, 1995). Brown is not alone in criticising the powerful effect the RAE has on academic management and priorities (Johnes and Taylor, 1992; Williams, 1993; Griffith, 1995; Jenkins and Gibbs, 1995; Smith, 1996).

The argument over whether there needs to be a direct link between teaching and research for high academic standards in higher education is more likely to be settled by funding allocations than by debate in the academic press. It is one of the main concerns of institutions in the Russell and 94 groups that the increasing number of HEIs competing for roughly the same amount of HEFCE research funding means those which have an international research profile find it difficult to maintain. Conversely, many new universities are worried that the gap between them and the old universities, as indicated in this chapter, will never narrow, because of the immense advantage of the old universities in having mature research facilities at the time when the new universities only began to compete for HEFCE research funding.

A stratified higher education system is widely envisaged. The National Commission on Education said: "Research, particularly equipment-intensive research in science and technology, will tend to concentrate more and more in a relatively small number of university institutions and, within institutions, in particular departments ... We do not see this as a bad thing" (National Commission on Education, 1993: 312). Ball, considering the system before the ending of the binary divide, wrote: "... the process of concentration and selectivity in fundamental research has hardly started. Before it is finished we shall probably have to identify a small subset of some twelve to fifteen research universities and recognize that the remainder of the existing system ... constitutes the 'teaching sector'" (Ball, 1992: 135). This prospect of research concentration was outlined recently by the report of the National Academies Policy Advisory Group: "We believe the increased concentration of the resources for research in a few universities follows inevitably from the severe and long-term constraints on the public funding for research" (NAPAG, 1996: 20). NAPAG proposed that concentration of funds would be accompanied by a professional development and teaching scheme, to improve the teaching role of staff in departments and institutions where research funding was withdrawn. The disadvantages of this proposal would be to accentuate the divide between research and teaching institutions; it would mean large numbers of staff no longer having the opportunity for research; the potential outcome of separating teaching and research in this way would be to impoverish students learning experience; academic standards, if they are influenced by the proximity to research, would suffer. These disadvantages may well outweigh the advantages of increased selectivity.

An alternative would be to establish regional research centres, perhaps based in departments which scored highly in the RAE:

> Such centres would provide the focus and locus for research-active staff in a particular subject or area from institutions throughout a region. Staff could be contracted or seconded ... and centres would be expected to establish mechanisms of dissemination and communication to inform all staff — teaching and research — of the work and findings of the centre. (Albury, 1995)

The attractiveness of this idea is that it would enable staff at institutions with a low RAE grade to take part in research and, in theory, avoid the rigid two-tier higher education system envisaged in the NAPAG report. The main problem is that institutions not chosen to be a regional "centre of excellence" would be unwilling to sacrifice their research funding. It would mean finding another method of allocating funding council research grants, to avoid the intensely competitive RAE and its associated funding mechanism, which forces institutions to outdo each other in recruiting highly research-active staff.

In the developing system of mass higher education in the UK, a gold standard is emerging which is based not so much on the overall comparability of an honours degree, but on the degree output of universities according to their performance in various kinds of assessment. The likelihood is that a two-tier, or even three- or four-tier, university system will develop, unless radical decisions are taken about the nature of research selectivity and the amount of funding given for university research. The question is not so much whether we can afford to have a broader base for research in our universities, but whether we can afford not to.

References

Albury, D. (1995) 'When Everyone's a Winner', *Times Higher Education Supplement*, 28 April.

Alderman, G. (1995) 'Superior Knowledge Comes With Age', *The Independent*, 12 October.

Association of University Teachers (1996) *Efficiency Gains or quality Losses?*. London: AUT.

Association of University Teachers (1997) *Universities: The Staff View*. London: AUT).

Ball, Sir Christopher (1992) 'Teaching and Research', in T. Whiston and R. Geiger (eds) *Research and Higher Education*. Buckingham: SRHE & Open University Press.

Barnett, R. (1990) *The Idea of Higher Education* . Buckingham: SRHE & Open University Press.

Brown, R. (1995) 'Logic of the Rhetoric', *Times Higher Education Supplement*, 8 December.

Cave, M. S. Hanney, M. Henkel and M. Kogan (1997) *The Use of Performance Indicators in Higher Education*. London: Jessica Kingsley Publishers.

Centre for Higher Education Studies (1994) *Assessment of the Quality of Higher Education*. London: Institute of Education.

Committee on Higher Education (1963) *Higher Education: Report* (the Robbins Report) Cm. 2154. London: HMSO.

Committee of Vice-Chancellors and Principals (1986) *Academic Standards in Universities*. London: CVCP.

Department of Education and Science (1991) *Higher Education: A New Framework*, Cm. 1541. London: HMSO.

Griffith, J. (1995) *Research Assessment: As Strange A Maze As E'er Men Trod*. London: Council for Academic Freedom and Academic Standards.

Halsey, A.H. (1992) *Decline of Donnish Dominion*. Oxford: OUP.

Higher Education Funding Council for England (1994) *Consultation Paper 2/94*. Bristol: HEFCE.

———— (1996) *1996 Research Assessment Exercise: The Outcome*. Bristol: HEFCE.

Higher Education Quality Council (1994) *Learning from Audit*. London: HEQC.

––––– (1995) *Graduate Standards Programme: Interim Report*. London: HEQC.

––––– (1996) *Graduate Standards Programme: Draft Report and Recommendations*. London: HEQC.

Higher Education Statistics Agency (1995) *Higher Education Statistics for the United Kingdom 1992/93*. Cheltenham, HESA.

––––– (1996a) *Students in Higher Education Institutions 1994-95*. Cheltenham, HESA.

––––– (1996b) *Resources of Higher Education Institutions 1994-95*. Cheltenham: HESA.

Hughes, C., and M. Tight (1995) 'Linking University Teaching and Research', *Higher Education Review*, 28(1): 51-65.

Jenkins, A. and G. Gibbs (1995) 'Scandal of Postgrad Army', *Times Higher Education Supplement*, 15 September.

Johnes, J. and J. Taylor (1990) *Performance Indicators in Higher Education*. Buckingham: SRHE & Open University Press.

––––– (1992) 'The 1989 Research Selectivity Exercise: A Statistical Analysis of Differences in Research Rating between Universities at the Cost Centre Level', *Higher Education Quarterly*, 46 (1): 67-87.

Kingman, Sir John (1993) 'The Pursuit of Truth', *Times Higher Education Supplement*, June 18.

Moodie, G. C. (1986) 'Fit for What?, in Graeme C. Moodie (ed) *Standards and Criteria in Higher Education* . Guildford: SRHE and NFER-Nelson.

National Academies Policy Advisory Group (1996) *Research Capability of the University System*. London: NAPAG.

National Commission on Education (1993) *Learning to Succeed*. London: Heinemann.

Royal Society Study Group (1993) *Higher Education Futures*. London: The Royal Society.

Scott, P. (1995) *The Meanings of Mass Higher Education*. Buckingham: SRHE & Open University Press.

Silver, H., and P. Silver (1986) 'The Escaping Answer', in Graeme C. Moodie (ed) *Standards and Criteria in Higher Education*. Guildford: SRHE and NFER-Nelson.

Silver, H., A. Stennett and R. Williams (1995) *The External Examiner System: Possible Futures*. London: HEQC.

Smith, D. (1996) 'Selection Perfection', *Times Higher Education Supplement*, 8 March.

Universities Funding Council (1992) *Research Assessment Exercise 1992: The Outcome*. Bristol: UFC.

Webb, C. (1994) 'Quality Audit in the Universities', in D. Green (ed) *What is Quality in Higher Education?*. Buckingham: SRHE & Open University Press.

Williams, B. (1993) 'Research Management for Selectivity and Concentration — With What Effect?', *Higher Education Quarterly*, 47 (1): 4-16.

Williams, G. (1986) 'The Missing Bottom Line', in G. C. Moodie (ed) *Standards and Criteria in Higher Education*. Guildford: SRHE and NFER-Nelson.

Higher Education in a Right State: Professionalising the Proletariat or Proletarianising the Professions

8

Patrick Ainley

The 'old maids of academicism' and the 'technical modernisers' march in different armies but to the same drum. [Friedrich Nietzsche]

Introduction

This chapter uses interviews with teachers in two very different higher education institutions to draw out contrasted reactions to change in the sector. These changes are related to changing government 'knowledge policies' (Bergendal, 1984), particularly in relation to the three Dearing Reviews of the 'National' Curriculum for state schools (1994), of 16-19 qualifications (1996) and of higher education (1997) — henceforth referred to as Dearings I, II and III (as in Ainley, 1996). These reviews can be seen as 'tidying up exercises' consequent upon the Conservative government's sudden switch in learning policy in the run up to the 1987 election. This new learning policy replaced a policy of *Training Without Jobs* (Finn, 1987), which had been administered during the 1970s and '80s by the Department of Employment as an answer to the rise of permanent structural unemployment since 1973. In its place, the 1988 Education Act and the 1992 Further and Higher Education Act marked a turn to what can be called a policy of 'Education Without Jobs' (Ainley, 1992). This policy is administered through the Department for Education which absorbed the Department of Employment in 1995. The new policy accompanies a 'transition from corporatism' (Ainley and Vickerstaff, 1993) to what has been called *The Contracting State* (Harden, 1992), widely seen as replacing the old, corporate welfare state with a post-welfare, workfare state. These changes in the form of the state have as profound implications for teachers in higher education as for everyone else.

The change in the state has in part been a response to still wider processes of class recomposition in society. Changing divisions of knowledge and labour. (Ainley, 1993) have eroded the previous rigid divisions between manual and mental labour, as between professionals and their clients. The current demystification of graduate-level professionalism holds teachers, doctors and other professional public servants increasingly accountable through more explicit contracts with the consumers of their previously self-regulated services.

Far from professionalising the proletariat, as the recent expansion of higher education pretends, the new learning policy in reality represents a proletarianisation of the professions. It runs concurrent with rampant qualification inflation and the general devaluation through expansion of the major part of a more differentiated Further and Higher Continuing Education (F&HCE) system. It parallels not only work reorganisation in the increasingly state-subsidised private sector, which especially squeezes traditional middle management, but also the dismantling of the traditional welfare bureaucracies in the increasingly semi-privatised state sector (including education) which have previously sustained the growth of the professional or 'service class' since the last war. The aspiration to professional education for all through a mass higher education system in a learning society is therefore *rhetorical*.

To contribute to a real learning society, rather than to what in reality is as yet only a *certified* one, this chapter argues in conclusion that teachers at all levels of the new system of F&HCE must abandon the defensive ideology of professionalism and transcend the polarised reactions to reform illustrated in the interviews with HE teachers that open this chapter.

The 'hard' and the 'soft': two models of higher education

The chapter reports research undertaken for the first systematic qualitative comparison of staff and student experiences across the former-binary divide in higher education, reported in *Degrees of Difference, higher education in the 1990s* (1994). Since this book was written the author has with a colleague undertaken further interviewing of staff and students in two similarly contrasted further education colleges, published in 1997 as '*The Business of Learning, staff and student experiences of further education in the 1990s*'. This further research now also informs this chapter.

In 1992, 20 teaching staff at East London and at Kent Universities were interviewed for comparison with the student experiences previously investigated at the two institutions. Staff represented all levels from lecturer to professor in the very different management structures of the two universities, which at Kent at that time still clung to the ideal of a collegial Oxbridge model of donnish democracy in comparison with the more centralised hierarchy at East London. At both places however, it was the shop-floor lecturer who was the target of investigation, as being representative of the reality of the situation on the ground and its likely future development.

The Oxbridge background of staff at Kent was evident in this sample, all except one of whom interviewed in humanities and social science had previously studied as under- or post-graduates at Oxford or Cambridge. This was not the case with the Kent University science staff interviewed nor with any of the staff interviewed at East London. Though there were some exceptions among Oxbridge-educated staff, one of two contrasted conceptions of higher education, and of the nature of their subject discipline within it, could be identified with the traditional university ideal that is symbolised by Oxbridge. Following interviewees' own usage, this view of HE can be termed 'hard' as against the 'soft' perspective to which it was opposed.

For in the course of research it was noticeable — at East London especially — that staff who made allowances for students, such as replacing an exam paper with a dissertation, or just by extending essay deadlines, were labelled 'soft' by colleagues who urged them to be 'hard' and uphold academic standards, and thus their conception of themselves as researchers and scholars rather than as mere teachers and of their institution as an academy and not a school. Staff who disregarded this advice were regarded as 'soft' by their academically 'hard' colleagues. As well as emotionally 'soft', staff who questioned the rules of the system and the standards by which they and their colleagues had been successful and which provided them with a valued identity, undermined their own position. Like turkeys voting for Christmas, they were regarded by the 'hard' majority at both institutions as perhaps 'soft' in the head, certainly lacking in 'hard' and rigorous logic!

The notion of 'hardness' relates to the masochistic nature of academic disciplines (sic) to which 'hard' cases feel they have subjected themselves, echoing the monastic origins of their craft, and which they sadistically inflict upon others. For in order to gain acceptance in academia, a subject has to be shown to be 'hard', like the 'hard sciences'. This means it is not only 'hard' for students to learn but also for their teachers to be qualified to teach it. Following Bailey, abstract and propositional knowledge (not skill) is, on an economic analogy, considered from this perspective the more valuable as it is increasingly rare and inaccessible, hard to find and refine — like gold. This involves a contradiction however, as knowledge (as distinct from the mystical experiences or revelations with which it is often confused) by definition only exists so long as it is shared. This accounts for what Bailey (1977: 27) described as the traditional academic community's:

> ...fragile sense of superiority... that curiously nervous elitism, which combines a firm sense of one's own superiority with a conviction that there is no way in which outsiders can be made to acknowledge it.

In this traditional and 'hard' view, university education is seen as a conversation restricted to academic peers into which students are initiated and by which general and analytic knowledge is handed down, essentially unchanged, from don to potential don. This task of academic vocational education is regarded by its proponents as a vital task, literally, to the preservation of civilisation as they know it and one that in the present economic and political climate is increasingly beleaguered on all sides.

From this point of view, higher education is seen as building upon students' previous schooling, or — exceptionally — college education, or even training in work, but is considered to differ fundamentally from them. Other university students (than potential dons) may incidentally benefit from a higher education so conceived but the university is not essentially concerned with them, even though only eight per cent of graduates went on to further study, according to the Association of Graduate Careers Advisory Services in 1992.

Similarly but also incidentally, it was considered by the 'hard men' (as they were mostly) that the wider society may also possibly benefit from the free enquiry, scholarship and research which was seen as vital to advance the frontiers of knowledge through gradual and organic accretion of the canon of texts, experiments or cases making up fixed subject-based knowledge. Communicating this subject-base either to students or a wider public is however not understood to be the essential purpose of a university, any more than are the practical applications of new ideas and the discoveries of research.

Instead, this academic ideal is based on the belief in knowledge for its own sake rather than knowledge for a purpose. So, the essential function of a university is, as described by the founder of educational sociology, Emile Durkheim (1938: 63), "for an organised body of professional teachers to provide for its own perpetuation" and that of the knowledge its individual members have collected. An individual's commitment in this conception is therefore, as one interviewee explained, "to research, to my subject, to my colleagues primarily". This implied the intensive study of one subject, closely related to research in that subject.

Selection for this vocation is seen as through a series of examination hurdles at which the majority ultimately fail. The function of education is thus not so much to teach as to establish the conditions in which the majority of students can fail and the minority sort themselves out to eventually succeed their examiners as the gatekeepers of 'quality' and 'excellence'. According to this view, the process of education is not lifelong but culminates in the 'final examination' in which the class of degree is used as an indication of the academic quality of the individual. This individual mental quality is viewed as innate, for students are seen as having distinct levels of ability indicated by the class of final degree they obtain — a mind is either an ordinary mind or 'a first class mind'. This label of a fixed state of grace is considered more important than the subject studied to obtain it. Even 20 or 30 years after graduation, a first class degree can be cited as demonstrating suitability for academic employment, although demonstrably the level of qualification for such employment is a function of the academic labour market at different times. In this sense, the degree is as final for the minority who continue their study after it as it is for the majority for whom it is the last exam they ever take.

The other model of education subscribed to by an overall minority of the staff interviewed at both HEIs corresponds with the original notion of polytechnic education — though only partially embodied in the polytechnics as they developed from 1965 to 1992 (see Pratt, 1997). It was not held by all the staff interviewed at East London, though a majority of them there subscribed to it, just as a minority of Kent interviewees also did. In addition, there was, as would be expected, a mixture of the two views sustained by many individuals in varying admixtures.

This second and 'polytechnic' conception of higher education sees the same higher cognitive skills, or general level knowledge, that are the object of the academic conception being derived not, or not exclusively, from abstract dialogue but from, or in combination with, various forms of practical experience. The process of acquiring generalised knowledge / skills is not therefore restricted to higher education institutions but is potentially realisable in society as a whole and can also take place in schools and FE. It could therefore be integrated with other forms of education and training in and out of employment and was not conceived of as essentially separate from it. Rather than closed save to a minority of individuals, all education was considered to be potentially open.

Primary loyalty in this conception was to students. Research interests were given equal weight with teaching rather than accorded primacy over it. Research, especially in the form of Independent Study, was not however regarded as the exclusive preserve of qualified professionals but as an activity open to students working collectively or individually at all levels from primary school project work upwards and, indeed, a natural and universal human activity.

Like their colleagues above, representatives of this conception assumed that they themselves were good professional teachers but the knowledge and skills that their students acquired were regarded as explicit, rather than — as in the rival conception — as implicit to the process of communicative transfer. Teaching was therefore more of a collaborative exercise undertaken with the students' active participation than one in which knowledge was handed down from teacher to students whose role was essentially passive. The nature of the curriculum was also not fixed but problematic because rapidly changing across subject boundaries and therefore also open to negotiation with students and others.

These two ideal-typical 'hard' and 'soft' positions with which interviewees could be identified have been discovered also among school teachers, described as 'lion tamers' by Hargreaves (1967) and 'progressivists' (in relation to what in the 1960s was called progressive primary schooling). They also correspond to Bernstein's (1977) distinctions between teachers subscribing to a collection code of strong classification and framing of the curriculum as against integrated curricula weakly framed and classified. Or the distinction between 'elitists' and 'expansionists' in higher education made by Halsey and Trow and summarised in Halsey (1992: 34).

In further education, Ainley and Bailey (1997) found a correspondingly 'hard' adherence by lecturers in technical subjects for whom it was important to their self esteem and professional identity that technical 'standards' were maintained, even if they were no longer required either by new forms of competence-based assessment or by actual practice in the trade. In the two colleges in which lecturers were interviewed, it is perhaps symptomatic — though it can be in no way statistically representative — that 'hard' attitudes were in a minority amongst the lecturers and managers who were interviewed in FE, whereas in Ainley's HE study they were an overall majority. (In both F and HE incidentally, the corresponding terms used by 'hard' academic staff for students are 'weak' for 'soft' and 'strong' for 'hard'.)

Shared problems, divided responses

While holding such opposed views as the above 'hard' and 'soft' positions indicate, all staff also voiced common concerns. At both universities they felt pressured by the external forces of the government and the market, by management interference and by lack of resources. The result, especially for women, was — as an East London lecturer reported — "Trying to do anything apart from work, trying to get the children to the dentist, for instance — it's a Herculean task". So that even a woman Professor at Kent stated, "My colleagues' morale is rock bottom and there are certainly moments when I think of getting out. The whole time one is struggling against not having enough money. It's as simple as that".

There was also a common perception that, as an East London fine art lecturer put it, "The most difficult problem for teachers at BA level now is the diversity of quality that's coming in. I mean, in the first year you've got some students who are really excellent and you've got some who, although they've got potential, can hardly cobble a sentence together. [So that] You can't take it for granted if you mention Plato, for instance, they'll know who you're talking about". Even at Kent, one law lecturer reported, "This year for the first time in lectures I've found myself pausing sometimes, wondering *will they understand*". In addition he added, "There is a twist to the problem of overloading in that the extra students we're getting take up more time". Students were generally seen as more demanding than in the past but what they demand is information to get them through their exams. Their teachers therefore complained of students' instrumental attitudes as they increasingly find themselves 'teaching to the grade' as in the USA (see Becker *et al.*, 1968). Many staff at both universities had rationed their contact time (again contributing to the universal student impression that staff were only interested in their research, while staff felt they were 'lecturing to a sea of heads' and 'dealing with numbers not people').

The common demand at both institutions was for an increase in resources. Both places were felt to be at a crisis point beyond which "I don't think you can go on increasing numbers and not have more staff or resources. It will go down beyond this point" (East London fine art lecturer). And "More students without more resources means worse education. That's all there is to it" (Kent law lecturer). This did not mean, as another interviewee stated, that "more necessarily means worse but if you are going to deal with more students you've got to do things differently in terms of resources and access to open learning and so on, all of which could actually lead to an increase in quality. But staff need time to make it work and you just don't have time to prepare for these numbers.. So there will be a decline in quality" (East London business studies lecturer).

Impending modularisation at Kent and semesterisation at East London were anticipated with foreboding by nearly all staff interviewed. As a result, nearly all interviewees were extremely pessimistic about likely future developments. For example, "What I think will happen? There will be more numbers without increase in resources. The staff student ratio will be squeezed so they won't get such a good education and the reliance upon non-staff directed methods of learning will go past the point at which those techniques are useful and go into the area where they represent a deterioration of the standard of education given" (Kent biology lecturer).

The responses to these shared circumstances varied by the 'hard' or 'soft' orientation of self to subject that has been outlined. Staff in both camps could agree that more resources were needed both to continue traditional approaches with larger numbers of students and to develop new approaches which were nearly always more staff intensive, at least initially. However, they soon diverged when it came to which direction and conception of education should be followed in future.

For instance, "I don't accept that everybody can't come to nice places like Canterbury. It isn't immediately practicable but it is something we should work toward rather than letting go of that aspiration and letting higher education be undermined as it is being at the moment. If we can't get it tomorrow it isn't an argument for accepting something less". Whilst conceding that it was 'elitist', such an ideal of extending unchanged minority HE to a majority of the population justified resisting any change in existing higher education. This was the position held by the majority of staff interviewed at Kent, like the law lecturer above. His opinion was bolstered by that of the Trotskyist groupuscule to which he belonged, which also advocated retaining 'A'-levels as a guarantee of 'standards'. This line implied that any acceptance of or adaptation to the new realities of more students without additional funding was seen as letting the side down. Such actions were regarded as setting the institution on the slippery slope towards becoming 'like a former-polytechnic' and so 'no longer a proper university', making the whole place like the despised Business School which yet provided so much of its funding through selling expensive courses to wealthy foreigners.

The minority of Kent staff who attempted such accommodations were, at best, superciliously regarded by the hard-line majority. That their dismissive views could be reciprocated is shown by the following 'soft' opinion, expressed jokingly by a computer scientist who declared that "Compared with English and other useless subjects like sociology, we're in a better position than them. I can understand why they think as they do but they could always put on courses in spelling and grammar for our students!".

This shows that some of the 'hard' nuts were not wrong to be suspicious of some of their 'soft' colleagues. They felt that to change traditional methods was to "surrender to the logic of the market', "subordinate education for its own sake to training for employment', or even "to drown in the post-modern flux". For them, because students were constituted as a market, to accede to student demand would inevitably weaken the academic content of courses because students would choose 'soft' options or merely what was vocationally prescribed. Instead, they had to be "dragged kicking and screaming", as the 'soft' computer scientist above put it, through "the great body of knowledge" that made up the organically accumulated curriculum and were not in a position to decide to do otherwise since, due to the cumulative nature of courses, students would not see the point of the exercise until they had completed it. It was therefore impossible to be more explicit about course content and HE was already in any case delivering the so-called 'personal and transferable skills' demanded by employers and government and traditional written examinations were a suitable way to assess them.

Aware of differences of opinion, many of the staff interviewed at Kent indicated that the options facing the institution in the new marketplace should be squarely faced by the collegiate body of staff who could then decide on what position to take,

> …where we can face a possible choice between, say, would you rather be a small liberal arts college or a large university with all subjects, and if you were a liberal arts college, say, then you'll have to get a large number of students from overseas, so you'll be rather like a finishing school, a bit twee but well-founded with decent working conditions. Or would you rather be a second-rate generalist university?

From the way this interviewee posed this choice, it is clear what his preferred alternative would be, and it is the impression of this study that it would have been shared by the overwhelming majority of Kent staff at that time.

At East London a similar division also constantly contested the future corporate identity of the institution in the marketplace. 'Soft' staff supported a continuation of the polytechnic ideal as originally established to be a service centre for local industry and the community from which it was intended to draw its students. They supported and were supported by entrepreneurial initiatives that led to employer participation in the institution and to a learner-managed learning framework for study and teaching. Funding for this approach came from the Department of Employment via the Enterprise in Higher Education Initiative. A survey of staff involved in this Initiative indicated that it attracted those who already possessed some professional interest or qualification in pedagogy or human communication or counselling and guidance. Many had also been involved in the former School for Independent Study.

The Enterprise in Higher Education Initiative developed so that it was designed to introduce student centredness and employer participation simultaneously, on the assumption that both aims were necessarily complementary. However, evaluation of the Initiative at both institutions suggests that at neither place did it successfully establish the connection between innovation in teaching and learning within the institution and mechanisms for employer/ education liaison. These latter were in any case rendered difficult due to recession and, at Kent, due to the lack of large local employers. More fundamentally though, the failure demonstrated that 'student centredness' as conceived by the 'soft' staff who entertained the notion, did not necessarily correspond, save in a minority of cases, with those same staff's notion of participation by employers with whom they often failed to make effective contact and use. This was due to misperceptions on both sides but was, it can be suggested, fundamentally because 'student centredness' was given primacy over vocational relevance by the academic staff involved in Enterprise-funded projects. [See also *From Enterprise to Quality, a case study of change in higher education*, paper to the Society for Research in Higher Education Summer Conference on 'Changing the Student Experience', University of Central England, Birmingham 4-5 July, 1995, to be published shortly by the Campaign for Academic Freedom and Standards.]

'Hard' staff, who were more strongly and openly opposed to any vocational relevance or 'employer interference' — as they saw it — in higher education, favoured, by contrast, the autonomous development of faculties and disciplines on the traditional university model. Funding for their approach came via research grants from the then-Department for Education. This reliance upon rival sources of external funding was heightened by the devolution of budgetary powers to faculties that would predictably sustain the already divergent orientations and cultures in each faculty. Confused managerial goals had been accentuated by this internal disagreement and the ultimate outcome was unclear at the time the research was reported, though East London as a whole seems to be moving towards an imitation of the traditional universities whose name it now shares but perhaps in a necessarily populist version of what Halsey called 'elitist teaching'.

The effort of former-polytechnics like East London to compete with the established universities they have joined in the academic marketplace is aided and abetted by those staff who see it as in their self-interest and in accordance with their self-perceptions as professional lecturers and researchers rather than as teachers, or 'facilitators' in the new jargon, and of their institution as a university in some traditional sense, rather than as a school or FE college. It is, however, an unequal competition to which the features that were distinctive of East London's polytechnic mission are being sacrificed. In order to recover and go beyond polytechnicism towards a new polyconceptualism that combines the best of both institutional positions, the ideal typical polarities of 'hard' and 'soft' self-conceptions among academic staff and students will have to be overcome. It is far from certain that this will prove possible.

Towards a 'certified' or a 'learning society'?

Nor is it certain that the new F&HCE that is developing in Britain today will contribute towards or merely hinder the development of new knowledge and a collective intelligence to meet the uncertain future now faced by individuals, society and the world. The new system of funding, through Councils for Further and Higher Education introduced by the 1992 Higher and Further Education Act, links central state support of universities and colleges to student numbers. This has encouraged the dramatic rise in student intake in both sectors, but this only explains the supply side of the equation. On the demand side, numbers enroling for higher education have consistently outstripped targets set by government despite a demographic drop in the numbers of young people that has increased the proportion of mature students.

The source of this demand is to be found in the economic and social 'restructuring' identified with the period of successive Thatcher governments, though the social changes they encouraged were the outcome of long-term trends that have yet to take final form (see Ainley, 1993). Basically, the traditional, tripartite social pyramid with distinct divisions between upper, middle and working classes has pulled apart. Paradoxically, this restructuring of class relationships may have reduced the awareness of many people in the new middle of society of material inequalities. Yet at the same time it has increased the distance between the two poles of richest and poorest, the latter including a so-called 'underclass' of the permanently unemployed. Education and training at all levels are heavily implicated through credentialism (or rather the lack of worthwhile credentials) in the more or less deliberate social and political construction of this 'new rough'.

Meanwhile, in the middle of society, the previously clear cut distinction between the non-manual middle class and the manually working class has been eroded, not only by the latest applications of new communication and information technologies but by the growth of services, especially in offices and selling. This has led to a confused situation in which many people see themselves not as part of the traditional working or middle classes but as individuals in a new 'respectable' middle, or working-middle of society.

Yet during the same period when these new social patterns became apparent, insecurity has been heightened for all employees and the self-employed, as well as for many small employers and business managers. Not only has everyone been affected by the increasingly marginal status of the British economy in crisis-ridden world markets, but also new methods of management and administration have been introduced at the same time. This 'enterprise culture' has permeated all levels of society save the real core of the employing class (see Scott, 1991). Growing insecurity for the rest heightens the importance of qualifications as supposed guarantees of permanent, core employment, increasing the demand for education for which many in the new respectable working-middle of society are willing to pay — or at least become indebted.

The 'enterprise solution' to Britain's problems was advanced by Mrs Thatcher's governments as a new form of modernisation and a way out of the apparent dead-end of corporate capitalism. The old mixed economy between private and state capital was replaced by a new mixed economy of state-subsidised private capital and semi-privatised state capital (see Ainley and Vickerstaff, 1993). The operational principal of this new enterprise state is one of franchise in which, like a holding company, parts are subcontracted out to be run independently by franchise holders on fixed, short-term, target-specific contracts. Civil service bureaucracies can thus be expanded and disbanded to meet demand. This leaves, as in the private sector, a securely employed core surrounded by a growing periphery of workers on short-term contracts. The new type of state is thus 'contracting' (Harden, 1992) in two senses. Power contracts to the centre as responsibility is contracted out. In the often heavily state-subsidised private sector too, processes of managerial decentralisation and labour-shedding have broken up former corporate monoliths into their semi-autonomous constituent units which act independently to adapt flexibly to rapidly changing market conditions.

In these new economic and social circumstances, the framework of National Vocational Qualifications intended to accredit both academic and vocational qualifications in one unitary system, has little to do with building the 'ladders and bridges' for progression and access for all, or with creating the skills needed for economic modernisation. Rather, they help to extend still further the period during which young people and others are removed from the labour market to be certified on courses of non-training and non-education for non-jobs. This outcome of expanding F&HCE in a recession became clearer as Dearing I rejected the attempt of the 1988 Education Act to impose a grammar school 'National' Curriculum upon all school pupils. By introducing GNVQ2s into schools at 14, Dearing I signalled a place in FE for those who fail the academic 'National' Curriculum that was confirmed by the suggestion in Dearing II of a 'work-based' route for 'non-academic' 14-year-olds. Meanwhile the defence of 'A'-levels by Dearing II clearly privileged the academic route as the royal road to 'quality' higher education via school sixth forms. Dearing thus resuscitated a tertiary tripartism of the most traditional type — gold, silver and bronze; 'A'-level, GNVQ, NVQ to be undertaken in sixth forms, FE and in work or on training respectively.

In fact, Dearing's reviews have less to do with any supposed correspondence of education of any type to the economy than with an attempt to restore a world that has been lost, where clear social divisions separated mental from manual labour and, within the last category, the skilled from the unskilled and unrespectable working class. The divisions of this tripartite world have of course been eroded not only by the loss of the heavy industrial base which sustained them but also by the growth of comprehensive schooling since 1964 and before (see Benn and Chitty, 1996). The Conservative reforms of education, particularly the 1988 Education Act, were widely seen as an attempt to return to a blue remembered past under the guise of encouraging 'diversity' and 'excellence', the Tories eventually openly endorsing 'a grammar school in every town' before the 1997 general election. Exhortations to 'parity of esteem' between Dearing II's three pathways therefore rang as hollow as when the phrase was first applied to the three types of state school — grammar, technical and secondary modern — to which pupils were to be allocated at 11-plus by IQ testing under the 1944 Education Act.

Still further 'diversity', which is a code word for discrimination and disqualification, is emerging in the new hierarchy of higher education that is likely to be confirmed by Dearing III (cf. Watson, this volume). For the new situation in higher education created by the 1992 Further and Higher Education Act can be seen as providing a model for the type of differentiated market that the Conservatives hoped to replicate in schools as well as FE. Indeed, only minor changes were necessary to produce such a competitive hierarchy in HE, as an elaborate pecking-order of universities already existed. There was also a submerged market in higher education, in which independent, self-governing universities competed with their various specialised course offerings for state-subsidised students. The removal of the binary division between universities and polytechnics, though welcome in the name of equality, completed this differentiated hierarchy at the same time as it removed the last vestiges of local accountability and democratic control over higher education.

It is predictable that, with the introduction (also in the 1992 Act) of separate costing for research and teaching leading to the concentration of research in specialist centres as the government proposes, there will be a new binary divide as the universities at the bottom of the pile become teaching-only institutions (cf. Court in this volume). Here 'skills' courses narrowly related to employment combined with generic so-called 'personal and transferable skills' already tend to be concentrated (see Ainley and Corbett, 1994). The widely predicted two-year 'associate degree' courses franchised to further education colleges may effectively draw another divide, so that a new binarism will be complemented by tertiary tripartism taking Dearing II's 'three pathways' up into HE. Another way of seeing this would be as a redrawing of the old binary divide so that FE becomes the last refuge of polytechnicism.

At the other pole of the widening spectrum are courses unrelated to any specific employment but serving as a cultural apprenticeship to higher management positions in business and finance, to top positions in the media and the core of civil service administration. Such courses also pander to the academic consumerism of overseas students and those who can afford to study for intrinsic interest alone. In place of flat-rate fees that are the same for all courses, fees raised to the full cost for such prestigious courses can be anticipated as colleges in the antique universities and elsewhere are tempted to privatise themselves out of the state system. As they have done before, they may also raise their entry requirements to preserve their elite status rather than admit more students who meet their old standards.

In this worst of both worlds, with the resulting competition all down the line to shadow the medieval flummery and academic obscurantism of Oxbridge, the distinctive contributions of the former-polytechnics are being lost, just as the ideals of the comprehensive schools are being submerged in the academic competition engendered by the 1988 Act. Meanwhile, in the forgotten college sector of HE, colleges that do not attain university status will merge or close. This may also be the fate of those new (and some not so new) universities that lose out in the competition for students and research funds. Mergers in their cases may be accompanied by collapse into regional learning centres ranged around the surviving management core of the old institutions.

The Private Finance Initiative, as the only means of raising capital funds, encourages this trend towards what can be called Virtual Universities and Colleges in which only the name plate over the door to the subcontracting providers of teaching and learning services indicates any institutional identity. Such reliance on virtual realities is seen by Frank Reeves in his book on *The Modernity of Further Education* where such processes have gone much further, as leading logically to what he calls 'the Marie Celeste college'. For, just as industrial managers continue to pursue the impossible goal of a 'workerless factory', Reeves (1995: 53) writes:

> One fantasy currently exciting management in further education is the possibility of a silent empty institution of the not-too-distant-future, where every student is enrolled on open and distance learning programmes while payment ... is transmitted electronically to the college account.

Universities and colleges ramifying over several 'sites' where students undertake learning in employment, community centres, or at home, are decentring themselves with the danger that, as learning institutions come to be everywhere, they end up being nowhere.

Certainly, FE colleges in competition with sixth-form colleges and schools are tending towards merger as their funding arrangements favour large institutions. A number have already been absorbed into the universities from which they franchise the initial level of degree courses and to which they feed students. The new pattern is clear in Birmingham where the traditional Ivy League University recruits 'oven-ready' students from the 'better' state and private schools nationwide. If they get jobs, students graduate to a national or international labour market. Meanwhile the former-polytechnic is fed mainly local and mature students by its linked FE colleges. There is in addition a US-style business school in the shape of Aston University.

However, neither the form that the extension of this new system of F&HCE will take nor its curricular content is yet fixed. And it should also be recalled that the previous and more modest expansion of HE coincided with the student unrest of the late 1960s (and that of FE and Youth Training with the urban riots of the early 1980s). Although the '60s student rebellions were associated with a very different period of expansion and relative prosperity, they were, as much as anything else, a product of frustrated expectations from a generation of students the majority of whose parents had not attended HE and for whom promises of access to new and more demanding job opportunities were unlikely to be met. With any continued stagnation of the economy, the same frustration is likely to recur, only this time for the far larger numbers graduating indebted and unemployed.

Meanwhile, academics are involved in new forms of work organisation in the administration and accounting of their own work. The threat to their previously relatively privileged way of life prompted hostility to Conservative government even amongst the most traditionalist of dons. Its policies were seen as undermining the professional ideal not only of academics themselves but also of the professions for which they prepare their students. Central to this conception of a profession is the expert and specialised knowledge which higher education supposedly imparts. Access to privileged knowledge is an aspect of professionalism likely to be stressed by higher educationists defining their teaching in compliance with the requirements of professional bodies and, increasingly, defining their own work according to externally specified measures of 'quality'.

Contrary to this preservation of specialised 'Official Knowledge', the latest scientific discoveries, together with new communication and information technologies, are interrelating previously discrete subject disciplines. As formerly specialised databases become accessible to information about other aspects of reality, academic experts, who had previously carved out a specialised niche for themselves in the intricate division of knowledge that used to obtain, find themselves suddenly exposed.

The academic community — if it is possible to speak of such a thing any longer — thus feels beleaguered not only by the state, but also by the market and the economy, all of which exert a more and more direct influence over higher education in place of the indirect effects they had previously. The assimilation of the universities by these external forces is partial and incomplete, taking various forms across different institutions and the various subjects and modes of study within them. The polarities of the process are illustrated however, in the comparison between staff at the two contrasted universities above.

'Flexibility' and 'adaptability' are the keywords of the new enterprising attitudes demanded by employers and encouraged by many university and college courses. Under the label of 'enterprise' its associated individual attributes of initiative and independence are accompanied for many employees and self-contracting workers by growing insecurity and isolation. This is a process of proletarianisation which goes unrecognised because it is not associated with the regimentation and uniformity of the factory proletariat of the past. Indeed, it appears to follow the opposite precepts of individual 'initiative' and 'independence'.

It is ironic that this proletarianisation of the professions is accompanied by an unprecedented expansion of the higher education with which so many professions sought to guarantee or to gain previously secure exclusive status. This expansion is not only, or even mainly, a rearguard action by education professionals to preserve their depreciated status — depreciated along with the value of their educational credentials. As has been argued, even as their devalued currency inflates, educational credentials become increasingly important, especially to parents seeking secure, 'middle-class' status for their children, but also for anybody trying to cling on to remaining secure employment in the shrinking core of both semi-privatised public and state-subsidised private sectors. Hence the phenomenal growth in part-time, adult courses of continuing professional development, often run off-site and out of hours using distance and open learning.

Moreover, as Aronowitz and DiFazio (1994) remark:

> ...the relative proletarianization of the technical intelligentsia does not signify that they have become a new working class so long as they retain the ideology and culture of professionalism, one of whose characteristic features is to foster self-blame for failure. (p. 225) [Yet,] The pervasiveness of self-blame reveals the degree to which the self-perpetuating features of the academic system are introjected by one group of its victims. (p. 256).

Both 'hard' and 'soft' academics shared a defensive ideology of professionalism. However, the 'soft' minority, in recognising the collapse of traditional distinctions between professionals and their clients (in this case, teachers and their students), were closer to a new definition of professionalism as autonomous practice. With its emphasis on professional self-responsibility, this version of professionalism only heightened self-blame and was regarded by the 'hard' majority as a management-inspired vision which surrendered genuine professional autonomy for 'managing yourself', or 'administering your own cuts'. As a defence against this management 'progressivism', which co-opted those 'soft' enough to go along with it, the 'hardliners' paradoxically resorted more readily to traditionally unprofessional trades unionism to defend what they conceded could be seen as elitist professional positions.

Yet, despite the chronic practical difficulties the rapid rise in students poses for overstretched institutions, the expansion of higher education presents HE staff with opportunities to enable greater numbers of students to share a culture of critical, scientific reason and general — as opposed to vocational — knowledge. If one third of the age range, as well as many more adults, can begin to think creatively, independently and logically due to their higher education experiences, this represents a major cultural change for society (Ainley, 1997). It also presents a challenge to the traditional academic culture of higher education. Staff can only meet this challenge if they can overcome the divisions between them that this chapter has illustrated.

Acknowledgements

Thanks are due to the staff at both institutions who gave their time to be interviewed. I am grateful to them above all for their being willing to put in the hands of a stranger what one of them called, 'the short-handing of a lifetime's experience' and to my colleague at Greenwich, Les Garner, who took the trouble to read and endorse the paper based on his own experience as a NATFHE representative of F&HE staff.

References

Ainley, P. (1997) 'Students in Britain in the 1990s', introduction to special student issue of *Youth and Policy*, May 1997.

———— (1996) 'What Dearing Could Have Learnt From The Scots, 'Parliamentary Brief', May and The Eternal Recurrence of the Same' (Dearing's latest review), *Forum* 38 (3): 44-45.

———— (1994) *Degrees of Difference, Higher Education in the 1990s*. London: Lawrence and Wishart.

———— (1993) *Class and Skill, Changing Divisions of Labour and Knowledge*. London: Cassell.

———— (1992) 'On the trail of that illusive first job', *Guardian*, 12 January, 1992.

Ainley, P. and Bailey, B. (1997) *The Business of Learning: Staff and Student Experiences of Further Education in the 1990s*. London: Cassell.

Ainley, P. and Corbett, J. (1994) 'From Vocationalism to Enterprise: Social and Life Skills become Personal and Transferable', *The British Journal of Sociology of Education*, 15 (3): 365-374.

Ainley, P. and Vickerstaff, S. (1993) 'Transitions from Corporatism: The Privatisation of Policy Failure', in *Contemporary Record, Journal of the Institute of Contemporary British History*, December 1993. (A shortened version is also in the July 1993 issue of 'Parliamentary Brief'.

Aronowitz, S. and DiFazio, W. (1994) *The Jobless Future, Sci-Tech and the Dogma of Work*. University of Minnesota Press.)

Bailey, F. (1977) *Morality and Expediency, The Folklore of Academic Politics*. Oxford: Blackwell.

Becker, H. et al. (1968) *Making the Grade: The Academic Side of College Life*. New York: John Wiley.

Benn, C. and Chitty, C. (1996) *Thirty Years On Is Comprehensive Education Alive and Well or Struggling to Survive?*. London: David Fulton.

Bergendal, G. (1984) *Knowledge Policies and the Tradition of Higher Education*. Stockholm: Almquist and Wiksell.

Bernstein, B. (1977) 'Class and Pedagogies: Visible and Invisible', in Karabel, J. and Halsey, A. (eds) *Power and Ideology in Education*. Oxford: Oxford University Press.

Durkheim, E. (1979) *The Evolution of Educational Thought: Lectures on the Formation and Development of Secondary Education in France* (trans. P. Collins). London: Routledge.

Finn, D. (1987) *Training Without Jobs, New Deals and Broken Promises*. London: Macmillan.

Halsey, A. (1992) *Decline of Donnish Domination, the British Academic Professions in the Twentieth Century*. Oxford: The Clarendon Press.

Halsey, A. and Trow, M. (1971) *The British Academics*. London: Faber.

Harden, I. (1992) *The Contracting State*. Milton Keynes: Open University Press.

Hargreaves, D. (1967) *Social Relations in a Secondary School*. London: Routledge.

Pratt, J. (1977) *The Polytechnic Experiment 1965–1992*. Milton Keynes: Open University Press / Society for Research in Higher Education.

Reeves, F. (1995) *The Modernity of Further Education*. Bilston College Publications in association with Education Now.

Scott, J. (1991) *Who Rules Britain?*. Oxford: Polity.

IV

ORGANISATIONAL CHANGE
IN THE NEW HIGHER EDUCATION

The Marketisation of Higher Education: Management, Discourse and the Politics of Performance

9

Cris Shore and Tom Selwyn

Introduction: the neo-liberal 'cultural revolution'

> Our specific policies are designed to get maximum value for money
> .... The aim is to achieve a key cultural change: better commu-
> nication, interaction and mutual understanding between the
> scientific community, industry and Government Departments.
> (HMG, 1993: 5)

The publication of the British Conservative Government's 1993 White Paper on
university funding represented a landmark in the history of higher education
in the UK. For the first time since their creation, all universities in Britain were
to have the quality of their education provision 'assured' thanks to the
introduction of rigorous systems of monitoring, inspection and assessment. All
this was part of a wider government agenda for re-structuring and modernizing
British higher education according to the principles and values of 'enterprise
culture' (Keat, 1991; Morris, 1991). To outside observers, it might have seemed
odd, therefore, that at the same moment that this much-praised project of cultural
change was taking root throughout the university sector, university staff and
professional associations, including vice-chancellors and principles, were warning
of a crisis in higher education borne of budget cuts, lack of investment and
declining morale — a crisis so dire that it now posed "a serious threat to the
economic future of the UK" (AUT, 1996: 1). However, arguments about levels
of funding sometimes obscure other important changes that have affected the
culture of higher education. As A. H. Halsey, one of Britain's most respected
sociologists of education, notes in a recent book, 'government meanness' and
'creeping managerialism' are also leading to a dangerous decline in academic
and professional standards (Halsey, 1995).

That the former Conservative government's reforms have succeeded in reshaping the structure, character and ethos of higher education is not disputed. What we do question, however, is the claim that these reforms have been beneficial to university teaching and research. Indeed, a growing body of professional opinion holds the reverse to be the case, and argues that the introduction of a quasi-market system into academia — often regarded as a panacea for the deficiencies in British universities — has been highly detrimental to the quality of education, and particularly to scholarship and the learning experience. The rationale driving these reforms was set out most explicitly in the mission statement of the recently created government 'quango', the Higher Education Funding Council for England (HEFCE). "The HEFCE's mission", it declares, "is to promote high quality, cost-effective teaching and research within a financially healthy education sector, having regard to national needs" In this context, it should be noted, 'national needs' was synonymous with the needs of the government. The mission statement concludes with the promise that the HEFCE will "encourage institutions to support these aims and ensure the effective and efficient use of their funds and assets, and delivery of value for money, through strengthening their managerial capabilities and the compilation of well developed strategic plans" (HEFCE, 1995: i).

'Value for money', 'cost-effectiveness', 'quality', 'efficiency' and 'strategic plans' are terms traditionally associated with commerce and industry rather than academia. What worries many educationalist today is not simply the wholesale introduction of the language of business and finance into the education sector, but the fact that these terms have now become the dominant discourse and organising principles of higher education (Selwyn and Shore, 1992) — and the yardsticks by which all universities must now measure their success or failure. As Will Hutton (1995: 216) observes:

> The universities and old polytechnics, now all 'universities', have been turned into factories for the production of degree-holders, their teaching staff ranked by their publications in specialist journals in a competitive system of performance tests upon which funding and even job prospects depend.

As the 1993 White Paper suggests, the past decade of government reforms were intended to bring about a neo-liberal 'cultural revolution' throughout the public sector, a revolution based on the ideological assumption that private sector activity in an unregulated market will invariably improve economic performance and efficiency. What these reforms have achieved, however, is not only the marketization of university practices and relations (resulting, some would contend perversely, in a decrease in economic efficiency); they have also consolidated a new regime of power and management and have created a world in which the New Right can divide and rule (Hutton, 1995: 21). Following Foucault (1991) we might call this the 'governmentalization' of universities; a process involving the subjugation of the universities and their staff to increasingly coercive systems of surveillance, bureaucracy, government intervention and the disciplinary forces of the free market.

Against this background the present chapter, which we offer as an essay in political anthropology, sets out to examine these processes and their effects on universities by analysing the linguistic and cultural dimensions of these reforms. We argue that the growing centralization and marketisation of higher education has brought about a progressive eradication and 'muting' of alternative voices and moralities. The coercive norms and totalising discourses of markets and management have induced a linguistic homogenization and ideological conformity within universities which, we contend, is seriously undermining their academic freedom and intellectual pluralism, marking what is potentially a dangerous step towards a new form of neo-liberal authoritarianism.

Our analysis focuses on two particular terms that have generated considerable rhetorical enthusiasm in contemporary mass higher education, namely 'quality' and 'performance'. These terms are worth studying not only because they are interesting in themselves but because they are integral components of the lexicon of comparable key terms, or 'KTs' — to which we will draw attention throughout this chapter (marking each 'KT' in parentheses) — which together contribute to defining and exemplifying this neo-liberal 'cultural change' in mass higher education.

University teaching as 'performance'

Over the past decade, the term 'performance' has achieved increasing saliency on the campus. Lecturers are subject to annual 'performance reviews' (KT) by their 'line manager' (KT); individuals and departments are required to become associated with 'performance targets' (KT); senior university staff, typically including those assuming titles associated with certain offices of church or state which are conspicuously performative in a ritualistic sense ('Dean', 'Rector', 'Chancellor', for example) have increasingly placed themselves on what has become known as 'performance related pay' (a key term which is presently in the process of being transformed or merged with *another* 'PRP', namely 'profit related pay').

'Performance related pay' is itself a peculiar cultural concept, the analysis of which provides a useful starting point for our critique. One of the special ironies of this method of payment is that the 'performances' — frequently referred to as new 'initiatives' (KT) included in the portfolios of those receiving it are frequently made up from the 'performances' or 'initiatives' of *others*! Thus, new courses or degrees, such as the proliferating number of Master's degrees in new universities, are typically products of the specialist experiences, skills, and enthusiasms of particular individual lecturers and/or networks of co-operating individuals. And yet it is precisely these sorts of 'programmes' (a key term with obvious links to the worlds of the theatre, concert hall and other sites of performance) which appear on the lists of 'new faculty initiatives', thereby attracting bonuses for those in receipt of 'performance related pay'.

The relationship between those on and those off 'PRP' (denotation by acronym is stylistically greatly favoured in contemporary educational discourse) in the same institution has the distinctive flavour about it of the relationship of the legendary organ grinder and his performing monkey. Furthermore, we may recall that in an allied branch of the public sector, the police, that the Chief Constable of Hampshire recently informed other chief constables that he intended to refuse to sign the Home Office's new 'performance related' contract for his job on the grounds that the idea of 'performance related pay' was 'absurd and objectionable' because it denigrated the concept of public service, undermined the solidarity of public servants, and implied that chief constables were motivated primarily by financial incentives (*Daily Telegraph* 24 April 1995).

All these arguments seem equally appropriate for higher education generally and its new caste of managers in particular. But perhaps the most trenchant argument the chief constable made, which is also the most relevant to us, was that 'performance related pay' inevitably leads to an emphasis on quantity over quality. Besides, can keeping the peace be measured in the same way as numbers of arrests made or parking tickets issued?

Our argument proper begins with the observation that 'performance' does, in fact, successfully describe an important aspect of the present culture of higher education. To begin to understand why, we need to define the term 'performance' itself. According to the *New Shorter Oxford Dictionary* the term 'performance' has two distinct clusters of meanings. The first refers to the action of fulfilling a promise or carrying out an order — as in "Thy will by my performance shall be served" [*All's Well that Ends Well*, 1601]. This sense of the term is mainly used now, according to dictionary definition, in relation to 'fulfilling the terms of a contract'. The *New Encyclopedia Britannica* develops this legal use of the term: performance in law is 'doing that which is required by contract'. Thus successful performance of an action specified in a contract discharges contractual obligations.

The *Dictionary* records that the second cluster of meanings centres upon the action of performing a ceremony, play, or public exhibition. Several other dictionaries and encyclopedias focus on performance in this sense. The *Batsford Dictionary of Drama* (Hodgson, 1988), for example, defines performance art as a 'form of fine art which employs live actors to create striking visual effects', while the *Macmillan Dictionary of Anthropology* defines the term as a 'concept used in the analysis of ritual and religion, drawing attention to the use made of performance in this sense by the anthropologist Victor Turner (Seymour-Smith, 1986: 221). In theatre language, performance is said to be a 'showing of a dramatic entertainment'.

How do these definitions apply to the use of the term 'performance' in contemporary higher education? To start with meaning 1: **Illustration 1** is a document inserted in the outlines of each course taught at a northern university, and is representative of similar documents used in comparable ways by universities elsewhere in the country: the 'Learning Compact' sets out the expectations of the behaviours of teachers and students at the university. This 'Learning Compact' has the look of a legal contract with the rights and obligations of teachers (here convenors) and students clearly and simply set out and would seem to fit well into a culture informed by such ideas as 'citizens charter'.

Illustration 1

LEARNING COMPACT

1. The convener of each course within a programme will issue every student enrolling on that course with a course booklet describing the nature and demands of the course, including

(a)   a calendar of all classes involved in the course and a week-by-week list of the topics to be covered by the course;

(b)   a list of required preparation for each week;

(c)   a description of the assessment criteria to be used during the course;

(d)   a statement of the nature, pattern and timing of the assessment;

(e)   a list of the dates and times by which all assignments must be submitted and details of the process for doing this;

(f)   a list of the dates and times by which each assignment will be returned to the students and details of the process for doing this;

(g)   a final date for collection of coursework by students, after which return cannot be guaranteed.

2. A register will be kept of attendance, and submission and return of all assignments for all courses.

3. Students are expected to:

(a)   participate fully in the learning process;

(b)   attend all classes and arranged tutorials;

(c)   provide the teacher with an explanation of enforced absences;

(d)   hand all coursework assignments in on time in accordance with published procedures;

(e)   attend all examinations at the published time and venue;

(f)   complete 100 hours of study (including assessed work and time-tabled activities) for each 10-credit course;

(g)   regularly check their communication channels (eg pigeonholes, noticeboards);

(h)   update their records with the University and Departments.

On closer inspection, however, it belies first impressions, for it is not as simple as it appears. Scratch a little and smiling mischievously out of the page are the twin demons of ambiguity and irrationality, not to mention possible illegality. Point (g), for example, states that there is a 'final date for collection of coursework after which return cannot be guaranteed'. Does that mean that, although not guaranteed, the return of coursework is possible? If so, how likely is the possibility? If it is *unlikely* to be returned, is it known what actually happens to the coursework? Is it, for example, shredded or otherwise disposed? Or just kept? And, if so, what are the legal implications? And, if the work is not disposed of, what is the purpose of the point in the first place?

Of course, documents such as the 'Learning Compact' are not legal documents in the strict sense of the term: not yet at any rate. Nevertheless the ambiguities, irrationalities, and mystifications of this and similar documents do inevitably raise real questions in the minds not only of students but also those lecturers responsible for teaching courses. These need to be addressed by *other* clarificatory documents, or 'commentaries'. As in the legal world itself, quasi-legal looking documents like this are giving rise to a cornucopia of quasi-legal looking commentaries. Take the student obligation (d) for example. Given the statistical certainty that some students do actually hand in assessments late, the problem arises: *on what grounds* may students 'legitimately' hand in assessments late? A Welsh college of higher education has produced a four page explanatory document entitled 'Extenuating Circumstances: Guidelines for students' in which 'extenuating circumstances' are defined (see **Illustration 2**). In this particular case these include "illness, bereavement, emotional difficulties, social, matrimonial or family problems, eviction/homelessness, experience of assault, robbery or other traumatic event, serious disruption to travel without warning, unavoidable involvement in legal proceedings, major computer problems affecting work which requires computer use", and so on. Helpfully, this particular document also lists those events and circumstances which do *not* constitute extenuating circumstances. These include "your car running out of petrol, leaving coursework to the last minute and missing the deadline because a printer would not print, failure to make alternative travel plans when you knew about disruptions in advance, losing work that you had not saved to disk", and so on. The question then arises as to the *evidence* — another long list follows; who the evidence should be presented to — another long list; and finally half a page on the work of the *Extenuating Circumstances Committee*:

> "You need to know that this committee is the only body which can make decisions about extenuating circumstances and that personal tutors play no role. The committee's decisions are then passed to Subject Field Boards."

Illustration 2

EXTENUATING CIRCUMSTANCES
<u>Guidelines for Students</u>

These guidelines are to assist you in the presentation of extenuating circumstances, so that fair decisions can be made about your work. If you need more specific guidance on how to present your own extenuating circumstances, you are advised to consult your personal tutor.

IF YOU SUBMITTED EXTENUATING CIRCUMSTANCES FOR SEMESTER A AND, HAVING READ THESE GUIDELINES, YOU DECIDE THAT YOU WISH TO RE-PRESENT THEM, SUPPLYING MORE SPECIFIC EVIDENCE OR EVIDENCE FROM A MORE INDEPENDENT SOURCE, YOU MAY DO SO. <u>THE DEADLINE IS 21st MARCH</u>.

<u>1. SUMMARY OF PROCEDURES</u>

It is possible that your career at the College will be plain sailing, that you will enjoy perfect health throughout, that all your work will be in on time, that you will have an uninterrupted attendance record and that no personal difficulties of any kind will hamper your academic achievement. We hope so. However, if you do experience problems, then you need to understand and comply with the new procedures for dealing with extenuating circumstances. Continuing students need to realise that these procedures are very different from those which operated before.

<u>Under the old system</u>, the exam board met at the end of each year to consider marks/grades and awards. In advance of the exam board you made any extenuating circumstances known to your personal tutor. He/she informed the exam board of these circumstances and, where appropriate, made a case, on your behalf, for acceptance of late work, for modification of marks/grades or for the award of first sits. The old system has gone!

<u>The new system</u> has three main components:

<u>The Extenuating Circumstances Committee</u>. This committee meets at the end of each semester to consider extenuating circumstances relating to all students in the Business School. Evidence of extenuating circumstances is presented to this committee by the Programme Administrators. The committee then decides:

- is the evidence admissible?
- is the illness or other problem to which the evidence relates sufficient to account for late work, impaired academic performance or failure to attend for assessment?
- what action should be taken?

Paradoxically, the idea of a 'learning contract' began as an innovative teaching method which was pioneered by liberal-minded progressive educationalists, at institutions including Bristol and Oxford Polytechnics. Only later were the terms appropriated by advocates of more authoritarian and managerial systems who found its emphasis on self-directed learning and its strategies for dealing with large classes particularly useful in bringing down unit costs (KT).

The relationship between the 'Learning Compact' (and its associated commentaries) and bureaucratic procedures are clearly reminiscent of relationships in the legal field: between Parliamentary Acts and legal processes and judgement based on precedent, for example. But what is also, quite strikingly, brought to mind are the similar relationships between texts and commentaries in the religious field — between Koran and Hadith, Torah and Talmud, for example. Furthermore, as in both legal and religious fields, there is what we may term a 'snowballing effect'. 'Learning Compacts' are followed by 'Extenuating Circumstances' Guidelines and these in turn give rise to a mushrooming industry of textual production, textual interpretation, and associated procedural debates. The equivalent of university *Yeshivot* (rabbinical centres for the study of the bible and Jewish tradition) are set up and a whole new bureaucratic caste is recruited to arbitrate on the complexities which inevitably arise from documents such as these. The room for debates is endless: what does 'participate fully' actually mean? What constitutes a 'traumatic event'? And so on.

The second cluster of meanings associated with the term 'performance' concerns ceremony, play, public exhibition and the participation in these by live actors. While teaching has always involved elements of performance, in contemporary mass higher education not only are lecturers themselves increasingly obliged to become 'performers' in this second sense, but the process of teaching itself has (necessarily, many would argue) become dominated by a concern with performative acts — and by the 'measurement' of these various kinds of performance — over other considerations. In backing-up this claim we cite the following growing practices in teaching:

i)   The use of acetates, films and videos

One of the standard pieces of equipment in any classroom today is the overhead projector. These are typically used to project summaries of arguments, or those aspects of arguments thought most critical by the lecturer (and hence often emphasised by 'bullet points' (KT). Films and videos have also become increasingly important to the day to day work of the university lecturer, a development that can partly be gauged by the fact that 'media departments' have been increasingly incorporated into libraries — themselves sometimes re-defined as 'learning centres'. While we are not in any way opposed to the use of these useful teaching aids, we would simply note that, in the current climate of bureaucratic surveillance and assessment, these audio-visual technologies have brought into existence important new norms by which 'effective teaching' is monitored and judged. The danger is when form comes to triumph over content: when it is no longer deemed sufficient to give a traditional lecture, however informative, inspired and intellectually challenging, if it does not include overheads or audio-visual material — or simplified handouts which alleviate students (now hailed as 'customers') from having to construct their own notes.

ii)   The triumph of 'communication skills' over disciplinary knowledge

A document was recently prepared by a Scottish university to aid students to 'evaluate' (KT) the teaching of lecturers on various courses. Students were invited to make ticks (signifying 'agreement') or crosses (signifying 'disagreement') in 17 columns constructed on the basis of specified criteria. These fell into two sections. The first, with 6 criteria, addressed what was called the 'content' of the course, namely whether it was understood, coordinated, was challenging, well prepared, whether the student felt that s/he had learnt something valuable, and whether the recommended readings were felt appropriate. The second, with 11 criteria, addressed the style of the lecturer: whether s/he was an effective *communicator, enthusiastic, stimulating, friendly and approachable, well organised, confident and self assured, helpful,* able to *hold my interest,* to give *lucid explanations,* enable *notes to be made,* and *used the OHP well.*

We need, simply, to notice that there are nearly twice as many columns devoted to the lecturer's 'style' and 'communication skills' as there are which deal with the 'content' of the course. And, furthermore, that several of the points referring to 'content' are themselves preoccupied with style.

iii)   Dolphins gambolling in clear blue water

That the politics of public performance and 'enterprise culture' are re-fashioning the character and ethos of higher education institutions may partly, but effectively, be demonstrated by considering the sharply increasing level of resources being spent by universities and colleges on advertising. One of the consequences of this has been an 'image inflation' — the 'war of logo against logo', to hijack Hobbes for a moment — with some quite remarkable consequences — such as the recent television advertisements commissioned by one University, at the cost of half a million pounds, which advertised the presumed enjoyment to be derived from following one of the courses on their selected module 'pathways' (KT) with vivid images of dolphins gambolling in clear blue water. The dolphin, it should be noted, was a definitive term in the political culture of the mid to late 1990s given its status as a virtually sacred animal to environmentalists and New Age movements, not to mention its symbolic associations with mystery and wisdom in ancient Greek mythology.

The fact that universities need ever more energetically to pitch for those 'clients' and 'users' (two KTs) referred to in the 'mission statements' (KT) of the all the major funding councils necessarily involve them giving ever more dramatic public performances. The comparison here, of course, is with the north American Indian *potlatch* during which tribes competed with one another for superior honour by engaging in competitive bouts of the burning of selected valuables.

iv)   'TQAs' — teaching quality assessments

The pinnacle of performative discourse is reached, however, during the visits made by inspectors from the Higher Education Funding Council to assess the 'quality' (a veritable corner stone of KTs) of teaching in an institution. For this occasion teachers and students quite literally 'put on a show' for which, in our experience, scripts are specially written, lines are learnt, and special scenic effects are laid on. Classrooms are painted and walls decorated with specially appealing photographs. These may include pastoral (in both senses) scenes involving students, or promotional images of various kinds. In one case the walls of a dining hall in an institution known to us, not noted before or since for the excellence of its food, was adorned with coloured photographs of unusually succulent looking vegetarian food arranged in *woks*. Interestingly, the appearance of these particular photographs not only appeared in time for a visit of the HEFCE inspectorate but coincided (we are still engaged in finding out whether by accident or design) with the *taking down* of the portraits of the rather solemn, grey haired, and be-robed former college principals. As one of the institution's managers was later to comment, 'Times change' (KT).

In short we find ourselves in educational spaces which have become theatres: where classrooms become 'stages', teachers and students 'actors' (performing to a script imposed upon them by government), and where inspectors, journalists and 'market forces' act as audience and critics.

Performance as a measure of ideological incorporation

What we have begun to demonstrate, albeit in a very preliminary and perfunctory way, is that university teachers and students are becoming increasingly incorporated into what might be described as structures of performance — in the two senses we have identified. Not only are teachers encouraged to develop the skills of the performing artist(e) but both they and their students are also increasingly placed within quasi-contractual looking relationships where rights and obligations are made explicit to each other in documents such as the 'Learning Compact'. 'Performance' has become a touchstone of the 'audit culture' of contemporary higher education.

The flowering of 'performance rhetoric' has, of course, been accompanied by growing organisational and bureaucratic structures. We have noted the 'Committee for Extenuating Circumstances'. There are other committees too. Many institutions of higher education have put in place what are called 'programme boards' (KT). These are committees made up of the staff and students of a programme at which a senior member of the management such as a Dean would also attend. The declared purpose of these 'boards' is to provide a forum for student 'feedback' (KT) about courses and to compile and issue 'reports' (a definitive KT), sent to other, higher, 'boards' at faculty level in order for the 'performance' of the 'programme boards' to be 'monitored' (KT). Reports are then issued from these 'faculty boards' for further 'monitoring', and so on.

University personnel are thus gathered into an expanding bureaucratic edifice of 'boards' and committees. Each monitors the other and at the apex there is a high command committee with a name such as the 'Academic Standards Committee' which, together with a Policy and Resources Committee, is likely to be one of the two most powerful committees in an institution. It is from these committees, and through them, that the new 'Management Teams' (KT) now control university business.

Let us summarize where we have got to in such a way as to allow us to make some additional commentary along the way. Three main points:

1. Teachers and students in contemporary HE have been increasingly drawn into 'rational' bureaucratic and quasi-legalistic frameworks of organisation. The primary principle around which both students and teachers have been invited to define their relationship is contractual performance. Without ruling out the possibility that they are implied (somewhere), we may observe that the rhetorical landscape of 'performance' does not include ideas such as truth, beauty, intellectual stimulation, knowledge, reason, or criticism. At any rate, there is no sense of these being in any way determining or guiding ideas in the contemporary culture of 'performance' and its bureaucratic elaborations. Furthermore, any sort of imagery made up of scholars drawn together by the excitement of the pursuit of such ideas and held together by a sense of internal moral obligation is conspicuously absent from this cultural landscape.

2. Linked to this is our major criticism: that the form of teaching has assumed dominance over content. One of the authors of the present paper had the enervating experience of being informed (by a Dean) that what is important these days is 'how a course is delivered'. The other author recalls an HEFCE inspector, during a TQA inspection visit, informing a colleague that though the lecture he had just observed was 'excellent', the lecture hall in which it had been given was not up to scratch and that therefore only a grade of 'satisfactory' would be officially recorded. The implication of this is that teaching quality is inextricably linked to levels of resource: that if a university's

infrastructure is poor, the 'quality' of its teaching provision can never be excellent. Deft use of classroom technology, including the liberal use of acetates, distribution of booklists and 'packages' of key texts, observance of calendrical and other temporal conventions are the thing nowadays. The spontaneous taking of a seminar group out for a stroll along a river bank in the summer, for example, is as far from the tightly laced 'performance' rhetoric as it is possible to imagine.

If reference to such companiable strolling in imagined groves of academe has little to with contemporary academic life, we may remember that in the West the idea of a university started with Socrates and Plato. The latter's *Academy*, the first university, was established in 387BC in a grove near Athens and gave us the term 'academic' (*not* a KT). Our highest academic degree, the Ph.D is derived from the idea of 'love for the goddess of wisdom' — *philo-sophia*. Without wishing to romanticise the academic tradition, we would simply note that the origins and strength of academia reside in the domains of contemplation, curiosity and intellectual freedom that stand outside the direct arena of market economics and the rationale of commerce.

3. Drawing 1. and 2. together, we could say that the staff and students of contemporary British higher education have become *performing artists* within tightly organised quasi-legalistic frameworks. They 'perform' (in *both* senses) to each other and, ultimately, to the HEFCE by way of its bands of roving inspectors. But, as noticed above, the 'quality' of teachers' 'performances' is adjudicated not only by management hierarchies within institutions and the HEFCE from outside, but also from a process known as 'student feedback'. This takes several forms but normally starts off by students filling in forms along the lines described above. Within the type of structures we have been outlining in British HE it is quite possible for student 'feedback' to become the subject of discussion at 'programme boards'. Given that these 'boards' are populated with 'managers' as well as students and lecturers themselves, the politico-cultural comparison seems to us to be with the Chinese cultural revolution when students were asked to 'report' on their lecturers in the same way that children 'reported' on their parents and villagers on their village elders. Just as happened in the cultural revolution itself, so public criticism of lecturers by their students at these semi-public 'programme board' meetings may unleash processes through which teachers may be subject to stigmatisation and social exclusion. At such moments, such 'boards' may turn into *charivari* type shaming rituals.

At this point we need to make clear our own commitment as teachers in Higher Education to good teaching and to the close co-operation between ourselves as teachers and our students. Indeed, we would not like to imagine a higher education system in which lecturers and students did *not* seek to work in such a co-operative way. Our discussion concerns the conditions under which such a system may flourish.

One such condition is that the teacher/student relationship is built upon and rooted in trust, confidentiality and professionalism. While acknowledging that the meaning of none of these terms is self-evident and that each begs a further question — what are the boundaries of confidentiality?; what are the parameters of professionalism in this case?; and so on — we would like to make two specific claims. The first is that the student/teacher relationship must lie at the heart of the higher education system's structure and values. The second is that what we are presently witnessing, precisely, is the *breaking down* of this relationship as it comes increasingly to be incorporated into quasi-legal, quasi-theatrical, managerially determined structures. Formerly grounded in face-to-face morality, the relationship is systematically being transformed in the new 'culture of performance' in such a way that it is becoming increasingly defined and organised by bureaucratic dictat. We return to this point at the conclusion.

Individuals and their activities are thus increasingly subject to the semi-public, semi-private gaze of varieties of technicians and specialists who themselves seem to occupy spaces which are part open to, and part hidden from, view. Thus, to pursue the example, 'student feedback' may appear, as we have described, in 'reports' which are discussed publicly in 'board meetings', but 'performance reviews' are compiled and consumed in domains which, away from public scrutiny and accountability, are altogether more shadowy and obscure. In our view it is Foucault's (1977) principle of 'panopticism' which is most relevant here, for the logic of both these activities leads in the direction of ever greater exposure of those working on the campus to the part known, part anonymous, gaze of bureaucratic agents. Ultimately the external norms concerning 'quality' and 'performance' become internalised. The result is that lecturers and their students are constantly made aware of the gallery they must play to — and perform to it even when the audience has gone home, so to speak. In other words, and unlike the performative role engendered by theatre or ritual, this kind of performance has a more long-term and negative influence in shaping subjectivity.

From 'performance' to 'quality'

What we have called 'the culture of performance' is, as we have already implied throughout the above, one of the 'outcomes' (KT) of TQAs. Teaching Quality Assessment is, of course, itself a KT, but in its acronymic form it is a *definitive* KT. There are two reasons for this. One is that acronyms look familiar and friendly, and are beguiling in their apparent simplicity. The other more specific reason is that in this case TQA is practically homonymous with 'TQM', 'Total Quality Management'. It is this idea which has defined the parameters within which the 'culture of performance' has flourished.

But before we make a few observations about 'Total Quality Management' itself, it needs to be noted that the term 'quality' has assumed a totemic status in contemporary management speak, appearing as it does in the management canons of many different institutional arenas. As Pfeffer and Coote (1991: 1) observe:

> currently it emblazons the packaging of products as diverse as toilet paper and smoked salmon... [it] litters the pages of health and social services journals. It was promoted by the Conservative government who regularly announced new quality initiatives. It became a byword of Labour's appeals to the electorate: 'the *quality* revolution'. It featured prominently in international and national guidelines on standards, at conferences where *quality* gurus came to recruit new disciples, and in innumerable training programmes claiming to teach people how to achieve it.

Thus, in higher education establishments Teaching Quality Audits are organised by the Higher Education Quality Council (HEQC). Hotels issue cards to their guests inviting them to nominate particular members of staff as 'Quality Winners' (as the Principal Hotel Group puts it). Local councils set up 'quality teams' in their Chief Executive Departments. In Camden this team publishes a quarterly newsletter for their staff entitled *Quality Matters*. A measure of the term's omnipresence is that the noun, as in 'good quality', has recently given birth to an adjective, as in 'quality service'. This is a usage which has not yet been incorporated into the latest edition of the Concise Oxford Dictionary — in which 'quality' is listed only as a noun. The fact remains however that 'quality' is everywhere with, Hydra-like, a seemingly inexhaustible appetite for its own reproduction and transformation.

English language speakers may be forgiven for feeling slightly puzzled at the weight of significance given the term, for there are many other simpler and better terms to describe the quality of things (such as good and bad, rough and smooth, for example). But in our view the answer to the question 'why quality?' lies not so much in any linguistic capacity the term may have, but in the political and economic signification it carries; and to understand that, one needs to know something of the history of the term as it has come to be used in American and then European management speak.

The idea of 'total quality management' has been used in modern management-speak primarily to serve a political project. In higher education, the aim has been to bring about a neo-liberal reform at the heart of which is the marketization of the university sector and the commoditization of education. Like 'performance', the seemingly positive and politically neutral term 'quality' has been appropriated by government to legitimate its imposition of a highly centralised form of management dedicated to the production and re-production of future citizens of the free market economy. In this usage both terms are, to use Foucault's terminology, 'discourses of power' or 'political technologies' for forging new kinds of subjectivities (see Foucault, 1980; Ball, 1990; Rose, 1990).

Binns (1992) has described how one of the sources of the idea of 'Total Quality Management' lay in the immediate aftermath of the second world war in Japan when the occupying American forces attempted to redraw a significant part of the culture of industrial relations in that country. The power of the trade unions was to be weakened and a new type of corporate culture introduced. Crudely, the aim of this institutional culture was to encourage the growth of a particular form of individualism and consumerism within the boundaries of Japanese firms' 'culture of quality', the overall strategic aim being to bring Japan into a framework of global capitalism dominated by America (Binns, 1992: 51).

The flowering of the idea of TQM in Britain echoes its usage in post-war Japan in the sense that the political programme of the 1980s was also dedicated to changing the overall 'culture' of economic management to respond to what was seen in Conservative circles as being the combination of factors associated with Britain's economic and political decline. Declining Britain was said to be governed by a 'corporate culture' in which trade unions and professional associations held too much power within a political and economic landscape determined to a significant extent by a public service ethic deriving from the early days of the Welfare State. To change all this, a rolling programme was set in train of remarkable internal consistency. Two of the foundations for this were the raft of union-weakening legislation and the privatisation of nationalised industries and services. In the process 'experts' (most definitely *not* a KT) of many different kinds, including educational specialists, were rubbished, the 'liberal 1960s' demonised, and TQM introduced into all kinds of institutions from commercial firms and government offices to universities.

The government believed that marketization would provide the solution to the problems of Britain. As part of the effort to transform the country, education, including higher education, was reformed. The reforms were driven by three principal factors. The first was the belief that deregulation and the introduction of a market system would naturally bring efficiency and raise productivity. The second had to do with the notion of 'accountability' (KT). The wholly admirable idea that those who spend public money should be 'accountable' was used to legitimate rule by government inspector. 'Coercive accountability' and ideological orthodoxy became the most pronounced features of this new system. The third derived from the political utility in disguising the sizeable cuts being made to the public sector, including the higher education sector. This was achieved partly by putting in place a regime in which inter-and intra-university rivalry and competition was stepped up under the 'quality' banner. Rounds of 'audits' and 'assessments' were arranged, including TQAs and a 'Research Assessment Exercise', or 'RAE' (KT). The 'RAE' gave rise to a climate likened by many to the football transfer market in which university was pitted against university and faculty members bought and sold according to the 'RAE's' own imperatives. In this way any lingering 'corporate culture' based on inter-university collegiality and co-operation was buried under the compelling logic of the market place in which universities fought each other. In the process, the idea of the desirability of universities exercising an independent voice was replaced by what some authors call a new 'culture of compliance' (Alderman, 1994; Shore and Roberts, 1995).

Conclusion: the 'CCCC' and beyond

To conclude, we would like to offer the following reflections. The first is that the 'performance culture' discourse we have described is part of a wider neo-liberal agenda informed by the ideas of TQM. This 'culture' (i.e., the rhetoric and associated organisational features we have outlined) has, in our view, much less to do with quality in any serious or recognisable sense than with the 'culture change' proclaimed by the apologists of TQM. The proponents of TQM set out to do that in Japan after the Second War and again in Britain in the mid 1980s. In our view the 'culture' it has gone some way towards producing is, to add just one further acronym to the forest of acronyms it has itself spawned, a 'CCCC': a 'culture of compliance and conformist consumerism'. It has done this by subjecting universities to the discipline of markets and managerialism, and by encouraging a system of division within, and competition between, university institutions and their staff, all of whom must now 'perform' to the gallery of funding councils, 'quality professionals', government bureaucrats and league-table observers.

The second is that under the cloak of the 'quality culture', government has adopted an ever more central role in the actual organisational processes of higher education institutions. An important element in the achieving of this has been the introduction, under the banner of TQM, of a 'culture of reporting' within bureaucratic structures defined by 'line management'. This has enabled government, together with its internal supporters, to identify 'lines of command' through which the new 'culture' can, as the TQM literature puts it, 'cascade down' (KT). After all, and as the acronym TQM itself reminds us, the replacement of the old 'corporate culture' of the failed post-war period by the new 'CCCC' has demanded a 'total' obedience to the demands of 'quality', to achieve which not only the 'culture' but the organisation of institutions has had to be totally redrawn. Let us emphasise the point yet again: what has been sought has been a 'total culture change': it is, we would like to suggest, a 'totalitarian' project.

Thirdly, the success of the 'culture change' we have begun to describe in universities has been achieved partly by some remarkable linguistic innovations and usages: deft employment of acronyms; the merging, mingling, and mangling of discrete senses of terms (such as 'performance') into single senses; the combining of formerly discrete parts of speech (turning the noun quality into an adjective, for example); and so on. But perhaps the single most striking *linguistic* achievement of the 'culture of performance and quality' has been the merging of management lexicons so that different types of institutions — from hotels to probation offices to stock exchanges to universities, and many points in between — are progressively being brought into the same linguistic universe. Everywhere we see different categories of people (including passengers, patients, parents, students, council tenants — anyone, in fact, in receipt of certain services) transformed via this linguistic homogenization process into the uniform and all-embracing category of 'customers'. We have already seen how hotel chains have their 'quality winners' and local authorities their 'Quality Newsletters'. But we could add that the Home Office have recently introduced 'performance related pay' to probation offices *(Guardian,* 11 April 1996), and that the language of 'performance' is closely associated not only with the law and with the theatre, as we have already pointed out, but also, and perhaps pre-eminently, with the financial markets and their institutions. As one newspaper reported recently, 'Britain's venture capitalists are pinning their hopes on new performance measurement surveys' *(Evening Standard* 4 April 1996).

Fourthly, leading directly on from this point, we would argue that there are senses in which institutions and associations which formerly have striven to maintain a degree of independence from each other — the judiciary, the city and associated financial institutions, the media, many parts of civil society including local government, as well as universities — have become bureaucratically and ideologically 'colonized' as a result of being pulled into the common linguistic and organisational 'culture' of 'performance' and 'quality'. In the process of this incorporation they are becoming increasingly no more than bit players in a culturally de-differentiated market place — the only arena of 'culture' recognised by TQM.

Finally, as far as the specific case of higher education is concerned, we would like to leave the penultimate words to David Bellamy and the last words to a student from the University of Sussex. Both talk of the 'changing culture' of contemporary mass higher education in the age of TQM, the 'quality culture', and the 'culture of performance' which we have discussed in this paper. In the view of the former:

> The 1993 science White Paper illustrates how far the prostitution of the universities is being pushed. It calls, fundamentally, for 'key cultural change' to accord academia with the needs of government and industry. It predicates competitive wealth creation, seeking interaction on an escalating scale, between scientists and businessmen involved in the business of selling in competitive markets. *(Guardian,* 9 April 1996)

For the latter:

> Universities today seem to play a very different role [from that which they played in the old university system]. Crammed full of students all studying lots of very little and obsessed more with their diminishing grant cheque and their part-time bar job than the development of new ideas, it is clear that the restructuring of higher education is about solving the problem of elitist education by getting rid of education itself. (*Times Higher Education Supplement*, 5 May 1996)

As historians and sociologists of education in future years come to chronicle the marketization of higher education at the end of the twentieth century, that may well be the conclusion some will draw.

References

Alderman, G. (1994) 'Who scores the college dons?', *The Guardian* (Education Supplement), 25 January 1994: 3.

Association of University Teachers (AUT) (1993) 'Letter to Council Members concerning quality assurance', LA/5061 (November).

Ball, S. (1990) 'Management as Moral Technology. A Luddite Analysis', in S. J. Ball (ed), *Foucault and Education: Disciplines and Knowledge*. London: Routledge.

Binns, D. (1992) *Administration, Domination and 'Organisational Theory': The Political Foundations of Surveillance at Work*. London: University of East London Occassional Papers on Business, Economy and Society.

Foucault, M. (1977) *Discipline and Punish*. Harmondsworth: Penguin.

———— (1980) *Power/Knowledge: Selected Interviews and Other Writings, 1972-1977* (ed. Colin Gordon). London: Harvester Press.

———— (1991) 'Governmentality', in G. Burchell *et al.* (eds) *The Foucault Effect*, London: Harvester Wheatsheaf, pp. 87–104.

Halsey, A. H. (1995) *The Decline of Donnish Dominion*. Oxford: Clarendon.

Her Majesty' Government (HMG) (1993) *Realising Our Potential. A Strategy for Science, Engineering and Technology*. London: HMSO, Cm 2250.

Hodgson, T. (1988) *The Batsford Dictionary of Drama*. London: Batsford.

Hutton, W. (1995) *The State We're In*. London: Vintage.

Jenkins, A. (1995) 'The Research Assessment Exercise, Funding and Teaching Quality', *Quality Assurance in Education*, 3 (2): 4-12.

Johnson, N. (1994) 'Dons in Decline', *Twentieth Century British History*, 5.

Keat, R. (1991) 'Introduction. Starship Britain or Universal Enterprise?', in N. Abercrombie and R. Keat (eds) *Enterprise Culture*. London: Routledge, pp. 1-17.

Morris, P. (1991) 'Freeing the Spirit of Enterprise: The Genesis and Development of the Concept of Enterprise Culture', in N. Abercrombie and R. Keat (eds) *Enterprise Culture*. London: Routledge, pp. 21-37.

New Shorter English Dictionary (1993) Oxford: Clarendon Press.

New Encyclopedia Britannica (1987) Vol. 9. Chicago: University Press.

Pfeffer, N. and A. Coote (1991) *Is Quality Good for You?*. London: Institute of Public Policy Research, Social Policy Paper 5.

Rose, N. (1990) *Governing the Soul: The Shaping of the Private Self*. London: Routledge.

Selwyn, T. and Shore, C. (1992) 'Education, Markets and Managers: A Clash of Cultures?', *Reflections on Higher Education*. 4, November: 88-95.

Seymore-Smith, C. (1986) *Macmillan Dictionary of Anthropology*. London: Macmillan.

Shore, C. and Roberts, S. (1995) 'Higher Education and the Panopticon Paradigm: Quality Assurance as "Disciplinary Technology"', *Higher Education Quarterly*, 27 (3) Summer: 8-17.

Wisdom and Understanding? Would you Like Fries with That? A View from Behind the Counter[1]

10

Simon Lilley

Introduction

This chapter considers and reflects upon a recent development in the supposed McDonaldization (Ritzer, 1993; 1996a; 1996b) of British university education: the introduction and use of standardised OHPs and lecture scripts as a significant pillar of course provision. According to colleagues this practice is becoming increasingly widespread. The particular product under interrogation here was intended to facilitate the teaching of 'organisational behaviour' in the ever-expanding university business school sector. The author was involved in the 'piloting' of this product when 'team-teaching' a course with one of its developers. After an examination of the product portfolio, both from my own 'user's' perspective and that of its designer, the chapter goes on to consider some of its implications, making particular use of the notion of *kitsch* (Broch, 1969a; 1969b; Cooper, 1986, Kundera, 1988; Linstead, 1996; Montgomery, 1991). This term seems to exhibit considerable 'interpretative flexibility', an asset that is fully exploited in the analysis that provides the discussion section of the chapter. The ambivalence of the conclusions that are tentatively offered reflects much of the wider debate surrounding the massification of higher education. However, a little further reflection reveals that this refusal of closure may be seen to be little more than an aggrandised form of the kitsch that our intellectualising diversion sought to escape. This somewhat depressing conclusion suggests that kitsch is not as localised and easily identifiable as our initial understanding intimated. Indeed, from the perspective adopted and developed here, kitsch can be seen to be virtually everywhere. In these circumstances, perhaps the best that we can hope for is to rob it of some its comforting power by making sure that we recognise it wherever we find it. This outcome is therefore the somewhat modest aim of what follows.

Meeting the demands of cost conscious 'consumers' (*aka* students)

Ritzer (1996b) provides us with a stark and, for many, nightmarish insight into possible futures for the McUniversity (see also Parker and Jary, 1995, for a more even-handed assessment). His contribution is something of a rhetorical *tour de force*, an appellation that applies equally to his oft-quoted McDonaldization thesis (Ritzer, 1993; 1996a; Parker, 1997). Ritzer's popular works are both entertaining and highly convincing. However, this *trompe-l'oeil* is achieved, as Parker (1997) notes through two key moves: a seemingly disinterested observer's or commentator's style and a rather acerbic wit, with the latter aspect being founded upon an unacknowledged, and hence untheorised, nostalgic cultural elitism, redolent of many other renderings of 'mass culturalism' (see Parker, 1997, for a list of exemplars of this tradition). Ritzer's discourse can thus hardly fail to prompt a 'Yes, I think that too' initial response from his mainly middle-class, liberal, Rortyesque, readers. It certainly worked on me! With this in mind, it would seem that his work merits some *detailed* attention.

For Ritzer (1996b), the future of the McUniversity may be extrapolated from novel modes of delivery and receipt of consumables visible elsewhere. The words, 'delivery' and 'receipt', are purposefully chosen here. They indicate the activity that Ritzer tends to ascribe to 'systems' of delivery against an assumed but undertheorised passivity on the part of the consumers of the products of such systems (see Parker, 1997).[2] According to Ritzer (1996b), apart from those who attend the 'elite institutions' such as 'Harvard and Oxford', both students and staff seem to have little alternative but to bend to the twin demands of increasing cost-consciousness and assured and demonstrable 'quality' that have already come to dominate many other spheres of consumption. 'Academics' who remain in faculty posts outside of the gilded cage of the elite institutions will increasingly find themselves reduced to the role of system administrators, ensuring and monitoring the cost effective purveyance of the products of those who still hold positions within them. We will seemingly be left with a few 'real' universities (those that always have been there) and a plethora of 'simulated' satellite institutions, the McUniversities. The latter may even produce satellites themselves (Ritzer, 1996b). Or at least that is 'the view from Maryland' (Parker, 1997). However, in Britain if nowhere else, the position seems somewhat different. 'Research', far from just being a sign of a golden age of academe that is soon to pass, seems to be a significant part of the problem. This is clearly somewhat paradoxical and the argument would therefore seem to warrant a little further unpacking.

Making space for the research race

Undoubtedly, governmental pressures to constrain the stretching of the fiscal purse have had an impact in the UK. But this has not immediately resulted in all but the 'very best' institutions and their inhabitants being reduced to teaching machines. The slow but sure effects of the research selectivity exercises have led to a somewhat more broadly contingent range of possibilities. Research, at least 'theoretically', is still an option for all.[3] With increasing class sizes, extending 'contact hours' and exponential increases in sources of 'knowledge', the desire to 'save time' at work,in order to feed those aforementioned knowledge sources and bask in the consequent kudos, seems unremitting. For as those in both the 'old' and 'new' British university sectors are continually made aware[4] , research is where it's at, and, perhaps more importantly, the money's there too. In Britain then, 'research' is not best understood as simply a casualty of increased teaching. It may also be seen to enact a villainous role in a play in which the 'quality' of teaching is victim.[5]

However, even within these circumstances, that tawdry business of teaching still has to be done — the job titles of Lecturer and Professor have to tie-in to something. And so a demand is created for a series of products that seek to lessen the burden on all concerned and ensure that time is available for the knowledge of the future to be 'better' than the knowledge of today. The temptation to buy time so that we can serve such noble ends is difficult to resist. And so it is hardly surprising if the supply of such products is starting to proliferate.

One such labour saving device is of course the widely used and much loved/ loathed 'standard' course text book. However the 'benefits' of these devices have recently been 'enhanced' by the introduction of pre-prepared, standardised OHPs and lecture scripts to accompany them. The implications of this development are the primary subject of this chapter and they are explored from a couple of complementary perspectives — those of the mouthpiece and the guinea pig.

I think it is important to note here that the deleterious effects of textbooks have not been a particularly big concern for me during my short academic career. I have used them, sparingly, but have not really given them much thought, beyond subjecting them to the traditional, sneering contempt that seems to be the *de rigeur* response for enthusiastic (relatively) young things like myself. However, during a recent stint of service teaching I was asked by one of the writers of the more successful of these tomes if I would be willing to employ and 'test out' some recent additions to her package — pre-prepared slides and lecture scripts. The text itself could not be described as particularly innovative, especially within a North American context.[6] It covers all that is seemingly required for teaching under- and postgraduates 'organisational behaviour' in university-based business schools. It contains all the expected, standard, time-validated knowledge[7] on those thorny 'human' problems of work and comes complete, for lecturing staff, with a workbook and a tutor's manual (see Fineman and Gabriel, 1994). The scripts and slides to facilitate the teaching of each 'subject' were as yet untested by either the developer or the ubiquitous 'user'. And that's where I came in.

The course was taught jointly with the tool's developer[8] and it is this aspect of the experience that may prove to be of particular interest to others. For this situation enabled a coupling of the joys of use with the justificatory marketing line produced by the developer. Thus the chapter will seek to juxtapose my own rationale for 'choosing' this device and my experience of its use with the views of its developer on its purpose and 'value' to the contemporary academic community.

On first sight then, the chapter may appear to present just another rubbishing of the denigration of 'knowledge' frequently seen to be entailed by the deployment of such devices. But such an analysis would miss the point and do little to serve the themes set out for this volume. In a world of mass teaching and money for research it would seem that there are no easy answers to the dilemmas of 'time management'. Tools that allow us to do what we currently do, not only with less effort but also with that 'shop-bought' glaze of professionalism are undoubtedly attractive to teaching staff. Indeed, in many circumstances they may result in 'better' service delivery to the (paying) customer. McDonaldization (Ritzer, 1993; Parker and Jary, 1995) is nothing if not successful. Standards *are* seen to be important by many and varied interested parties, and the knowledge 'product' provided here is certainly that.

But perhaps more interestingly, opportunities to do what we currently do 'better' should force us to reflect upon what it is that we currently do and why it is that we do it. Other 'academics' with whom I have discussed this product seem to have extremely polarised views on the subject. Pre-produced OHPs and scripts are seen as either boon or bane, but rarely if ever are they routinely accepted. Why should this be the case? What threats do they harbour and what opportunities do they promise? Indeed, could this polarisation of views be more usefully seen as a dissimulation, a chimerical non-argument that serves to occlude and hence a safeguard an underlying but perhaps somewhat unsavoury agreement about the nature of knowledge and its relations to the power associated with the bodies that peddle it (see, for example, Baudrillard, 1983; Burke, 1969; Foucault, 1970)? These are the sorts of questions that the chapter will be seeking to address and whilst unlikely (and unwilling) to provide any definitive answers, the novel combination of approaches adopted may allow some rather unusual insights to emerge. The devices under consideration look likely to stay with us, whether we like them or not. They would therefore seem to merit a little more attention than just uncritical acceptance or rejection, as indeed would our reactions to them. The latter therefore form the subject matter of the following section.

Choosing the product

The course on which the new products were initially deployed was a compulsory one for second year engineering degree students. A change in the rules for obtaining 'Chartered' status had apparently resulted in such students being required to take a basic course in management. The course was titled 'Management and Organisational Contexts'. Only one book was recommended (indeed mentioned!) as relevant for the course, the standard Organisational Behaviour text we mentioned earlier. This book itself had apparently emerged out of a number of years teaching to 'straight' management students and the author was in the process of repeating this transformative production with another one of her lecture courses. For her, lectures were a test bed for text books and a large proportion of her income was derived from the royalties for such products.

The producer of the product, let's call her 'Dr Deadpan', spoke warmly of Ritzer's (1993) notion of McDonalidization, but not with the tone of acerbic critique that informs the original rendering. Rather she saw a potential for wider applicability of the McDonalds way: "Make them all the same but make sure you leave the buyer with a nice taste in their mouth". She saw great virtue in a standard knowledge product[9] . It gave 'us' the opportunity to 'know' when students 'knew' the material, providing some objectivity in a dangerously subjective field. And it also saved 'us' time which she recognised as an increasingly scarce resource in the all-too-familiar conditions of the 'New Higher Education' (NHE) (Parker and Jary, 1995). Dr Deadpan did however point out that a number of other 'young lecturers' to whom she had offered her tools had been less than enamoured with the approach and, whilst she was somewhat surprised by this reaction, she claimed to understand it. Some had even expressed deep 'disgust', so she was very insistent about the fact that 'it was up to' me whether I used the products or not. However, the course was the department's *bete noir* and I, as the most junior member of staff with an 'interest' in the area had been 'chosen' to provide it. Dr Deadpan was doing me a favour by offering to share it with me and it seemed churlish to turn down her assistance. Moreover, I had no intention of teaching the course again so was unwilling to put too much investment into course design and of course, given the conditions and subjectivities of the NHE, I thought I could get some research out of it! In short, I agreed to play the game.

In keeping with our McDonalds metaphor, Dr Deadpan and I had a meeting to consider whether the students should receive a 'thick' or a 'thin sandwich'. The latter would apparently have involved a brief consideration of all the subjects in the 'comprehensive' mother text, the latter a 'deeper' consideration (i.e. both chapters on each subject) of a smaller range of topics. Pedagogic integrity forced us to opt for the latter, but it is important to realise what sort of depth we are talking about — the students were examined by a long series of short answer questions. With our programme outlined, we had little additional contact concerning the provision of the course. We both attended the introductory session, which Dr Deadpan led, and from then on did one session each of the two that were scheduled per week. Thus, I was the first to unleash the new aid to knowledge on the unwitting consumers.

Ciphering the product

Session Two, which 'I' 'provided', concerned 'Perception'. The hundred and twenty or so engineers gathered in the lecture theatre as I strode forward with my pre-prepared package. I had thirty-four overheads and an accompanying script. There was also space for an exercise in which the class divided into twos and made observations and concomitant character inferences of and on each other. Dr Deadpan had made it clear that I didn't have to use all of them or stick with the script. But it was easier to do so and more faithful to my research aims.

Perhaps inevitably, for someone with a self-image at least partially constructed around notions of 'brightness' and youthful self reliance, I felt like a complete fraud from the start. It was nigh on impossible to disguise my distaste for the material and the 'pat' answers it provided to what seemed to me to be rather deeper questions. No amount of humorous illustrations of little people mis-perceiving each other seemed likely to make up for this. And I could feel the students picking up on my distaste and feeding it back to me — non-verbally at first but gradually more vocally. I then had to either defend the (to me at least) indefensible or agree with their complaints and apologise but say that this was what they had to know. I chose the latter course of action and became more and more aware of my slide along the slippery slope to intellectual prostitution.[10] It is very difficult to convincingly present someone else's words and ideas as your own (or perhaps worse, as *the* truth), as anyone who has ever listened to a pub band cover version will attest. More worrying still was the deadening effect on the mind. It was incredibly hard to inject critique into the performance as it seemed to ruin the flow, which was about all it had going for it. Indeed, even that was lost when, expecting a slide showing the triangulated perceptual tease 'Paris in the the spring time' (the scripted version) —

Paris
in the
the spring time

—which the 'normal observer' tends to read as 'Paris in the spring time', supposedly demonstrating the active role played by experience in perception — I found myself showing a slide of a triangulated 'Pull the the rabbit out of the hat'.

Pull the
the rabbit
out of the hat

This minor perturbation in the expected example left me completely flummoxed. Obviously a change had been made in the slides but not recorded in the script (perhaps the 'Paris…' example has become so overused that is too familiar to work, or maybe it is easier to add a nice little clip art picture of a rabbit/hat combination than it is to pictorially represent the shifting seasons in the French capital — who knows?) but at the time, in front of a class, I simply could not grasp this and I spent two or three whole minutes (which felt like an hour at the time) flipping between gabbling and silence as I desperately tried to recover the situation and regain that all important flow. All in all, it was not a happy or rewarding experience, but I persevered for almost the entirety of the course. To have done otherwise would have both jeopardised this research and the other pieces I was working on at the time. And of course, in the current research selectivity environment, that would never do! My reaction was not exactly a surprise to me, but its vehemence did make me stop and think. What precisely had I found so distasteful about the product and the experience of its use? And, perhaps more interestingly, what distasteful aspects of self recognition did this 'scapegoating' (Burke, 1969) transference enable me to occlude? With the indulgence of the reader I reflect upon this navel gazing below.

Exploring the source of my disdain

If I had to choose just one word to describe both the 'knowledge' I 'gave' those poor students and the format of its delivery it would have to be *kitsch*. According to my *Concise Oxford Dictionary* (1977) kitsch is "worthless pretentiousness in art" although in its more common usage it seems also to refer to those rather tacky products, perhaps best exemplified by the treats available at British seaside 'gift' shops, that seek to cost-effectively fulfil a desire for ornaments and mementos in and of our lives. Kitsch then is certainly 'nasty', at least from an aloof, elitist perspective, but it seems to satisfy some extremely widespread needs, and as such it would certainly not seem to be necessarily limited to the spheres we have considered so far. For example, Steve Linstead (1996, drawing heavily on Cooper, 1986) has considered the kitsch in and of much that is written under the heading of administrative science. As he notes:

> Kitsch works because it reminds us we are not alone, and it is so powerful because it capitalizes on a fundamental lack: the desire for the other which motivates social structure (Cooper, 1983; Linstead and Grafton Small, 1992). Kitsch offers quick and easy access to the longed-for world of the other, which becomes *our* world, and which

> is reassuring no matter how cheap and nasty it may be.... we don't need to be *persuaded* by it, just to share and participate in it is sufficient — it works without us having to think about it. [original emphasis]

Linstead's usage here starts to take us away from at least the worst excesses of an elitist notion of kitsch as it seeks to broaden the purview of the term. However, it is important to note that any usage of the term, much like the notion of the 'mass' we considered earlier (Parker, 1997), necessarily instigates a rhetorical separation between the author and less enlightened 'victims' of the phenomenon, regardless of the number of politically correct and noble caveats that surround that usage. This broadening nevertheless does increase the 'democracy' of the term, potentially inviting all comers to take up their place in the victims' fold. Superficially this would lead us to suggest that different groups and individuals, in different places and times, create and appropriate different 'types' of kitsch. However, although we may agree that the content of kitsch changes all the time, it is important to note that at a deeper level its effects remain constant. And kitsch is all about effects (and affects) as our initial quote from Linstead makes clear.

To help substantiate his position, Linstead (1996) cites Montgommery's mobilisation of Broch (1969a; 1969b) in which kitsch appears as "the disintegration of art into commodity, creativity into a demand for known effects and affects" (Montgommery, 1991: 10).[11] Kitsch is all about creating and satisfying a demand for comfort. Throughout changes in form, kitsch remains stable, as both the reflection and reconstitution of those truisms and clichés that together make up the taken-for-granted and unarguable, or what we more frequently term 'common sense'. And it is perhaps the variations in this supposedly 'common' sense, across space and time, that allow us to apply the term to a vast range of cultural artefacts.

In this sense then, kitsch is a *lack* of challenge to shared and consequently comfortable understandings, an active acceptance to bypass activity. It is not however to be confused with a lack of critique. Kitsch can accommodate critique as easily as praise. For as Burke (1969; see also Lilley, 1997) notes, the substance of critique is praise (and *vice versa*).

> Literally a person or a thing's sub-stance would be something that stands beneath or supports the person or thing... [and thus the word]...used to designate what a thing *is* derives from a word designating what a thing is not. (Burke, 1969: 22-23)

Critique, as much as praise, is a way of putting the stop on the "permanent hermeneutics of oneself" (Foucault, 1985: 371, cited in Linstead, 1996) — such as the navel gazing we have engaged in here — that constitutes Being (Heidegger, 1977). For when whether we are for some*thing* or against it then at least *we* can convince ourselves, however temporarily, that we know where (and therefore what) *we* are. Kitsch is the costume in our charade of identity that assuages the interminable problems of self. It...

> ...short circuits this agonising and continual process by providing simple and clear models and defining the unacceptable un-ambiguously. (Linstead, 1996)

And the same is therefore true of the critique that is constituted by this paper. It is to this particular form of kitsch that we turn in our conclusions.

Concluding kitsch

As Kundera (1988: 135, cited in Linstead, 1996) notes, kitsch... "is the need to gaze into the mirror of the beautifying lie and to be moved to tears of gratification at one's own reflection". I have read my Foucault (1970 etc.) and those other critical theorists with more of a capital 'C'. I 'know' that knowledge and power, or ideology and hegemony, are intimately related. And I can see how Dr Deadpan's texts and tools help to legitimate, and hence perpetuate, many of the distributions of property and properties to which I feel myself opposed. Indeed my ability to see this is in large part dependent on the ability of others to see the same things — others with whom I am happy to ally. 'Sexy' others, 'radical' others, others who claim to be against the things that I see myself as standing against, others whom I would like to be like. But does that release me from the mirror of kitsch? Does it allow me to be different from those I have been seeking to attack? Unfortunately, it would seem that, at least in certain crucial respects, the answer has to be a resounding 'no'. For as Burke (1969: 406–407) points out:

> When the attacker chooses for himself the object of attack, it is usually his blood brother; the debunker is much closer to the debunked than others are.

All of which leads to a somewhat sobering conclusion.

In other circumstances I do not and would not teach the sort of stuff that Dr Deadpan peddles. Being a proper post-modern pedagogue I refuse to give the students answers (except, of course, at exam and assessment time!). But as the good Doctor herself pointed out: "Some people like to stand up and say more complicated things that the students don't understand but they do so to make themselves look clever rather than to help the students". And so it would seem that this is the ideal that *my* mirror provides: that of a heroic crusader who seeks to use his superior powers, defined by his difference, to enable the less worthy to become more challenging, more active and more creative. This then is the identity of my charade. By allying in critique with others who share 'my' concerns, I can cleanse myself as I 'ritualistically alienate' (Burke, 1969) those other 'others' who do not: those whose aims, at least from 'our' perspective, seem more pedestrian and perpetuative of the current status quo. But when I am aware of the process, as I have become through this reflective diversion, it no longer works. For the 'charismatic' power of the 'scapegoating' process lies precisely in the invisibility of its action (Burke, 1969). Worse still, I also 'know' that as an 'intellectual' I will be the last to see those deeper 'discursive formations' that constitute the present *order of things*, the 'real' status quo behind the 'simulations' (Baudrillard, 1983) that serve to distract my well-meaning attentions. And given that 'knowledge', the path that I have chosen here — to attack the good Doctor and her prescriptions — is revealed as kitschistic in the extreme.

Notes

1 This chapter has benefited from the comments of participants at the international conference on *The Dilemmas Of Mass Higher Education*, held at Staffordshire University in April 1996. It has also received a useful commentary from the editors of this volume, much of which has been incorporated into the final text. The paper was originally presented under the title 'Organisational Behaviour? Would you like...', but the editors believed that this could lead to the impression that McDonaldised teaching is only an issue for business education. The new title is intended to rectify this potential misunderstanding, although the subject matter largely remains constant. Any errors that remain in the final version, despite these helpful interventions, are of course my own.

2 Ritzer's contribution to the Staffordshire Conference appeared superficially to differ somewhat in this regard from his earlier work (1993; 1996) through a reliance on the notion of cost-conscious consumers shaping the possible organisational responses he identifies. However this shift is something of a chimera. The 'mass' of students and their cost conscious desires seem largely prefigured by the sorts of 'choices' foisted upon them by other contemporary consumption systems.

3 Obviously, it is still more of an 'option' for some, even at present, and these differentiating pressures look likely to, if anything, intensify in the future.

4 Most frequently and effectively by themselves and their peers. See Parker and Jary (1995).

5 The 'teaching quality' exercises are intended to prevent the worst excesses of this process but judging by the degree of derision to which they are subjected by the academic staff who are their objects, they are at best a palliative and at worst a bureaucratic distraction that leaves even less time available to invest in a high 'quality' of interaction.

6 It is exceedingly difficult to escape the snide anti-American tone of much of the mass culturalism discourse. To do so is simply to miss out on too much xenophobic fun! See Bryson (1995) for a recent and frequently hilarious boundary crossing example of this genre!

7 This is no first edition!

8 Or maybe jointly with the development tool, depending on one's views on actor network theory!

9 She happily admitted that her main sources in producing her textbooks were American Organisational Behaviour texts of the sixties and seventies which she bought in second hand book shops. These texts apparently had 'better and clearer examples and theories', presumably being untrammelled by the confusing distractions of recent 'developments' in the field (c.f. Fineman and Gabriel, 1994).

10 It is important to note the extremely poor press that prostitutes as a whole receive through the sort of linguistic turn engaged in here. As Brewis et al. (1997), amongst others point out, prostitution is a multifaceted 'business' with many players involved for many different reasons. It is presumptuous and condescending to assume that the providers of such services are only involved because they have to be and/ or because they have little or no self respect. These reasons may indeed account for the involvement of many, but certainly not all. My use of the term here then is particular. I refer to sense of selling oneself that is expressed by some prostitutes as problematic. I certainly am not referring to the positive, self enhancing view of prostitution that is expressed by some of its providers.

11 As should be readily apparent, referencing of the sort engaged in here is deeply kistschistic.

References

Baudrillard, J. (1983) *Simulations*. New York: Semiotext(e).

Brewis, J., Linstead, S. and Sinclair, J. (1997) 'Any time, any place, anywhere. 24/7 and the organization of sex work', paper presented to the *After Dark Conference*, Egerton House Hotel, March 1997.

Broch, H. (1969a) 'Evil in the System of Artistic Values', in G. Dorfles (ed) *Kitsch: The World of Bad Taste*. New York: Universe Books.

——— (1969b) 'Notes on the Problem of Kitsch', in G. Dorfles (ed.) *Kitsch: The World of Bad Taste*. New York: Universe Books.

Bryson, B. (1995) *Notes from a Small Island*. London: Black Swan.

Burke, K. (1969) *A Grammar of Motives*. Berkeley and Los Angeles: University of California Press.

Cooper, R. (1983) 'The Other: A Model of Human Structuring', in G. Morgan (ed) *Beyond Method*. London: Sage.

——— (1986) 'Notes on Organizational Kitsch', Working Paper, University of Lancaster.

Fineman, S. and Gabriel, Y. (1994) 'Paradigms of Organizations: An Exploration in Textbook Rhetorics', *Organization*, 1 (2): 375-400.

Foucault, M. (1970) *The Order of Things*. London: Tavistock.

——— (1985) 'Sexuality and Solitude', in Marshall Blonsky (ed) *On Signs*. Oxford, Basil Blackwell.

Heidegger, M. (1977) *The Question Concerning Technology and Other Essays*. New York: Harper.

Lilley, S. (1997) 'Stuck in the Middle with You?', *British Journal of Management*, 8 (1): 51-60.

Linstead, S. (1996) 'Administrative Science as Kitsch', paper presented at the *Translations* Conference. Malahide, Co. Dublin.

Linstead, S. and Grafton Small, R. (1992) 'On Reading Organizational Culture', *Organization Studies*, 13 (3): 331-355.

Montgommery, S. (1991) 'Science as Kitsch: The Dinosaur and Other Icons', *Science as Culture*, 2 (1): 7-58.

Parker, M. (1997) 'Nostalgia and Mass Culture: McDonaldization and Cultural Elitism' in M. Alfino, J. Caputo and R. Wynyard (eds) *McDonaldization Revisited: Essays on the Commodification of Culture*. Westport, CT: Greenwood.

Parker, M. and Jary, D. (1995) 'The McUniversity: Organization, Management and Academic Subjectivity', *Organization*, 2 (2): 319-338.

Ritzer, G. (1993) *The McDonaldization of Society*. Thousand Oaks, CA.: Pine Forge.

——— (1996a) *The McDonaldization of Society* (Revised Edition). Thousand Oaks, CA.: Pine Forge.

——— (1996b) 'McUniversity in the Postmodern Consumer Society'. Paper presented at the *Dilemmas of Mass Higher Education Conference*, Staffordshire University, April.

Economics Divided: The Limitations of Peer Review in a Paradigm-Bound Social Science

11

Frederic S. Lee and Sandra Harley

Introduction

Prior to 1986, the year of the first Research Assessment Exercise (RAE), funding for research in British universities was built into funds per student on the assumption that all academics were engaged in research and scholarship as part of their role as academics. Additional funds for specific projects were available upon successful application from the Research Councils according to the principle of dual funding. However, beginning in the 1970s, the University Grants Committee (UGC) found that the government grant for the funding of teaching and research in British universities was declining in real terms. Moreover, in the early 1980s the universities fell victim to heavy cuts in public expenditure and it became apparent to many administrators in the field that excellence in research could not be maintained without applying some principle of selectivity in funding. Somewhat reluctantly, therefore, the UGC agreed to a research selectivity exercise whereby research funds were distributed to different departments according to the UGC's assessment of its degree of excellence (see Court, this volume).

The first exercise was an ad hoc affair with the UGC hurriedly appointing its assessors and only a small proportion of research monies dependent on their ratings.[1] The second exercise was carried out by the UGC in 1989 with a larger proportion of research funding dependent on the ratings of duly constituted subject panels to whom departments were to submit much refined applications; and in 1992, its successor, the Universities Funding Council (UFC), carried out a third exercise. In 1992, over 90 per cent of the UFC's research funds was distributed by its successors, the Higher Education Funding Councils (HEFCs) for England, Wales, Scotland, and Northern Ireland, according to the ratings of its subject panels and the pre-1992 universities had to compete for that money

185

with the ex-polytechnics or the new universities. As for the 1996 RAE, British universities prepared their submissions in an even tighter financial climate brought about by an average of 5 per cent reduction in real terms across the sector for 1996/97 (Universities Funding Council, 1989; Phillimore, 1989; and Higher Education Funding Council for England, 1993).

The first exercise seemed to have little impact on economists and their research. However, by the time of the 1989 RAE, the so-called "Diamond List" of core mainstream economic journals had been drawn up and there was a strong belief amongst economists that this list was used by the assessors to inform their judgement of the quality of research in economics departments in British universities. Certainly attempts were made to extend this list for use in the 1992 RAE, though this modified list remained, like its predecessor, "unofficial,". The existence of these lists, whether official or not, has produced considerable discontent amongst British economists, for reasons not at all unrelated to the research rating received by their departments (Diamond, 1989; Minutes of Conference of Heads of University Departments of Economics, 4 November 1989, 21 May 1993, and 21 May 1994; and Harley and Lee, 1997).

At the 1994 Royal Economic Society Annual Conference a special session was held at which the chairman of the economics panel for the 1992 RAE gave his view of what the panel did and also received questions from the floor. One question asked was how did the panel regard economic research which fell outside the domain of mainstream economics. The answer was, in part, that the assessors did not discriminate against non-mainstream research and that the research assessment exercise should not be used by economic departments to do so. He added that he did not believe British economists would actively discriminate against non-mainstream economists and their research. However, at the same conference a flyer appeared which announced that one old university was in the market for nine economists who would raise its economics department research profile in mainstream economics (see *The Guardian* 29 March 1994).[2] Advertisements for posts in other institutions similarly specified that applicants must be working within mainstream economics and linked this explicitly to either maintaining or improving their ranking in the assessment exercise.[3] Therefore, it would appear that economics departments were in their hiring practices discriminating positively towards mainstream economists and their research as a way to maintain and/or enhance their rating in the next research assessment exercise. As a result, it would be plausible to assume that non-mainstream economists and their research were being discriminated against; but this is precisely what the chair of the economics panel believed would not happen.

This contrast between his belief about British economists and their actual performance in a few chosen instances is so stark as to warrant further investigation. One area of research, which is the concern of this CHAPTER, is to examine the peer review system which underlies the RAE and its institutional impact on economists and their research.[4] The argument to be advanced is that the theoretical and methodological divisions within economics, combined with the institutional arrangement of the RAE and peer review, has produced a state of affairs which poses a serious risk to the future existence of non-mainstream economics within economics departments in British universities. After briefly establishing that economics is split into two distinct camps, the next three sections describe the nature of peer review, recount the establishment of the economics assessment panels for the 1989, 1992, and 1996 Research Assessment Exercises and the method of assessment they used, and assess the assessors in terms of pre-eminence in research and subject coverage. Utilizing the material in the previous sections, the discussion in the following section centers on the shortcomings of the peer review process in the 1989 and 1992 RAE and their consequences for the assessing of the quality of non-mainstream research publications. The next section utilizes survey data to examine the situation of non-mainstream economics in economic departments after the 1992 RAE. The final section concludes the article with a discussion of the 1996 RAE and the future of non-mainstream economics.

Economics divided: mainstream vs. non-mainstream

Economics can be divided into a mainstream, called neoclassical economics, and a non-mainstream, which broadly consists of Marxian, Post Keynesian, Institutional, and Sraffian economics. The distinction between neoclassical and non-mainstream economics can be broadly conceived in terms of theoretical and methodological concepts such as relative scarcity, rationality, atomistic individualism, equilibrium, and ergodicity which are central to the former but are not to the latter. This difference is succinctly expressed in their definition of economics. Neoclassical economists define economics broadly as the study of how people and societies deal with scarcity; whereas the non-mainstream economists support various combinations of the following definitions— economics is the investigation of the nature and causes of the wealth of nations, of the laws of motion of capitalism, and/or of the behavior, institutions, and culture which underlie evolving capitalist economies. The fact that neoclassical economics has splintered into various quasi-competing research programmes, such as public choice economics, experimental economics, game theory, transaction costs economics, and new classical economics, in the last twenty years does not negate the reality that a common basic theory, method of approaching economic issues, and language exists among neoclassical economists. Recognition of this broad division between mainstream and non-mainstream economics has been acknowledged in articles in the *Royal Economic Society Newsletter* (Culyer, 1994), in letters circulated to British economists (e.g. see Presley, 1994), and in a survey of British economists carried out by Harley and Lee (1997). The division between mainstream and non-mainstream economics is also *reflected* in the journals in which economists publish. That is, core mainstream journals (see Appendix A) form a virtually closed self-referencing system *vis-à-vis* core non-mainstream journals, by which we mean that core mainstream journals contain articles which nearly exclusively cite articles which appear in other core mainstream journals. In contrast, the core non-mainstream journals (see Appendix B) form a distinctly more open self-referencing system in that core non-mainstream journals cite both mainstream and non-mainstream journals.[5]

Peer review

Central to the assessment exercise is the peer review system, which can be defined as a system by which the intellectual excellence of a piece of research is judged by a committee or panel of researchers working in, or close to, the field in question. According to researchers on peer review, for the system to work it is necessary that each member of the panel be pre-eminent in the specialism(s) which they have to evaluate; that the pre-eminent panel members be selected from across the relevant academic community; that the actual method of selection is open, democratic, and involves as much of the academic community as possible; that involvement in peer review be voluntary as opposed to forced under threat of financial sanction; that feedback be provided automatically to all applicants; that an appeal system exists; that the panel be open to unorthodox and interdisciplinary research; and that the peers do not as individuals or as a group have an interest, financially or otherwise, in the outcome. The UGC fully accepted the peer review system since, in their view, there was no substitution for the sensitive and subtle judgement by experts in the field.[6] Accordingly, it suggested that the choice of peers for the 1989 research assessment exercise be made with regard to "the range of specialised expertise needed to cover the spread of research in the subject area to be assessed"; to "the spread of institutions being assessed"; to "age and current active involvement in research"; and to "evidence of wide knowledge of the conduct of research in the relevant subject area" (Universities Funding Council, 1989: 15). The UFC and the HEFCs also adopted similar guidelines for the 1992 and 1996 assessment exercises. On the other hand, the UGC, UFC, and HEFCs were not concerned that the methods of selection of the panel-peers were not open and democratic, that no feedback would be given to the departments (but not the case for the 1996 RAE), that university economists and their departments were financially 'forced' to be peer reviewed, and that the peers may have an interest in the outcome of their deliberations; neither were they explicitly concerned about the issue of less orthodox research. As we shall see below, these omissions have had a serious impact on the peer review process in such a paradigm-based discipline as economics (Advisory Board for the Research Councils, 1990;

Smith, 1988a and b; Universities Funding Council, 1989; Lock, 1985; Roy, 1982; Hubbard, 1995; Higher Education Funding Council for England, 1994 and 1995a; Griffith, 1995).

Economics Assessment Panel and method of assessment

It could be argued that the process by which the economic panels for the 1989, 1992, and 1996 RAE were appointed was not open or democratic in that the majority of economists had little say in, or understanding of, the selection process. The make-up of the 1989 panel consisted of two appointments made by the UGC, four economists recommended by the Royal Economic Society (RES), one economist recommended by the Scottish Economic Society, two non-economists, and two observers from other panels.[7] As for the five economists not appointed by the UGC, four were selected from a list of five names sent to the UGC by the RES. To obtain the five names, the Society solicited nominations from members of its standing committee of the Conference of Heads of University Departments of Economics (CHUDE). The CHUDE Steering Committee considered all the nominations that came in and recommended to the RES Executive Committee what it thought to be a balanced slate of five names for transmission to the UGC. The fifth economist on the panel was nominated by the Scottish Economic Society and supported by the CHUDE Steering Committee. The names of the panel assessors were not made public until after the exercise was completed (Minutes of the Conference of Heads of University Departments of Economics, 5 November 1988 and 4 November 1989; Standing Committee, 25 February 1989 and 14 October 1989; and Feinstein, 1995).

The selection of economists for the 1992 panel was slightly different in that the UFC did not directly appoint any of the panel members. Rather it solicited nominations for all panel members from subject associations, professional bodies, and learned societies, including CHUDE and the RES. Since the UFC's timescale from first seeking nominations for the assessment panels to announcing who the panel members were was only two months, the Steering Committee of CHUDE decided to seek nominations only from its members. Some seventy names were proposed by the Heads, of which twelve or so commanded substantially more support than the remainder. Taking into account subject coverage and geographical spread, the Steering Committee selected eight or so names which they forwarded to the RES who in turned forwarded them to the Council. From the names submitted, the UFC and its economic advisors selected the chair for the economics panel, and then in consultation with the chair they selected the rest of the panel. However, two economists declined to serve on the panel and were simply replaced by the chair after some consultation. The identity of the initial panel members was made known in July 1992 and updated later in November (Minutes of the Conference of Heads of University Departments of Economics, 9 May 1992 and 7 November 1992; Standing Committee, 22 February 1992 and 19 September 1992; and Universities Funding Council, 1992; and Higher Education Funding Council for England, 1993).

The selection of economists for the 1996 economics panel involved a three-step process. First, the four funding bodies, Higher Education Funding Council for England, Scottish Higher Education Funding Council, Higher Education Funding Council for Wales, and Department of Education Northern Ireland, drawing upon the advice of the previous chair, appointed his successor. At this same time the Steering Committee of CHUDE sought nominations from its members and the names of the five economists with the most nominations were forwarded to the new chair for consideration. He accepted the CHUDE list. Drawing upon the nominations submitted by other learned and professional bodies and in consultation with the chairman of CHUDE, and the previous chair, the new chair also appointed four additional economists to the panel. The identities of the panel members were made known in July 1995 (Higher Education Funding Council for England, 1994 and 1995A; and Standing Committee, 25 February 1995 and 15 May 1995).

Central to the RAE is that the method of assessment used by the various panels produced ratings which meant the same thing across all subject areas. It is also essential to the Exercise that the method of assessment used by a panel produced ratings which meant the same thing across all departments within a subject area. For the 1989 RAE, the members of the economics panel initially read all the submissions and gave each of them an independent mark.[8] Each department was also assigned one member of the panel who considered its submission in detail. A lengthy meeting was then held where the individual submission marks were considered in conjunction with the department reports and a rating for each department determined. Similarly for the 1992 RAE, each submission was read by each panel member from which a provisional ranking of the departments derived. For the twenty borderline departments, each of them was allocated two panel members who also read and reported on the cited publications, as well as considering other aspects of its submission. This second evaluation was used to determine the final rating of the borderline departments. The 1996 economics panel largely followed the methods used by the 1992 panel (Griffith, 1995; Higher Education Funding Council for England, 1993 and 1995B; Minutes of the Conference of Heads of University Departments of Economics, 4 November 1989 and 21 May 1993; and Feinstein, 1995).

Panel assessors

The main criterion for the selection of economists to the assessment panel was pre-eminence in research in one or more of the subject areas of economics. While it is difficult to concretize pre-eminence in research, one indication of it, in light of the emphasis economists place on journal publications, would be the number of publications a panel member has in core mainstream or non-mainstream journals. Using the *SSCI: Source Index* as the basis, it is possible to determine the number of journal publications of each of the 1989, 1992, and 1996 panel members published for the period 1966 to 1994, the percentage of the publications which appeared in core mainstream and non-mainstream journals, and the percentage of core mainstream journals in which the publications occurred. A summary of the computations is presented in Table 11.1.

Table 11.1   Journal publications 1966–1994 of RAE panel members

Assessment Panel	1989	1992	1996
Number of publications as listed in the *SSCI: Source Index* for the *period* :	*1966 –1988*	*1971 –1992*	*1971 –1994*
	93	162	235
% of publications in MAINSTREAM journals	76%	76%	65%
% of publications in NON-MAINSTREAM journals	4%	3%	10%
% of CORE MAINSTREAM journals in which publications occurred	51%*	68%**	66%**

*   (excluding International Journal of Industrial Organization, Empirical Economics, European Journal of Political Economy, and Recherches Economiques de Louvain).

**   (excluding Empirical Economics, European Journal of Political Economy, and Recherches Economiques de Louvain).

 It is clear from the table that as a group, the assessors on the 1989, 1992, and 1996 panels were well-published and that over half of their publications appeared in core mainstream journals.[9] Thus, they would appear to fulfill the criteria of pre-eminence in mainstream research at the time the Research Assessment Exercises took place.
    However, a closer examination revealed that six of the nineteen panel members had published on average less than three articles, whereas the other thirteen members had on average published twenty-eight articles. Hence, it could be argued that nearly a third of the panel members had not fulfilled the criterion of pre-eminence in research.

The secondary criteria used to select panel members was subject coverage. Table 11.1 shows that overall the 1989, 1992, and 1996 panel members published in only 51%, 68%, and 66% of the core mainstream journals respectively; while a closer inspection of the data shows that none of the 1989, 1992, and 1996 panel members actually published in more than 36% of the core mainstream journals. The mainstream journals in which the panel members had not published were mostly specialist, applied, and interdisciplinary journals. Thus, none of the assessment panels can be said to have covered all of mainstream economics as represented by the core mainstream journals.[10] Furthermore, the Tables reveal the near absence of publications in non-mainstream journals by members of all three panels (except for the lone Post-Keynesian economist on the 1996 assessment panel), which suggests that the panel members *may* not have the expertise or knowledge to judge the quality of non-mainstream economics submissions. This point is reinforced in Table 11.2 below, which is based on the references the 1989, 1992, and 1996 panel members (excluding the Post-Keynesian) made in their published articles. Finally, except for the Post-Keynesian, almost none of the non-mainstream references of the remaining eighteen panel members suggest that they were familiar with Marxian, Sraffian, or Institutionalist economics.

Table 11.2   1989, 1992, and 1996 panel members' references

Total number of references	7,953
Percentage of references to core mainstream journals	37%
Percentage of references to core non-mainstream journals and other publications	1.4%

Peer review, a divided economics, and the Research Assessment Exercise

The unilateral managerialist imposition of the RAE on university economics departments and their economists, coupled with financial penalties for non-compliance, gives the exercise a distinct air of authoritarianism, by definition contrary to the spirit of peer review. Nevertheless, the nomination of economists for the 1989 and 1992 economics panels could have been reasonably open and democratic and thereby fulfill an important criterion of the peer review process, but this was not the case. As noted in Section 4, the decision by the RES, CHUDE, and The Standing Conference of Heads of Economics in Polytechnics to solicit nominations only from the heads of economics departments meant that the large majority of economists were judged by "peers" whom they had no involvement in selecting and whom they might not, therefore, recognize as such. The behind-closed-doors selections of two economists to the 1992 economics panel simply highlights the undemocratic nature of the process by which the members of the economics panels were selected. Moreover, most economists did not actually voluntarily agree to have the peers on the economics panels assess their research and this also undermines the legitimacy of the peer review process and hence of the assessment exercise itself. The legitimacy of the peer review process and the assessment exercise was further undermined because the economics panels did not provide reasons and explanations for the results they reached for each department and there was no way for a department to actually appeal against its rating if it thought it unfair.[11]

If the above were *all* the faults with the peer review process operated by the RAE, the end results of the Exercise would probably have had little more adverse effect on the future of non-mainstream economists in economics departments and their research than on their mainstream colleagues. But, as established in the previous section, not all the members of the 1989 and 1992 assessment panels were qualified to evaluate all areas of economic research. This clear violation of the central tenets of peer review further undermines the legitimacy of the peer review process underlying RAE. Moreover, given the method of assessment used by the 1989 and 1992 economics panels, these faults had serious consequences for the assessing of the quality of non-mainstream research publications. That is, for the method of assessment used by the two panels to produce comparable ratings of publications and departments, it was necessary that each panel member be relatively familiar with the economic subject matter in each and all submissions. However, the panel members in neither Exercise had published in more than 36% of the core mainstream journals, had not in their references to their publications cited all of the core mainstream journals, and were unfamiliar with the subject matter of non-mainstream economics. Therefore, one can only wonder how a panel member could have rated a publication in non-mainstream journals, such as the *Cambridge Journal of Economics, Capital and Class, Journal of Post Keynesian Economics*, or *Journal of Economic Issues, vis-à-vis* a publication in mainstream journals, such as *The Economic Journal, Review of Economic Studies, European Economic Review*, or *Kyklos*.[12] Similarly, one can only wonder how the members of either panel could believe that they could reach a comparable rating for each department when the department submissions contained subject matter with which the panel members were not entirely familiar.

In one sense, the 1992 panel members realized that they failed on both accounts when they admitted that they ranked journals differently and dealt with interdisciplinary research unsatisfactorily. Moreover, by not explicitly taking steps to ensure that the assessing procedures were open to non-mainstream research, they could not help but be biased when rating them.[13] For example, a survey of the 1992 RAE publication submissions of seven 5-rated, eight 4-rated, eleven 3-rated, and three 2-rated university economics departments revealed twenty-five publications in non-mainstream core journals. Four of those publications were in three 5-rated departments, none were in 4-rated departments, fourteen were in eight 3-rated departments, and seven were in two 2-rated departments. Thus it appears that if a department publication submission included a significant proportion of publications in core non-mainstream journals, it would most likely receive a 2 or 3 rating (Minutes of the Conference of Heads of University Departments of Economics, 4 November 1989, 21 May 1993).

Interestingly, members of both panels stated that there were no profound disagreements with regard to rating individual publications or departments as a whole or that there was any discrimination against non-mainstream research. While such claims would startle knowledgeable researchers on peer review, it is only to be expected for economics.[14] It has already been established that core mainstream journals form a closed self-referencing system and that mainstream economics has come to resemble a paradigm-bound normal science where the practitioners only converse with themselves. As a consequence, the community of mainstream economists have a vested interest in mainstream economic theory and, by their very adherence to it, cannot see the evidence which might support an alternative view. It is not that new knowledge is not rewarded within mainstream economics. Indeed all academic labor processes, by their very nature, demand intellectual innovation and reward it in the reputations which are achieved by individuals amongst their peers. The knowledge which is produced, however, has to fit in with that which is already established. In paradigm-bound mainstream economics what is defined as knowledge at all has to conform with the neoclassical theoretic core, otherwise it is regarded at best as irrelevant, at worst as incompetent and unscientific. It is this kind of orthodoxy which has been achieved by mainstream economics and with it the attitude that those outside the mainstream are generally inferior economists whose research lacks any real economic value (Flemming, 1995; Feinstein, 1995; and Harley and Lee, 1997).

The overriding propensity of mainstream economists to judge all economic research *vis-à-vis* the theoretic core of neoclassical theory meant that it was relatively easy for the members of the 1989 and 1992 economic panels to produce "comparable" ratings of publications and economics departments. That is, it was not important for the panel members to have detailed knowledge of all areas of economic research. Instead, all that they had to do when evaluating a research publication submission was to judge it on its congruence with the theoretic core of mainstream economics and ignore its other substantive content. Since the adherence to and/or understanding of the theoretic core was more or less the same for all panel members, as indicated by their journal publications (see Table 11.1), they could independently arrive at the same evaluation of a research publication submission and of a department as a whole. Therefore, it is not surprising that they had no profound disagreements with regard to rating individual publications or departments. Panel members could evaluate non-mainstream publications, with which they were relatively unfamiliar, in a consistent manner — that of being incongruent with the core of mainstream economics and hence of lesser value than mainstream research.

Non-mainstream economics after the 1992 Research Assessment Exercise

The combination of peer review and the RAE has produced an institutional arrangement in the form of an economics panel which, because of its control over funding, has the power to affect the type of economic research carried out by British economists. Since the selection process promoted by the RES and carried out by CHUDE ensured that the members of the 1989 and 1992 economics panels were, with one possible exception, mainstream economists, the message that the panels sent out was that research in mainstream economics and publications in core mainstream journals was what was necessary for university economics departments to maintain or increase their research funding. This message was reinforced by the evaluation of research submitted to them and the ranking of departments. Consequently, since the 1992 RAE, economic departments have taken steps in the areas of recruitment policy and the direction of both departmental and individual work to emphasise mainstream research and de-emphasise and discriminate against non-mainstream research (Minutes of the Conference of Heads of University Departments of Economics, 4 November 1989; and BBC, 1995).

For example, a survey of economists located in economics departments in British universities, Harley and Lee (1997)[15] showed that while the recruitment policies of some of the older universities have always emphasised mainstream research and publications in core mainstream journals and a desire not to hire non-mainstream economists (and these were the ones rated most highly by the RAE), there has been a noticeable shift towards a mainstream recruitment policy in others, with a concurrent positive disinclination to recruit non-mainstream economists (all quoted in Harley and Lee, 1997):

> ...research rating potential a prime consideration. Idea of looking for non-mainstream people now inconceivable.

> ...the authorities are looking for mainstream economists to bolster their credit rating in the Research exercise.

> ...recently, main criterion seems to have been ability to publish in mainstream journals — in the past, judging from the composition of the department, things were different.

> ...formerly head-hunted non-mainstream economists. Now no
> longer sought by my department....I was appointed professor in
> 1989. I would probably not even be included in an interview shortlist
> now.

Furthermore, large numbers of British economists felt themselves directly affected
by the 1989 and 1992 economics panels' apparent view that national and
international research excellence was restricted to mainstream economics and
publishing in core mainstream journals:

> ...the whole concept of 'core journals' has got a firmer grip on the
> profession than say 10 years ago. What counts about an article now
> is where it's published rather than what it says.

> ...research geared towards potentially core-publishable papers.
> Down-grading of lower-power interdisciplinary related conferences
> and research.

> ...awareness of (supposed!) criteria for RAE permeates all research
> and publication activities.

> ...our department has a very strong view about what "journals"
> count and applies this vigorously.

> ...pressure to do the sort of work [publishing in core journals] which
> will assist the department in its ratings.

The survey revealed that the de-emphasis of and discrimination against non-
mainstream research in the pursuit of research funding by economics departments
had spilled over into the hiring of non-mainstream economists and the teaching
of non-mainstream economic courses. The most immediate and visible evidence
of this was found in the actual hiring of economists by fifty-seven of the fifty-
eight departments which participated in the 1992 RAE for the period 1992 —
1994. Advertisements for posts ranging from lectureships to chairs predominantly
favored mainstream economists while the criteria for making appointments
narrowed to publications in core mainstream journals. This resulted in interviews
where candidates were directly asked in which core mainstream journals they
intended to publish. It also meant that non-mainstream economists on probation
or temporary contracts were coerced into doing mainstream research (quoted
in Harley and Lee, 1997):

> I am a Marxist, but since I am on probation until January 1 have been
> forced to do mostly mainstream research or else I know I wouldn't
> be made permanent.

> I personally have been interviewed at other universities where it has
> been clear that publishing in core journals is the criteria.

...in my inquiries regarding other posts at older universities I have been asked about research interests and the RAE and journals have been signalled. At a selection committee of a large older university I was recently asked directly which journals I aim to publish in over the coming 2 years.

...on advice from a present colleague, when I applied for my current post, I stressed my ability to teach mainstream micro. I also told them that my research interest was general equilibrium. Subsequently I "came out" and pointed out my research as Marxist equilibrium. I doubt I would have got my present post had I not pursued this little deception.

Consequently, while forty-three of the fifty-eight economic departments had non-mainstream economists, only sixteen departments have hired non-mainstream economists (see Table 11.3). More significantly, although non-mainstream economists constitute at least 20% of academic economists in British economic

Table 11.3

1992 RAE Rating:	5	4	3	2	1	Not rated
No. of Old University Economics Departments	10	13	21	3	—	6
No. of New University Economics Departments	0	0	1*	7	3	15
No. of Old University Economics Departments hiring Mainstream Economists — 1992–94	1	1	6	3	—	3
No. of New University Economics Departments hiring Non-Mainstream Economists — 1992–94	—	—	1	4	—	8
No. of Mainstream Economists*** hired 1992–94	69	69	139	39	7	40
No. of Non-Mainstream Economists*** hired 1992–94	1	1	15	14	-	16

*   De Montfort University has been included.

**   Thames Valley University and Buckinghamshire College of Higher Education each received a "1" rating, but we have no responses from them to our questionnaire.

***   These are subjective estimates of respondents; they include both permanent and temporary appointments.

(Questionnaire Survey, October 1994)

departments, of the 354 economists hired on temporary and permanent contracts by the fifty-seven hiring economic departments, less than 9% were non-mainstream economists. Finally, the disaggregated data on which Table 11.3 is based shows that three of the sixteen departments have hired 50% of the non-mainstream economists and that the sixteen departments as a group have hired more mainstream than non-mainstream economists (48 vs. 31). Thus the impact of the RAE on hiring has been to reduce the employment possibilities of non-mainstream economists in British university economics departments and to "pressure" those departments most open to non-mainstream economists to hire mainstream economists as well.[16]

Conclusion: the future of non-mainstream economics

The UGC established the RAE as an institutional mechanism to provide it with a rationale for distributing research funds among university departments of a given subject area. Central to the Exercise is the assessment panel made up of pre-eminent peers who rate the research excellence of a department and thereby determine the amount of research monies it will get. Perhaps not initially intended to affect the areas of research carried out by British academics, the assessment panels in fact have that capability through their control of the allocation of research monies. Before the RAE, the dominance of mainstream economics in British economics departments and among British economists was largely due to the degree to which the leadership of the Royal Economic Society had maintained control over the 'reputational' system that is central to the organization of academic work. The advent of the RAE with its economics panel could have posed a potential threat to this dominance. It did not. Instead, by virtue of their already dominant position, the leadership of the RES was able to capture the process by which assessors were appointed to the economics panel. In particular, the Society actively supported the establishment of CHUDE in 1987, whose most important activity was the selection of RES-acceptable candidates for the economics panels. Consequently, the assessors appointed to the 1989 and 1992 panels had the characteristic of being overwhelmingly mainstream economists and of holding significant positions within the RES, such as a member of the Council or Executive Committee, Treasurer, or President, being on the editorial board of *The Economic Journal*, and/or being a member of the CHUDE Standing Committee.

Since the paradigm-bound view that the quality of non-mainstream research is largely inferior to mainstream research was for the most part accepted by these assessors, the two panels financially rewarded departments who did mainstream research and published in core mainstream journals and, in consequence, damned those who did not. The real threat of financial sanction by the economics panel has, in light of the declining financial support for universities and research, driven British economic departments to discriminate against non-mainstream research and the hiring of non-mainstream economists as well as to restrict if not eliminate the teaching of non-mainstream economics to students. For example, evidence from our survey suggests that following on the departure of a member of an economics department who took particular interest in teaching a non-mainstream course, effort was generally not made to retain the course by hiring a suitable replacement:

> We had a senior member of staff who was a Marxist — but it would be unthinkable to replace him with a Marxist economist on retirement. Hence his course in Marxist political economy was dropped. (quoted in Harley and Lee, 1997)

Evidence from our survey also suggests that many departments do not make an effort to retain Marxian economics courses when their enrolments decline or to offer M.A. and M.Phil. programmes which contain non-mainstream modules.[17] The partially engineered decline in student demand for non-mainstream courses reduces any pressure on economics departments to hire non-mainstream economists and thereby provides an additional rationale for their exclusion (Minutes of the Conference of Heads of University Departments of Economics, 5 November 1988; Standing Committee, 22 February 1992; Murphy, 1994; and BBC, 1995).

The cleansing process that is under way in British economics departments was not altered by the 1996 RAE. As before, the selection process was not open; there was behind-closed-doors selection of four panel members; not all panel members were pre-eminent in research; and the panel members were not qualified to evaluate all areas of economic research. Furthermore, the RES through CHUDE guided the selection of economists to the economics panel, with the predictable outcome that all but one panel member held a leadership position within the Society, helped edit *The Economic Journal*, and/or was a member of the CHUDE Standing Committee. With the exception of a Post Keynesian and a development economist, the remaining panel members were part of the closed self-referencing group of mainstream economists who publish in core mainstream journals; were influenced by articles, arguments and concerns contained within these core mainstream journals; and were not influenced by the arguments and concerns of economists who publish in the core non-mainstream journals. Finally, the assessment criteria delineated by the 1996 panel emphasises the members' *subjective* but professional judgement of the quality of journals and of published works, and publications in internationally reputed journals (Higher Education Funding Council for England, 1995b).

The combination of panel members' intellectual allegiance to mainstream economics with the panel's assessment criteria made it, therefore, unlikely that the presence of one non-mainstream economist would be able to challenge the profession's historical tendency to reward mainstream and discourage non-mainstream research. This turned out to be the case. The nineteen economic departments in the old and new universities which improved their 1992 research ratings in the 1996 RAE deliberately hired almost exclusively mainstream economists (82 versus 7 non-mainstream economists), with the seven most noted examples hiring 48 mainstream and only 2 non-mainstream economists between them. On the other hand, the ten economics departments which did not improve upon their 1 to 3 ratings in the 1992 RAE hired 37 mainstream *and* 17 non-mainstream economists. Thus, the message is clear; improvement in research rating is highly correlated with the near exclusive hiring of mainstream economists. Hence, it is more than likely that economics departments will attempt to improve their rating for the next RAE by even more positive discrimination towards mainstream economists and mainstream economics independent of any non-mainstream representation on the panel.

The ongoing discrimination against non-mainstream economists and their research has resulted in few young non-mainstream economists obtaining university teaching and research positions. As a consequence, within ten years or so, the number of non-mainstream economists in British university economics departments will decline significantly.[18] Such a decline will result in the virtual disappearance of non-mainstream economists from the vast majority of economic departments, with the remainder ageing and increasingly invisible. For non-mainstream economics to have a chance of surviving in British economics departments, we suggest — at the very least — the democratization of the peer review process underlying the RAE by opening-up the selection of the economics panel and making it accountable to all its constituents. The extent to which this is possible in the context of an authoritarian management-led research selectivity exercise is open to question; but without it we believe there is no future for non-mainstream economics.

Notes

1. The 1986 RAE consisted of the UGC asking British universities to complete a four part questionnaire covering various aspects of their research income and expenditure, research planning, priorities, and output. The responses received were considered by the UGC's subject subcommittees and were rated against a variety of scales and standards (Phillimore, 1989).
2. A further advertisement in *The Guardian* (June 14, 1994) noted that the appointee to the Chair in Economic Theory must be an active researcher, contributing at the leading edge of *mainstream economic theory*; and in another advertisement in the November 8, 1994 *The Guardian* stated that the appointee must be an active researcher, contributing at the leading edge of mainstream macroeconomics, either theoretical or applied.

3. In 1994-95 we obtained some twenty job specifications by sending for details of posts advertised in the educational press. Out of these, only three did not specify an area of interest within mainstream economics or make reference to ranking in the 1992 RAE.

4. A second area of research would be to examine the impact of the RAE on the work and employment of academic economists in economic departments in both the old and new universities in the UK. The working hypothesis of the research would be that the existence of lists of core mainstream journals which are believed to count most in the ranking exercise poses a serious risk to academic diversity within the discipline—see Harley and Lee (1997).

5. The authors obtained their evidence for these statements from the *Journal Citation Reports* of the Social Science Citation Index. The evidence can be obtained from the authors upon request.

6. There are, however, alternative approaches to peer review -see Roy (1982 and 1984) and Lock (1985).

7. The process of working with learned societies as well as directly appointing individuals is the customary way peer review panels are selected in the UK. Direct democratic elections of peers, which in fact occurs in Germany, is not thought to be an appropriate way of choosing researchers for peer review panels in the UK (Advisory Board for the Research Councils, 1990).

8. This claim made at the 4 November 1989 meeting of CHUDE is at variance with the comment made in personal correspondence by one panel member who said that he based his provisional assessment on the documentation and bibliographies and did not read the published research at all systematically.

9. In addition, the panel members published and/or edited over fifty books between them.

10. This point is further reinforced by scanning the references of the articles published by the panel members. The 1989, 1992, and 1996 panel members referenced over 80% of the mainstream journals; however, most of the references were restricted to the smaller set of journals in which their own work appeared. The little referenced and un-referenced journals were the specialists, applied, and interdisciplinary journals. The ignored journals included the *Journal of Development Economics, Journal of Financial Economics, International Journal of Industrial Organization, Public Finance, Regional Studies, Urban Studies,* and *Journal of Transport Economics and Policy.*

11. For an extended discussion of this point with regard to the clinical dentistry panel, see Griffith (1995).

12. This also applies to the subject matter of history of economic thought, comparative economic systems, regional economics, and transport economics, one can only guess how they rated publications in *Journal of Asian and African Studies, History of Political Economy, Regional Studies,* and *Journal of Transport Economics and Policy* vis-à-vis publications in *The Economic Journal* for instance. This point is important

since the managing editor of *The Economic Journal* has stated that he rejected submissions in history of economic thought when he believed that the emphasis was on the history as opposed to the economics (Hey, 1995, 1996A, and 1996B).

13. The Advisory Board for the Research Councils made this general point in their review of peer review (Advisory Board for the Research Councils, 1990, p. 31).

14. Lack of consensus when rating the value of a piece of research, bias against individual researchers and particular subjects, bias against researchers at low-status institutions, cronyism, discrimination against certain types of research (such as applied research and non-orthodox research), making major errors of assessment, and making assessments which lack scientific rigor have long been noted as possible problems with peer review; and no peer review system can be said to have completely escaped them. Furthermore, peer review presupposes that *everybody* in the research "community" shares the same value scale as to what is good and bad research which is reasonably unique. Such consensus has never existed in any research community and certainly does not exist in a divided research community such as economics. Finally, it has been widely acknowledged that peer review can be mechanism used by those who support the ruling paradigm to reinforce their hegemony (Peters and Ceci, 1982; Roy, 1982 and 1984; Lock, 1985; Smith, 1988B; Leslie, 1990; and McCutchen, 1991).

15. In 1994 we sent out a total of 1000 questionnaires to British economists asking them a series of questions about the impact of the RAE on their own research and department recruitment and research policies. Some 380 questionnaires were returned from 79 universities. For further details about the survey and its findings, see Harley and Lee (1997).

16. This point is reinforced by looking at the NR in Table 11.3. This shows that 21 British universities did not have their economic "departments" assessed by the 1992 economics panel. Even though eleven of the departments have hired approximately one-third of the non-mainstream economists, they hired two and half times as many mainstream economists. Therefore, the survival of non-mainstream economics outside of economics departments is problematical as well.

17. This point is driven home by the following comment on the Scottish doctoral programme:

> All the old universities in Scotland have agreed to accept PhD candidates only through this programme which has a highly neo-classical masters component. Thus, no Scottish economist can, as far as I can see, avoid being trained as a purely neo-classical economist. I have no knowledge of any attempts by the organisers to extend recognition of any schools beyond the mainstream ones (Quoted by Harley and Lee, 1997).

18. Nearly 60% of the non-mainstream economists who responded to our survey have been in higher education since before 1979.

References

Advisory Board for the Research Councils (1990) *Peer Review*. London, Advisory Board for the Research Councils.

BBC (1995) Radio 4: *File on 4 — Research Assessment Exercise*, November 28.

Conference of Heads of University Departments of Economics (1988–1994) *Minutes*, Royal Economic Society.

Culyer, T. (1994) 'A Proposal for a Checklist of Reputable Economics Journals for the UK Profession', *Royal Economic Society Newsletter* 87, October: 16-17.

Diamond, A. (1989) 'The Core Journals in Economics', *Current Contents* 21: 4-11.

Feinstein, C. (1995) Personal communication, 25 September.

Flemming, F. (1995) Personal communication, 18 September.

Griffith, J. (1995) *Research Assessment: As Strange a Maze as e'er Men Trod*. Report No. 4, Council for Academic Freedom and Academic Standards.

Harley, S. and Lee, F. A. (1997) 'The Academic Labour Process and the Research Assessment Exercise: Academic Diversity and the Future of Non-Mainstream Economics in UK Universities', *Human Relations*.

Hey, J. D. (1995) 'Managing Editor's Annual Report on the EJ', *Royal Economic Society Newsletter* 88, January: 2-3.

———— (1996a) 'The Economic Journal: Report of the Managing Editor', *Royal Economic Society Newsletter* 92, January: 3-5.

———— (1996b) Letter to J. Toporowski, 22 February.

Higher Education Funding Council for England (1993) *A Report for the Universities Funding Council on the Conduct of the 1992 Research Assessment Exercise*, June.

————(1994) *Conduct of the 1996 Research Assessment Exercise: Panel Membership and Units of Assessment*, June.

————(1995a) *1996 Research Assessment Exercise: Membership of Assessment Panels*, July.

———— (1995b) *1996 Research Assessment Exercise: Criteria for Assessment*, November.

Hodgson, G. (1995) 'In Which Journals Should We Publish?', *European Association Evolutionary Political Economy Newsletter*, 11, January: 6-8.

Hubbard, P. M. (1995) Personal communication, April 11.

Leslie, C. (1990) 'Scientific Racism: Reflections on Peer Review', Science and Ideology, *Social Science and Medicine*, 31 (8): 891-912.

Lock, S. (1985) *A Difficult Balance: Editorial Peer Review in Medicine*, London, The Nuffield Provincial Hospitals Trust.

McCutchen, C. W. (1991) 'Peer Review: Treacherous Servant, Disastrous Master', *Technology Review*, October: 29-40.

Murphy, P. S. (1994) 'Research Quality, Peer Review and Performance Indicators', *The Australian Universities' Review*, 37 (1): 14-18.

Peters, D. P. and Ceci, S. J. (1982) 'Peer-Review Practices of Psychological Journals: The Fate of Published Articles, Submitted Again', *The Behavioral and Brain Sciences*, 5: 187 -195.

Phillimore, A. J. (1989) 'University Research Performance Indicators in Practice: The University Grants Committee's Evaluation of British Universities, 1985-86', *Research Policy*, 18: 255-271.

Presley, J. (1994) Letter to David Greenaway, November 8.

Robertson, J. (ed) (1992) *1991 Social Science Citation Index: Journal Citation Reports*. Philadelphia: Institute for Scientific Information, Inc.

—— (1993) *1992 Social Science Citation Index: Journal Citation Reports*. Philadelphia: Institute for Scientific Information, Inc.

—— (1994) *1993 Social Science Citation Index: Journal Citation Reports*. Philadelphia: Institute for Scientific Information, Inc.

Roy, R. (1982) 'Peer Review of Proposals — Rationale, Practice and Performance', *Bulletin of Science and Technology in Society*, 2: 505-422.

—— (1984) 'Alternatives to Review by Peers: A Contribution to the Theory of Scientific Choice', *Minerva*, 22: 316-328.

Smith, R. (1988a) 'Peering into the Bowels of the MRC–II: Review Systems', *British Medical Journal*, 296, 20 February: 556-560.

—— (1988b) 'Problems with Peer Review and Alternatives', *British Medical Journal*, 296, 12 March: 774-777.

Standing Committee (1989-1994) Conference of Heads of University Departments of Economics, Minutes, Royal Economic Society.

Universities Funding Council (1989) *Report on the 1989 Research Assessment Exercise*, December.

—— (1992) *Research Assessment Exercise 1992 Membership of Assessment Panels*, 24/92.

Appendix A   List of Core Journals (Diamond, 1989)

American Economic Review

Brookings Papers on Economic Activity

Canadian Journal of Economics

Econometrica

Economic Inquiry

Economic Journal

Economica

Economics Letters

European Economic Review

International Economic Review

Journal of Development Economics

Journal of Econometrics

Journal of Economic Literature

Journal of Economic Theory

Journal of Financial Economics

Journal of International Economics

Journal of Labour Economics

Journal of Law and Economics

Journal of Mathematical Economics

Journal of Monetary Economics

Journal of Political Economy

Journal of Public Economics

Oxford Economic Papers

Quarterly Journal of Economics

Rand Journal of Economics

Review of Economics and Statistics

Review of Economic Studies

Possible Additions to the List (UK.)

Oxford Bulletin of Economics and Statistics

Journal of Industrial Economics

The Manchester School of Economic and Social Studies

Bulletin of Economic Research

Scottish Journal of Political Economy

Applied Economics

Possible Additions to the List (European)

Scandinavian Journal of Economics

International Journal of Industrial Organisation

Recherches Economiques de Louvain

Weltwirtschaftliches Archiv

Empirical Economics

European Journal of Political Economy

Kyklos

Interdisciplinary or Specialist Journal in which

Economists Frequently Publish

Public Finance

Regional Studies

British Journal of Industrial Relations

Economic Modelling

Urban Studies

Journal of the Royal Statistical Society

Journal of Transport Economics and Policy

Appendix B   Core Non-Mainstream Journals

SSCI Non-Mainstream Journals
[All the journals listed below are fully covered in the SSCI]:

American Journal of Economics and Sociology

Cambridge Journal of Economics

Economy and Society

International Journal of Social Economics

Journal of Economic Behavior and Organization [This follows the classification in Hodgson, 1995]

Journal of Economic Issues

Journal of Economic Studies [This follows the classification in Hodgson, 1995]

Journal of Post Keynesian Economics

Monthly Review [Monthly Review is addressed to a non-specialized readership, thereby affecting the extent to which it is cited in specialist academic journals)

New Left Review

Review of Social Economy

Science and Society

Other Non-Mainstream Journals
[All the journals listed below are either selectively covered by the Social Science Citation Index or are not covered at all:

British Review of Economic Issues

Capital and Class

Contributions to Political Economy

Eastern Economic Journal

International Papers in Political Economy

International Review of Applied Economics

Review of Political Economy

Review of Radical Political Economy

On Whether it is Better to be Loved than Feared: Managerialism and Women in Universities

12

Heather Clark, Jim Barry and John Chandler

The participation of women in higher education is patchy, passionate and peculiar because we are living through a period in which vigorous reforms are taking place with a view to establishing fair or equal chances in what remains, despite many slights and denials, one of the most attractive careers for women in paid employment in modern society. (Halsey, 1995: 216)

Introduction

This chapter focuses on two developments in higher education in Britain: the increasing numbers of women to be found in academe and the role of managerialism in university life. Neglected for many years, interest has been shown recently in both of these areas, though consideration of the relationship between women and managerialism in the academy is still somewhat thin on the ground.

Our purpose is to consider women's presence and their relationship to managerial control, exercised as it is presently in universities almost exclusively by men, through a case study of two institutions: one new and one old university. Using material from interviews with female academics and administrators we explore their accommodation, resistance and opposition to forms of control being exercised in universities in Britain today. Because of the limited empirical base of our research we make no grand claims for generalisability. Instead we offer speculations on the role of women in the changing context of university life which continues to be subjected to the rigours of economic restructuring and clamour of management-speak in a context of increased political and public surveillance.

Women in higher education

Writing in 1980, Sandra Acker set out to consider the question of women's prospects in universities. Noting that little "research [had] been done on the everyday experiences of women academics", she nevertheless identified problems for women as deriving from the competing demands of career and family, male control and marginalisation.

In 1993, returning to the issue, she documented the position of women in the lower level, insecure, ranks of British universities, noting that still the "literature on academic women in Britain [was] rather sparse, probably reflecting a tendency to consider them members of an elite rather than a disadvantaged group worthy of feminist concern" (Acker, 1994: 135-7). What accounts there were tended to occupy themselves with role conflict and discrimination or cast women as a reserve army or as subjected to patriarchal control, reflecting Liberal, Socialist and Radical feminist concerns respectively; with an almost deafening silence surrounding ethnic composition. Yet women, she suggested, seemed unlikely to be in a position to do very much about this: "women academics are too scattered to provide a critical mass" (p. 148).

From available research we know that women traditionally have been under-represented in higher education in Britain, although the gap has been narrowing and is smaller in the 'new' universities compared to the 'old' (Halsey, 1995: 221-222). A gap is also in evidence in a large number of other countries as shown in **Table 12.1**.

Women are also poorly represented in senior academic and administrative positions in Higher Education (c. f. Lie and O'Leary, 1990; and Lie and Malik, 1994: p209). This is in common with women in other occupations and professions in Britain (Hansard Society, 1990); and even those who are in the university sector, particularly in lecturing and research, are more likely than men to be found in vulnerable fixed-term contract employment, as part-time lecturer, teaching associate or assistant and contract researcher: posts which are usually "low paid [as well as] very often female" (Davies and Holloway, 1995: 15; and Morley, 1994: 194). Furthermore, whilst universities have not always been hospitable places for women, the increasing emphasis on the quantity of research output generally, along with intensified forms of work, leave "weekends and evenings as the only realistic time when personal research can be carried out", something detrimental to women with domestic responsibilities (Davies and Holloway, 1995: 12-16).

Published research also tells us that women (as well as men) in the Higher Education Sector along with Further Education are suffering stress, associated with styles of management; with the Educational Press now carrying stories of bullying. Earley's (1994: 11-12) study into stress for NATFHE, the University and College Lecturers' Union, whilst more representative of Further Education, found poor communication and 'macho management' not uncommon, with one Higher Education lecturer (gender unspecified) referring to a "confrontational and

Table 12.1   Relative position of women in higher education

	% of Faculty who are Female	% of Full Professors who are Female
Poland	31. 7	16. 9
Bulgaria	30. 8	12. 0
France	27. 1	11. 4
USA	26. 0	14. 0
Turkey	25. 0	20. 0
Russia	24. 3	11. 3
Norway	24. 2	9. 3
China	23. 8	11. 0
Greece	20. 5	6. 3
UK	20. 5	4. 9
Australia	18. 6	7. 4
E. Germany	18. 6	4. 9
W. Germany	16. 6	5. 2
Botswana	13. 9	—
Netherlands	13. 2	2. 3
Pakistan	11. 8	4. 2
Iran	11. 0	5. 9

Source: Lie and Malik (1994: 208)

dictatorial management style" and another commenting that "Middle managers have forgotten they are dealing with people". One respondent remarked "all jobs have some degree of stress but sometimes this stress is 'artificially' caused by managerial actions and attitudes". As the third largest area of local authority expenditure and the second (with Health) largest central government expenditure (Ferguson, 1994: 93), education has clearly not been immune from political interest, with "the methods of managerial capitalism…entering and re-shaping the academy" (Morley and Walsh, 1995: 1).

There were clearly political concerns voiced from at least the early 1980s to seek efficiencies and economies from universities (Parker and Jary, 1995: 322) and the importance of the Jarratt Report (1985) should not be overlooked. Parker and Jary (1995: 324) emphasise perhaps the most significant aspects of Jarratt's proposals as being:

> ...the centralization of executive control, the linkage between budgetary and academic considerations and the decentralization of accountable budgets to the lowest level.

Jarratt's (1985) observation that "[the] crucial issue is how a university achieves the maximum value for money consonant with its objectives" (p. 12) certainly underlines an economic agenda to be pursued vigorously by a Vice-Chancellor who is not only an "academic leader but also ... chief executive" (p. 36), ensuring that "strategic plans" link "academic, financial and physical aspects" into "one corporate process"(p. 36). Jarratt makes it quite clear that in their view "universities are first and foremost corporate enterprises" (p. 22). In a discussion of the role of Head of Department, Jarratt makes a telling comment:

> Ideally the [Head of Department] should be both a manager and an academic leader. However the most eminent and able academic, as judged by the standards of research or teaching, is not always the person most fitted to manage a department. We take the view that it is preferable to retain the two functions in one person. In circumstances where this is impracticable, we believe the head of department must possess the requisite managerial capabilities and that he [sic] should be encouraged to delegate some part of the responsibility for academic leadership to others. (Jarratt Report, 1985: 28)

In some respects, this issue parallels that raised by Machiavelli some five hundred years ago in the quotation that provides our title: whether (as a 'ruler') it is 'better to be loved than feared'[1]. That is, how should a manager, in order to be effective, be seen by the managed? This is a perennial problem for managers whose practices have (historically) oscillated, reflecting the changing face of fashionable theories of control.

These concerns are congruent with developments reflected in the literature on the public sector more generally, which discerns a growing pre-occupation with forms of managerial control, legitimated by a new discourse of managerial culture-speak and accompanied by a questioning of the conventional political wisdom of the so-called Social Democratic settlement associated with the work of Beveridge and Keynes.

Managerialism in the public sector

Recent trends towards the recruitment of private sector managers in the public sector, together with attempts to transform bureau-professionals into managers and increase the representation of business expertise on boards (Newman and Clarke, 1994: 25), are in tune with policies designed to roll back the frontiers of a dependency-creating welfare state and introduce the disciplines of the market.

But the questioning of the welfare discourse went beyond political considerations, with economic factors playing at least an equal part. Whilst we note Clarke *et al.*'s (1994: 1) caution that claims concerning cuts in levels of welfare provision may be overstated, there seems little doubt that an underlying economic agenda was linked to the political one (Cochrane, 1993: 118) in the context of a deepening global recession and a New Right obsession with efficiency, marketisation, business cultures and 'value for money'. This is the context in which ideas about managerialism in the public sector gained currency.

Cutler and Waine (1994: x, 22) see public sector managerialism — favoured by Conservative governments over New Right ideology — as "characterised by the belief that the objectives of social services such as health, education, personal social services or social security can be promoted at a lower cost when the appropriate management techniques are applied", and as appearing in four distinct manifestations: performance management, quasi markets, compulsory competitive tendering and pay determination. It also embraced private sector "values", leading Cochrane (1993: 106) to suggest that "managerialism [had] become the evangelism of the new age, linking private and public sectors", changing or attempting to change the very language of the public sector in the process and seeking the importation of managerial techniques and business values to support entrepreneurial strategies of privatisation, marketisation, flexibility and delayering of 'superfluous' levels of supervisors and managers in the precipitate scramble for efficiency.

In the public sector, the apparent respectability (and no doubt the promise) of the framework has been seen as particularly attractive to senior public servants, enabling attention to be given to "matters of morale and staff development" (Pollitt, 1990: 171-172). With managerial values cascading down from on high, the new charismatic leaders, imbued with entrepreneurial spirit, could show vision and flair and reveal the way out of the corporate wilderness, diverting attention from the fears of external threat to individuals and organisations alike and re-asserting in the process their own authority and "right to manage" (Clarke and Newman, 1993: 436).

The adoption of techniques of "culture management" (Pollitt, 1993: 187) is associated quite specifically with the likes of the management guru Tom Peters in some texts and is taken to herald the arrival of a "new managerialism" (c. f. Clarke and Newman, 1993; and Newman, 1994: 185) with some authors sensing a New Public Management (Hood, 1991: 3); though students of management will recognise features of earlier schools such as Human Relations and Organisation Development lurking in the background and operating both alongside and integrated with "continuing elements of neo-Taylorism" (Pollitt, 1993: 187). Indeed, the combination and co-existence of so many different strands of managerial tradition and practice leads us to wonder just how much there is in all this which is 'new' and what sway it holds. Yet the emphasis on cultural change in the recent attempts to control public sector organisations may well represent a new mood (Newman, 1995: 16-21), even if itself reminiscent of earlier neo-Durkheimian, Mayoite managerial thinking (Axtell Ray, 1986).

In many respects, of course, the management gurus who pronounce on the merits of 'strong' corporate cultures are merely offering a variation on the old theme of control. The elements which comprise much management thought and practice — Taylorism and Human Relations — offer 'overt coercion' or 'psychological persuasion' to what some will see as the same end. Yet there are differences which may be experienced differently, particularly in an era seemingly more sensitive to individual rights and freedoms. The language of the corporate culture merchants, who espouse empowerment and participation, may well have struck a chord with a generation of public service professionals with aspirations for an extension of social rights and citizenship — even if the harsher underlying realities of control remain yet unspoken.

The new 'management prophets' (Höpfl, 1992: 22) thus not only call for obedience — they also expect to be believed. Yet reports on lecturers in the higher (and further) education sectors in Britain suggest that they see through the Prince's new clothes. As one of the respondents in our research commented:

> I send the papers and it is as if they disappear into a black hole, I never get a response. [Theirs is an] autocratic approach. It's not the way I like to work.

Another put it this way:

> The changes to jobs [in organisations generally] count against women… it's all about quantity, there's no more quality… Women put a lot into communicating and more effort into helping others… so women will suffer trying to maintain overall standards. Women do an all-round job and will continue to try and do this…they find it hard to have a single minded goal, unlike men.

However, their comments, which seem to sense an iron fist in the velvet glove of the new prince, suggest more than a managerial style — new or otherwise — they point to perceived differences in terms of gender.

Masculine managerialism

The connection between a managerial cast of mind and masculinity is one made specifically by Clarke and Newman (1993: 431) who argue that:

> Historically…management has been archetypally masculine, associated with both behaviour and predispositions which resembled loosely packaged testosterone.

White (1995: 197) also notes the association of traditional leadership style with 'military hierarchies' and masculinity. Whether this remains true when managers espouse doctrines of culture-speak is an interesting question, especially as the new language is peppered with terms such as 'participation', 'empowerment' and 'team-working'. On the face of it this seems at one remove from the aggressive orientation being suggested and performance controls being advocated.

Indeed, on a superficial level at least, the pre-occupation with culture-management seems congruent with some expectations about women's preferred styles of management — a link made quite explicitly by Lunneborg (1990: 197) in her discussion of the work of Tom Peters. It is also in tune with Rosener's (1990: 120) research, sponsored by the International Women's Forum, which contended that women managers in non-traditional, medium-sized organisations developed what she called 'interactive leadership' styles which encouraged participation, shared power and influence, enhanced other people's self-worth and got them excited about their work; though the organisations she looked at were experiencing rapid change and may have been atypical.

There are, nonetheless, two difficulties in particular in linking managerialism and masculinity. First, the notion that women have a preferred style of leadership which is somehow 'participative' and 'caring' draws on a stereotype (some would say 'ideal-type') which may not be recognised by everyone and which can lead to gender-labelling of particular jobs, which in turn can result in women being ghettoised. Whilst the literature on the psycho-social moral development of young women may see an 'ethic of care', against a male 'logic of justice' (Gilligan, 1982), there is evidence to suggest that women are as capable as men of being purposeful, competitive and ambitious (Lunneborg, 1990: xviii;) and equally prepared to "succeed in business by being hard-nosed over ethical niceties" (Burke *et al.*, 1993: 24).

Second, there seem to be many 'masculinities' and 'patriarchies'. Hearn's (1992: 3) comment makes the point well, "there are effectively lots of patriarchies, dominated by different types of men, operating simultaneously, overlapping, interrelating, contradicting". The equation of managerialism with masculinity is thus at best problematic, though the simple fact of male predominance in senior organisational positions in the public sector does seem to have led to the experience of marginalisation by women who are made to feel outsiders — something apparent from our own research and noted for women in senior positions in other organisations (c. f. Coe, 1992; Faludi, 1992; and Marshall, 1995).

If there is a growing preoccupation with managerialism and control in Higher Education it seems to have been manifested in differing ways. As we have seen, it has been accompanied by some financial restructuring in an attempt to render universities more responsive to the dictates of the market, and "as pressures mount on the university system and resources shrink, responses are increasingly couched in the pervasively masculine language of management" (West and Lyon, 1995: 63). It seems as though women are more adversely affected than men, although it is fair to say that universities are presently not particularly comfortable organisations for either women *or* men.

One of the first things from our interviews that struck us was the general concern with the ways of working which *were* seen as managerial and authoritarian, imposed, and at odds with the ways of working favoured by women. Senior male academics and administrators were seen by our respondents as largely part of a male club, benefiting from a managerialism which seemed to value aggression and individualism over common good despite the rhetoric of participation and empowerment. One woman told us how senior male academics in one university department took turns to be 'top management' in order to compete with one another in the hope of advancing their careers. Another commented, "men say we cannot stand still, we have to move on to get on — why?".

We also have reference to a 'male world of committees' in Higher Education where men play 'boys games' scoring points off one another endlessly to 'massage their egos'. Women, we were told, were made to feel outsiders. They were bewildered at the sheer amount of time 'wasted' in what they saw as pointless posturing and tilting at windmills, engaged in for its own sake and creating considerable levels of both anomie and alienation (Clark, 1991) for the women concerned. As Kerman (1995: 139), herself the only female member at academic and other meetings, comments:

> I was accustomed to being made to feel out of place — I recognised as exclusion devices, the opening lewd joke, made with an eye cast in my direction, the detailed discussion of football tactics before we got down to business, the chairman (sic) who began with his feet on the table. They were tiresome, but they did not really bother me as they appeared to confirm that the meeting was changed because of my presence. Certain things could not be said because of my being there, certain other things could be said.

This may be evidence of a 'new' patriarchal managerialism or may be indicative of a historically sustained process of marginalisation exercised over women by powerful men (Rich, 1979: 136-7 and 154). Given the relative dearth of research into women in Higher Education, noted earlier by Acker, it seems difficult to answer this question directly, though our own inclination is that combinations of managerialism and masculinity have articulated together historically in different organisational contexts (Maile, 1995: 77), particularly given accounts such as Newman's (1995: 16-21) recent discussion of cultural forms of managerial control in the public sector. From our interviews there is certainly sufficient evidence to suggest that women are presently suffering discrimination and disadvantage and feel outsiders in male-dominated cultures (at least as far as we are able to generalise) in both new and traditional universities. We are unable, nevertheless, to offer any firm conclusions on its likely different historical configurations.

Whether or not there is a new managerialism in Higher Education it would appear that the women in our research are responding to patterns of male behaviour which are operating through managerial control processes.

Accommodation and resistance

Accommodation and resistance are often different sides of the same coin (Anyon, 1983: 26), with members of subordinate groups responding to control and domination in a variety of often subtle ways (Baker Miller, 1983). The individualising of a problem makes it personal, both in experience and response, putting pressure on the individual to conform. It is this which lies behind the encouragement of independence and exhortation to self-reliance found in the 'Managing Diversity' and 'Human Resource Management' literature (Liff and Wajcman, 1996: 84; see also Rajvinder et al., 1995: 31) which can be interpreted as an invitation to aspiring managers to try a variation on the old recurring theme of 'divide and rule'.

Accommodation and resistance need not, however, be lone cries in the wilderness of self-subjugation and often represent innovative and meaningful coping mechanisms to keep hope alive and demonstrate spirit and dignity. Our interviewees displayed just such qualities in their individual reactions following, in many respects, the behaviour of female lawyers in a study which drew on the work of Gilligan (1982). Jack and Jack (1988) sought to explore the ways in which women dealt with the demands of the legal profession. Being lawyers required the women to operate in a world regulated by principles, abstract reasoning, case law and precedent — suspending for the duration of a case the full apprehension of a client's often tragic personal circumstances.

The women lawyers (along with some men) coped by adopting one of three strategies: emulating the traditional male role, splitting the self, or attempting to reshape the role. Our respondents behaved in similar ways. When emulating the male role in response to the expectations of male colleagues they denied the relational part of themselves and suffered as a result — one losing a partner along the way and exhibiting some of the 'classic' signs of stress. Another of our interviewees 'split' her 'self' in response to the concerns of colleagues who saw the expression of care as evidence of weakness. This proved very difficult for her to cope with, saying that she felt she was not really being 'herself', and seeking solace and renewing her self-image when away from work. We also have evidence of attempts to alter expectations of the job to encompass both reason and emotion as requirements of the role; though here again our respondents encountered problems, with one of them seeing her career chances vanishing as a result.

From our interviews we did gain a sense that some men in academia were seen as working and coping in similar ways to women, suggesting a need for further research to consider the role of gender and the experience of managerial control. Certainly the experience of an issue as a private trouble (Wright Mills, 1959: 14-15) individualises a problem and is invariably accompanied by guilt and self-doubt. But above all, perhaps, it tends to disempower, until recognised as a public issue. As Anyon (1983: 34) explains:

> Daily accommodation and resistance does not seek to remove the structural causes of.... contradictions. For such transformation women need collective action.

Collective opposition

We noted earlier in the paper Acker's observation that women academics were too scattered to provide a critical mass, yet our research in one new British university, backed up by published research on another (Butler and Landells, 1994), suggests that this may not entirely be the case. Our research revealed concern from women academics and administrators over issues such as lighting in car parks and corridors and campus security provision which were seen to affect them adversely as women. What was perhaps most interesting was that consciousness about these issues and the collective mobilisation around them which ensued cut across administrative and academic categories, as well as categories based on ethnicity and age. As a group, the women concerned refused to recognise formal hierarchies or name 'leaders' to enquiring male managers who they suspected would target them individually to pressurise or harrass.

The group took different forms in different circumstances, sometimes comprising different women, and clearly did not involve all the women in the university. Nor did the male hierarchy which opposed them comprise *all* the men, with some male colleagues expressing their concern and support. Yet the women *confronted* the men who held senior positions in the institutional hierarchy on issues which they argued affected them *as* women — only to be met with incomprehension and bewilderment by the men in power. Eventually the demands for improved lighting and security were met, but not until a long and bitter struggle had been played out, twisting and turning for the men on issues of resources and priorities and for the women on personal safety. There was considerable emotional cost to the women involved and, as far as we know, the group remains presently dormant and may or may not reappear in the forms it took before. As a loose-knit network, operating without formalities, there are no guarantees or predictions possible.

Powell (1990: 272-3) notes that networks develop based on trust, reciprocity, mutuality and co-operation; in academe we note a male 'invisible college' dating back to the 17th century (O'Leary and Mitchell, 1990: 59). Research shows that women may use networks to further their careers but that they are likely to use them to foster relationships, support one another and share concerns about women's disadvantage (Greenglass, 1993; and Lie and Malik, 1994: 212).

This means that women's under-representation in universities and professional autonomy need not, in and of itself, act as a disincentive to networking in order to share experience and a sense of collective power (Morley, 1994: 202); we note for example the development of WHEN, the Women in Higher Education Network (Davies et al., 1994). Networks may even develop in (or through) the research process itself (White, 1995) as evidenced by Butler and Landell's (1994: 25-26) work on the sexual harassment of women academics. As they show, women were able to 'raise consciousness'; it freed them to break 'their silence and…the taboo'. It also led to the researchers themselves being encouraged to share their work "as part of a network of people, struggling to effect change in Higher Education".

But there are costs. Butler and Landells (ibid.) comment that their research "both empowered and intimidated us", identifying them as "feminists working in a University". This is paralleled by the experience of women in our research. Once labelled a "troublemaker" — and the term 'feminist' may carry more of a connotation for the women so categorised by men — you are vulnerable. Even with support, even in collective action, the consequences are experienced alone. It may be that collective and individual responses are not as separable as they seem to be, their combination offering considerable opportunities for change.

Yet we should not forget that the collective opposition found in our research was located in a new university. This may be significant since new universities differ from traditional universities in a great many respects, not simply in terms of their larger female presence. They have a history of involvement with Local Authorities and more of a 'public sector' image than traditional universities whose elite 'ivory tower' persona would at least suggest that they are less likely to be vulnerable to the incursion of managerialism, new or otherwise. Indeed, greater financial independence and autonomy may just provide a buffer against the harsher economic realities confronting new universities whose lecture theatres and seminar rooms groan under the sheer weight of student numbers.

But if traditional universities seem more comfortable places to work in, we should not lose sight of the potential for men to behave badly, obsessed with maintaining their 'quality' ratings and 'letting go' those staff targeted as insufficiently research active. As we saw earlier, such concerns may have quite deleterious effects on women academics taking on ever-widening burdens of responsibility.

Speculations

The complexity recounted here is perhaps to be expected. The women in our research negotiate their lives as people with a number of different identities, any one or combination of which may be salient at particular moments in time. Where they came together as women in a new university they did so around particular policy issues — security and lighting — which said much about their concerns over personal safety and drew on their experiences as women; which is why the men by and large, although themselves different in many respects from each other — with some sharing the concerns — failed generally to grasp the meaning for those adversely affected. Equally, the study by Butler and Landells focused on the policy issue of sexual harassment which affected women *as* women.

This does not mean that the women will not mobilise around other issues — indeed, in terms of racial discrimination they may well feel an affinity with certain men and draw on the experience of other identities; as men will sometimes seem to act *as* men or *as* managers, or *both* and occasionally work supportively with women. This need not entail a drift into a variant of post-structuralism or postmodernism. Alcoff's (1988) attempt to retain the category 'woman' in her use of a politics of identity to meet the challenge of deconstruction offers the insight that agency may be conceptualised through the affirmation of a collective self, historically and socially constituted. It is this which Alcoff shares with Bondi (1993) and de Lauretis (1990) who sees difference and disagreement as indicative not of post-feminism, but of a flourishing social movement, whose networks are dynamic and fluid rather than fixed and formally organised.

There is no guarantee that consciousness will somehow develop in a particular way however. As Marshall (1995: 193) puts it, in her study of women managers, several of her "research participants commented that — contrary to popular belief — other women were not necessarily instant allies or people with whom they had an affinity". This should not really surprise us. Our research has shown simply that women came together around particular issues which affected them as women — at which point they affirmed their identity as women who shared common disadvantage and came to a collective appreciation of their situation. That the opportunities for movement mobilisation are "structured by the features of institutional life" (Piven and Cloward, 1977: 23) should not detract from the fact of their joint action as women — it simply reinforces it, showing how they took action to seize (and even create) opportunities in the situation in which they found themselves. It may be that this is what a social movement is — operating, as Melucci (1988) puts it, through the submerged networks of civil society, rendering power visible and thereby negotiable, or at least contestable, whatever the cost. Moreover, retention of the notion of a women's movement, a social movement for change, based on a shared consciousness of both differing and similar identities in creative tension, may be the most helpful way of keeping in view the broader picture of structured disadvantage that characterises social, economic and political life in a climate currently hostile to women (Liff and Wajcman, 1996: 91).

In this sense we can interpret the actions of the women in our research as challenges to forms of masculinity which operate through processes of managerial control. It is difficult to disentangle 'gender' from 'office' in all this, but then perhaps we should not try. What our research does show is that the power holders, who happen to be male, enact managerial processes which take specific material forms to control performance and espouse the ideology of empowerment which is conjured up to legitimate its presence.

On this count, managerialism is ideological in a Marxist sense of the term, wheeled in to justify and mystify, mouthed by "hired prize-fighters" (Marx, 1976: 97) who play the deadly serious game of measuring and monitoring, discounting the un or non-accountable in the lottery of monetised existence.

In another sense, of course, this does make it all 'work' even if from a distance, and may be why there is the ever-present fear of an iron-fist concealed in the velvet glove, sensed by some of our interviewees who tremble in the climate of fear and dread of the unemployment queue and the grim reality that we *have* to get on with it — after all what else can we do? It is as well to remember Jarratt's concern that the Head of Department should be both a manager and an academic leader, but that if 'he' cannot be *both* ,then a *manager* 'he' should be.

What then of the future, seen from a context in which 'donnish dominion' (Halsey, 1995) is said to be in decline? Are we set for the proletarianisation of academe (Weber, 1918) in the wake of a managerial offensive in line with so many beleaguered public sector institutions? Maintenance of tradition may be more feasible from within the financially secure walls of old Universities where life seems to continue at one remove from everyone else's reality, although questions need to be asked about the nature of a tradition before rushing to its defense. Women's increasing presence in academe has had a number of effects, not least the making visible of male power and privilege.

If the future promises greater access to previously under-represented groups of students — which would include, for example, those from working-class and different ethnic backgrounds as well as more part-time and female students — then the needs of the new 'consumers' will likely be more diverse and there may be more demand for the growing numbers of women already under greater pressure to 'perform' across a wide range of teaching, administration, research and pastoral care responsibilities (see Cotterill and Waterhouse, this volume). Demands on women in academe seem likely only to increase as students seek out a sympathetic ear in these increasingly Kafkaesque towers of the future — an ear already bent to listen to the din surrounding 'quality' in teaching and research, and proclamations of 'empowerment'.

Acknowledgements

This is an amended version of a paper presented to the 14th International Labour Process Conference, Aston University, England, 27-29 March, 1996 and The Dilemmas of Mass Higher Education International Conference, Staffordshire University, England 10-12 April, 1996. We would like to thank the participants of both Conferences for their helpful comments and the editors for their helpful comments on an earlier version of this paper.

Note

1   ... *whether it is better to be loved than feared or the reverse. The answer is that one would like to be both the one and the other; but because it is difficult to combine them, it is far better to be feared than loved if you cannot be both.* ... *The bond of love is one which men, wretched creatures that they are, break when it is to their advantage to do so; but fear is strengthened by a dread of punishment which is always effective.* Niccolo Machiavelli [1514] (1975) *The Prince.* Harmondsworth: Penguin: quote pp. 96-97.

References

Acker S. (1980) 'Hierarchies, Jobs, Bodies: A Theory of Gendered Organizations', *Gender and Society* 4 (2) June: 139-158.

Acker S. (1994) *Gendered Education.* Buckingham: OU Press.

Alcoff L. (1988) 'Cultural Feminism Versus Post-Structuralism: The Identity Crisis in Feminist Theory', *Signs* 13 (3): 405-436.

Anyon J. (1983) 'Intersections of Gender and Class: Accommodation and Resistance by Working-Class and Affluent Females to Contradictory Sex-Role ideologies', in S. Walker and L. Barton (eds) (1993) *Gender, Class and Education.* Lewis: Falmer Press: 19-37.

Axtell Ray, C. (1986) 'Corporate Culture: The last frontier of control?', *Journal of Management Studies,* 23: 287-297.

Baker Miller J. (1983) *Toward a New Psychology of Women.* Harmondsworth: Penguin.

Bondi, L. (1993) 'Locating Identity Politics', in M. Keith and S. Pile (eds) (1993) *Place and The Politics of Identity.* London: Routledge, pp. 84-101.

Burke, T. , Maddocks, S. and Rose, A. (1993) *How Ethical is British Business?: An analysis of the sensitivity of Senior Managers and other professionals to ethical issues in business.* University of Westminster Research Working Paper, Series 2, No. 1.

Butler, A. and Landells, M. (1994) *Telling Tales out of School: Research into sexual harassment of women academics,* University of Plymouth Equality Research Group Working Paper, No. 1.

Clark, H. (1991) *Women, Work and Stress,* University of East London Occasional Papers on Business, Economy and Society, Paper No. 3.

Clarke, J., Cochrane A. and McLaughlin, E. (eds) (1994) *Managing Social Policy.* London: Sage.

Clarke, J. and Newman, J. (1993) 'The Right to Manage: A Second Managerial Revolution?', *Cultural Studies,* 7 (3): 427-441.

Cochrane, A. (1993) *Whatever Happened to Local Government?.* Buckingham: Open University Press.

Coe, T. (1992) *The Key to the Men's Club: Opening the doors to women in management.* Corby: The Institute of Management.

Cutler, T. and Waine, B. (1994) *Managing the Welfare State.* Oxford: Berg.

Davies, C. and Holloway, P. (1995) 'Troubling Transformations: Gender Regimes and Organizational Culture in the Academy', in L. Morley and V. Walsh (eds) *Feminist Academics: Creative Agents for Change*. London: Taylor and Francis.

Davies, S. , Lubelska, C. and Quinn, J. (1994) *Changing the Subject: Women in Higher Education*. London: Taylor and Francis.

De Lauretis, T. (1990) 'Upping the Anti (sic) in Feminist Theory', in M. Hirsch and E. Fox Keller (eds) *Conflicts in Feminism*. London: Routledge, pp. 255-270.

Earley, P. (1994) *Lecturers' Workload and Factors Affecting Stress Levels: A Research Report from the NFER*. London: NATFHE.

Ferguson, R. (1994) 'Managerialism in Education', in J. Clarke *et al.* (eds) (1994) *Managing Social Policy*. London: Sage.

Gilligan, C. (1982) *In a Different Voice: Psychological Theory and Women's Development*. Cambridge, Mass: Harvard.

Halsey, A. H. (1995) *The Decline of Donnish Dominion*. Oxford: Clarendon Press.

Hansard Society (1990) *The Report of The Hansard Society Commission on Women at the Top*. London: The Hansard Society.

Hearn, J. (1992) *Men in The Public Eye*. London: Routledge.

Hood, C. (1991) 'A Public Management for All Seasons?", *Public Administration*, Spring, 69: 3-19.

Höpfl, H. (1992) 'The Making of the Corporate Acolyte: Some Thoughts on Charismatic Leadership and the Reality of Organizational Commitment', *Journal of Management Studies*, 29 (1), January: 23-33.

Jack, D. and Jack, R. (1988) 'Women Lawyers: Archetype and Alternatives', in C. Gilligan *et al.* (eds), *Mapping the Moral Domain*. Cambridge, Mass: Harvard University Press: 263-288.

Jarratt Report (1985) *Report of the Committee for Efficiency Studies in Universities*. Committee of Vice Chancellors and Principals.

Keith, M. and Pile, S. (eds) (1993) *Place and The Politics of Identity*. London: Routledge.

Kerman, L. (1995) 'The Good Witch: "Advice to Women in Management"', in Morley, L. and Walsh, V. (eds) (1995) *Feminist Academics: Creative Agents for Change*. London: Taylor and Francis, pp. 131-144.

Lie, S. , and Malik, L. (1994) 'Trends in the Gender Gap in Higher Education', in S. Lie, L. Malik and D. Harris (eds) *World Year Book of Education 1994*. London: Kogan Page, pp. 205-213.

Lie, S. and O'Leary. V. (1990) *Storming the Tower*. London: Kogan Page.

Liff, S. and Wajcman, J. (1996) '"Sameness" and "Difference" Revisited: Which Way Forward For Equal Opportunity Initiatives?', *Journal of Management Studies*, 33 (1): 79-94.

Lunneborg, P. (1990) *Women Changing Work*. New York: Bergin and Garvey.

Maile, S. (1995) 'The Gendered Nature of Managerial Discourse: The Case of a Local Authority', *Gender, Work and Organization*, 2 (2): 76-87.

Marshall, J. (1995) *Women Managers Moving On*. London: Routledge.

Melucci, A. (1988) 'Social Movements and the Democratization of Everyday Life', in J. Keane (ed) *Civil Society and the State: New European Perspectives*. London: Verso, pp. 245-260.

Morley, L. (1994) 'Glass Ceiling or Iron Cage: Women in UK Academia', *Gender, Work and Organization*, 1 (4), October: 194-204.

Morley, L. and Walsh, V. (eds) (1995) *Feminist Academics: Creative Agents for Change*. London: Taylor and Francis.

Newman J. (1994) 'The Limits of Management: Gender and the Politics of Change', in J. Clarke *et al.* (eds), *Managing Social Policy*. London: Sage.

——— (1995) 'Gender and Cultural Change' in Itzin, C. and Newman, J. (eds) (1995) *Gender, Culture and Organizational Change*. London: Routledge.

Newman, J. and Clarke, J. (1994) 'Going about Our Business? The Managerialization of Public Services', in J. Clarke *et al.* (eds), *Managing Social Policy*. London: Sage.

O'Leary, V. and Mitchell, J. (1990) 'Women Connecting with Women: Networks and Mentors', in S. Lie and V. O'Leary (eds) (1990), pp. 58-73.

Parker, M. and Jary, D. (1995) "The McUniversity: Organization, Management and Academic Subjectivity', *Organization*, 2 (2): 319-338.

Piven, F. F. and Cloward, R. A. (1977) *Poor People's Movements: Why They Succeed, How They Fail*. New York: Pantheon Books.

Pollitt, C. (1990) *Managerialism and the Public Services: The Anglo American Experience*. Oxford: Basil Blackwell.

——— (1993) *Managerialism and the Public Services: Cuts or Cultural Change in the 1990s* (2nd edition). Oxford: Basil Blackwell.

Powell, W. W. (1990) 'Neither Market nor Hierarchy: Network Forms of Organization', reprinted in G. Thompson, J. Frances, R. Levacic and J. Mitchell (eds) (1991) *Markets, Hierarchies, Networks: The Coordination of Social Life*. London: Sage, pp. 265-276.

Rajvinder, K. , Fullerton, J. and Ahmed, Y. (1995) 'Managing Diversity: Succeeding where Equal Opportunities has Failed', *Equal Opportunities Review* 59, January/February: 31-36.

Rich, A. (1979) *On Lies, Secrets and Silence*. London: Virago.

Weber, M. (1918) 'Science as a Vocation', in H. H. Gerth and C. Wright Mills (1948) *From Max Weber: Essays in Sociology*. London: Routledge and Kegan Paul, pp. 129-156.

West, J. and Lyon, K. (1995) 'The Trouble with Equal Opportunities: the case of women academics', *Gender and Education*, 7 (1): 51-68

White, J. (1995) 'Leading in their own ways: Women chief executives in local government', in C. Itzin and J. Newman (eds), *Gender, Culture and Organizational Change*. London: Routledge, 193-210.

Wright Mills, C. (1959) *The Sociological Imagination*. Harmondsworth: Penguin.

Speaking Confidentially, or How Long Have I Got? The Demise of the Personal Tutorial in Higher Education

13

Pamela Cotterill and Ruth L. Waterhouse

An imperfect safety net

We would like to explore some of the contradictions surrounding the role of personal tutor in higher education. We argue that these contradictions reside in the changes which are contingent upon the recent period of reconstruction in this sector (Morley and Walsh, 1995; Davies, Lubelska and Quinn, 1994; Mace, 1993; Williams, 1992; Ball and Eggins, 1989). At the time of writing, we are conscious of the deliberations of the Dearing Committee into Higher Education. Expected to be published in July 1997, the National Committee of Inquiry into Higher Education (the Dearing Report) has a wide brief. The Committee covers issues such as the economic role of higher education; teaching, quality and standards; information technology; research and the use of staff and cost effectiveness. We expect the Committee's findings to have a substantial impact on the issues discussed in this chapter, although it is difficult to fully anticipate them. It is interesting to note, however, that women are not fully represented on the Committee and that the issue of student support was placed on a secondary agenda to be examined in the autumn rather than the summer of 1996. Given the emphasis on information technology and greater efficiency, we expect that student support, whilst human in origin, will be virtual rather than empirical.

Given this, our interest in the role of the personal tutor is timely. We are particularly interested in what we regard as the deskilling of this role; one that has often had an ambiguous but generally accepted position within the diverse institutions which constitute higher education (Morley and Walsh, 1995). As tutors who began our academic careers in the former polytechnic sector and who are now teaching Women's Studies and Sociology in a 'new university', we have long had experience of working with students drawn from a wide

223

range of backgrounds. We are particularly familiar with the problems and challenges encountered by those students who have traditionally been denied access to higher education. (Montgomery and Collette, 1996; Mirza, 1995; Corrin, 1994; Matthews, 1994; Edwards, 1993). Such students frequently, although not intrinsically or inevitably, require the support system offered by the personal tutorial. It can and does operate as an imperfect safety net.

As we have moved through the processes associated with modularisation, semesterisation, growth in student numbers and an increasing focus on learning rather than teaching communities, we have witnessed a decline in this support system. Time allocation for personal tutorials has either been reduced or has disappeared from our official staff timetables. It was always a struggle to register this time officially but prior to recent changes we were usually successful in doing so. Furthermore, the title Personal and Academic Guidance Tutor (PAGT) is increasingly referred to by a kind of collective slippage as Academic Guidance Tutor (AGT). Consequently, the 'personal' which, as feminists, we also know to be the 'political' is subjected to an unconscious process of 'invisibilisation'. As Women's Studies tutors whose teaching programmes focus on both public and private worlds, we find this stripping away of the personal intensely disturbing. Despite rhetorical claims that higher education is concerned with the whole person we find that our institutions are rapidly dehumanising people into FTEs (Full-time Equivalents). In an era labelled 'post feminist' and with the assumption that we are 'all equal now' (Coppock *et al.*, 1995), we are in danger of becoming post personal. Our students are not, of course, 'all equal now' and their personal lives continue to impact upon their public, educational lives. The 'playing field' has never been level and, as we know, many inside the field are forced to be spectators. A considerable number — due to class, 'race', and gender factors — are not even allowed near the turnstiles. Mass higher education was supposed to make entry into the playing field equal for all those who could benefit. Debt, family responsibilities and personal hardship continue to ensure that the expansion of higher education is strictly limited. Furthermore, it has been argued that 'mass' education has provided more opportunity for the middle class, including middle class women, but that the working class remains underrepresented in British universities (Evans, 1995). Others have questioned whether 'mass' education has ever been about equality, suggesting that open access policies have more to do with funding than with wider opportunity (Mirza, 1995; Humm, 1994).

Learning communities

The problems of mass higher education have engendered a number of innovatory responses. Within our own institution these have involved attempts to look at different teaching and learning strategies, with the emphasis increasingly on the latter. This emphasis on learning has been encapsulated in the term 'the learning community' and we and our colleagues have been urged to engage with 'building the learning community'. As we understand it, the movement from teaching communities to learning communities involves a shift towards greater use of distanced learning techniques (Nicholls, 1997). The new technologies of learning have opened up the way for more homebased, privatised study. This will, no doubt, be welcomed by some of those who are tied to the home by domestic and other responsibilities. Indeed, it is possible to envisage a future where the university is not a place where people congregate but something which exists primarily in cyberspace. This may be good news for students isolated by their personal responsibilities. However, we argue that the higher education experience is also about the social interactions it makes possible — social interactions not only between groups of students but also between students and tutors. It has been suggested that many students entering higher education want a social relationship with their tutors and to feel that tutors care about them as people (Edwards, 1993).

By the millennium, the institution in which we teach and do our research will have taken considerable steps towards building a learning community. According to the recently published *Strategic Plan 1996-2000* those working within its remit will be committed to the "development of the whole person" (Staffordshire University, 1996: 4). Academic staff, in particular, will be engaged in developing a culture in which "support is readily available to help students deal effectively with the range of challenges that face them including both educational and personal issues" (p.10). We welcome such statements. Yet it is already the case that academics have been counselled against investing too much time in personal contact with students. We, however, *are* urged to improve our individual and collective research profiles.

Following the Research Assessment Exercise, many universities categorise staff according to whether they are 'research active'. Those who are 'research active' are valued because their work is quantifiable in monetary terms whilst the 'research inactive' find themselves locked into teaching/administration/ pastoral care roles. The drive for research activity exacerbates the division of academic labour in higher education and, as we have argued elsewhere, encourages a competitive working environment where time devoted to students is reduced in an effort to find time for research (Cotterill and Waterhouse, forthcoming). We argue, therefore, that the rhetoric of 'personal growth' and the 'whole person' runs counter to the actual processes which are at work in higher educational establishments today. In the changing world of universities, new managerial regimes have replaced academic autonomy. The institutional response to academics faced with more students and fewer resources has been the demand for quantifiable products through teaching quality audit and pressure to publish (Evans, 1995). Furthermore, we believe that the existing gap between rhetoric and experience will escalate as we move towards learning as opposed to teaching communities and that, without a committed investment of more human and material resources, the students in the learning community will feel as abandoned as the ex-mental patient in the 'caring community'.

More with less?

In common with many other higher education establishments, our own institution has been concerned to respond to a decline in the unit of resource. This trend is likely to continue into the future. As tutors we are exhorted to do more and to do it better with less. We have become increasingly concerned about the impact of this approach on the quality of our professional relationships with students. This has particular significance for the personal tutorial process.

It is our view that there has already been a devaluing of both the person and the personal in higher education. It is also our view that this loss will be exacerbated unless steps are taken to remedy the situation. The loss permeates many aspects of the higher education experience but it is exemplified by the devaluation afforded the personal tutorial. We argue that the demise of the personal tutorial is a loss not only to the students concerned but also to ourselves as academics and teachers. Our own wholeness is interdependent with our ability both to regard students as whole and to treat them as such. It is difficult to do this in a system where students are rapidly becoming numbers on assignment forms or an anonymous collection of faces.

At first sight, increases in the numbers of students might be seen in terms of market success *and* success in the promotion of equal opportunity. However, as Epstein (1995) points out, 'equal opportunity' has a hollow ring if we cannot support our students through their degree courses. This is not simply because more students means more demands on our time (although, of course, it does): it is because, in the academic division of labour, pastoral care is accorded little importance. Whilst we can see some value in the concept of 'learning communities' and the techniques which support them, we remain sceptical about their application given the present political and economic climate.

Comparisons between community care programmes and learning community programmes are inevitable in that both appear to be driven by fiscal considerations (Radcliffe, 1996; Williams, 1992). The rhetoric of both is often couched in liberal-humanist, even radical language. However, it has been argued convincingly that 'New Right' thinking (which provided the justification for community care policies) is now common currency in higher education (Epstein, 1995). Abbott and Wallace (1992) point out that the politics of the 'New Right' combine two seemingly contradictory ideologies: economic liberalism and moral conservatism emphasising individual responsibility. The introduction of 'learning communities' in higher education is a clear example of 'New

Right' thinking which stresses individual responsibility by placing the onus to learn on the students and, at the same time, provides the justification for reducing state spending on education. Consequently, when monetary concerns drive the implementation of such programmes, they become scarcely recognisable as the innovatory and empowering schemes they arguably have the potential to be.

Student empowerment or 'fuck off and find out'?

As students are increasingly ushered into learning as opposed to teaching communities, we cannot help wondering what these communities will look and be like. As sociologists we have no choice but to recognise that the term 'community' is not only a hotly contested one but one loaded with political meanings (Walker, 1991; Finch and Groves, 1985; Wilson, 1982). We know that it can mean many things and that it can also be empty and meaningless in practice. The term has been attached to both actual and imaginary utopias and dystopias. It is often an ideological rather than an empirical term, implying that if we call something a community that is what it is and that it is undoubtedly to be equated with a 'good thing'. But communities are defined by their boundaries. They consist of insiders often at the expense of outsiders. Despite the commitment to mass higher education there will continue to be many outsiders. We argue that without a strong, hence highly valued, personal tutorial system many of those who initially make it through the turnstiles will be ejected before the first interval (i.e., the end of their first year). As academics we have found ourselves reluctantly moving away from responding to students in a holistic fashion. We are exhorted to meet with them less; to hold fewer tutorials and seminars. Students must be empowered to take responsibility for their own learning. This has a radical ring to it but it has long been experienced by students as the 'fuck off and find out' model of education. Furthermore, modularity and semesterisation ensures that our contact with students is fragmentary. It is a rare experience to see more than a handful of students through from their point of entry to graduation. The personal tutorial system remains but it remains as a piece of plaster to stick over the gaping wound which sometimes becomes the student's experience of the higher education world. The student's trauma becomes too great and s/he leaves the institution. This, we would argue, is a loss for us all.

We are not suggesting that it was ever easy to treat students as whole persons. Any system which is hierarchical and requires us to assess and evaluate others carries within it depersonalising tendencies. We are acutely aware of the dangers of romanticising the old system or indeed any system. The personal tutorial system, as past students will no doubt testify, was always incomplete and flawed. Like the proverbial curate's egg, it was only good in parts. For many students the personal tutorial was not a positive experience. For some, especially where the relationship broke down or was never established, it was either a negative or a non- experience. There were always those students who, for personal reasons, conscientiously and consistently avoided it. Others writing about students' experiences of higher education make similar comments. For example, Rosalind Edwards (1993) in her study of mature women students found that some did not look for a personal relationship with their lecturers. For these women, contacts with lecturers were sought only in relation to their formal academic progress. Further intimacy was neither looked for nor desired.

We certainly do not claim to have provided a successful system for all. But for those for whom it worked it sometimes made a difference between academic survival or academic disaster. Our role in this we recognise as modest. Academic survival often had more to do with the way the student used the tutorial as part of an overall and rational strategy than with the individual skills and qualities of the tutor. But this was not always the case. Sometimes the individual competencies of the personal tutor, his or her ability to empathise with the student, did help some students overcome certain obstacles. The personal tutor did make a difference — sometimes enabling the student to discover or re-discover valuable personal qualities of his/her own. Frequently, the personal tutor contributed to the process of confidence building, confidence often being in short supply yet so crucial in facilitating student progress.

Despite official policies and programmes to the contrary, we would argue that the recent changes in higher education have resulted in a culture which systematically devalues personal tutor relationships. The traditional academy has always valorised the public world over the private and thus ignored emotions and emotional work. Nevertheless, in the newer 'red brick' universities and the former polytechnic sector, the personal tutor system was an acknowledged part of (some) academics' work. However, "in the intellectual climate of post modernism" (Evans, 1995: 79) with its rising tide of individualism and personal responsibility, the role is no longer regarded as politically or economically expedient. There simply isn't the money or the time. The tendency to depersonal- isation is, we recognise, common to all bureaucratic systems. Higher education is no exception although managerial systems have certainly become more pronounced in recent years. However, there is resistance. Talking ('coming in for a chat') is a process not easily transformed into a quantifiable product, but the importance of talk is held onto by a considerable number of students and academic staff. Those who attempt to maintain this kind of personal contact are, however, regarded as the 'old guard' or 'academic dinosaurs'. As Women's Studies teachers and feminists, we are committed to resisting the depersonalising of academic roles, although this is difficult within the increasingly bureaucratic administration in which we work. Furthermore, new and complex management structures have obscured areas of responsibility and often it is unclear where resistance might be most effectively directed.

Increasingly, the educational relationship is envisaged as one pertaining to student and computer rather than student and tutor. For some students and tutors, this will be preferable. Tutors will be freed for research and students will be freed from a hierarchical relationship in which an abuse of power sometimes took place. But others, ourselves included, will experience this process as a loss — not only of the valuable resources which are located in individual tutors, but of the interesting dynamics fostered by the personal tutorial relationship. Some of us do not wish to be freed for research if this 'freedom' takes us away from contact with students. In writing this, we are aware that we have to examine our motives for wishing to retain the personal tutor relationship. There is a danger that we need it more than students do. We may be holding on to it out of a need for control in uncertain times. It is something which we know and feel safe with; an area in which we can demonstrate some skill and even possess some influence. Yet the personal tutorial role was never easy. It required the ability to empathise, listen attentively and intervene with sensitivity whilst refraining from the temptation to take over. It was not an easy option and most of us understood that we were always in a process of becoming competent personal tutors. We learnt something fresh about the role with each new student. It was certainly not a comfortable or cosy role to play.

'How long have you got?'

Barbara Adam (1990) points out that time management is central to the organisation of Western industrial life. The temporal organisation of bureaucracies and institutions is taken for granted and all activities within them are paced and timed. Within the academy, such activities are prioritised according to the time resources of managers and lecturing staff. Access and availability to students are determined by a process of selection which values some activities more highly than others. Time given is carefully measured and assessed in terms of professional and personal gains and losses. As Adam (1990: 109) points out:

> Once we ask who structures whose life, what rules are being adhered to, and how these processes occur, then timed social life becomes fundamentally embedded in an understanding of the structural relations of power, normative structures, and the negotiated interactions of social life.

In other words, time is to do with control and power: some members of society control time, others must wait. Students have little control over university teaching timetables and still less over the availability of lecturers outside these contact hours. The unequal status of students in relation to those who teach them is made explicit in the process of who waits for whom. In waiting situations, the power lies with those who impose the waiting and not with those who must wait.

As lecturers we are increasingly encouraged to manage our time better as though time management was an individual problem. One of the least comfortable aspects of the personal tutorial role concerns our use of time in relation to individual students. In our experience, critical reflections on our competency in this role involves 'time fretting'. By this we mean the anxiety experienced over how much time we are able to or should spend with an individual student and his/her unique problems. Unlike some colleagues in other institutions, we have found students to be almost unfailingly considerate and courteous towards us as tutors (Barnes-Powell and Letherby, forthcoming). There are exceptions but they are rare. Students are also tolerant of our shortcomings in the personal tutor role. They are particularly considerate concerning the use of what they see as 'our time'. The frequently expressed question 'how long have you got?' is particularly pertinent here. It usually carries with it two important meanings. The first is a factual enquiry as to how much time we can actually spend with them The second meaning is an implicit one which can be read as 'my problems are so complex it could take all day'. Most students know that you have not got all day to 'spend' on them, that they are lucky if you can spare half an hour. Such a question is therefore often full of self-irony and parody. They know they will have to settle for less than as 'customers' or 'clients' they are really entitled to. They settle for what they can get whilst the tutor is left to 'time fret' as she makes her way home at the end of a busy day.

We are reminded here of a character in a Jean Rhys novel (1971) who agrees to meet what has become known as the 'Jean Rhys woman' to listen to her life concerns. In the book, Julia Martin (the 'Jean Rhys woman') turns to an old friend, a man she had an affair with when she was nineteen, for help and support. She wants to explain that her life has been very hard; to tell him about her baby who died 'for the simple reason that you haven't enough money to keep it alive...'.

> Then he said, trying to be kind: 'Look here, you can tell me all about it, because I've got loads of time — heaps of time. Nearly three quarters of an hour. (p. 80)

Rhys used this as a device to show how women are seldom listened to by men, especially middle class men who devalue the personal and emotional. Such men do not hear the distress of women even though they have been the agents of the problems in the first place. We have commented on the feminisation of personal tutorial work elsewhere (Cotterill and Waterhouse, forthcoming). Whilst women undertake the bulk of emotional support work, we would not argue that all men disengage from this process. However, whatever the gender of the tutor, students today fare rather worse than the Jean Rhys woman. This is so even with tutors who have a personal and political commitment to enabling students realise their potential. We have much less than an hour to spare. We know they require and deserve more than we can give. Hence we 'time fret' in our 'spare time'.

Confidentially speaking

Earlier in the paper we suggested that the role of personal tutor has been deskilled. We would like to demonstrate that deskilling process by focusing on just one element of the personal tutorial relationship — the issue of confidentiality. As with many other professional relationships, the role of personal tutor carries with it the responsibility of confidentiality. Whilst the PAGT is concerned primarily with the academic progress of the student, it has generally been accepted that this progress may be compromised by personal distress and trauma. It has traditionally been the case that some students have elected to disclose serious personal concerns to their tutors in recognition that their academic careers are being jeopardised by those concerns. As Montgomery and Collette (1996) point out, these students may then be defined as 'problem students' because of the nature of the disclosure. Such disclosures are rightly granted the confidentiality which surround the doctor/patient relationship; the counsellor/client relationship etc., and the rules of confidentiality are there to foster and protect the sense of trust which should be a feature of such relationships. They should operate to protect the students, who find themselves in vulnerable personal circumstances, from abuse from both peers and those who occupy higher places in the institutional hierarchy. However, academia has traditionally stressed the importance of objectivity, thus devaluing subjective emotion and feeling (Evans, 1995).

The post-modern university, with its ethos of individual responsibility and personal choice, is simply 'old wine in new bottles'. Here the rhetoric of 'equal access' and 'education for all who can benefit' does not reassure and only partly obscures a harsher reality: those who cannot cope should not stay. It is not surprising, therefore, that very often the talk which transpires between personal tutor and personal tutee concerns 'underground knowledge'. It is only 'given' to the personal tutor on the understanding that the 'gift' will not be passed on. In most relationships formed within a bureaucratic setting, however, confidentiality is far from absolute. Most professional bodies contain ethical codes which either permit or compel confidentiality to be broken in specific circumstances and to specific people (British Sociological Association, 1993; British Association of Counselling, 1985). Usually this confidentiality is broken with the 'client's' knowledge and permission — but not always. Confidentiality is sometimes broken without the client's knowledge and consent where, for instance, a higher law demands it or where someone else's life would be endangered if the information were withheld. However, this is neither a routine nor a common feature of most professional relationships. Normally, confidentiality is sacrosanct. It is a valued privilege of the professional relationship. The professional is trusted as someone who has the competency to practice confidentiality in both the individual's and the institution's interests. This is done in the knowledge that the professional relationship could not flourish otherwise (Banks, 1995; Hugman and Smith, 1995).

Many students encounter a range of problems over the three years of higher educational study (Fisher, 1994). These can range from medical to diverse domestic problems. Traditionally, the former has been documented by a medical certificate, the latter by a brief statement confirming the existence of domestic problems without any further disclosure of details. Increasingly, however, as institutions of higher education take on the role of institutions providing a service for the 'mass', the demand for elaborated documentation has grown. This demand comes from the Examination Boards and is particularly acute during the examination periods. As the gap between academics and students widens, the call for more formal demonstrations (proofs) of mitigating circumstances has increased: a discrete statement from the personal tutor is rarely sufficient to satisfy the Examination Boards and their Chairs who require increasingly detailed documentary evidence to be supplied either by a medical practitioner or by a trained counsellor. The informed opinion of the academic tutor is not enough. Furthermore, the onus for presenting proof of extenuating circumstances lies with the student rather than the academic staff. Whilst this undoubtedly carries some benefits (some staff proved unsympathetic or incompetent in their role as personal tutors) it carries a number of costs. In the name of parity of treatment, confidentiality is broken. Confidential knowledge is shared with a third party, a party whom most students will never have met let alone learnt to trust with delicate knowledge about themselves. Furthermore, the credibility of a personal tutor skilled in managing knowledge received in a confidential setting is undermined and implicitly brought into question. This is particularly so, where, as in our own institution, a centralised body is being created to adjudicate on matters of extenuating circumstances affecting academic performance. As we understand it, this body will not call on the expertise of teaching staff. Yet, at the same time, the centralised hierarchy exploits the personal tutor. Its rigid demands for documentation and monitoring increase her/his administrative work in a context which devalues this activity in favour of research.

Iatrogenesis in higher education

As experienced personal tutors, we have long been aware that many personal circumstances fall outside the remit of medical certification or intervention by the overstretched counselling services. As sociologists we are rightly wary of medicalising social and personal problems. (Illich, 1976) Yet in order to protect student interests we often find ourselves in the insidious position of urging them to seek medical certification for something which will be individualised as 'depression' but which has its roots in their socio-political situation. There is a real danger, therefore, that higher education establishments are fostering routines and practices which are iatrogenic. Alternatively, we may find ourselves attempting to persuade students to contact counselling services when it is entirely inappropriate. Clearly we do not force students to contact either the medical or the counselling services but students quickly learn that they ignore our reluctantly given advice at their academic peril.

'Our hands are tied'

There are, however, many students who resist this advice. They do not wish confidential information to be passed further up the line out of the personal tutorial context. Frequently they have disclosed information which, if known more widely, would render the student vulnerable to social stigmatisation. Goffman has called this a 'spoiled identity' (Goffman, 1968). The information may pertain to rape, sexual abuse, lesbian and gay sexual identity, drug use or HIV status. In such cases, high levels of mutual trust have to be reached by both parties before the information is communicated. It also takes considerable courage by the student and considerable sensitivity by the tutor. The disclosure may be seen to be a very special form of narrative which concerns the student's individual life history and life concerns. It is not given away easily or lightly. It is spoken to a particular audience in a particular context. Sometimes it is told only when the personal tutor had disclosed something about his/her own life history which has enabled the student to reciprocate with a story s/he both wants and needs to tell. As Women's Studies teachers we are particularly conscious of the risks involved here. In our teaching practice we frequently require students to draw on personal experience in order to explore theoretical and political issues. And yet we are conscious that we have an unequal relationship with our students and that for some students exposing the personal is not necessarily a liberating experience. Similarly, like other feminist teachers, we are also selective about which personal aspects of our lives we are prepared to reveal in the classroom (McNeil, 1992). Whilst the personal tutorial is a relatively more private setting, there are similar risks involved. The tutor will have imparted fragmented knowledge about their own lives on the basis that the student will treat it confidentially. The student may then disclose their own fragmented life history secure in the knowledge that the confidence will be reciprocated. Whilst our own experience suggests that such confidences are respected by both sides, we are also aware that verbal guarantees of confidentiality can only be given and accepted on trust (Finch, 1984).

Yet for the narrative to count in terms of mitigating circumstances, it must be documented and passed on to the Chair of the Examination Board. It is not that we as personal tutors do not trust such chairs to deal with the information confidentially and sensitively. It is the fact that we alone are not to be trusted to use this knowledge professionally and that the student is called upon to trust someone they do not know. In most cases students want us to pass on the information. Most illnesses and bereavements are easily documented, but even here there may be difficulties. The illness may be one which carries a stigma as in the case of AIDS or the bereavement may concern a gay or lesbian partner. In making the bereavement visible the student's hitherto 'invisible' sexuality is inadvertently 'outed'. Whilst we as tutors may know that the Chair can be trusted not to be 'homophobic', the student — despite reassurances from us — cannot possibly *know* this for her/himself. In cases of rape, sexual abuse and domestic violence, the student may have overcome enormous emotional obstacles in disclosing such information to even the most empathetic of tutors. There is an understandable reluctance to let the information go any further.

We have both experienced the distressing situation of sitting on examination boards where students we personally knew had serious personal problems were dismissed as 'poorly motivated'. Some failed modules as a consequence, a small minority failed an entire degree. Before coming to these boards we have spoken to students explaining the consequences if they do not divulge this information. Frequently we have expressed the view that 'our hands are tied' if such refusals persist. We will not be able to assist them to achieve the result they so clearly merit. In one case, a highly talented student obtained a third class degree because she chose not to disclose her HIV+ status to the Board. The havoc that the knowledge of her HIV+ status had played on her ability to concentrate ensured that she constantly handed in work late which, despite extensions, ultimately resulted in penalties. These penalties were undeserved but inevitable given the inexplicable lateness of her coursework delivery. This is a frustrating and saddening situation. It is unjust for the student concerned and leaves us in possession of an 'underground knowledge' which cannot be deployed constructively. As personal tutors we not only 'time fret' but we fret about these lost student narratives.

We empathise with the students' reluctance to pass their 'underground knowledge' to the 'overground'. Students, even when very distressed, possess excellent reasons for not wishing their confidentiality to be shared with a third party. They are very rarely acting irrationally or irresponsibly. Ostensibly, it might seem that our hands are tied by the students' refusal to allow the information to be divulged. We argue, however, that in reality our hands are tied by a system which no longer credits us with the ability to judge whether a student's circumstances are extenuating or not. Whilst these issues are made explicit within Women's Studies, we would argue that they are of paramount importance across disciplines — although some disciplines may not recognise them.

'Send three and four pence, we are going to a dance'

It is all too easy to dismiss students as acting recklessly or foolishly when they deny examination boards the opportunity to assess the impact of their personal circumstances upon their academic progress. Students, however, possess sound reasons for this reluctance. There is, for instance, the fear that they will be regarded as engaging with 'special pleading'. The majority of students wish to be judged on their academic performance alone and often, despite our assurances to the contrary, dismiss the extenuating nature of their current circumstances. Other students are aware of the impact of stigma on their lives and experience a sense of transparency of the self when disclosing details of their hidden, stigmatised status. Already in possession of a temporarily fragile sense of self and identity, they do not wish to be further threatened by letting their 'story' pass from their control. Their story is their own and under some circumstances it may be all they feel they control or own at the moment of telling it. There is also the fear of miscommunication or misunderstanding. The apocryphal story of the command 'send reinforcements we're going to advance' which was passed down to the bottom line as 'send three and fourpence we are going to a dance' warns us of such dangers. Students have no way of knowing that the third party, having received an accurate documentation, will interpret it with the wisdom and compassion it deserves.

This is not to claim that personal tutors are more than usually blessed with wisdom and compassion. Most of us have to work very hard to achieve the latter and probably never will achieve the former. We do, however, have a rich experience of working with students who are struggling to not only achieve their degrees but to realise personal ambitions and that much vaunted quality — personal growth. We have developed some skills along the way and we are reluctant to give them up as we struggle to perfect them

'In the boning halls'

In a recently published lyric[1], the Irish singer/songwriter Christy Moore refers to 'the boning halls' of contemporary society. Here the 'carcass is stripped down to the bone' as 'all the flesh is ripped off a country'. In the 'boning halls' everything is destroyed and everything laid bare to the bone. Sometimes it does indeed feel that the public sector, including higher education, is being subjected to the harsh deliberations of the 'boning halls' ... that the rich resources residing within human beings are being wantonly plundered and subjected to a rendering process.

Yet we would argue that there is room for resistance in the 'boning halls'. It is important not to abandon everything to cynical despair or a fatalistic lament about good times gone. They were never really *that* good for most people anyway. It is clear from our experience with prospective students, that many still hold onto a vision of education as an experience allied to self and social development. Whilst, like others (David, 1989; Skeggs, 1994), we have encountered students who view education as a commodity in itself with a marketable qualification as the end result, we have met many who clearly identify education as a means to self-discovery. For these students a return to education is about missed opportunities now to be taken. Such recruits, whilst clearly excited, if sometimes daunted, by the possibilities opened up by new technologies of learning see them as being essentially complemented by the skilled and personal contacts with teaching staff. As most of our feedback forms suggest, students want to have more time to exchange ideas and knowledge with each other. They *do* want to be at the centre of a teaching and learning environment. They also, despite our many failings, want to have more time from us. Indeed, there appears to be a disturbing contradiction between students' expressed needs and the increasingly contractual nature of teaching and learning in higher education (Edwards, 1993, Lilley, this volume). But time alone whilst a help is, understandably, not enough. Time for and with students must be supported by a culture in which there is mutual respect and trust. It is difficult for students to respect and trust their tutors when some of the knowledge and skill acquired by those tutors is systematically devalued. We want our students' personal narratives of both success and failure to continue to be heard. This requires a relatively 'safe place' which can and should be fostered by the personal tutorial. Resistance is fostered and fuelled by collective and individual narratives. For some students, the narrative begins in the personal tutorial, but it certainly doesn't end there.

Dearing do or don't?

At the time of writing, the 1997 General Election is imminent and there is a notable lack of discussion about the future of higher education. Although education is high on the agendas of the three main political parties, the focus is on schooling rather than post compulsory education. The Dearing Committee is not due to report its findings until after the general election but already it appears to be emphasising links with local and business communities and with schools and further education colleges. Whilst we would not wish to pre-empt the outcome of the Committee's deliberations, any focus on structures to the detriment of processes runs the risk of losing sight of the personal needs of those who are to be offered the opportunity of 'education for life'. We will be interested to see whether the Dearing Committee does or does not address the issues we have highlighted here, which we believe are central to a holistic educational experience. Only then can we truly claim to educate for life.

Note

[1] Christy Moore (1996) *Boning Halls*. Taken from Graffiti Tongue, Grapevine, Newberry Recordings Ltd.

References

Abbott, P. and Wallace, C. (1992) *The Family and the New Right*. London: Pluto Press.

Adam, B. (1990) *Time and Social Theory*. Cambridge: Polity Press.

Ball, C. and Eggins, H. (eds) (1989) *Higher Education into the 1990s: New Dimensions*. Milton Keynes: Open University Press.

Banks, S. (1995) *Ethics and Values in Social Work*. London: Macmillan/BASW.

Barnes-Powell, T. and Letherby, G. (forthcoming) 'All In A Day's Work: Gendered Care Work in Higher Education', in D. Malina and S. Maslin-Prothero (eds) *Speaking Our Place: Women's Perspectives on Higher Education*. London: Taylor and Francis.

British Association for Counselling (1985) *Code of Ethics and Practice for Trainers*.

British Sociological Association (1993) *Guidelines for Good Professional Conduct*.

Coppock, V., Haydon, D. and Richter, I. (1995) *The Illusions of 'Post Feminism': New Women, Old Myths*. London: Taylor and Francis.

Corin, C. (1994) 'Fighting Back or Biting Back? Lesbians in Higher Education', in S. Davies, C. Lubelska and J. Quinn (eds) *Changing the Subject: Women in Higher Education*. London: Taylor and Francis.

Cotterill, P. and Waterhouse, R. (forthcoming) 'Women in Higher Education: The Gap Between Corporate Rhetoric and the Reality of Experience', in D. Malina and S. Maslin-Prothero (eds) *Speaking Our Place: Women's Perspectives on Higher Education*. London: Taylor and Francis.

David, M. (1989) 'Education', in M. McCarthy (ed) *The New Politics of Welfare: An Agenda for the 1990s*. London: Macmillan.

Davies, S., Lubelska, C. and Quinn, J. (eds) (1994) *Changing the Subject: Women in Higher Education*. London: Taylor and Francis.

Edwards, R. (1993) *Mature Women Students: Separating or Connecting Family and Education*. London: Taylor and Francis.

Epstein, D. (1995) 'In Our (New) Right Minds: The Hidden Curriculum and the Academy', in L. Morely and V. Walsh (eds) *Feminist Academics: Creative Agents for Change*. London: Taylor and Francis.

Evans, M. (1995) 'Ivory Towers: Life in the Mind', in L. Morely and V. Walsh (eds) *Feminist Academics: Creative Agents for Change*. London: Taylor and Francis.

Finch, J. (1984) 'It's Great to Have Someone to Talk To': The Ethics and Politics of Interviewing Women', in C. Bell and H. Roberts (eds) *Social Researching: Politics, Problems, Practice*. London: Routledge and Kegan Paul.

Finch, J. and Groves, D. (1985) 'Community Care and the Family: A Case for Equal Opportunities', in C. Ungerson (ed) *Women and Social Policy*. London: Macmillan.

Fisher, S (1994) *Stress in Academic Life: The Mental Assembly Line*. Buckingham: Open University Press/SRHE.

Goffman, E. (1968) *Stigma: Notes on the Management of Spoiled Identity*. London: Penguin.

Humm, M. (1994) 'Equal Opportunities and Promoting People', in M. Evans, J. Gossling and A. Seller (eds) *Agenda for Gender*. Canterbury: University of Kent at Canterbury (Women's Studies Committee), pp. 28-35.

Hugman, R. and Smith, D. (eds) (1995) *Ethical Issues in Social Work*. London: Routledge.

Illich, I. (1976) *Limits to Medicine: Medical Nemesis*. (2nd edition) London: Marion Boyars.

Mace, J. (1993) 'University Funding Changes and University Efficiency', in *Higher Education Review*, 25: 7-22.

McNeil, M. (1992) 'Pedagogical Praxis and Problems: Reflections on Teaching about Gender Relations', in H. Hinds, A. Phoenix and J. Stacey (eds) *Working Out: New Directions for Women's Studies*. London: Falmer Press, pp. 18-29.

Matthews, J. (1994) 'Empowering Disabled Women in Higher Education', in S. Davies, C. Lubelska and J. Quinn (eds) *Changing the Subject: Women in Higher Education*, London: Taylor and Francis, pp. 138-147.

Mirza, H. S. (1995) 'Black Women in Higher Education: Defining a Space/Finding a Place', in L. Morely and V. Walsh (eds) *Feminist Academics: Creative Agents for Change*. London: Taylor and Francis, pp. 145-156.

Montgomery, F. and Collette, C. (1996) 'The Patience of a Saint and the Cunning of the Devil: Teaching Women's Studies in the 1990s', *Teaching in Higher Education*, 1 (1): 21-29.

Morley, L. and Walsh, V. (eds) (1995) *Feminist Academics: Creative Agents for Change*. London: Taylor and Francis.

National Committee of Inquiry into Higher Education (*The Dearing Report*). July 1997.

Nicholls, A. (1997) 'Towards New Horizons. Distance Learning: Your Flexible Friend', *The Guardian Higher*, 21 January: ii-iii.

Radcliffe, J. (1996) 'Community Care and New Public Management: The Local Government Response', *Local Government Studies*, 22 (4): 153-166.

Rhys, J. (1971) *After Leaving Mr McKenzie*. London: Penguin.

Skeggs, B. (1994) Women's Studies in Britain in the 1990s: Entitlement Cultures and Institutional Constraints. Paper given at the Women's Studies Network (UK) Association Conference, University of Portsmouth, July.

Staffordshire University (1996) *Strategic Plan 1996/2000*.

Walker, A. (1991) 'The Social Construction of Dependency in Old Age', in M. Loney, R. Bocock, J. Clarke, A. Cochran, P. Graham and M. Wilson (eds) *The State or the Market: Politics and Welfare in Contemporary Britain*. London: Sage.

Williams, G. (1992) *Changing Patterns of Finance in Higher Education*. Buckingham: Open University Press/SRHE.

Wilson, E. (1982) 'Women, the "Community" and the "Family"', in A. Walker (ed) *Community Care: The Family, the State and Social Policy*. Oxford: Basil Blackwell.

Complicated Money: Funding Student Participation in Mass Higher Education

14

Patricia Walters and Elaine Baldwin

Introduction

Recent substantial increase in participation in higher education is accompanied by radical changes in the way the maintenance costs to students are financed. The old maintenance grant system never covered all the financial costs of being a student. The full grant rarely covered all expenses and 'means testing' was based on the assumption of a parental contribution, more or less substantial. The family as a resource therefore was an inherent part of the grant system, as were assumptions that vacation jobs would generate disposable income. Over the past decade a Student Loan Scheme has been devised, initially to supplement the grant system but now widely considered as an eventual replacement of the grant system. Loans are not means-tested. A student can claim up to £2,035 annually to be repaid over a period after graduation. In a sense, therefore, the concept of a formal parental contribution is being phased out. Nevertheless the ceiling on the loan is not so high as to eliminate the need for most students to obtain some degree of material support from family and employment. Family resources and employment income are, and will be, needed and provided for the maintenance needs of students. Moreover, the end to state provision of tuition fees, with scope envisaged for elite institutions to charge top-up fees, will leave students and their families as significant providers. The family, therefore, will remain a key source of the funding for students in mass higher education. At the same time, student employment and its contribution to student income is likely to grow.

Given its centrality as a resource, albeit often tacitly assumed, we would argue that the full significance of the family in the higher education process needs more exploration. We suggest that some of the more subtle, less quantifiable or overt aspects of the family dimension of resourcing have not been recognised. Finding the financial wherewithal to enter and to complete higher education involves individual students and their families in a series of economic transactions. But these, like many economic transactions, cannot be understood independent of their social context. Students and their families operate within a set of complex and variable constraints which influence both the generation and disposal of resources necessary to finance students' education.

Student income derives from a highly mixed bag of resources. Commentators are agreed that the 1990s have seen students turning to a greater variety of sources to help fund their way through university. Thus:

> ...their own savings, parental funding and term-time working are increasing in importance alongside the more traditional sources of funds such as Student Loans, grants and loans and overdrafts from financial institutions. (Barclays Bank; 1996: 1).

> There has been a marked change in the composition of student income since 1988/89. The proportion of support available through grants has declined with a corresponding increase in the proportion from student loans. At the same time, the proportion of income earned, borrowed from commercial creditors, or withdrawn from savings has also increased. ....In 1995–96 three fifths of student income came from grant, parental or spouses' contribution, student loan or Access/Hardship Funds. Two fifths came from other sources. (PSI, 1996: xiv)

Clearly much of the impetus for this growing mixture has been the policy changes of the 1990s. The Education (Student Loans) Act, 1990 aimed at reducing students' reliance on maintenance grants as their major source of income whilst establishing loans as a significant supplementary income source. Further students' eligibility for social security benefits during vacations was withdrawn and the government introduced another source of funding for students: discretionary Access Funds, administered by the education institutions, which aim to help students with financial difficulties or those whose access to full-time higher education might be jeopardised for financial reasons.

The vast majority of students have to engage in complex income generation: financial limits on particular sources prevent any one source providing the necessary wherewithal. Compared with the average student income in 1995/96 of £4,907, the maximum maintenance grant level was £2,340, the maximum student loan level was £1,695, the average disbursement from Access funds to those receiving one is confidential and unknown. Policy directions and economic calculations do not, however, exhaust explanations for the complex and mixed nature of student income. There are also social explanations. Students occupy an heterogeneous social situation largely because they are transitional: transitional between being part of the parental household and being largely independent of it; transitional between being funded by grants of money donated by parents or spouse and/or the state and having income from employment earnings. Students, to attain necessary income, are constrained to comply with the expectations, however unspecific they might seem, of a variety of social institutions — the state, their family, banks, employers and the quasi-public bodies of the Student Loan Company and Access Funds. In their combination of money from different sources students are thus hedged about by a variety of different discourses about money. The reasons for this lie in the particular transitional space occupied by students. Student income is an instance of what Zelizer (1989) calls 'special money'. It is a meaningfully constructed currency, qualitatively different from purely instrumental, rationalised money. It is shaped by the social sphere of transition in which it circulates. It can be argued that, within that sphere, student money is affected by the gender and social class of student 'money handlers'. This perspective on income is well-established sociologically. The recognition of the importance of social and cultural factors in areas that are conventionally regarded as economic has a long history in sociological analysis (Mauss, 1966; Veblen, 1970) and has been revived recently in the work of Cheal (1988) and Fukuyama (1995). The implication of the sociological view of money is that it is never 'just' or 'only' money, but that it is always imprinted with social value and infused by prevailing social relationships. In combining the elements of their income, students are negotiating a process of transition and defining social identity. Aspects of this process of combination will now be explored.

Parental and family money

Assumptions about the family membership of students have been built into the state system of maintenance grants. Students commencing higher education up to the age of twenty six years are assumed to be the financial dependants of their parents and either their parents' or their spouses' income is assessed for maintenance grant purposes. After the age of twenty six only a spouse is so assessed. Currently, according to the PSI study (1996: xv), about three quarters of all students are assessed for a parental or spouses' contribution and a third of all these are awarded a 'full' grant with no assessed contribution. The remainder have assessed contributions based on their parents' or spouses' income which averaged £1,236. The great majority of students expect to receive that contribution in full, although one in six expect a shortfall. In practice many students actually receive more that the assessed amount so that actual contributions averaged £1,467 in 1995, close to a third of average student income.

In such a system it is possible to see parental contributions to student income as structured by expectations that they are grants and consequently patterned by norms of regularity, dependability and being free of any tight performance schedule on the students' part. Whilst many parents are guided by such expectations in the money that they provide, interviews with students in the University of Salford (Walters and Baldwin, 1996) made it clear that many parents seek to tie the money that they give to particular expenditure. Student responses showed that money from the parental source is viewed by students and parents as very directly related to the provision of basic support for a student career, most usually accommodation or food. Parents often seek to ear-mark money for such purposes, sometimes by making direct payments — for example paying the rent — or for a shopping expedition to buy household supplies. The considerable support that most students receive from parents bears the hall-mark of family social processes: resources are managed in 'moral systems' (Finch and Mason, 1993), feelings of rights and obligations structure access to resources (Pahl, 1989) and ideas of 'what might be' construct and inform relationships: there is a negotiated mixture of encapsulation, support, autonomy and independence between student and family.

Gifts play a significant role in these relationships. Aspects of this are revealed by the PSI (1996) study of student finance: it found that family gifts constituted about ten per cent of student income and that this was a considerable increase from the two earlier surveys 1988/89 and 1992/93. However, whilst income from gifts was important, the study found that gifts were a considerable element only in the income of students under twenty six. They were a particular way of transferring resources to 'quasi-independent' households. Furthermore, the researchers calculated the income from gifts by asking students about gifts in 'cash' and in 'kind': it was the researchers who insisted that students attach a monetary value to the gifts. Young students are the recipients of all kinds of gifts from their families. Sometimes the gift is money, but just as often the gifts are clothing, food — in the form of meals as well as actual gifts of food, holidays, phone cards, air miles. The giving of gifts symbolises the on-going affective relationship between parents and children; they are a mark of an expected, continuing close, though nevertheless changing, relationship. In formal terms these transfers of resources from parents to children are real contributions to student and educational economies. Paradoxically, their economic significance is not always recognised by the givers or the recipients. Students see the aid that they receive as a continuation of the diffuse care due to family members. Interviews with University of Salford students (Walters and Baldwin, 1996) found that it was unusual for students to have a clear sense of the variety and amount of goods and services that they received: only close probing revealed that they were recipients of a great deal of the kind of support detailed above. The point is that they do not immediately categorise this as an economic transaction.

The contributions to students' maintenance made by parents and family appear to constitute a form in which 'pure' money is translated into other media. The translation signifies the ambiguity of the transitional state: in part, parents exercise control and limits though ear-marking contributions; in part, they concede the freedom of monetary allowances. The gifts that they give signal the family as ultimate resource for the student, but they also put a distance between the student and the role of dependent.

Student loan and debt

The take-up of student loans has increased rapidly during the nineties. During 1995/96 just over half of all students had borrowed from the Student Loan Company; the average loan being £1,243. This is a considerable increase from 1992/93 when 35% of students had taken out a loan, worth an average £541. Students' attitudes to the accumulation of debt via student loans appear to be changing. In the early 1990s, surveys of student opinion recorded that students did not see it as 'real', heavy or serious debt compared with commercial debts (National Westminster Bank, 1994). More recently, the larger amounts of money at stake and the clear evidence (despite the early maladministration of the Student Loan Company) that, politically, student loans are here to stay, has led to students considering them both as having a serious cost and as being seriously necessary.

The years of being an undergraduate student are years of developing a practice and tolerance of indebtedness (National Westminster Bank 1994). Students increase their propensity to take out student loans beyond the first year of study (PSI, 1996: 64). There is evidence that parents seek to dissuade students from undertaking loans: a mixture of reasons are in play — parental fear about long-term debt, the challenges that a relatively large lump sum poses to careful management, the monetary unaccountability that it inserts into the parent/ student relationship. Parents are most successful in their dissuasion where the parental income is high and also where students live at home. The net result of the latter of these 'background' features is that female students and ethnic minority students are less likely to undertake loans (PSI, 1996: 64). Students, however, do not need parental consent to receive the loan and they may well relish the apparent independence from parents that it offers. Within the operation of the scheme itself there are incentives for the student to take the full amount of the loan. Students cannot, within the same academic year, make a series of applications for fractions of the full loan: hence there is an incentive to apply for the full amount. There is also an incentive to apply for the student loan in the first place because students who have not applied for a loan are ineligible to apply to the special 'Access' hardship funds. Hence taking a student loan starts to assume the guise of financial prudence. Whilst uptake of the student loan is, as indicated earlier, selective in terms of variation in students' family location, it is becoming widespread through the student population. Thus whilst there is a systematic association between parental social class and take up of Student Loans, in 1995 over half the students in each of the classes identified in the PSI study had taken out Student Loans (PSI, 1996: 63-4).

This is an indication of the rapid spread of the practice of taking out Student Loans: a spread likely to increase as the political push behind Loans intensifies. In economistic discourse students are being constructed as individual investors, in some kind of partnership with the State, anticipating the individual as well as the collective benefits from degree level education. There is now much discussion about which kind of repayment schemes best relate loans and future income (Barr and Crawford, 1996). A theme that is surfacing in discussion of schemes is that in some cultural enclaves — working class students, women students, students from ethnic minorities have been noted — there is resistance to acting rationally as investors. Amongst students generally however, reluctance to take out loans is talked about if not acted upon. It is possible that acting economistically is tempered by social considerations arising from the complexities of students' transitional status.

Student employment

There has been a dramatic increase in term-time student employment, supplementing the more traditional pattern of vacation employment. Various recent investigations provide a range of data that build up a composite picture of students' activity rates and a characterisation of the jobs that they do. Rates of student employment measured at any one point of time are lower than rates based on incidence over a period of time. Hakim's (1996) analysis of student employment from S.A.R. census data reckoned that at the date of the 1991 census week (1420 April), the rate of all students aged 19–24 years who had a job was 7.5%. She argued that an upper limit for annual student work rates (ever had a job in the previous 12 months) could be estimated by doubling the current measures. Hakim (1996) reckoned that the 1995 NUS finding that, in 1994, 31.6% of 20–24 year olds in full-time education were in employment was 'on the high side' because it was a measure based on a period of high employment — the summer vacation, *and* it incorporated reference to jobs held some time in the previous year. Other studies, however, undertaken a few years after the 1991 census, tend to confirm the higher figures (PSI, 1996; Barclays Bank, 1996; Ford, 1995; Walters and Baldwin, 1996). Where earlier comparative data is available, the indications are of a substantial rise in the number of students taking employment. Thus the PSI Study:

> In the 1995/96 academic year 69 per cent of young students (aged under 26 when they began their course) had either worked in term time or in one of the two short vacations — a rise from 47% in 1992/3.... (PSI, 1996: 35).

And, where data is available that distinguishes between vacation and term time working, the indications are that whilst vacation work is still the most predominant form of student employment, term time working is now substantially established. A study of a sample of second and third year University of Salford students (Walters and Baldwin, 1996) explored work histories over the previous twelve months. It established that 37% of the students were working in the current semester and that 79% of them had worked during the previous summer vacation. Taking the previous twelve months as a whole, 24% of the respondents had worked during all relevant semesters and 38% only worked during the summer vacation: additionally, 12% of the students had had no employment and 26% of the students had worked in a pattern of duration that fell outside the three other patterns.

The contribution that earnings make to student income has risen markedly during the 1990s and now stands around 15% of student income (PSI, 1996). Research is also starting to focus on the employment conditions of student jobs and the possible impact on student academic performance. Using both quantitative and qualitative data, Ford *et al.* (1995) reckoned that the 'employment profiles' of student employment was wide-ranging — from 'one-off' employment, through limited hours on campus, to substantial hours (in excess of 20), split shifts and multiple jobs. From census analysis, Hakim (1996) concluded that three main jobs accounted for the employment of over half of students — catering (waiters, waitresses, bar staff and cooks), sales work (mainly as sales assistants, retail cashiers, check-out operators and some petrol forecourt attendants), and miscellaneous other service jobs (most commonly kitchen assistants, counter-hands, cleaners and shelf fillers in supermarkets). Hakim argues that whilst these are female dominated occupations nationally, as far as students are concerned they are the source of jobs taken by young men and young women equally. More detailed, local, evidence casts doubt on the generalisation that there is no difference in the kind of jobs taken by male and female students. Certainly evidence on the work patterns of male and female students at the University of Salford (Walters and Baldwin, 1996) reveals strong differences. Female students were almost twice as likely as males to be working in the semester in which they were surveyed and twice as likely as male students to have worked consistently through all previous semesters. There was very little difference between male and female students over summer vacation work. The percentage was high in both cases, with both men and women students who had worked in the previous summer vacation showing a very similar distribution of weekly pay: about half earning under £100 per week and about half earning between £100 and £200.

Employment undertaken during the academic year offers income possibilities to students that seem free of the financial and social costs attaching to other sources of income. Students access employment income through their own volition: income from it is unambiguously theirs and they consider themselves free in the disposal of their earnings. The PSI Study (1996: 21, 31) shows that the proportions of students in each of the five social classes taking employment in the academic year was higher than those taking Student Loans and that in the case of employment there was little class variation. Compared with debt, student employment in vacation and term time is often discussed in very positive terms. The social valuation of part-time work amongst students is not that it is merely necessary but that it is 'socially competent', involving skills of time organisation, job search, negotiation. Students portray their skill and competence in building up their portfolios of part-time jobs, often starting at school: some national department stores encourage students to transfer between their home and university towns. Term time and vacation work have connotations of choice, independence from parents, and student control over finances. Young women students in particular seem more likely to seek out and more able to find these labour market opportunities.

There is, however, a downside to the picture which in part was highlighted by the NUS (1996) survey of student work. In general, the report emphasises the low pay, poor conditions of student employment, often compared with more permanent employed workers alongside them. It draws attention to the particular vulnerabilities of students as term time workers by emphasising some of the contrasts between term-time working and vacation time working which emerge from the data. Thus:

> During term time, the majority of student workers are working unsociable hours at night, in the evening and at weekends though their pay statuses show they receive little in the way of enhanced rates for doing so. During the vacations the majority of students work during the day, but nearly half are also working nights and weekends. (NUS, 1996: 15)

Students working during term time seem more likely to work in pubs, restaurants and clubs than those working in the vacation. If anything, vacation work seems more likely than term-time work to have some kind of a family connection. This is revealed by nearly 40% of students reporting that they got their employment through friends or family.

In terms of the 'control' exercised by students on their finances through employment, the NUS survey emphasises that financial desperation makes students vulnerable. Even aside from such stark terms of description there is the point that neither students nor universities exercise any control over the supply of part-time jobs, or the terms on which they are offered/accepted. Some universities are in relatively employment rich local economies, whilst others are not.

Student financial difficulties and crisis management

For most students the acquisition of financial management skills is as necessary as academic ability to the successful completion of a degree programme. Indeed, the two are frequently linked since financial difficulties may undermine or call a halt to academic study. Students in higher education are engaged in complex juggling of a variety of means of support to meet a variety of needs. There is seldom sufficient margin for students to take their eye off financial concerns and if mistakes are made or if an element of the resource system fails then a crisis can readily develop. Special funds administered by Universities are relegated to deal with cases of severe financial difficulty. There are restrictions on the use of these funds and a university must give an account to HEFCE of their use. In cases where funds are denied to students it seems that parents sometimes pick up the bills. What is clear in the student applications made to Access Funds is that students are reluctant to ask parents for financial help in a crisis because this involves an explicit re-negotiation of a relationship of support that was often tacit and diffuse. Parental help in circumstances of severe hardship may result in students losing most of their discretion and being highly constrained in their use of money.

Students who declare themselves to be in acute or drastic financial difficulty reveal the impact of family circumstances. The family situation with which students enter higher education is significant. Mature students (those over twenty six years) — particularly those with their own partner and child(ren) — enter higher education with the responsibilities and commitments of this stage of life. Often the purpose of higher education is to enable such a student to improve their (and their family's) life chances, but they often enter higher education with financial obligations, the repaying of credit card and store card debts, hire purchase agreements — all the means by which individuals seek to manage on-going requirements on limited resources. The change to student status for mature students shifts their pattern of resourcing. The legal provisions of the benefit system — as well as the economic consequences of a student grant and loan — often adversely affect the support to which student and their families are entitled. The recalculation of, for instance, housing benefit, or free school meals for children, often leaves the student with less support than they expected. Moreover there are, typically, additional expenses such as childcare costs which students have not had to pay previously. The shift in obligation and resourcing of such students causes chronic financial difficulties. Such students do not receive or expect long-term regular support from their families of origin. In fact such support would be beyond the means of most families of origin. In this situation students seek employment to overcome their difficulties but, again, family circumstances play a part. Single parents often find it impossible to find sufficient work to enable them to cover the expenses of childcare and their household commitments.

Younger students (those aged seventeen — twenty five) usually enter higher education from a different family situation. Typically they are still part of the household of their family of origin. They often enter higher education with some savings (PSI, 1996) or at best with little debt. Financial crises for such students seem to have some common origins. Many such students in crisis do not recognise the special characteristics of the resources that they are managing. Young students in severe financial hardship appear both to enter crisis, and to compound it, because they treat all resources as undifferentiated. For example, they use the Student Loan or the Student Grant in its lump sum form to pay off overdrafts and credit card debts. As a result they have no income other than more bank and credit borrowing plus any money from employment. Students are engaged in a complex transaction of 'robbing Peter to pay Paul'. When banks decide to call in an overdraft or credit agencies cap borrowing or enforce repayments students face severe difficulties.

There is a time dimension to student financial crisis which is an outcome of the various time cycles within which students operate. Students reveal the incidence of crisis according to a timescale within student careers. Strategies of management are often based on paid employment, enough of it being undertaken during term time to keep things in balance; employment in the vacations, particularly the summer vacation, contributes to clearing overdrafts and credit card borrowing and to starting the next academic year afresh, free of claims on grants and loans. This accumulation of money in vacation is typically made easier by students living at home where parents freely give day-to-day domestic support at no cost to the student. Students operate within a number of time frames. There is the cyclical time frame of the nine-month academic year within which students seek to manage their earnings and borrowings so that they balance the books or incur a manageable deficit. There is the time frame of the twelve-month calendar year, in which substantial earnings are made to renew the academic year.

Alongside this cyclical movement of deficit and renewal is chronological, cumulative time. It seems that the management strategy often runs into difficulties in the final year of a degree programme. In spite of their intentions, few students manage to clear all their debts by the beginning of the final year, hence there is accumulated debt from year to year. Paid employment, the major means of dealing with the debt, is less desirable for final year students who wish to concentrate on their studies; further, the time frame of this particular academic year does not allow the ultimate summer vacation for replenishment. The time of greatest academic anxiety often coincides with the time of greatest financial anxiety.

Conclusion

Issues of student funding are often posed in dichotomous terms of either public funding or private funding. Historically and contemporarily, however, in Britain public and private funding, individual and state finance have been combined in the resourcing of student maintenance: and combination of public and private finance will be what happens in the future. Nevertheless, as we have indicated, there have been changes: in the range of sources, in the balance of public and private money and in public discourse which has moved to highlighting the importance of individual private funding. The proposals of the Dearing Committee emphatically underline the current power of this discourse. Dominant discourse however, whilst it highlights and structures practice, also obscures elements of social practice. Currently students and their families are being constructed as individual investors in the enterprise of higher education. They are *also* family members, affected by family processes which are social and not narrowly economic and which involve the negotiation of dependence and independence, constraint and autonomy.

The final chapter of a recent authoritative survey of student finance sponsored by the Department of Education and Employment (PSI, 1996) is entitled 'The Balance of Student Finances', signifying the report's concentration on the interrelation of the various financial components of student's low income. Our present chapter supplements such an account by a perspective which emphasises that the balance — sought and often achieved by students — is not only a financial composite but is also the result of social processes involving the creation of student money, a form of special money. The social character of student money is that it is mixed and complex as a result of the inherently transitional state of studentship. Students act not only economistically, seeking to create working balances of finance, calculating the relative advantage or disadvantage of particular combinations of finance. They also act socially, negotiating their social identity as family members in a stage of transition in an immediate and a long-term time frame. Policy making over student finance, student loans in particular, often makes assumptions about these processes. We suggest that more explicit consideration of them along some of the lines that we have started to explore, would give us a more socially nuanced reading of some of the consequences for students likely to issue from post-Dearing proposals. For instance, a highly publicised proposal to the Dearing Committee of 'Individual Learning Accounts' repaid through the National Insurance system focuses attention on the connection between the immediate experience of education and a future labour market experience. Family processes and experience can, however, be as concerned with short-term outcomes and horizons as with long-term horizons. Student concern with negotiating autonomy and independence in the short term of early adulthood can, we argue, lead to a strong disposition to combine higher education and employment. Certainly student employment and its manifold connections with family negotiations and cultural values, with educational achievement and later careers, is under-explored among the unfolding issues of student funding.

References

Barr, N. and Crawford, I. (1996) 'Student Loans: Where are we now?', Discussion Paper, WSP/127, London School of Economics.

Cheal, D. (1988) *The Gift Economy*. London: Routledge and Kegan Paul.

Finch, J. and Mason, J. (1993) *Negotiating Family Responsibilities*. London: Routledge.

Ford, J., Bosworth, D. *et al.* (1995) 'Part Time Work and Full Time Higher Education', *Studies in Higher Education* 20 (2): 187-202.

Fukuyama, F. (1995) *Trust: The Social Virtues and the Creation of Property*. London: Hamish Hamilton.

Hakim, C. (1996) *Working Students*, Working Paper 8. London: Department of Sociology, The London School of Economics and Political Science.

Hutson, S. and Cheung, W-Y. (1992) 'Saturday Jobs: Sixth-formers in the Labour Market and in the Family', in C. Marsh and S. Arber (eds) *Household and Family: Divisions and Change*. London: Macmillan.

Mauss, M. (1966) (2nd edition) *The Gift: Forms and Functions of Exchange in Archaic Societies*. London: Routledge and Kegan Paul.

National Union of Students (NUS) (1996) *Students at Work*, A report on the economic conditions of students in employment. London: National Union of Students and GMB.

National Westminster Bank and Exeter University (1994) *Student Money Matters*.

Pahl, J. (1989) *Money and Marriage*. Basingstoke: Macmillan Education.

Policy Studies Institute (PSI) (1996) *Student Finances: Income, Expenditure and Take Up of Student Loans*. London: PSI.

Veblen, T. (1970) (2nd edition) *The Story of the Leisure Class: An Economic Study of Institutions*. London: Allen and Unwin.

Walters, P. and Baldwin, E. (1996) *Student Resources and Higher Education at the University of Salford*. Report to the Research Committee.

Zelizer, V. A. (1989) 'The Social Meaning of Money: "Special Monies"', *American Journal of Sociology*, 95 (2): 342-377.

V

HIGHER EDUCATION:
A NEW COMPACT?

Commodification and Control in Mass Higher Education: A Double Edged Sword

15

Margaret Edwards

This chapter seeks to explore the notion that the transformations which are taking place within our higher education system indicate more than a transition from elite to mass forms. The changes we are experiencing within universities signal something beyond mere notions of wider access and increased cultural opportunities.

We cannot understand the full import of the rapid transformation which we are experiencing within higher education at the present time without considering the changing relationship between higher education, knowledge and society. For example, Barnett (1994. 22-23) claims that, in the past, higher education held a privileged position wherein it produced the knowledge which was then made available to society at large. However, that relationship has now changed, as he states:

> Crudely speaking, society is coming to determine the forms of knowing that it wishes for itself. It is no longer content to leave their definitions to the academics; ... or even their production. Higher education, furthermore, is having to respond to the epistemological agenda being put to it by the wider society.

Barnett (1994: 14) claims that this changed relationship is indicative of the 'one-dimensionality' of late capitalism whereby reductionism and 'operationalism' flourish and "higher education has turned to favour some forms of knowing and marginalized others". Winter (1995: 129), similarly argues that higher education is "inevitably bound up with the political and economic forces of capitalism" which emphasizes profitability, the commodity form and a 'market logic'.

The type of evidence and argument offered by Barnett (1994) and Winter (1995) does give some insight into the changes which are taking place within higher education. For example, Winter (1995: 135) highlights the manner in which "the products of education and those of manufacturing industry are comparable". Similarly, Barnett (1994) highlights the observable shift from 'knowledge as process to knowledge as product'. However, we need to develop the debate to investigate the factors which have arguably precipitated a change in the status of knowledge. By the same token, we need to examine why knowledge has become commodified. We also need to consider the implications of commodification for the control of higher education.

Knowledge as a commodity

The rapid changes which are taking place within our education system can be perceived as being reflective of fundamental changes within advanced industrial societies such as our own. The debates concerning the trajectory of modern societies are many and varied; are we moving towards a post-industrial era; a post-fordist era; an information society; a post-modern era? Whatever the argument, one feature is consistent within many approaches and that is the notion that knowledge is becoming a commodity. Castells (1989), Jameson (1991) and Lyotard (1984) all identify the manner in which knowledge has entered the domain of the market. This line of argument appears to be sustained by claims made by Barnett (1994) and Winter (1995).

It is not the intention to give a detailed account of the various perspectives within the debate which surrounds informational developments and the potential trajectory of the modern world. Attention will however be paid to the claims made by Jean-François Lyotard and by Frederic Jameson.

It will be argued that, from a postmodern perspective, Lyotard's work offers insight into not only the changed status of knowledge but also the alternative model of 'narrative legitimation' which now serves to underpin knowledge and information (see also Lawson, this volume). Obviously, any change in the status and legitimacy principle of knowledge will impact upon higher education, which has historically been charged with a duty to "lay open the whole body of learning and expound both the principles and foundations of all knowledge" (Lyotard, 1984: 33).

The 'principle of legitimation' which was historically conferred upon universities was premised upon the notion that 'there was meaning to know'; as a consequence, the 'disinterested pursuit of learning' was encouraged. Lyotard (1984) insists that 'the history of knowledge and its institutions' is underpinned by two principal metanarratives: a speculative or philosophical narrative, and a political narrative of emancipation. However, these metanarratives are, for Lyotard, 'value-laden' insofar as they involve partial and subjective ideas about human emancipation and social progress. As a consequence, the whole Enlightenment project which is perceived as being based upon 'pure' knowledge is actually premised upon a language game which takes human emancipation to be the end goal.

Lyotard (1984) proceeds to focus upon the status of knowledge in a postmodern era which displays an 'incredulity regarding metanarratives'. He argues that within postmodern culture "there are many different language games — a heterogeneity of elements, they only give rise to institutions in patches — local determinism". This 'incredulity' is precipitated by two key features.

Firstly, the status of knowledge is impacted upon by the growth of new technologies and the consequent switch from ends to means which, together with the protection given to capitalism during the Keynesian economic regime, have served to recharge capitalism. As Lyotard (1984: 38) indicates, this renewal "has eliminated the communist alternative and valorized the individual enjoyment of goods and services".

Secondly, and perhaps more importantly he identifies 'internal erosion of the legitimacy principle of knowledge'. As Lyotard (1984: 39) claims:

> What we have is a process of delegitimation fuelled by the demand for legitimation itself. The "crisis" of scientific knowledge, signs of which have been accumulating since the end of the nineteenth century, is not born of chance proliferation of sciences, itself an effect of the progress in technology and the expansion of capitalism. It represents, rather, an internal erosion of the legitimacy principle of knowledge. There is erosion at work inside the speculative game, and by loosening the weave of the encyclopaedic net in which each science was to find its place, it eventually sets them free ... The classical dividing lines between the various fields of science are thus called into question — disciplines disappear, overlapping occur at the borders between the sciences, and from these new territories are born.

Within the postmodern condition, knowledge finds itself the victim of delegitimation and the universalising pretensions of the intellectual exercise are called into question.

Science as a unified body breaks down as its legitimacy as a metalanguage is disputed:this results in a splintering of science into a "cloud of specialisms each with its own incompatible mode of proceeding, or language game". The problem as Lyotard (1984: 40) sees it is that the new language games are added to old and no-one can speak all languages. Consequently, the claim to universality becomes even more remote, intellectuals are no longer perceived as having a "special calling to supervise the game of praxis" and, as Lyotard (1988: 301) indicates:

> ... it is probable now and for the foreseeable future [that] we as philosophers, as much as we may be concerned by politics ... are no longer in a position to say publicly: 'here is what you must do' ... This is not to say that there are no longer any intellectuals but

that today's intellectuals, philosophers in so far as they are concerned by politics and questions of the community, are no longer able to speak in the name of 'unquestionable' universality.

Where then resides the 'principle of legitimation' for knowledge within the postmodern condition? Lyotard (1984) argues that the question of legitimation is reformulated around the concept of performativity. If we cannot have truth we can at least settle for performance improvement; efficiency rather than emancipation becomes the game rule. As Usher and Edwards (1994: 175) usefully indicate, "even while the modern totality fragments[,] the postmodern condition allows a non-epic legitimation of knowledge to optimise the efficiency of the system". It is within this economic system and under the game rules of efficiency that education establishes its *raison d'être*. As Lyotard (1984: 36) argues, "knowledge is no longer the subject but in the service of the subject". The 'principle of performativity' becomes the legitimating factor for knowledge production.

The university no longer holds a position of autonomy: it becomes 'a subsystem of the social system' and as such is no longer responsible for the creation of ideals but the creation of skills which will allow the social system as a whole to operate 'to the best performativity'. Lyotard (1984) insists that its mission is no longer that of nurturing an elite group 'capable of guiding the nation towards emancipation'; rather it now has a dual mission wherein it is charged with not only the reproduction of professional and technical intelligentsia but also 'job training and continuing education'.

Thus for Lyotard (1984: 51) the postmodern condition confronts us with a situation wherein knowledge is commodified. He says:

> The question (overt or implied) now asked by the professional student, the State or institutions of higher education is no longer "Is it true?" but "What use is it?" In the context of the mercantilization of knowledge more often than not this question is equivalent to: "Is it saleable?" And in the context of power-growth: "Is it efficient?"

It can be argued that Lyotard's 'narrative analysis' offers a useful insight into the changing function of higher education in the late twentieth century. However, his postmodern framework serves to emphasize the relativism of knowledge and information, rejecting the notion of any underlying grand narratives. As a consequence his approach does not explain why knowledge and information have become 'subject to the mechanism of the market'.

Consumer culture and commodification

Arguably Frederic Jameson's work gives more insight in terms of causation. As Bertens (1995: 10) states:

> A key feature in [Jameson's] interpretation of postmodernism as the
> superstructure of the current socio-economic order is the ever
> increasing penetration of capitalism into our everyday existence or
> to put it differently the ever- increasing commodification of both the
> public and the private .... The onslaught of commodification that
> is characteristic of late capitalism has in the view of theorists such
> as Jameson and Jean Baudrillard even managed to obliterate the
> classically Marxist distinction between economic and cultural.

If we accept this claim then it is possible to discern the transformation taking
place in the field of higher education as reflective of the dynamics of capitalism.
Initiatives such as modularity, credit accumulation and transfer schemes (CATS),
Enterprise in Higher Education (EHE) and the growth of managerialism tend
to be accepted as necessary elements of a 'mass system' can alternatively be
viewed as "an expression of the inherent developmental logic of late capitalism"
(Winter 1995: 133) whereby knowledge and information become commodities
and students become consumers, and where the 'cultural authority' of academics
is usurped by the market. As Winter (1995: 129) indicates:

> A bereft humanity seems to be condemned for the time being to
> organise *all* its affairs within the general parameters of capitalism,
> whose apparent claim is that matters of value and priority must be
> adjudicated simply by the forces of supply and demand.

Arguably, mass systems do not need to be facilitated by modularity and credit
transfer schemes. Nevertheless, these now familiar features of higher education
— along with quality assurance procedures and the growth of corporate enterprise
culture — do serve to facilitate commodification at three levels. Firstly, modularity
and credit transfer schemes are consumer oriented insofar as they allow customer
choice and flexibility. Secondly, the application of quality assurance procedures
to core activities of teaching and research assists commodification from within
by providing performance indicators which serve not only to facilitate consumer
choice but also to promote competition between institutions. Thirdly, the culture
of corporate enterprise (Becher and Kogan ,1994; McNay, 1995) which is in evidence
in many of the 'new' universities arguably expedites the 'industrialization' of
higher education. Within this scenario, Winter (1995) states that higher education,
once perceived as 'craft work' gives way to the pressure of 'highly capitalised
production' and results in changes within the labour process which equate with
a 'proletarianization' of the academic profession (Halsey, 1992; Winter, 1995).

  If we accept these arguments, then we must accede to the notion that higher
education has become or is in the process of becoming commodified and we must
consider in more detail the implications of that process in terms of control and
autonomy.

However, we must be alert to the fact that an explanation couched merely in terms of a correspondence between the demands of a capitalist economy and the 'products' of higher education will leave us with a partial understanding. Can commodification be adequately explained by focusing upon economic factors and the demands of capitalism? We must consider this question more fully if we are to gain an adequate understanding of the relationship between higher education, knowledge, and society. An approach which gives primacy to the capitalist economy has the potential to deflect analysis away from the extent to which higher education institutions have to preserve the legitimacy of their endeavours, as Apple (1988: 123) reminds us:

> The educational system is not an instrument of the capitalist class. It is the product of conflict between the dominant and the dominated. Education is at once the result of contradictions and the source of new contradictions. It is an arena of conflict over the production of knowledge, ideology and employment, a place where social movements try to meet their needs and business attempts to reproduce hegemony.

Thus an approach which only focuses upon the commodification of higher education as a feature of the intensification of late capitalism would tend to reify capitalism and as a consequence deflect analysis away from the extent to which particular institutions and stakeholders use dominant discourse and 'technologies of power' to manipulate consent.

Control and autonomy in higher education

Education in general has historically had to serve 'many masters'. Ranson (1994) has argued that education serves a multiplicity of functions: education for the individual; education for society; education for the polity; education for the economy.

The priorities within education change over time depending upon changes and demands within cultural, political, and economic dimensions of society. Nevertheless, the higher education sector has always appeared to have more academic autonomy than the compulsory state sector.

Nonetheless, Becher and Kogan (1994: 177) argue that there is a 'quadrilateral of interests' which relates to the British higher education system:

> ...each emphasising their own value positions with which higher education must negotiate, and within which it must find its own path. One group of values is professional and derives from academic norms and aspirations. Another is governmental and is concerned with the demands of the state, which can range in different times from those of theocracy to those of the economy. A third is that of the market as it seeks particular skills in its workforce and particular forms of knowledge for conversion into wealth production. And,

finally there is that of public and social utility at large, whose interests may lie both in increased educational opportunities and in the maintenance and enhancement of a civilised society.

It would appear that this 'quadrilateral of interests' is constructed in terms of value positions held within the academic community, the state, the market and society at large. However, whilst Becher and Kogan (1994) usefully identify the four key forces, their notion of a quadrilateral is misleading, in as much as it infers independent forces and does not fully convey the dynamics and interplay of the various value positions. Arguably, a more powerful model for examining the process of commodification and related issues of control within higher education is the 'forcefield analysis' model developed by Kurt Lewin (1948). In this model, the current situation is perceived as a temporary equilibrium which is arguably held in position by two sets of forces: 'driving forces' which push change along and 'restraining forces' which resist or pull back against change.

The questions which need to be addressed here are these: how and why have the balance of forces shifted between the various value positions highlighted by Becher and Kogan (1994) in order to promote commodification and bring about a change within control in higher education?

To answer these questions we need to adopt a theoretical approach which can access an understanding at the level of the individual and at the level of the institution or plurality. Whilst Becher and Kogan's 'quadrilateral of interests' is couched in terms of pluralities, groups and structures we must bear in mind that individual agency has a role to play in bringing about change. As Apple (1988) argues we cannot legitimately talk of an 'imposition theory' whereby changes are imposed in an arbitrary manner by dominant groups; how, if this is the case, could we talk of a 'popular higher education' (Ball and Eggins, 1989)? For Apple (1988: 128), imposition theory is inadequate because:

> What it forgets is that most institutions not only came about because of conflict, but are continuously riven by conflict today. Furthermore, people employed in these institutions at all levels often have their own interests they try to pursue based upon their own material circumstances and histories. Many times, these interests will cohere with those of dominant groups, perhaps especially now when capital and the right are resurgent. At times, though these same people will mediate, transform, and attempt to generally set limits on what is being imposed from outside. They will also try to employ such 'impositions' for their own ends, and that will have a good deal to do with their own class, race, and gender location.

So with this argument in mind, let us consider each element in the 'quadrilateral of interests' to establish how mediation, transformation and imposition are occurring.

Transformation and the academic sommunity

It can be argued that it is the academic community itself which has borne the brunt of the recent transformations in higher education. The progress from an elite to a mass system and the concomitant moves to modularity, credit accumulation, semesterisation, along with a growth of competence based and vocational learning, and the introduction of quality control procedures have had a massive effect upon academics in general. These changes have meant increased work loads both teaching and administrative and a loss of autonomy as it relates to the learning experience. As Winter (1995: 134) states:

> ...gone is the general authority of the individual 'educator' (parent figure or cultural crusader): instead HE staff are purveyors of commodities within a knowledge supermarket.

Can these changes be seen as an unwarranted imposition from outside the arena of higher education? Firstly, it must be recognised that not all universities have had to bear the innovations discussed above. For example, modularity, credit accumulation, and competence-based learning are arguably more likely to be embraced wholeheartedly by the 'new' as opposed to the 'traditional' universities. Similarly, when these innovations have been introduced they have often been modified and customised by individual institutions to meet their own needs. As Tapper and Salter (1992: 32) suggest, the 'economic ideology of education' cannot be imposed on all universities. They argue:

> The State has to be aware of the fact that the ability of individual universities to combine knowledge and status into a form of socio-political power varies considerably. Oxford and Cambridge have far greater status to lend to a knowledge area than does the average university. In addition, the social and cultural advantages of having attended one of the ancient universities reinforces these other differences and results in a university system which is highly differentiated in terms of the amount of socio-political power possessed by individual institutions. Any attempt by the state to impose ideological, financial or administrative pressure upon the universities is therefore likely to produce a different response from different institutions.

Secondly, the academic community in general has concurred with the notion that wider access to higher education is advantageous for universities and for society albeit that this is typically underpinned by liberal humanist rather than economic motivations (see Lawson, and Parker and Courtney, this volume). It can be asserted that in general the academic community would aspire to the traditional liberal ideal that emphasizes the pursuit of knowledge for its own sake including the advancement of knowledge as well as the transmission, as this would allow them to maintain "their hegemony over the higher education sphere" (Tapper and Salter, 1992: 11).

Thirdly, the splintering of disciplines and the overlapping identified by Lyotard (1984) serve to provide many academics with opportunities for research and career advancement which they might not have had in the 'traditional' university. One only has to consider the splintering of sciences into a range of faculties or the growth of thematic degrees such as 'Environmental Studies', 'European Studies' or 'Women's Studies'.

Fourthly, the 'postmodern condition' has arguably created 'space' and opportunities within higher education for groups who would not in the past have had a voice. In particular, the work of feminist academics is being more readily recognised. Similarly, the promotion of experiential learning within higher education has allowed feminist academics to further promote their own pedagogical ideals.

Finally, the requirements of the internal and external quality assurance and enhancement procedures have arguably provided opportunities for academics to embellish their own professional development by way of increased research activity and staff development in teaching and learning.

It may appear that of the stakeholders in higher education, the academic community has had most to lose by recent innovations. But it can be argued that sufficient numbers of the community have 'bought into' the range of discourses which accompany these changes or 'employed impositions for their own ends' to make the transformation a viable proposition.

Transformation and the state

When we consider the role played by the State as a stakeholder in higher education we must be alert to the fact that the State gains its legitimacy from the people (Lyotard 1984). However, a liberal democratic state such as our own which is also situated within a capitalist economic system has to balance the public demands based upon 'person rights' with economic demands based upon 'property rights' (Bowles and Gintis 1986, Apple 1988).

In terms of a move to mass higher education, one can see that it has been very much within the State's interest to promote this action both in terms of 'people rights' and 'property rights'. There appears to be an articulation between economic and social demands which has served to promote an ethos of mass higher education which is acceptable to employers, students and parents. However, this ethos is not underpinned by the notion of a liberal humanist education which perceives education as an end in itself but more as a progressive vocationalist one which also emphasizes use value (Lewis, 1994).

However, in the past the State has had little control over universities. Salter and Tapper (1994: 186) state:

There was a tradition of university independence from the State (
in spite of ever greater dependence upon the State's financial input),
so the universities were not expected to rush lemming-like to fulfil
specific societal demands. For example, while the State would expect
a positive response to increased demand for higher education, or
pleas for the expansion of research that allegedly would benefit the
economy, the universities could rely upon respect for their autonomy,
as well as the potential status that they had to confer, as significant
bargaining counters.

Arguably, this is why the Robbins Report, which was seen as the State's first
attempt to bring higher education in line with economic requirements, was not
successful. Halsey (1992: 14) claims that "the Robbins Report was more a
consolidation of Victorian expansion than the beginning of mass higher
education". Similarly, Tapper and Salter (1992: 13) assert that the Report's
requirement that unlimited expansion be "guided by a high quality and expensive
form of elite education" was problematic. They suggest that "the fact that the
reality and the ideology are fundamentally irreconcilable made no difference to
the attempt to legitimate the former with the latter".

Nevertheless as the British economy declined rapidly in the 1970s and the
early 1980s and the legitimacy of the State itself was threatened, it was recognised
that the autonomy of the universities must be reduced and that higher education
must be made to confront its role as a functional subsystem of society (Lyotard,
1984). For, as Barnett (1994: 20) says, "the academic corps has so immersed itself
in its disciplinary interests that the problems of the wider society have been
neglected".

The 'academic corps' could not fully withstand the 'attack' on its autonomy
on two counts. Firstly, the disciplines could no longer hold a claim to universality
and a 'disinterested pursuit of learning' because of the delegitimation created
by a postmodern rejection of grand narratives. The grand narrative of speculative
unity which had privileged universities and had provided "the basis for justifying
academic freedom and the 'retreat into the ivory tower' to pursue the development of knowledge unconstrained by concerns for its relevance" (Usher and
Edwards 1994) no longer provided aegis for the academics. As Tapper and Salter
(1992: 16) indicate, "the legitimating power of the traditional liberal ideal relied
heavily on ideas with an 'absolute' status" and the academic community could
no longer use this as an 'ideological protection' against the 'application of
economic values to education'.

Secondly, despite their autonomy, universities relied heavily upon the state
for funding and cuts in public expenditure introduced by the Conservative
government in the early 1980s had a drastic effect on university budgets. As
Halsey (1992: 5) indicates, "between 1980 and 1983 the universities had to reduce

their budgets by approximately 15 per cent, and there were further resource cuts in subsequent years". Autonomy was difficult to maintain when funding was tightly restricted.

Thus changes engineered by the State and articulated within two key White papers — *Higher Education: Meeting the Challenge* (April 1987) and *Higher Education: A New Framework* (May 1991) — are being assimilated by the higher education sector. As Barnett (1994: 20) indicates:

> Higher education has begun to show a paradigm shift in reorienting its knowledge functions, its research projects, its curricula and its wider mission towards the wider society. 'Paradigm shift' is becoming an empty phrase, used all to readily to describe the first signs of any social change. It is justified here since there are indications of academe, in its most intimate recesses, thinking explicitly of the world beyond in framing and delivering a curriculum.

Transformation and market values

When considering the market as one of the 'quadrilaterals of interest' we need to examine how market values have impacted upon higher education and how universities have sought to mediate their relationships within a market framework.

If we accept the arguments of Jameson (1991) and Winter (1995) we must acknowledge that knowledge is now a commodity like any other and as such can be bought and sold and those who produce it are regulated by a commercial environment which is encompassed by the notions of competition and supply and demand.

One could argue that this state of affairs eminently suits the State insofar as it reduces the autonomy of higher education and makes it more accountable to its customers i.e. students and employers. Similarly, it provides the potential for 'privatisation' which will allow the State to unburden itself of much of the cost of a mass system. As Becher and Kogan (1994: 183) indicate:

> Market models are designed to privatise what some would consider and overprotected sector of public activity and to force its activities into open commercial competition... The system must be broken of its heavy dependence on tax payers money and forced to sell itself to its immediate clients, the intending students and the employers of graduates.

Whilst the notion of market values entering the world of higher education may be more than acceptable to the State it would appear to be diametrically opposed to the values held by academics who still maintain a claim to academic freedom. However, as Becher and Kogan (1984: 184) claim, "the assumption that higher education should behave entrepreneurially is not intrinsically antipathetic to academics". They argue that competition is 'endemic in the system' witness the battle for ratings within Research Assessment Exercises, the competition for best students and best qualified staff. As a consequence, what might appear to be the external imposition of a market framework can offer opportunities for the academic community to employ the impositions for their own ends. As Schuller (1992: 33) indicates:

> One of the consequences of the intensified competition and the context within which it has been created is what might be called, not too unhappily, the commodification of academic relations.

Transformation and social and public values

The fourth aspect of the 'quadrilateral of interests' identified by Becher and Kogan (1994) is that of social and public utility and when examining the values which sustain social and public utility, we again need to address the issue of legitimacy.

Halsey (1992) indicates that universities are 'intrinsically inegalitarian institutions' insofar as they serve to maintain social stratification by controlling access to a highly prized intellectual culture. Nevertheless the inegalitarian aspect of higher education has in the past been counterbalanced by the fact that legitimacy was conferred upon the higher education system by the populace because universities were concerned with the unfettered production of knowledge for the betterment of society. The majority of society would never experience a university education but they acknowledged the right of the higher education system to set the 'epistemological agenda'.

However, that right to set the 'epistemological agenda' has come under attack for two reasons. Firstly, there is now a recognition that an advanced society such as Britain cannot afford to allow its population to remain 'educationally polarized' (Ball, 1989; Halsey, 1992; Barnett, 1994). A widening of educational opportunity (Halsey, 1992) can ensure that social order is maintained. Similarly, a more relevant curriculum which encourages transferable skills, continuing education and job training (Lyotard, 1984) can improve the economic system's performance.

Secondly, as Usher and Edwards (1994: 196) suggest:

> ...in the postmodern moment the educational is recast as the cultivation of desire through experience(s) as a condition of and a response to the economic and social fragmentation initiated by uncertainties of scientific and foundational knowledge, the limits of technical rationality and the consequent failings of the modern project.

Usher and Edwards (1994) claim that uncertainty has led to an upsurge in public support for experiential learning which can be defined as 'learning from and through experience'. As Hart (1992: 191) indicates, "this means not only that the individual learner must be able to recognize and actualize the educative potential contained in experience, but also be able to organize her experiences in such a way that they are or become educative". Two strands need to be developed when considering the transition to experiential forms of learning, one which stems from the 'postmodern condition' and one which can be linked with commodification and the 'cultural logic of late capitalism'.

A key element of the postmodern condition is the rejection of universal rationality and truth as espoused within the 'Enlightenment project'. "The disinterested producer of knowledge is no more", state Usher and Edwards (1994: 198): "in the postmodern moment we are all producers of knowledge but through participation and immersion not detachment". This dramatic change in the epistemological agenda in turn creates the 'space' for social movements other than those based upon class e.g. feminism and anti-racism.

Obviously, this has implications for the relationship between society and higher education. In a world of multiple realities the academic's position is weakened and, as Usher and Edwards (1994: 199) claim, "it is the consumer (the learner) rather than the producer (the educator) who is articulated as having the most power in the situation and given the greater importance".

Individuals who in the past would have seen no 'accommodation' within the realm of the university now look to it to give validity to their 'experiential learning' and "the accreditation of prior learning, workbased learning, learner centred curriculum frameworks, encouragement for the autonomous learner all embody, recognise and give expression to the validity of experiential learning" (Usher and Edwards 1994: 203).

It can be argued that this type of learning has the potential to break down barriers in higher education, opening up the higher education system to allow more in terms of equal opportunity. Similarly, experiential learning serves to promote the notion of 'life long learning' and provides the potential for a more critical pedagogy (Freire, 1985; McLaren,1995).

However, experiential learning, which is becoming a feature of innovative practice in higher education, also sits neatly within the discourse of competence and vocational education. In terms of public utility it allows higher education to open up the ranks to mature students, part-time students and those seeking continuous education and retraining. As a consequence the pedagogical base of experiential learning facilitates the production of the flexible worker and the life long learner who will readily police themselves in the service of an advanced capitalist economy:

> Support for experiential learning brings together different wings of conservatism it combines the anti-education culture, and particularly hostility to the 'progressive' practice of teachers, lecturers and tutors, with a more socially authoritarian desire to assert control over the outcomes of experience. In this way, power of the consumer and the market is asserted over that of the producer and the education system, thereby transforming experience into a commodity to be exchanged for credit towards qualifications. (Usher and Edwards, 1994: 204)

When we examine the 'quadrilateral of interests' as a whole we can arguably observe a strong tendency for State, market and social and public values to create the 'driving forces' for the creation of a commodified model of mass higher education. The academic community as a 'restraining force' has not mounted strong resistance to this model and has to an extent employed the imposition of this model for its own ends. Delegitimation of the higher education system has been avoided and the legitimacy of the State has been preserved insofar as it has opened up an elite system, brought it more into line with economic demands and sought to lift the burden of funding from the tax payer. Social and public demands are beginning to be met by the widening of university access and the development of experiential learning within the university curriculum.

Nevertheless, it would appear that this consumerist model does accord most readily with the interests of the market and economic demands. However, because these interests cohere so readily with other elements of the quadrilateral we must support Apple (1988) in his argument against an imposition theory which is economically reductionist.

Democratising higher education — some contradictory tendencies

Is it then the case that a re-articulation of the relationship between higher education, knowledge and society has created a 'democratic' higher education? Or, conversely, has that re-articulation created a commodified form of higher education which is based upon 'operationalism' and, as Barnett (1994: 15) states, the "regeneration of capital (which) requires not knowledge *per se*, but abilities to exploit and if necessary discard knowledge"?

Apple (1988: 122) exhorts us not to oversimplify any theory that links education to the social formation. He argues that capitalism must be perceived "not simply as an economy but as a way of life". He claims:

> This requires an approach not only to the economy but one that is a theory of the social totality, of the complex and contradictory interconnections within and among the economic, political and

cultural/ideological spheres, with the economic being even more powerful in times of crisis.

To understand the changes which have taken place within higher education in recent years, the move towards commodification, the altered relationship between society, knowledge and higher education, we need to confront the operations of power within society; not in a reductionist manner which only addresses class dominance but in a manner which relates the changes to discourse analysis and hegemonic struggle.

Thus, it is essential that we draw on the work of Foucault and more importantly Gramsci in our efforts to comprehend the power relationships which arguably underpin the re-articulation between higher education and the social totality. As Holub (1992: 29) claims:

> Foucault and Gramsci agree ... on one issue; that power is not imposed from above, but that operations of power and their success depend on consent from below.

At one level, Foucault's analysis of discourse gives us a purchase on the manner in which individuals buy into discourse and find meaning and the way in which 'regimes of truth' are constructed:

> The world is perceived differently within different discourses. Discourse is structured by assumptions within which any speaker must operate in order to be heard as meaningful. Thus the concept of discourse emphasizes the social process that produce meaning. (Ball, 1990a: 3)

It can be argued that individuals use discourse to make sense of their lives, they identify with fundamental features of a discourse and utilise these to form or reform their own world view. For example, the discourse of 'experiential learning' has been embraced by learners and educators alike as an empowering feature of education (Usher and Edwards, 1994). Experiential learning is seen by learners as an enabling feature which allows them to have control over what they learn and how they learn; within this discourse their prior experience is recognised and valued. In particular, this form of learning is embraced by groups whose knowledge and experience has in the past been marginalised, e.g. women and ethnic minority groups. Similarly, this same discourse is embraced by 'the new middle classes' insofar as it allows them to promote their own values. Neo-conservative governments have also bought into this discourse because it serves to promote a form of vocational education with use value. As Usher and Edwards (1994: 203) state, "Neo-conservative governments, the new middle classes and oppositional forces struggling for equality and against oppression have all felt able to support initiatives based upon the validity of experiential learning". As Ball (1990b) has pointed out, a strange alliance indeed.

Individuals feel empowered by the discourse of experiential learning and this is precisely how 'regimes of truth' are constructed. As Usher and Edwards (1994: 89) indicate, "Foucault is challenging the notion that the exercise of power is simply oppressive, a negative force which weighs on us and stops us from doing things we would otherwise do". However, Foucault also recognises that whilst discourses have the potential to 'empower' they also have the potential to 'disempower'. Usher and Edwards (1994: 98) describe how this disempowerment can take place:

> In this process, knowledge is an aspect of regulatory power which operates 'externally'. At the same time, regulation can take the form of self-regulation, where knowledge is self-knowledge. At one level, this produces 'empowered' subjects; individuals who are empowered by learning and knowing more about themselves. However, subjects 'disempower themselves in the very process of 'self-empowerment', because this very power of learning about oneself is also the condition for self-regulation; one learns the limits of one's own possibilities — limits which are a function of discourses rather than 'natural' factors.

Within the articulation of experiential learning we have then the potential for disempowerment and the potential for the creation of 'docile bodies'. That element of experiential learning which lends itself to competence base assessment and behavioural objectives can serve to construct a "compliant body of practitioners … and a processed group of graduates" (Dwyer, 1995: 472). Thus whilst Foucault emphasizes that "power is not one-sided, the understanding of power which informs the image of 'docile bodies' belies this" (p. 472).

It can be argued that Gramsci takes a more insightful approach to power relationships. Whilst he agrees with Foucault on the ubiquity of power relationships, he sees power has having a directed focus. As Holub (1992: 29) indicates:

> If power is everywhere it is not everywhere in the same form and to the same degree … Some social groups possess more economic, social and cultural power than others and since the imbalance of power is neither easily challenged nor readily changed there is a directedness to power relations.

Gramsci exhorts us to think in terms of dominant discourse and the manner in which discourse can be utilised to establish hegemony. Thus any notion we may have about a re-articulation of higher education, society and knowledge in terms of a democratic higher education must be tempered by a recognition that there is:

> …a transportability of such a discourse as person rights not only from one sphere or site to another but to an opposing and often reactionary

group which is able to use such meanings for its own purposes ...
there is no guarantee that the trajectory of such 'transportable
discourses' is necessary in a progressive direction. (Apple, 1988:
125-126)

Thus when we examine the recent repositioning of higher education we need
to be aware that those changes which may have signalled the democratisation
of the university system — wider access; consumer choice; credit accumulation
and modularity; experiential learning and accreditation of prior learning;
Enterprise in Higher Education (EHE) projects — may similarly have the potential
to create a system which is totally subsumed within the commodity form. For
example, the manner in which experiential learning and competency based
learning can create 'docile bodies' has already been identified. However, as Usher
and Edwards (1994: 204) indicate, it also serves to reduce the autonomy of the
education system:

> Experiential learning is largely circumscribed by employers' needs
> for particular kinds of labour and consumers. Experiential learning
> unsettles the established order, but this can only go so far in order
> that the limits of social order are maintained. The regulation of
> experience is a means of by-passing experienced practitioners and
> negating the powers of their professional judgement ... experiential
> learning is opened and closed in the same moment.

Similarly, as this reduction in autonomy takes place, the strength of the 'academic
community' as an hegemonic force is weakened by a whole range of strains and
tensions arising from the commodification of academic relations. As Schuller
(1992: 34) claims competition for resources, the growth of managerialism, the
fragmentation of knowledge, strains on academic loyalty are indicative of a break
down in the 'collective web' of interdependent academic exchange. He states
"the shift is away from a collective web towards a network of individualised,
bilateral and monetarized relationships".

It can be asserted that the democratising potential of recent changes in higher
education has been 'reappropriated by the right's hegemonic project'): the
transition to mass higher education arguably being used as a vehicle for
supporting a re-energised capitalism under the guise of the popular discourse
of democracy, as Apple (1988: 121) claims:

> The key to winning, to establishing hegemony is usually that group
> which can establish the parameters of the terms of the debate, that
> group which can incorporate the competing claims of other groups
> under its own discourse about education and social goals.

Concluding remarks

What then of the future — is the ground lost to the 'right's hegemonic project' in higher education irretrievable? Is there a potential to regain ground and to reinsert a genuine democracy within higher education?

The answers to these questions will rest, in the first instance, upon the reaction of the academic community. They need to have a general awareness of the impact of commodification and they need to fully explore the issue for, as Schuller (1992: 39) indicates, "their freedom to explore such an issue, and the habit of critical enquiry to which they aspire, should enable them to do so. If they do not, one consequence may be a reinterpretation, by others of that very freedom to do so".

The inner motivation of the academic community has been that of the discipline (Barnett, 1994): it has arguably been inward looking and has not fully appreciated or noted the impact of the restructuring and repositioning of higher education which has been taking place in recent years. If, as Barnett (1994: 22) argues, "higher education … has changed from being and institution *in* society to becoming an institution *of* society", then the academic community needs to fully recognise and act upon this. The 'ivory tower' mentality must be dispelled and academics must confront the fact that they are no longer in a privileged position shielded from the vicissitudes of the market.

However, accepting that they are part of an institution of society does not foreordain that they should function on an operationalist basis. We have already briefly discussed the manner in which academics can "mediate, transform and attempt to generally set limits on what is being imposed from outside" (Apple, 1988: 120). Docile bodies do not have to be the natural outcome of mass higher education.

The academic community has it within its power to produce graduates who are more than operationally competent and more than academically competent. As Barnett (1994: 179) claims, the educational aim for the new century must be couched in terms of "life world becoming" and "higher education as self - construction" rather than the "know-how of operational competence and the know-that of academic competence".

In order to achieve outcomes based upon 'reflective knowing', academics have to be prepared to realign their own conceptions of knowledge, they must become 'reflective practitioners' who are prepared to involve themselves in a dialogical process. As Barnett (1994: 192-193) indicates:

> It will be apparent that a pedagogy and a curriculum of the kind argued for … places definite and considerable responsibilities on academics and educators. In an education for academic or operational competence, the responsibilities are definite but limited; on the one hand, to enable individuals to live comfortably in

disciplinary territories and, on the other hand, to bring students to a mastery of the identified skills. In higher education for life, the educator's responsibilities are not merely expanded but are susceptible to continuing redefinition and expansion and even challenge.

If we are to procure a democratic higher education system which meets the needs of society — a society in which 'capitalism is a way of life' — then we need to think in broader terms than an open access, mass higher education system which prepares individuals for work in an advanced economy. Within this formation 'democratic effects are not automatic' (Apple, 1988); rather, this formation permits a competitive market-oriented approach to flourish and negate 'person rights' at the expense of 'property rights'. The mission of higher education should be focused upon the extension of 'person rights' and the creation of a 'learning society' oriented not merely to the requirements of the economy but to the requirements of individuals by giving them 'ability to act on the world' (Brown and Lauder, 1992).

References

Apple, M. (1988) 'Facing the Complexity of Power', in M. Cole (ed) *Bowles and Gintis Revisited*. London: Falmer Press.

Ball, S. (1990a) *Foucault and Education Disciplines and Knowledge*. London: Routledge.

——— (1990b) *Politics and Policy Making in Education: Explorations in Policy Sociology*. London: Routledge.

Ball, C. and Eggins, H. (eds) (1989) *Higher Education into the 1990s*. Buckingham: The Society for Research into Higher Education and Open University Press.

Barnett, R. (1994) *The Limits of Competence: Knowledge Higher Education and Society*. Buckingham: The Society for Research into Higher Education and Open University Press.

Becker, T. and Kogan, M. (1994) *Process and Structure in Higher Education*. London: Routledge.

Bertens, H. (1994) *The Idea of the Postmodern — a History*. London: Routledge.

Bowles, S. and Gintis, H. (1986) *Democracy and Capitalism: Property Community and the Contradiction of Modern Social Thought*. New York: Basic Books.

Brown, P. and Lauder, H. (eds) (1992) *Education for Economic Survival: From Fordism to Post-Fordism?*. London: Routledge.

Castells, M. (1989) *The Informational City: Informational Technology Economic Restructuring and the Urban-Regional Process*. Oxford: Blackwell.

Dwyer, P.J. (1995) 'Foucault Docile Bodies and Post-Compulsory Education in Australia', *British Journal of Sociology of Education* 16 (4).

Freire, P. (1985) *The Politics of Education*. South Hadley: Bergin and Harvey.

Halsey, A. (1992) *The Decline of Donnish Dominion*. Oxford: Clarendon Press.

Harvey, D. (1991) *The Condition of Postmodernity*. Oxford: Blackwell.

Holub, R. (1992) *Antonio Gramsci: Beyond Marxism and Postmodernism*. London: Routledge.

Hart, M. (1992) *Working and Educating for Life: Feminist and International Perspectives on Adult Education*. London: Routledge.

Jameson, F. (1991) *Postmodernism or the Cultural Logic of Late Capitalism*. London: Verso.

Lewis, T. (1994) 'Bridging the Liberal Vocational Divide: An Examination of Recent British and American Versions of an Old Debate', *Oxford Review of Education* *2(2)*.

Lewin, K. (1948) *Resolving Social Conflicts*. New York: Harper and Brothers.

Lyotard, J. F. (1984) *The Postmodern Condition: a Report on Knowledge*. Manchester: Manchester University Press.

—————— (1988) 'An Interview', *Theory, Culture & Society*, 5 (2-3).

McLaren, P. (1995) *Critical Pedagogy and Predatory Culture*: London and New York: Routledge.

McNay, I. (1995) 'From the Collegial Academy to Corporate Enterprise: the Changing Cultures of Universities', in T. Schuller (ed) *The Changing University*. Buckingham: The Society for Research into Higher Education and Open University Press.

Ranson, S. (1994) *Towards a Learning Society*. London: Cassells.

Robbins Report (1963) *Higher Education: Report of the Committee Appointed by the Prime Minister under the Chairmanship of Lord Robbins.*

Salter, B. and Tapper, T. (1994) *The State and Higher Education*. The Woburn Press.

Schuller, T. (1992) 'The Exploding Community? The University Idea and the Smashing of the Academic Atom' in I. McNay (ed) *Visions of Post-Compulsory Education*. Buckingham: The Society for Research into Higher Education and Open University Press.

Tapper, T. and Salter, B. (1992) *Oxford Cambridge and the Changing Idea of the University*. Buckingham: The Society for Research into Higher Education and Open University Press.

Usher, R. and Edwards, R. (1994) *Postmodernism and Education*. London: Routledge.

Winter, R. (1995) 'The University of Life PLC: The Industrialization of Higher Education?', in J. Smythe (ed) *Academic Work — The Changing Labour Process in Higher Education*. Buckingham: The Society for Research into Higher Education and Open University Press.

Culture and Utility: Phrases in Dispute

16

Andrew Lawson

A spectre is said to be haunting the modern university: the spectre of Excellence. According to Timothy Clark and Nicholas Royle, editors of the *Oxford Literary Review*, a viscious new ideology of "operational competence" has steadily displaced the old, liberal humanist model of the university: the Enlightenment ideal of autonomous rational enquiry in which students are acculturated to "the values, modes of questioning and knowledge of a particular discipline" (Clark and Royle, 1995: 5). Academics have allowed their liberal faith to be taken over by a managerial ethos of 'quality' which measures intellectual work by 'performance indicators', career points and research ratings, along with an entirely non-referential concept of 'excellence' (a floating signifier if ever there was one). The student curriculum has been made over in the image of the worst aspects of the 'free market', in which individual disciplines compete with each other for a limited pool of "clients" or consumers. In the process the very ethos of disciplinarity is betrayed by the vagaries of student 'choice'. In short:

> Within the very institution traditionally believed to embody certain
> enlightenment ideals, academics are living daily through their own
> version of Adorno and Horkeimer's dialectic of enlightenment.
> (Clark and Royle: 8)

Like Odysseus lashed to the mast, academics are forced to hear the sirens sing but watch the crew row on: forced to repress their authentic human nature and submit to the tyranny of Reason, now degraded to a utilitarian techno-science, itself based on the most crudely reductive means-end rationality. The university lies in ruins: it is a ruined institution on burnt-out ground.

I think that Clark and Royle's editorial audit reports an agon: the agon of Culture and Utility, a agon which is not, however, resolved. I think this agon is a version of what Jean-Francois Lyotard calls the *differend*: "a case of conflict between (at least) two parties, that cannot be equitably resolved for lack of a rule of judgement applicable to both arguments" (Lyotard, 1988: xi). The conflict is between heterogeneous phrases or language games which inhabit the same discursive space. What is disturbing is not that there is a discourse of utility and a discourse of culture, two rival logics suspended in relation to each other, their boundaries clearly defined. What is literally monstrous is that the language of culture and the language of utility invade each other's space, producing all kinds of effects of oscillation and slippage (mission statements are notorious, easily parodied examples of this kind of heteroglossia.) In the differend of culture and utility, it is no longer possible to be in secure possession of one's language, to be in control of the story one tells about oneself — one finds oneself ventriloquised by another discourse: uncanny, decentered. In this paper, I will be examining two related themes: first, the class basis of the agon of culture and utility and its continued grip on the politics of higher education; second, the failure of the university to make itself into a public sphere, and its consequent inability to unlock the differend and act as an agent of social change.

Culture and utility: a brief history

The utilitarian ideal of operational competence is, it turns out, far from new to the university. Indeed, the history of higher education in England for at least the last two centuries has been dominated by a debate between 'academic' and 'vocational' positions. As Robert Young (1992) shows in "The Idea of a Chresto-mathic University", this debate, although sterile and circular, is far from irrelevant: for behind the terms "academic" and "vocational" lies a history of cultural and political struggle. The English university is founded not on the Kantian principle of reason, but on a division between cultures and classes. Young's evidence provides a history of the differend in its English context: it reminds us that phrases in dispute have a history and perform an ideological function.

Oxford and Cambridge, founded as ecclesiastical corporations, had a monopoly of higher education for six centuries, and no one there pretended that what they taught had any particular use. Oxford's intake was restricted to those members of the Church of England who could afford the fees; its curriculum consisted almost entirely of the classics, or what Milton derided as "a scraping together of so much miserable Greek and Latin" (qtd. Young, 1992: 105). By the late eighteenth century, Cambridge had fallen into the decay described by Wordsworth in *The Prelude*. In 1809, in an article in the Whig journal, the *Edinburgh Review*, Sidney Smith declared that the game was up: "this long career of classical learning, we may, if we please, denominate a foundation; but it is a foundation so far above ground, that there is absolutely no room to put any thing upon it". "The proper criterion of every branch of education", Smith declared, is "its utility in future life". If this were true, there could be no place for a lifetime's study of "the intrigues of Heathen Gods" (qtd.,Young: 102).

Smith's calumnies against Oxford and his appeal to utility were immediately answered by Edward Copleston, who argued in a series of pamphlets that a classical education, in its very lack of specificity, prepared the student for every- thing: "without directly qualifying a man for any of the employments of life, it enriches and ennobles all. Without teaching him the peculiar business of any one office or calling, it ennables him to act his part in each of them with better grace and more elevated carriage" (qtd., Young: 102). Copleston thus provides the first rationale for what are nowadays known as transferable skills. But Copleston also expresses the supreme ideal of an English higher education: the disinterestedness purchased by culture. This virtue, of course, is the exclusive property of a parti- cular class: the English gentleman, who does not need to soil his hands in any vulgar trade, because he lives on the income produced by those who do.

Smith versus Copleston is, for Young, the founding moment in a cultural and political dialectic of (non)enlightenment. The monopoly of Oxbridge is broken in 1826 by the founding of the University of London, the first English university to teach useful knowledge, on the radical utilitarian principles of Jeremy Bentham. This dialectic of (non)enlightenment structures the history of English higher edu- cation, and takes the form of a binary opposition formed under the heading of Oxbridge versus London, or 'Arts' versus 'Science', a game of University Chal- lenge. The Oxbridge team are made up exclusively from the conservative upper class, whose other institutions are the Tory Party and the Church of England. For them, the University sustains the state by embodying its religious and cultural heritage in an elite education for the ruling class. The aim of the university is the transmission of truth. Knowledge is an end in itself, as well as promoting the higher form of conduct of the gentleman. Its prefered expertise is pedagogy, and its favorite subject is, not suprisingly, the past, particularly the classics. The London team is made up exclusively of the radical, dissenting middle-class. For this group, the university sustains the community by offering a democratic, secular education: education is a liberating force for disadvantaged groups, e. g. "nonconformists, women, the poor, colonized peoples'" (op.cit.: 107). Knowledge is useful and practical, promoting progress as well as greater equality. Its preferred expertise is research, and its favorite subjects are anything up to date, theoretical, and scientific.

Young observes a lacuna in this game of Culture vs. Utility. London's emphasis is on "political amelioration": in other words, the possibilities of education for liberating individuals, rather than effecting change in the capitalist order. If Oxford's role is to legitimize the status quo for the ruling class, London's role is to help the middle classes to live with it. But there is, Young says, a "striking absence of a politics of higher education that can be identified with the working class" (op.cit.: 107). This is hardly suprising, given the desuetude of the rest of the education system in the first half of the nineteenth century. While the radical utilitarians of the middle class were founding the University of London and breaking Oxbridge's monopoly, the working classes were still trying to get primary schools. (In England the idea that education is good for the nation as a whole is a relatively recent one.) This lacuna, Young argues, "accounts for the extent to which the issues of 'truth' versus 'use', arts versus sciences, continue to dominate the politics of education" (*op.cit.*: 107).

What I take Young to mean by this is that higher education is a stalemated game between contending teams: the conservative ruling-class and the utilitarian middle classes. And, in a society of chronically scarce resources, it is in the interests of *both* teams to keep the game in stalemate. The utilitarian middle-classes are prepared to let a few meritocratic individuals from the working-classes into higher education: such a reward confirms their own ideology of self-reliance and hard work. Likewise, the conservative ruling-class are prepared to let a few meritocratic, middle-class individuals into Oxbridge: they will learn to become gentlemen. Whenever pressure comes from whoever is occupying Downing Street for wider access, expansion, meeting the needs of industry, etc., the 'Arts' versus 'Science' debate is replayed, one more time. This is an in-house debate: towards the end of the twentieth century, the working-classes are still trying to get a decent secondary education (and nursery schools).

Young's strategy is to perform a characteristically elegant deconstruction of the binary opposition of Culture and Utility, by proposing the terms "useful uselessness" and "useless usefulness". The 'liberal' education proposed by Cardinal Newman from the camp of Culture produces a form of knowledge which is, in Newman's words, "capable of being its own end" (*On the Scope and Nature of a University Education* (1859), qtd., *op.cit.*: 108). In other words, this knowledge has no specific use. But it does produce the figure of the "gentleman", the man with "a cultivated intellect a delicate taste, [and] a candid, equitable bearing in the conduct of life" (qtd., *op.cit.*: 109). Newman argues, *pace* Copleston, that a liberal education is of "great secular utility, as constituting the best and highest formation of the intellect for social and political life" – that uselessness is useful. Newman's gentleman is ideally placed to become the colonial adminstrator, and Young goes on to show how a notion of culture as sublimely disinterested is pressed into political service by Coleridge and Arnold, whose idea of culture as "sweetness and light" is supposed to "do away with classes" (qtd., *op.cit.*: 111). By the same token, arguments for utility as the criterion of higher education are forced to acknowledge the claims of culture. Adam Smith, in *The Wealth of Nations*, espouses the free market system, and inveighs against higher education as "tedious and expensive", a shelter for "exploded and obsolete systems" (qtd., *op.cit.*: 115; 116). But the very material betterment produced by the free market also leads to the intellectual and moral decay of the populace, through the effects of the division of labour. Young observes that, here, "[k]nowledge outside the orbit of a strict criterion of utility has to be invoked in order to provide something beyond the system that can save it from its own consequences" – higher education alleviates alienation, in Marx's words, "in prudently homeopathic doses" (*op.cit.*: 120; qtd., *op.cit.*: 117).

"What becomes clear", Young concludes, is that both ideas of the university, the University of Culture and the University of Utility, may seem to be set in opposition to each other as conservative and radical. But both "are equally necessary to the state, as is the conflict between them". Culture vs. Utility is the regulator of the system, absorbing slack as well as pressures for change, claiming to balance the claims of the vocational and the academic in a purely in-house debate which leaves the arrangements underpinning society unchanged. "To enter into that conflict by resisting one with the other is to remain blind to the extent to which they are interimplicated and therefore not in any sense alternatives" (*op.cit.*: 121). "The question today's philosophers therefore need to ask is this: In what ways and with what effects can the university, both inside and outside the market economy, useful and useless, function as a surplus that that economy cannot comprehend?" (*op.cit.*: 121-22). For Young, the question of the university becomes one of proposing a new form of knowledge which cannot be co-opted or appropriated by the binary opposition of culture and utility.

What I think has to kept in mind as the corollary of Young's analysis is summarized by Martin Trow: "[a]ll recent developments in British higher education are played out against a backcloth of cultural values marked still by an anti-industrial bias among the elite" (Trow, 1987: 89). Trow attributes this thesis to Martin Weiner and Correlli Barnett, but the case was made, of course, by Anderson (1992). Anderson describes how the aristocracy emerged in England as the first capitalist class, and never ceded dominance to the middle-class who began to rise, as it were, in their wake. Although landed aristocracy and industrial middle-class form an alliance, it is the values of the aristocratic elite which remain the ruling ideas of society as a whole. Seen in this perspective, higher education is a strategic point, not in a war of position in which the values of one class struggle for clear dominance over the other, but instead a space of cosy complicity and cohabitation. Ideas about democracy and material improvement have always been weaker, in this sphere, than ideas associated with hierarchy and tradition (when an Englishman makes his money, he tends to want to retire to a country estate; likewise, the landed gentry are adept at opening their homes for appreciation by the masses). The strongly marked ideological role of culture in English education is to act as an antidote to the deleterious effects of utility, whether these be the alienating effects on the individual of the division of labour, or the possibility of class warfare. To be in the camp of culture is thus to be always already positioned in an essentially conservative role, implicitly hostile to the full unleashing of productive forces, the only way in which the material and cultural happiness of the many is likely to be secured (Marcuse, 1969). Leftist critics of culture opposed to the status quo will therefore have to consider how far their advocacy of purely cultural values is immune to culture's ideological effects. Given this state of affairs, it might be worthwhile continuing the historical narrative of what I'm calling the differend of Culture and Utility, and in particular, reading the key moment in the debate: the Robbins Report of 1963.

The Robbins trap

Noel Annan's account of the whole sorry shambles has some lessons for philosophers (Annan, 1991). Annan picks up the story in the 1950s, when reform of higher education proceeded on the 'human capital' argument, that to ensure economic growth a modern trading nation had to invest in a highly trained, diversified, and flexible workforce. Harold Macmillan, the virtual incarnation of the upper-class duffer, appointed Lionel Robbins to chair a committee on higher education. The problem was that Culture's team, although stalemated, was incomparably stronger than that of Utility. Higher education was still a profoundly elitist institution, the university still essentially a Victorian finishing school for the gentleman administrators of the Empire from which Britain was in the process of disengaging, an engine of governance rather than enterprise and technology, steadily limiting its intake to 3-4% of the relevant age group.

The expansion of the 1960s which was supposed to produce human capital (see O'Neill, this volume) and usher in an era of material progress was unable to overcome the stalemate: indeed it proceeded in the terms of a deadlocked debate, already bankrupt. The Robbins Report is a virtual summation of the differend of culture and utility, and, insofar as it succeeded in shaping the British higher education system, its institutionalization. Among the objectives Robbins identified as "essential to any properly balanced system" were "instruction in skills suitable to play a part in the general division of labour" – skills essential to the "maintenance of a competitive position" for the British economy (Robbins Report, 1968: 6). But Robbins gives equal stress to "the transmission of a common culture and common standards of citizenship [...] that background of culture and social habit upon which a healthy society depends". The Arnoldian sense of this common culture of citizenship is strongly marked in Robbins' statement of aims and principles: society depends on a common culture, more especially "in an age that has set for itself the ideal of equality of opportunity". But this isn't just a matter of providing more university places for students "from all classes". It also means providing, "in the atmosphere of the institution in which the students live and work, influences that in some measure compensate for any inequalities of home background" (*op.cit.*: 7). (The report is well aware of these inequalities, noting that "the proportion of young people who enter full-time higher education is 45 per cent for those whose fathers are in the "higher professional" group, compared with only 4 per cent for those whose fathers are in skilled manual occupations" [*op.cit.*: 51]). Acquiring culture, then, will sweeten the bitter pill of the inequalities of home background that may become starkly evident to the universities' new recruits, once they come into contact with their better educated, better equipped, and better positioned peers.

There is, in fact, a pronounced scepticism running through the Robbins report towards merely utilitarian arguments for higher education, as well as any attempt to quantify its costs and benefits to the nation in economic terms. The aim of investing in the nation's human capital "is not productivity as such but the good life that productivity makes possible" (*op.cit.*: 204). But Robbins makes some very easy, not to say complacent, assumptions: that higher education will perforce increase productivity, and that both higher education and increased productivity will, together, secure the "good life" for the nation's citizens. All this is to be achieved by simply expanding access to higher education (at a relatively modest rate) without any significant alteration to the nature of the system as it had evolved over the course of a relatively brief period of time.

First of all, the price Robbins had to pay to get the universities to agree to even a relatively modest expansion was 'parity of esteem'. In other words, all universities would be funded equally, and all would be based on the elite model which had evolved under the state's patronage: full-time, three year degrees, maintenance grants to ensure students could have independent, gentlemanly means, the sacred 1: 8 staff-student ratio. But what Annan calls the "golden age of the don", was a luxury the ailing British economy couldn't afford. Robbins was told to assume a increase of 4% per annum in productivity. Instead, the economy quickly entered a four-year downturn. Instead of producing human capital, higher education was actually a drain on resources. Secondly, the gestures Robbins made towards increasing the resources given to science and technology did not have the intended effect of sparking the "white heat of the technological revolution" prophesied by Harold Wilson a few weeks before the publication of the report. Robbins noted that Britain had a lower proportion of graduates in technology than its major competitors, and recommended the establishment of the Colleges of Advanced Technology (CATS) as "technological universities" (*op.cit.*: 131). But no new relationships between the remaining technical colleges and the universities were established. In 1965, Toby Weaver, Deputy Under-Secretary at the Department of Education and Science observed that, while a few institutions were privileged to become universities, Robbins cast the technical colleges in "too modest a role and failed to give [them] a sufficiently stable and clearly defined place" (qtd., Venables, 1996: 161).

In the face of declining competitiveness, the differend of culture and utility entered another session. Weaver persuaded Antony Crossland to make a speech on the occasion of the 75th anniversary of the Woolwich Polytechnnic, denouncing "our snobbish caste-ridden hierarchical obsession with university status", and announcing the government's intention to create up to thirty more polytechnics. (qtd., *op.cit.*: 162). Crossland attempted to elaborate "a system of higher education" in the sense defined by Robbins, arguing that "in Britain the system must be based on the twin traditions which have created our present higher education institutions". These twin traditions were "the autonomous sector, represented by the universities", and "the public sector, represented by the leading technical colleges and the colleges of education" (qtd., *op.cit.*: 162). The "public sector" was defined by Crossland as being "under social control, directly responsive to social needs". No one had phrased the differend quite as acutely as this: by implication, the "autonomous" university sector was not responsive to social needs. The elite University was to retain its dominant position in the higher education system, ringfenced in possession of Culture, while the *arriviste* agents of Utility were sent off to build the new Jerusalem.

Of course, it did not work. The polytechnics were made in the image of the universities and granted the all-important 'parity of esteem': full-time, 3 year degrees, maintenance grants, etc. The consequence of the Robbins Trap (diagnosed by Martin Trow) was "academic drift", itself the consequence of a failure to reform England's uniquely specialized post-16 education. Robbins expected the proportion of students in science and technology to increase by 8%. In fact, this proportion fell by 3% (Scott, 1988: 38). Starved of sixth-form entrants in the sciences, the polytechnics were forced to expand their arts courses, with the social sciences helping to fill the gap. Futhermore, even after the expansion of the 1960s and 1970s, higher education was offered to no more than 1/6th of the relevant age group. An ostensibly meritocratic system, in which anyone capable of benefiting from higher education should be entitled to it, was in fact regulated by a rigorous principle of selection on the basis of educational qualifications and social background. If the tacit assumption of the first phase of Victorian expansion was that the University was "a finishing school for the sons and perhaps daughters of the elite [...] a decoration rather than an engine of economic growth", what happened after Robbins was that more of the daughters of the elite joined the sons (Halsey, 1992: 5).

Robbins has been described as a "liberal document" by Peter Scott, in the sense that "its prescriptions were rooted in an aristocratic rather than utilitarian view of the purposes of higher education" (Scott, 1988: 34). The expansion of higher education proceeded as part of "a moral tradition which regarded reform as far more than material improvement [...] The good life was still imagined as the godly life, lightly disguised in the secular clothes of postwar prosperity" (*ibid.*). Robbins was part of what Scott calls "an organic tradition" of public reform, its values neither those of "privatized individualism" nor "critical opposition", but "a perhaps instinctive loyalty to ancient Whig rhythms of public thought and to an assured civil religion" (*ibid.*). I think these descriptions are essentially accurate. But what is even more striking about the world Robbins created is the way it exactly mirrors the class-basis of English education: the continued hegemony of aristocratic values, the uneasy alliance of gentleman and capitalist, cultured elite and utilitarian middle-class, the ability of aristocratic ideals of culture to offer both an enticing prospect of the good life, and a means of "compensating for" or defusing the tensions of a class society based on manifest inequalities of opportunity. Not given a hearing at the differend of Culture and Utility are the very things that would break the stalemate: the planned development of productive forces which is the indispensable material basis for the happiness of society as a whole, and the fullest possible participation in a higher education which aims at promoting both technical skills and the skills of critical thinking and aesthetic enjoyment essential to the exercise of liberty and citizenship.

Robbins did produce a decisive change in the political and administrative context of higher education, the possibilities of which were not grasped at the time, but may yet prove to be decisive. Scott argues that the Robbins Committee "made it impossible ever again to imagine universities and other advanced colleges as a loose collection of small exclusive isolated semi-private institutions" (*ibid.*). Robbins created a higher education system wedded to state patronage and still with a high degree of autonomy: the University Grants Committee acting as a buffer between the universities and its Treasury paymasters, dispensing funds in the form of substantial, quinquennial grants. There was at least the possibility, then, of higher education establishing itself as a public sphere: an autonomous realm with the ability to make its voice heard in society at large. This did not in fact happen, for three reasons. First, the universities thought they could shelter behind the "public sector", leaving it to "take the brunt of governmental guidance and direction", while they preserved their cherished autonomy (Trow, 1987: 85). In fact, the polytechnics evolved into *de facto* universities, making the abolition of the binary divide a formality when, in June 1992, it finally happened. Secondly, the universities suffered a slow decline in their autonomy as a *sector* because of a complacent insistence on their autonomy as *institutions*: there was no effective leadership or governing structure capable of unifying the sector and providing it with coherent policy (*op.cit.*: 89). Third, the universities failed to respond positively to demands for change from its own student constituency: demands which, if taken seriously, could have made higher education more democratic and more popular. The failure of higher education to willingly make the transition from elite to mass system, to diversify its provision and demonstrate its value, led to a new session of the differend: the "thousand lessons in disillusion" provided by the Thatcher Revolution, and the rise of a militant utilitarianism (Halsey, 1992: 105).

Two May events

"In May 1968, students, supported by the tax-payer suddenly appeared, armed with sociological jargon, not as aspirants to, but as subverters of suburban respectability" (*op.cit.*: 180). For Halsey, the student revolt showed that the social sciences had really arrived: but as a means of challenging the state and 'smashing the system' rather than perpetuating middle-class hegemony:

> The second dramatic May, of 1979, carried into Downing Street a group of Conservatives, armed with stern nineteenth century theories of society – pro-market and anti-state – determined to restore a manageable order. Among them Sir Keith Joseph was convinced that low productivity, as well as antipathy towards business enterprise, patriotism, and familial piety, had been irresponsibly taught to students by left-wing dons. (*op.cit.*: 180)

Margaret Thatcher was the almost predestined nemesis of Culture and its worst nightmare: the enemy of both Arnold and Marx, Utilitarianism incarnate. Lower-middle class (a grocer's daughter), a science graduate (with a 2nd class degree), *nouveau riche* (she married money), a nonconformist (brought up as a Methodist), a believer in Victorian values (prudence, diligence, temperance, self-reliance, responsibility), regularly smeared by the liberal Establishment as a suburban philistine: if she hadn't existed it would have been necessary to invent her. Thatcher formed an alliance with a renegade don from the camp of Culture, Sir Keith Joseph, and another, even more brutal philistine, Norman Tebbit, to "turn the country round".

It was becoming clear very soon after Robbins that expanding an elite system was an expensive option. In 1969, Labour education minsiter Shirley Williams suggested self-administered economies by the universities, with a predictable response. In 1973 the Heath government ended quinquennium funding. The Thatcher government began to turn the screw in 1981, with the UGC forced to adminster a 14% cut in resources over three years. Playing the unfamiliar role of downward *dirigisme*, the Committee decided on "selective" cuts. Even as the government expressed its wish that more resources should be switched to science and technology, the Committee cut the grant to Salford University, a former CAT, by over a third. The result of this hamfisted gesture was the abolition of the UGC in 1988, and the establishment of the University Funding Council, the first step in a move to a more 'contractual' system of funding, based on the measurement of 'performance indicators' (Trow, 1988: 86-7). The differend, formerly conducted behind closed doors by a discreet committee, became a public shouting match. Dons were accused by Utilitarians like Martin Weiner and Correli Barnett of producing a dubious return on the nation's investment, even of frustrating the industrial spirit, in yet another replay of the differend of Culture and Utility. In turn, FR Leavis's fulminations against 'technologico-Benthamism' were revived by Fred Inglis, who chanted that "genteel deutero-fascist managerialism" was now the order of the day.

For Robert Young, the chief lesson of this period is that the critical theorists of the left found themselves outflanked by Thatcherism. They had spent years pointing out that Culture was ideologically contaminated, an instrument for obfuscating class division and ensuring the continuation of the status quo. "When theorists found themselves wanting to defend [the humanities] against successive government cuts they discovered that the only view with which they could vindicate themselves was the very one which, in intellectual terms, they wanted to attack" (Young, 1992: 113). The academic left thus found itself pressed against the "limits of a purely oppositional politics" (*ibid.*). It was left to the right to defend the humanities: in an act charged with symbolism, Oxford refused Thatcher her traditional honorary degree.

But it is also clear that the perpetuation of the differend prevents certain things happening: preeminently, the granting of any positive or distinctive contents to either culture or utility. Utility's case is either debased into the means-end rationality of 'performance indicators', or dressed up in dubious arguments about 'human capital'. Culture is given no definition other than a gentlemanly disinterestedness, the distinction acquired by the possession of cultural capital in the pursuit of the 'good life'. As Young argues, what is needed is some point of leverage, some reformulation of the university, which will allow the binary opposition of Culture and Utility to be deconstructed. But this will have to be more than a merely formal deconstruction of the terms 'culture' and 'utility': it will have to address and contest their ideological function in the historical context of both the institution of the university, and the system of higher education created by Robbins. In the remainder of this paper, I will suggest that doing this means reconceptualizing the academic community as a *public sphere*, and redefining the goals of liberal education as the goals of *critical citizenship*.

Conclusion: a new public sphere?

How might the university function as a public sphere, that is to say, an open forum for rational, critical deliberation on the common good? Alisdair MacIntyre argues that the possibility of such a forum has evaporated: "what modernity excludes is the possibility of the existence of an educated public" (MacIntyre, 1987: 17). This is because there is no longer any agreement on what the standards of rational thought are, "or upon what subject-matters it is important that thinking should be exercised" (*op.cit.*: 16). The modern university is broken on the dilemma of culture and utility: the "two major purposes teachers are required to serve", namely "to shape the young person so that he or she may fit into some social role", and "teaching young people how to think for themselves" are, "under the conditions of Western modernity, mutually incompatible" (*ibid.*). MacIntyre's arguments are based on a particular model of a historical bourgeois public sphere which has great normative power: "the remaking of the Scottish universities" in the first half of the eighteenth century by Moderate clergy, lawyers, larger farmers and smaller gentry, prosperous merchants, and schoolmasters. Since this public composed of the male middle classes shared the habit of debate about the common good, common standards of debate based on Scottish "common sense" philosophy, and a common body of canonical texts, one and the same education could fit individuals for their social role *and* make them enlightened. According to MacIntyre, there are three factors which now make this educated public impossible: 1) the specialization of knowledge means educators can no longer deliberate together; 2) the public itself became "a heterogeneous set of specialized publics" through the division of labour, eroding civic values and loyalty to society as a whole; 3) there was an increase in the size of the groups excluded from the bourgeois public sphere: "both the owning and employing class and the labouring class" in manufacturing industry, producing "a class structure which made the educated class impotent and functionless in the face of the new class conflicts" (*op.cit.*: 25; 26; 28).

But MacIntyre's account contains more than its fair share of nostalgia and resignation. It ought now to be possible to rethink and reimagine the public sphere as a space which is not necessarily dependent on the shared habits of a cohesive social group. One influential attempt to do this is Nancy Fraser's rewriting of Habermas's "bourgeois masculinist" conception of the public sphere from a materialist feminist perspective, which encompasses the following points.

1) Taking issue with the assumption that "it is possible for interlocutors in a public sphere to bracket status differentials" and to deliberate "as if they were equals", Fraser argues that the bourgeois public sphere operated according to "protocols of style and decorum that were themselves correlates and markers of status inequality", and served, particularly, to silence the voices of women (Fraser, 1993: 9; 10). It would be more appropriate "to unbracket inequalities, in the sense of explicitly thematizing them" (*op.cit.*: 11).

2) Opposing the assumption that "the proliferation of a multiplicity of competing publics is necessarily a step away from, rather than toward, greater democracy", Fraser argues that "in stratified societies, arrangements that accommodate contestation among a plurality of competing publics better promote the ideal of participatory parity than does a single, comprehensive, overarching public sphere" (*op.cit.*: 9; 13; 14). She asserts that "communication across lines of cultural difference is not in principle impossible", although it requires "multicultural literacy [...] acquired through practice" (*op.cit.*: 17).

3) Fraser argues that the assumption that "discourse in public spheres should be restricted to deliberation about the public good" actively prevents participants from clarifying their interests, and stresses instead the idea that "preferences, interests, and identities" can be "discursively constituted in and through" public deliberation (*op.cit.*: 9; 20).

4) Finally, Fraser questions the assumption "that a functioning democratic public sphere requires a sharp separation between civil society and the state", since this conception ideally facilitates the development of a *laissez-faire* economics and limited government inimical to participatory democracy. Instead,

Fraser advocates the proliferation of "strong publics" in the form of "self-managing institutions" constructed as "sites of direct or quasi-direct democracy" (*op.cit.*: 9; 25).

I think that Fraser's arguments are very suggestive for the kind of critical practice which could be shaped within the institution of the university as public sphere.

1) Unbracketing or thematizing status inequalities means, of course, a curriculum which raises questions of the relationship between discourse and power. But more than that, the curriculum should, in Gerald Graff's phrase, "teach the conflicts", allowing students to see what is at stake between interpretations, value systems, and cultural norms. This does not mean assuming there is a universal language for expressing conflicts. Students should be able to express *themselves* in the medium of academic discourse, which means neither the valorization of the vernacular nor the slavish adoption of latinity: being able to think and speak for one's self does not mean talking like a book. What follows on from this is that students should have some influence in the debating and shaping of an open-ended curriculum: something which is in danger of becoming a professional piety in the sense of a belief never actually practiced. Underpinning all of the above considerations is the principle that higher education should be available to anyone who can benefit from it, a guiding principle of Robbins which took decades to be taken seriously and is still far from being fulfilled.

2) As Fraser observes, multicultural literacy means being able to identify what cultures have in common as well as what differentiates them: this means that neither the antagonism of essentialisms nor a merely abstract recognition of inscrutable difference should be the norm of an educated public.

3) The University can be a space in which rational deliberation and aesthetic self-fashioning take place alongside each other: where identities are formed in the negotiation between alternative possibilities which are newly apparent in a heterogeneous public, through "self-cultivation, self-direction, self-understanding, and creativity" (Students for a Democratic Society, 1992: 451).

4) The university is located in the public sector, but this does not mean that it is sealed off in some kind of "market shelter", that it possesses the distance from production taken to be definitive of professional status in an "autonomous self-directed community" of students and scholars. It's this final assumption which I want to emphasize, because it virtually defines even the most updated versions of "liberal education", for which questions about accountability to the public at large are "second order", and it is the assumption which drives the differend of culture and utility (Barnett, 1988: 109).

I have been arguing that it is the ideological function of 'culture' in English society to resist the claims of utility: 'culture' is the ruling idea of a bloc essentially hostile to democratization and modernization and loyal to notions of tradition and hierarchy. 'Culture', thus defined, encourages individuals to "keep their wants inchoate" in Jane Mansbridge's resonant phrase: culture preoccupies individuals in a marketplace 'negotiation' of identity whose radical or emancipatory potential is one of the contemporary pieties of Cultural Studies (qtd., Fraser, 1993: 11). Education, on the other hand, is one of those "group needs that could not expect to be satisfied by a self-regulating market", and so calls for regulation by the state (Habermas, 1992: 132). The distinction between private and public needs and interests, and the shifting terrain they occupy is therefore of central concern to the university. By critical deliberation on this issue in the manner outlined above, the university has the potential to act again as the space for deliberation over public ends, and specifically over the principle of utility in a world of "meaningless work and idleness," where "superfluous abundance" exists alongside mass starvation and environmental catastrophe (Students for a Democratic Society, 1992: 448). It seems likely that increased access to higher education will only sharpen the contradiction of the bourgeois public sphere: that its claims to universal equality, access, and self-realization are based on the perpetuation of relations of inequality, exclusion and domination. When increasing numbers of people are trained to become skilled and purposive agents of their own destiny, the 'cultural' palliatives of heritage and tradition offered in place of modern, democratic society will appear increasingly shopsoiled and derisory. The university could then become the space where the possibilities of a radical democratic transformation of society can be once again be imagined, debated, even to some extent implemented. The university might be the place where the differend is finally brought to an end and the principle of utility, the greatest happiness of the greatest number, is reclaimed, rephrased and reimagined: the place where people join together to debate what is needed for the public good.

Acknowledgements

I am grateful to members of the School of Arts Research Forum at Staffordshire University for the opportunity to debate some of the issues raised in this paper, and to Derek Longhurst for the term "critical citizenship".

References

Anderson, P. (1992) [1964] 'Origins of the Present Crisis', in his *English Questions*. London: Verso.

Annan, N. (1991) *Our Age: The Generation Who Made Post-War Britain*. London: Weidenfeld and Nicholson.

Clark, T. and Royle, N. (1995) 'Editorial Audit', *Oxford Literary Review*, 17: 5-11.

Barnett, R. (1988) 'Institutions of Higher Education: Purposes and 'Performance Indicators', *Oxford Review of Education*, 14 (1): 97-112.

Fraser, N. (1993) 'Rethinking the Public Sphere: A Contribution to the Critique of Actually Existing Democracy', in B. Robbins (ed) *The Phantom Public Sphere*. Minneapolis and London: University of Minnesota Press.

Habermas, J. (1992) [1962] *The Structural Transformation of the Public Sphere: An Inquiry into a Category of Bourgeois Society*. Trans. T. Burger with the assistance of F. Lawrence. Cambridge: Polity Press.

Halsey, A. H. (1992) *The Decline of Donnish Dominion*. Oxford: Oxford University Press.

Lyotard, J-F. (1988) *The Differend: Phrases in Dispute*. Trans. George Van Den Abbeele, Minneapolis: University of Minnesota Press.

MacIntyre, A. (1987) 'The Idea of an Educated Public', in G. Haydon (ed) *Education and Values: The Richard Peters Lectures*. London: Institute of Education, University of London.

Marcuse, H. (1969) *Essay on Liberation*. Boston: Beacon Press.

Robbins Report (1968 [reprint of 1963]) *Higher Education: Report of the Committee Appointed by the Prime Minister under the Chairmanship of Lord Robbins. 1961-63, Cmnd. 2154*. London: Her Majesty's Stationery Office.

Scott, P. (1988) 'Blueprint or Blue Remembered Hills? The Relevance of the Robbins Report to the Present Reform of Higher Education', *Oxford Review of Education*, 14 (1): 33-48.

Students for a Democratic Society (1992) [1962] 'Port Huron Statement', in R. Griffith (ed) *Major Problems in American History Since 1945*. Lexington, Mass. and Toronto: D. C. Heath and Co.

Trow, M. (1987) 'Comparative Perspectives on Higher Education in the United Kingdom and United States', *Oxford Review of Education*, 14 (1): 81-96.

Venables, P. (1996) [1965-66] 'Dualism in Higher Education', rep. in M. Shattock (ed) *The Creation of a University System*. Oxford and Cambridge, Mass.: Basil Blackwell.

Young, R. (1992) 'The Idea of a Chrestomathic University', in R. Rand (ed) *Logomachia: The Conflict of the Faculties*. Lincoln: University of Nebraska Press.

Does Higher Necessarily Mean Better? Reinvigorating the Humanities and Social Sciences

17

Grahame Thompson

Introduction

In a climate of review and reassessment, universities are increasingly being challenged to justify and account for themselves. The establishment of the Dearing Committee has no doubt hastened this process. Nowhere is this more so than in respect to the teaching of the humanities and social sciences. The period since the 'conservative turn' in intellectual and policy matters has seen an unprecedented attack on the role that many academics had thought the university was traditionally there to exemplify, namely the genuine pursuit of a disinterested knowledge and the embodiment of enlightened liberal values. A deep sense of unease has now fallen over many humanities and social science departments as they are increasingly subject to internal performance assessments, funding retrenchments, public attacks upon their research output and teaching competence, and even a questioning of the reason for their very existence in a time of severe economic austerity. As the 'commercialisation' of the university proceeds apace, the pressures to gather outside funding seem destined to overwhelm what shrinking time there still remains for the actual teaching of students and the conduct of research. Teaching time itself is under intense pressure as a massive expansion in the numbers of students admitted to the universities has coincidentally taken place without a commensurate increase in resources.

In fact these processes are perhaps unwittingly part of a wider move that will result in the whole of the education system becoming a machine of mass mediocrity. Politicians and managers are relentlessly bureaucratising all aspects of the production and distribution of knowledge in the pursuit of so-called academic 'quality' and 'accountability'. A mind-numbing conformity to administrative procedures is what is called for, which is presented as the supreme good. The creative and innovative capacities of teachers are increasingly frowned upon, treated with suspicion and sometimes open hostility. Politicians may be satisfying a public demand for mass higher education, but without any conception of what this is supposed to accomplish other than to create a certificated mass workforce. A growth of hidebound specialisms has displaced broad intellectual curiosity and replaced it with narrow-mindedness and a narrowly-focused academic industry.

The general growth of managerial commercialism in universities and other teaching establishments is in danger of turning them from cultural institutions into businesses. The implications of this can be seen clearly in the case of the Art Schools and Teacher Training Colleges, both of which are in decline. The Art Schools are increasingly being used as mere conduits for a overtly commercialised and aesthetically dubious 'hype'. How far are pickled fish and the like an answer to the 'crisis of modernism', rather than a prime indicator of its symptomatic implosion? The relentless attack on the credibility of teaching has so undermined confidence that the Training Colleges now face their worse ever crisis or recruitment. And the Schools themselves face an even more relentless drive to uniformity, mindless testing and centralized managerial bureaucratic initiatives. Unfortunately, we see all these features manifest in many other contemporary public and private arenas.

It is possible that these features and trends are part of a wider transformation in the nature of the social order in general. One way to characterise this is to name it as a 'kakistocratic social order'. The concept of a kakistocracy is defined by the *Webster's Dictionary* as "government by the worst men", but it is better characterised as *government by the least able*. The problem is that as the least able climb the ladder of 'success' and become a critically important mass in positions of authority, it becomes extremely difficult to dislodge them. Those few genuine creative and innovative institutions that manage to survive in a kakistocratic order are themselves increasingly vulnerable, as they too are threatened with being overwhelmed by careerists who are increasingly attracted to their success and who wish to firmly attach themselves to it.

This may all sound depressingly pessimistic. And at one level it is. But a moment's reflection should bring home its essential truth. The trouble is that the kakistocrats are not only the 'least able': they are often the most cunning and devious as well. This is not a contradiction — one of the pervasive features of a kakistocratic social order is the lack of intellectual ability of its leaders combined with a depressing ability for them to effectively manoeuvre into positions of authority and 'success'. Look, for instance, no further than those who now run our privatized utilities and corporations. The former, who were previously the equivalent of managers of municipal water or gas works, now present themselves as international businessmen and award themselves salaries accordingly. But in fact they operate in highly sheltered and almost risk free commercial environments. Unfortunately, these attitudes are increasingly adopted in a wider range of organizations and institutions.

The issue pursued in the rest of this chapter is what might be an appropriate response to these trends. I confine myself here to the domain of higher education, and within this to the social sciences and humanities in particular. Four main responses to the predicament posed by the attack from the new right and its kakistocracy can be discerned which, while distinct, are not unrelated to one another.

Responses

The first I term a 'politics of despair'. It is to deeply lament these developments and react to them quite negatively. A resigned disaffection is the result. It leads to a seemingly endless lament on the part of disillusioned academics, heard in senior common rooms, at course or departmental meetings, indeed at every conference attended. What chance do we have to delay or divert these trends when faced with a determined and powerful opponent in the form of our political and funding masters and their internal managerial allies? None, or very little, is the standard response. Perhaps this is the most pervasive of the reactions. For instance, for all intents and purposes, opposition from academics to internal and external 'quality control' has collapsed as the language of this 'technology of governance' has been accepted and embraced by all (even though most academics realise its futility?).

A second reaction is a variation on the first. This involves a 'politics of exposure'. It leads to detailed investigations and 'revelations' of the moves being made by those opposed to a 'liberal education' — broadly speaking, ultra-conservative forces — whether in terms of some shadowy 'national intelligence' gathering regime or the more overt New Right think-tanks and their allies. But as the embrace of the bureaucratic techniques referred to above widens within higher education, the politics of exposure might also expand to include our administrative masters as well as ultra conservative political forces. However, what is distinctive about this response is that exposure as such is somehow seen to constitutes the limit of an adequate defence.

The third reaction is one of the main positive ones. It is to offer a fight back, but a fight back in the name of the traditional values and roles ascribed to universities as part of an enlightened and universalistic liberal intellectual and governmental programme. This I will term 'the politics of nostalgia'. Such a politics of nostalgia reasserts the value of a university education as part of a process of subject formation which views the individual as mobilised into a universal and emancipatory humanitarian project — the historical destiny of the enlightened liberal subject set within a utopian political programme ("follow us and we will liberate you from your shackles").

A final response — a variation on the third just outlined — is to invoke the 'politics of relativism'. The aim here is to defend an educational strategy based upon different *perspectives* on the same or similar problems. In this case, great care needs to be taken to invoke a defensible definition of relativism, one which does not just duplicate the attacks of the opponents of the relativisation of truth on their own ground by accepting that there is a genuinely real domain of Truth to begin with against which different interpretations of it can be quite reasonably and legitimately measured. This is the position adopted by so called 'philosophical realism', a strong element in the present configuration of forces arrayed along this oppositional dimension.

Now, while one would not necessarily wish to completely dismiss any of these positions, they do not seem to offer an adequate analysis either of the historical role of the university or of a defence that can be mounted within the academy for a progressive interdisciplinary based education in the humanities or social sciences. For the purposes of much of the rest of this chapter, I concentrate upon the latter two 'positive' positions outlined above with which to conduct a critical engagement. To construct an adequate response to the challenges facing a progressive disciplinary and interdisciplinary education in the humanities and social sciences will require a re-examination of the ascribed role of the university and higher education more generally. This re-examination is designed to buttressed the existing approaches with a set of telling arguments that re-legitimize the position and future role of the university.

University education as production-good or consumption-good?[1]

The usual manner in which the output of the universities is considered is, broadly speaking, as a *'production-good'*. Thus higher education is seen almost exclusively as an element in the inputs that go to make a viable and productive economic structure. On a more general note, it is the *production* of knowledge that is considered the most important aspect to the whole process of knowledge-power relationships. This emphasis on the production side has served to obscure the *utilisation* or *consumption* side of that process (which is developed further in a moment). In fact, however, one might argue that the conditions for the production of knowledge are less of a problem in a modern society than are the conditions for the effective utilization of that knowledge once produced. In one way or another, the production and distribution of knowledge remains a remarkably open process in Western societies, despite all manner of attempts (both commercial and governmental) to control it. Much less effective is the efficient utilization of that existing knowledge base once it is in 'open circulation'. A striking proportion of any knowledge-base just 'goes to waste'. This is where differential and particular social institutional arrangements have an important impact on the way knowledge can be, and is, effectively utilized for the good. These are highly nationally specific in the case of their impact upon economic performance, for instance. Some countries display an institutional arrangement that is highly conducive to the utilization of the available knowledge base for productive economic output, while others have an inherited institutional arrangement that is just unable to make effective use of this base. More on this later.

The main way the connection between the universities and the economy is made in respect to the production-good argument is via the operation of the labour market. The labour market is structured around competences and qualifications, and it is the educated outputs of the universities that play a major part in organizing this structure of inputs to the economy. Clearly, this is the site of a long and continuing debate focused around whether the higher education system actually provides the 'right' set of input skills needed for the economy. By and large, employers have consistently complained that it does not. But if such employers are asked to be more specific (which perhaps surprisingly they often are), they generally have little idea of exactly what educational skills they do require, other than as expressed in vague terms and in general notions. Thus, whatever system of higher education were in place, complaints would invariably emerge, and it is probably wise to ignore these as far as is possible.[2]

Increasingly, governments have jumped rather uncritically on the production-good band-wagon, aided by university administrators, academics and economists alike. A good many reports have been produced that try to point to the relationship between educational standards generally — and university qualifications of various kinds more particularly — and economic performance. Now, it would be foolish to suggest that there is absolutely no relationship between the levels of educational competences of a population and its level of well-being or economic development. The problems emerge, however, when the objective becomes to demonstrate a *close or strong* relationship between these two, and particularly between them when the outputs of various types of graduates are involved. Admittedly, *some* studies have shown some *correlation* between these two, particularly where it is science and technology graduates that are concerned. But this has not settled the issue of whether such correlation implies a *causation* running from the number or type of graduates to the rates or levels of economic growth, or the actual robustness of such correlations. By and large, a scrutiny of a large body of analysis and evidence, particularly country cross-sectional analysis, reveals that there is no consistent and robust causal relationship involved here.[3]

Indeed, this conclusion is bolstered by the difficulty of finding such strong causal relationships between a wider variety of specific economic inputs and national economic performance. Thus, if one compares measures like the amount of research and development expenditure, or other types of investment thought to be of particular importance in generating growth, or the numbers of patents taken out, or levels of technology, and the like, then again little consistent relationship emerges. In fact, much more important for economic performance than these specific input categories is the more general institutionalized operation of the labour market in terms of outcomes over wage negotiations (centralised *versus* de-centralized bargaining arrangements), the operation of the financial system in terms of how effective and closely it links the raising of finance with a long-term investment strategy for industry, the forms of corporate governance, and the nature of the national political settlement between the dominant social interest groups or 'partners' over negotiated outcomes to distributional disputes.

What, then, are we to conclude from this discussion about the dominant line of argument linking the universities to the economy? Contrary to the main thrust of this argument, it is suggested here that higher education be considered not so much as a production-good but increasingly as a *'consumption-good'*. Thus, just as they enjoy and demand fast cars and large houses, people also like and demand good quality higher education, particularly in the case of the humanities and the social sciences. The benefits they perceive from such higher education may not be tied very closely to their supposed labour market effects in terms of enhanced opportunities in employment, but as a benefit in its own right, and as a way of understanding and engaging with an increasingly complex and interdependent world.

If I may speak for a moment from experience, I work in a nationally organised university of 'the second chance' that has two hundred thousand undergraduate and other students, most of whom already have jobs. These students seem less interested in gaining their degree for employment purposes (though they are by no means totally disinterested in this!) than in pursuing their study for its own sake. Without wishing to exaggerate, in the humanities and the social sciences in particular, the Open University seems to have tapped a market for good quality, heavily interdisciplinary based undergraduate education, that is demanded as much for its benefit in explaining the nature of ideas and a complex world as for the enhanced employment prospects a degree might offer. This leads me to believe that the output I am involved in producing has less to do with traditional notions of a production-good, as described above, but more to do with a consumption-good that is demanded much in its own terms. What is more, I suspect this is a form of demand that will grow in the future.

Why is this? The problem is that the kinds of mass consumption demands that we have become accustomed to in the post-Second World War period are not necessarily those that will hold into the future. Of course, one is not suggesting that such demand patterns will change overnight, or for all, very quickly. The distribution of income and wealth is too uneven for that. But the problem with the main popular cultural leisure-based consumption patterns of the post-II World War era is that they were (are) popular because they were (are) novel. But novelty itself presents the problem that could be its undoing. Shopping, mass entertainment TV, mass-travel, 'drugs, sex and rock and roll', or what-have-you, are all very well and will continue to have their place. But for how long will they maintain their hold over the imagination of a population rapidly increasing in 'intelligence'? This may sound fanciful, but my proposition is that as the plateau of educational competence and achievement rises, itself the result of the first ever experiment in mass-secondary education that was conducted in the post-Second World War years (however unevenly and slowly this has spread), then the realm of ideas and understandings of a complex world will become as attractive a pursuit, if not more so, as more shopping or more mass entertainment *per se*. The nature of what is considered pleasurable and even hedonistic is thus likely to change.

If this admittedly rather speculative argument has any merit it is that it alters the nature of how one must begin to construct a case for higher education. Even if students continued to take a hard instrumental attitude towards their own studies and pursue particular subjects because they think these will enhance their prospects in the labour market, there would be no justification on the part of the university authorities to directly link this to an argument about an increase in national competitiveness. Uncomfortable though this might be, the nettle should be grasped.

Let us begin with what might seem to be the most disturbing implications of the issues outlined so far. If fast cars and large house are paid for directly in the market place, why should not the same conditions of distribution now apply to higher education? But the point about the term 'consumption-good' as used above is that it is not *necessarily* to imply that it means a total *commodification* of higher education in the humanities and the social sciences. Contrary to an argument directly by analogy, just because fast cars and large houses are bought and paid for in a market does not necessarily mean that the same must apply to good quality education. Note here that an emphasis is put upon the notion of no *necessary* implication. It may well be, therefore, that the question of paying directly for higher education is raised anew by the consumption-good argument considered here. But to reiterate, there is no necessary implication for how it is to be provided. There are good arguments from economics about education being a collective good of some kind (so called 'public-goods' or 'merit-goods')[4] , which have a long and respectable pedigree as justification for the public provision of education. There seems no reason why these should be any less compelling, when applied to the case of consumption-good as used here, than in the case of the conventional production-good example. Indeed, in a moment I explore an explicit argument in these terms for the education-as-consumption-good example. To do this, however, requires us first to examine afresh the historical and contemporary nature of the university.

The university: what is it?

As mentioned in the introductory remarks to this paper, one defensive way the university is presented is to conceive of it as a bastion of enlightened and universalistic values, the quintessential institution of the liberal emancipatory project (see Lawson, this volume). No doubt there is at least some residual truth in this conception. But I would like to pose the nature of the university in a different manner to highlight some of its rather less enlightened characteristics and other neglected aspects of its operation and significance.

The problem is that, for much (perhaps most) of its history, the university has been a bastion of conservatism and reaction rather than of liberalism and the Enlightenment. How can we make sense of this if we insist on conceiving it in the manner of the 'politics of nostalgia' discussed briefly above? This point is not necessarily to decry the project of the Enlightenment as conducted within the university, but just to recognise that it has been pursued (of necessity in some instances), and continues to be pursued, in many other arenas at the same time. Thus for much of its history the Enlightenment project has been conducted in such areas as the publishing house, through the medium of the pamphlet, in independent institutions like the Royal Society of Arts and the Royal Academy in Britain, within the institutions of the legal profession in terms of judgements and case histories, within the hospitals and non-university educational establishments (Parker and Courtney, this volume), even within the penal system and political parties. In the US the form of the Congressional hearing has offered another site where this project has been at least in part pursued, and this is duplicated in the case of the Royal Commissions in the UK and other Parliamentary procedures of scrutiny and accountability. A good many of these alternative arenas were set up precisely because of the indifference or open hostility on the part of the university to their intended investigations and work. Thus we should neither exaggerate the universities own commitment to enlightened values nor underestimate the importance of other arenas in fostering these values.[5]

In addition, it is important to recall why the great universities of Europe were founded in the thirteenth and fourteenth centuries. They were designed to fulfil quite utilitarian tasks of the time, namely to train men of medicine, the law, and of religion. In many cases this continued to constituted the main rationale for university education in the humanities and the social sciences well into the nineteenth century (such that these distinctions were operative in that period). It was only then that, in British universities for instance, education in the humanities and social sciences was first comprehensively overhauled. But this was not done in the name of some belated Enlightenment project. Again it was for very instrumental reasons: now to train home, and particularly colonial, administrators rather than ecclesiastics, doctors or lawyers.[6]

When one recognises these features of intellectual life one is of necessity forced to reconceptualise the nature of the university. One way to do this is to conceive of it as a mechanism of governance, and as an institution of 'governmentality'.[7] As a mechanism of governance the university — like any other institution of governance — is characterised by multiple objectives, often conflicting, and employing diverse forms of calculation designed to meet those objectives. These are always historically and socially contingent. As an arena of governmentality, the university can be linked to all those diverse strategies and technologies that serve to produce a certain type of 'self-hood'; the construction of the self-referential subject able to mediate the mentalities of conduct, types of 'vocational' training, and the forms of self-discipline commensurate with the wider technologies of governance and power circulating at any time.

These ways of re-posing the nature of the university move away from conceiving of it as a unitary entity with a single (almost trans-historical) purpose — the construction of an enlightened and humanitarian being. They also enable us to make another argument for the humanities and the social sciences without feeling this would compromise a general principle. Thus, accepting the instrumentality and utilitarian features of the university of the past provides the basis for arguing that a large section of the contemporary working population required to make a modern society function — such as administrators, teachers, professionals, those in the arts, managerial personnel, civil servants, etc. — find their natural training home within these kinds of departments. This 'vocational' aspect to the university is one that needs a more robust defence. The competences of this large group of the working population, fulfilling a vital and unavoidable set of tasks and providing for an equally important set of functions, are for the most part the products of the humanities and the social sciences departments, and they can be justified as products of the university in perfectly good faith. Nor need this be linked to the increasingly discredited argument about the necessary economic performative implications of such a training task now fulfilled by the university. Social science and humanities departments may no longer be producing a critically rounded enlightened subject but rather a set of prosaic administrative and informed functionaries, who are of vital importance nevertheless.

But there is yet another positive consequence of this reconceptualisation of the role of the university for a contemporary defence of the social sciences and humanities. This is to invoke a rather old fashioned *'civic virtue'* argument about the reason for the existence of universities. This plays into a slightly different but related point to the one made by the Enlightenment project justification for a traditional university education considered briefly above. It does so in a specific and particular context, however (not in terms of a universal subject), and one designed to pay close attention to the nuances of contemporary New Right argument.

Perhaps the universities still play a major role in the construction of the 'civic person-hood', and indeed of the 'civilised person' in terms of conducts, manners and the virtue of toleration.[8] There are great *social* benefits (not just private benefits) to be had from the efficient fulfilment of this task, not least benefits associated with the proper conduct of civic duties. The issue behind this is the mechanisms available to assess competing social programmes, economic and political projects, civic and administrative initiatives, aesthetic and moral concerns, and the like, that emerge into the public domain, or that are pressed into it. If there remains a commitment to political and democratic pluralism (even if only a residual commitment), there must be a mechanism that guarantees a range of informed voices available to debate the merits or otherwise, consequences and implications, and so on, of the inevitable emergence of these kinds of social initiatives. What the humanities and social sciences do, at least in some large part, is provide a means by which expertise amongst the general public and an informed opinion can be generated to enable a scrutiny and assessment of these matters. The New Right as well as New Labour is particularly keen (in the UK at least) for there to be a more 'active citizenry' in respect to many social welfare and administrative functions. But the expertise to conduct these functions does not just drop out of thin air. It must be taught, and it should be remembered that it *is* already taught in the context of humanities and social sciences education.

In relation to this, another positive argument for higher education arises quite naturally. It provides a potential mechanism of social equality. The system can open up an opportunity for those not provided with a voice on such civic matters to gain one. It can act to draw-in those from different socio-economic strata, refreshing their competences in the skills needed to fulfil a range of necessary civic duties and responsibilities. Thus the importance of a 'training for citizenship' can be stressed as against the neglect fostered by either paternalism or the idea that these skills are simply acquired naturally.

Here the importance of a diverse and multi-layered higher education system for the generation of a 'plurality of voices' also should be stressed. Suppose we were all members of one large university institution. Under these circumstances, the conditions for sensible and robust debate would be stifled. It is notoriously difficult for members of the same institution to publicly disagree with one another. Thus, to generate an effective debate requires a range of institutions, differentially placed within the social milieu, that can generate a variety of positions in debate. The reduction of the universities to a homogeneous dull uniformity undermines this objective.

The final upshot of these arguments is to link the consumption-good model of higher education, elaborated earlier, to these civic virtue and training mechanisms. Part of the reason for a strong interest in the interdisciplinary study provided by the humanities and the social sciences is to precisely gain the intellectual confidence to engage with, initiate and partake in debates and discussions about the major social and political issues of the day. This constitutes a strong reason for its demand. Such a 'training for citizenship' remains a major and absolutely necessary and legitimate *public* responsibility which needs to be strongly reasserted under present conditions where there is a renewed public emphasis from New Labour and others on citizen responsibility, personal accountability and so on. The construction of 'civic persons' and of 'civilised persons' requires the humanities and the social sciences as the mechanisms for this 'training for citizenship' (see O'Neill, this volume).

The need for a stronger model?

This may all sound reasonable and even feasible, set as it is within the existing contours of the contemporary university. But the implications of a kakistocratic social order referred to above could easily be its undoing. Perhaps we need a new and different conception of the university to re-energise its project and role for late capitalism.

The key question here is whether the university, as an institution of culture and ideas, can co-exist with a trend towards potential mass mediocrity and managerial commercialism? Any society that refuses the implications of a leadership through ideas and a cosmopolitan cultural milieu based upon merit, honesty and the promotion of ability of the 'best' is destined for marginalisation and decline. Thus, the only way out may be to promote a 'new elitism' based upon these principles. To say this, however, is to risk the approbation of the intellectual equalisers and the perspectivisers, as well as to be highly controversial politically. But perhaps it should be said. The issue is not to in any way promote a new *social* elitism, based upon birth, social position or contacts. Rather it is to promote an *intellectual* elitism, where those with ideas, with intellectual creativity, and with capacities for cultural innovativeness, are given a space to think and encouraged to offer advice and find solutions to the pressing politico-economic problems of the day. These ideas can neither be imposed upon citizens nor used to 'talk down' to them. On the other hand, there would seem to be the necessity for an intellectual elite; not all citizens either have the ability, the time nor the inclination to generate such ideas. It is just foolishly utopian to think otherwise.

Perhaps the best metaphor for any such re-invigoration of the university would look to the craft production of the medieval guild. Craft, in its widest connotations, embraces skill, dexterity, and excellence. Its ethical principles — which were so integral to its 'production' principles — involved honour, integrity in performance, honesty, grace and competence. The guild form of organization — which has its contemporary equivalent in the modern day 'networking' form of social coordination — offers a way of recouping the 'best' from a diverse institutional resource that characterises the present sorry intellectual state of the university sector.[9]

Conclusion

This chapter did not set out to unmask or engage with the enormous political obstacles and difficulties facing the continued teaching of a critically informed and interdisciplinary based humanities and social sciences. This does not mean that I am unaware of these difficulties and obstacles. Rather, the problem is to find ways — many different ways — to circumvent these or at least to partially undermine them. In this respect, one of those strategies must be to provide good argumentation. This was one of the objectives set for this chapter. Perhaps there has been too much stress laid upon the political obstacles facing the humanities and social sciences in the university and not enough imaginative thinking about how to defend them through realistic but honest argument. Here I have tried to redress that imbalance. A lot of this might sound naive and fanciful but until it is intellectually explored we will never know. It is time the academic community went on the offensive with some clear, positive and forward looking arguments for its existence.

But in addition there was another objective set for the chapter. This was to highlight a possible significant shift in the contours of the contemporary social order, one characterised as being the development of what was termed a kakistocracy. This unwelcomed event is having profound effects upon the nature of the university (and on the social order more widely), which prompted a discussion of a very different model for the university involving a radical change in its purpose and function. As far as can be judged, the jury remains out on this issue, but its potential, and highly controversial, implications need much further thought and investigation.[10]

Finally, will the advent of a New Labour government and a post-Dearing political climate change matters much? One is tempted to say not, and the early signs seem to indicate that they will just exacerbate matters. The Labour government has simply fallen in behind the 'reforms' of the education sector initiated by the previous Conservative governments. Only if the Dearing Committee can come up with convincing ways in which the universities can escape the clutches of an over bureaucratised and centralized management structure does it hold out much hope for a reversal of the trends identified in this chapter. Here the 'ambiguity' surrounding the university-as-consumption-good argument will be posed afresh. 'Financial independence' might enhance the capacity of the university sector to re-new its plurality, but it could so easily simply re-establish a *social elitism* as the same time. Finding a way of securing an intellectual renaissance for knowledge and ideas, without this being just a disguise for the least able to rule in a different style, remains the fundamental issue.

Notes

1   In this section, I declare a personal note which might help clarify the nature of the argument being made. As an economist, I approach the question posed by this heading in that capacity. The aim here is to more adequately re-conceptualise the economic arguments that are prevalent within both popular and professional discourses about the nature of the connection between the Universities and the current concern with 'economic competitiveness'.

2   Historically, in the UK at least, it has been the public authorities, the universities, but most importantly of all the *schools*, that have provided the impetus for any changes or initiatives in the development of educational competences and skills, not commercial organisations. The latter have generally been the most conservative and backward in terms of their perception of what educational outputs are needed for an advanced industrial economy.

3   See Edgerton (1996) for a discussion of this literature in the context of the relative demise of the economic performance of the British economy.

4   Public- and merit-goods are those which meet the criterion of non-excludability and non-divisibility in their consumption; the 'consumption benefits' derived from these goods can be made available to all at no extra cost if they are to be supplied to any single consumer, and such consumption benefits cannot be divided in any sensible way as between the consumers.

5   One problem in the contemporary period is that many of these other sites for the pursuit of the Enlightenment project (or any other similar project, for that matter) are also increasingly in disarray. Substitute sites for a civic education and critical thought, like the political parties, the media, Parliamentary Commissions, etc., are also in decline.

6   See Hunter *et al.* (1981) for an elaboration of these ideas.

7   Readers will recognise that these terms arise from a Foucauldian reading of the nature of institutional activity.

8   I owe much of the following discussion to Jeffrey P. Minson (1993).

9   For the genesis of these none too systematic remarks about craft production, a 'guild constitution', and networking see: Black (1984, 1992); Franklin (1971); Nicholls (1993); Thompson (1993).

10   I intend to explore this issue and others in Thompson (1999).

References

Black, A. (1984) *Guilds and Civil Society in European Political Thought from the Twelfth Century to the Present.* London: Methuen.

────── (1992) *Political Thought in Europe, 1250-1450.* Cambridge: Cambridge University Press.

Edgerton, D. (1996) *Science, Technology and the British Industrial 'Decline', 1870-1970.* Cambridge: Cambridge University Press.

Franklin, J. H. (1971) 'Sovereignty and the Mixed Constitution', in J. H. Burns (ed) *The Cambridge History of Political Thought, 1450-1700.* Cambridge: Cambridge University Press.

Hirst, P. (1993) 'Is the University the Enemy of Ideas?', *AA Files.*

────── (1994) *Associative Democracy.* Cambridge: Polity Press.

Hunter, I. *et al.* (1991) *Accounting for the Humanities: the Language of Culture and the Logic of Government.* Griffith University, Brisbane: Institute for Cultural Policy Studies.

Minson, J. P. (1993) *Questions of Conduct.* London: Macmillan.

Nicholls, D. (1990) *The Pluralist State.* London: Macmillan.

Thompson, G. (1993) 'Network Coordination', in R. Maidment and G. Thompson (eds) *Managing the United Kingdom: An Introduction to its Political Economy and Public Policy.* London: Sage.

────── (1999) *Between Markets and Hierarchies: The History of Network Coordination in Theory and Practice.* Oxford: Oxford University Press.

Civic Capital: Education and the National Economy

18

John O'Neill

> A society is rich when material goods, including capital, are cheap, and human beings dear; indeed, the word 'riches' has no other meaning. (R. H. Tawney, 1924)

For some time, the educational institutions in the UK have been subject to a process of 'nationalisation' in keeping with the modern form of liberal democratic governmentality (Miller and Rose, 1990). Whether or not it espouses a left-right ideology, the government of the day will put forward to the people any number of 'policies' on industry, housing, crime, health, research and education. At the same time, these policy proposals will be framed in terms of a moral language of efficiency, excellence, quality and competition. Necessarily, certain key-words will convey the coherence of government policies — hence, 'growth' and 'competitiveness' will dominate, while 'social justice' and 'equality' will get unavoidable but weak mention. The integrator in the government's appeal to its citizens will lodge in the language of individual autonomy, enterprise and merit. Governmentality, therefore, represents the distinctive practice of modern ethics in the strategic alignment of politics and economics.

Broadly speaking, the welfare state is the proper field of modern governmentality. We can expect changes in policy emphasis with respect to its dominant components — employment, health and education — but not the end of the welfare state (Pierson, 1991). With respect to education, then, it is not surprising that the UK has set up such elaborate provisions for national accounting in the provision of teaching and research. This puts considerable controls on the teaching profession, upon designated researchers and, of course, upon students and their families. What is at stake is the need to combine the values of social justice with the values of educational proficiency (Commission on Social Justice, 1994). What must be rejected is the 'third position' adopted by the sceptics who believe that the present expansion of the educational system already exceeds the talent available to it and is therefore a waste of national resources.

I shall, therefore, enter the debate by taking on the theory of human capital formation since it represents an appealing strategy for the alignment of education with current demands upon the national economy.

Human capital theory

All older industrial societies are now recasting their approach to human capital formation. Whether or not this exercise is due to the past sins of the welfare state or to the new puritanism of the market, we are engaged in a great national debate about investment in human capacities. We cannot allow this debate to be directed solely by marketeers to whom the mass media give such loud voice. Nor can this debate be decided solely by economists, demographers or sociologists. No social science is privileged in the national exercise of reconstituting our civic capital. It is vital to our national reconstruction that we avoid the fragmentation and opportunism that are the stock in trade of interest groups. What we need is a strong political concept of the civic mosaic that is emerging in our national response to the forces of globalization.

Surprisingly, what we are looking for can be found in the literature of educational economics. Thus, when Theodore Schultz (1971) introduced the notion of human capital theory, he cut through the wall between the material and spiritual arguments for education by showing that not only are there good economic reasons for investing in education but that *human capital* is in fact a major component in physical capital formation, economic growth and social welfare:

> It is my contention that economic thinking has neglected two classes of investment that are of critical importance under modern circumstances. They are investment in man and in research, both private and public. (Schultz, 1971: 5)

Schultz argued that it was time to revise the dominant assumptions that labour is a factor of production 'free of capital', despite its considerable increase in skill, while capital itself is nothing but physical capital (see Kiker, 1971). What follows, we suggest, is that classical capital theory has ignored the considerable amount of *civic capital* invested in both labour and capital. No one has expressed this argument more vigorously than R. H. Tawney whose tireless advocacy of worker education as a civic, if not civilizing, necessity remains as relevant to today's debate as when he first took up the educational struggle early this century:

> It is foolish, above all, to cripple education, as it is crippled in England for the sake of industry; for one of the uses of industry is to provide the wealth which may make possible better education. If a society with the sense to keep means and ends in their proper places did no more than secure the investment in the education of children of a fraction of the wealth which to-day is applied to the production of futilities, it would do more for posterity—it would in a strictly economic sense, 'save' more 'capital'—than the most parsimonious of communities which ever lived with its eyes on the Stock Exchange. (Tawney, 1982: 81)

As I see it, Schultz's observations on the economic functions of education involved a step forward in human capital theory by taking a step backwards to Adam Smith's concept of *civic capital*. What this involves is the recognition that the wealth of nations depends upon all of the social institutions that set a value upon human capital rather than diminish it in favour of rent and profits. This civic approach allows for a more expanded concept of capital activity than the relentless promotion of technological change. It broadens our concept of labour from that of an appendage to machinery to the larger activity of human capital formation enhanced by private and public investment in knowledge and research. This conceptual advance also recovers the history and politics of labour's struggle against its reduction to a mere factor of production stripped of its communal knowledge and craft skills. In addition, the historical narrowing of the morality of capital investment to risk and profit taking may be revised through the recognition of civic capital requirements that underwrite economic growth. In short, a fully developed theory of human capital requires us to formulate the broader concept of civic capital which we shall attempt in this essay.

Civic capital theory

> It is possible for the personnel as well as the material equipment of industry to be undercapitalised, and a nation which has the courage to invest generously in its children 'saves', in the strictest economic sense, more 'capital' than the most parsimonious community which ever lived with its eyes on the Stock Exchange. (Tawney, 1924: 144)

The current restructuring of the capital ideology, content and practice of education must be placed in the context of the breakdown of the tripartite social contract in North America and the UK (Sklar, 1988). What is redefining education is not simply the global economy unless the national economy is interpreted to demand a redefinition of social democracy (Dale, 1989). Education is now in a twist because it has responded to demands both for social efficiency and for social justice. Once business draws the state to itself more than to the people, then the educational system will be reframed in terms of the market model of 'choice' (parents, students, vouchers systems), of 'national' standards and downloading an employment-driven 'core curriculum' into the earliest years of schooling. Educational reform turns the class struggle into a struggle over the class room. Here the administration of a core curriculum is the focus of the struggle to align teachers and students with a system of schooling that services business needs rather than social and political ideas of citizenship (Emberley and Newell, 1994). The twist in the New Right educational reforms is that they reintroduce disciplinary schooling — and all in the name of market freedom and competitiveness. But the prospect of a dual education system only confirms the dual labour economy that has emerged ever more sharply from globalization. At the same time, it would confirm a double shift in human capital theory.

Through its concentration upon the production of technical and administrative knowledge (Apple, 1995; Edwards this volume), capital theory is already moving away from its earlier concept of the social expansion of knowledge and skills. At the same time, the relation between capitalism and civic education is increasingly depleted. Yet vocationalism and qualificationism are touted as responses to both the expansionary and contracting phases of an economy that no longer attempts to provide full employment (McBride, 1992). Can we really expect a training contract between capital and labour — mediated by schools and universities — to restore the loss of civic cohesion that is evident with the breakdown of the corporate pact that we have had for the last fifty years? What evidence do we have that global capital needs to contract with anything but a small percentage of the world's skilled labour force, while taking advantage of cheap labour, regardless of its socio-political condition? Despite flexibility, we can expect a severe increase in worker discipline promulgated in the name of consumer sovereignty. For sovereign consumers are simply docile workers in another guise.

The challenge before us is to restate the case for the complementarity between civic solidarity and national wealth production without either 'selling' our schools or reducing them to global labour camps. This means we must reassert the difference between a few individuals having a lot of wealth and a nation that is wealthy because its toleration of individual gain is tempered by its provision for modest livelihoods whose generality is itself a school of civility. We must restate what we can reasonably expect from the market and what we can reasonably ask of government. The current subordination of government to the economy is not an effect of democratic will but of elite financial institutions whose own state withdrawal hides behind populist rhetoric of anti-governance and anti-taxation. Moreover, the anti-inflation policies of the debt mongers will not achieve economic growth merely by shedding the welfare state. Nothing in fact guarantees the stability, efficiency or fairness of markets except for a state framework. Capitalists themselves know this but merely want to reduce its cost to themselves even after they have excluded society from state provision. Therefore we cannot tolerate the evisceration of the national state if we are to recast our political, economic and educational institutions in a civic mode. Rather, as we restructure work, school and family institutions, we shall need to reconfigure welfare state agencies — even to expand them in some directions, especially in the case of children and youth. We cannot separate economics from social policy, assigning the latter to sparrow status, picking up the crumbs from the capitalist table.

The complementarity between social and economic policy far exceeds the terms of right and left political ideologies. This is because an expanded civic concept of human capital formation exceeds the old order concept of factors of production separated from any notion of civic intelligence. The uncertainty in human capital formation is a fact of life on both the collective and personal levels. For this reason, it is in the national interest to subsidize the *civic mind* so that its perspectives are not limited either by the short-sightedness of market profits or of personal diffidence. Since class, race and gender inequality are so injurious to the civic mind as a national capital investment, it is absolutely necessary to include health, family and social justice improvements in an expanded concept of civic capital investment.

If we map the field of civic capital formation (Figure 18.1, page following) to show the interplay between human capital, social justice and economic growth, we need also to underline the exchanges between the inputs on both the human capital and policy capital sides. These capital exchanges reinforce one another so that personal and social income supplement each other, raising the value of human beings *vis-à-vis* physical capital while reducing social inequality, ignorance and injustice. To the extent that this can be achieved, the goals of civic society reinforce economic growth precisely because of its expanded concept of civic capital formation. The structure and flow of civic capital formation cannot operate in abstraction from the systemic exchanges that impinge upon it from the wider economy. The overlapping systems of exchange that mediate the global economy and national formations of civic capital also make it clear that we cannot simply read off the connections between economic growth, education policy, curriculum and pedagogy as do the vocationalists and market education ideologists.

The continuous enlargement of the concept of human capital has still to progress towards the understanding of a civic investment concept of capital to secure general welfare beyond the scope of market investments. This is needed because we risk great swings in our faith in education as the prime mover in the economy and in our personal lives (Oaks, 1986; Blaug, 1970; Jones, 1993). Excessive credentialism at the expense of job-relevant skills cools business attitudes toward educational institutions. Students themselves become disaffected and disillusioned by the mismatch between the economy and their education. The result is that educational institutions experience considerable swings in their public relevance — and perhaps never so much as when they tie themselves to

CIVIC CAPITAL

HUMAN CAPITAL	SOCIAL POLICY CAPITAL
HEALTH	NATIONAL HEALTH SERVICE
EDUCATION	NATIONAL EDUCATION
INFANT CARE; CONTINUING EDUCATION FROM SCHOOL TO UNIVERSITY	EDUCATIONAL LOANS ACCESSIBILITY
EDUCATIONAL TAX INCENTIVES	

JOB TRAINING

(HEALTH AND EDUCATIONAL
    SUPPLEMENTS) WITH ACCESS TO
    CONTINUING EDUCATION

PERSONAL INCOME	SOCIAL INCOME
INCREASE IN HUMAN/PHYSICAL CAPITAL INVESTMENT RATIO	REDUCTION IN SOCIAL INEQUALITY, INJUSTICE AND IGNORANCE

ECONOMIC GROWTH

Figure 18.1   Civic capital formation

economic trends that dissolve due to economic restructuring that puts so many people's career goals in jeopardy. Whatever the connection between education and economic growth — to some it is a fact, to others a myth — the relationship is certainly fraught with all the troubles of growth, down-turn and restructuring in the economy. What is best said is that an educated citizenry is a civic asset with potential benefit to the political and economic life of a nation. An uneducated economy will not absorb educated labour. For the same reason, students may not absorb education that they fear will not be wanted in the economy. This is the vicious circle of educational and industrial underdevelopment.

We cannot speak of the extension of mass higher education without asking what sort of 'mass' is being produced by the economy (Jones and Hatchet, 1994). There is, for example, considerable debate as to whether the post-Fordist economy demands a more flexible and more knowledgeable labour force — putting pressure upon 'higher' education to reflect just these needs in its curriculum and recruitment policies (Brown and Lauder, 1992). In addition to the problem of youth unemployment, it can be argued that the average level of labour is depressed and that there is considerable de-skilling and underskilling created by the organizational restructuring of global production. Here the working class romance of education, mobility and social justice completely breaks down. In fact, it may even be coming apart for the middle-class whose credentialism is increasingly a strategy to combat its own over-production and risk of falling into a lower class. The point is that unless the structure and content of higher education is changed its expansion merely serves to under-produce working class students while over-producing middle class students. As long as it neither alters students' capacity to cope with shifts in the economy nor improves their sense of civic solidarity, higher education will remain part of the social problem rather than its solution. Above all, unless our educational system abandons its concept of the disposable, degradable child whose sacrifice is the linch-pin of its class system, it is very unlikely that any vocational scheme will alter the tradition of educational demoralization for the masses on one side and of educational affirmation of its elite, on the other side (Connell, 1993).

What is squeezed in the narrow economistic redefinition of human capital theory is the possibility of working-out some mosaic of elite, efficiency and civic functions in the higher education system. The redefinition of the educational system very much depends upon how we understand its civic conscription. It is quite possible for the university to invoke the rhetoric of the community's economic interest in its expansion but to do little to alter its own internal priorities. Rather, the university must embrace the common status of citizenship and the acquisition of civic education for the challenges of modern citizenship. But this means that a civic university must resist political pressures to reduce the educational covenant to one of entitlement or clientship. The ideal of civic education is to promote public intelligence as the best guarantee of the autonomy of the university to which it owes its own life.

Learning in a civic society

It is quite worrying that the vocational tide seems well set against general education. Student anxiety is understandably aggravated by general courses that seem to have no such pay-off as dangled before them by the vocationalists. Paradoxically, it is precisely the anxiety of the generalist that, if carefully tutored, proves to be the greatest asset in the shifting worlds of work and morals (Scott, 1984). So we must defend the generalist approach at all levels of education as a vital factor in any national response to social change. This response is deeper than the buzz words of pluralism, relevance, accountability, two-tiering, and so on. It places education at the centre of civic society — neither above it nor on its margins. By drawing schools and universities into the civic centre, we open them to a public that has opened itself to them so that everyone may thrive. If we throw our schools into the market, our children will enter them by a gate no wider than the eye of a needle. What is endangered in this prospect is the opportunity to open up a civic university culture broader than the class uses of symbolic capital that endlessly recode the split between manual and non-manual work, as well as the femalization and coloration of service tasks. Here we have in mind something more grounded than the shibboleths of the so-called 'learning society' through which the business world imposes its employment demands, distributing flexibility, adaptability and personal investment in terms of its own bottom-line concepts of career and profit.

Even when the state invites parents and students to enter the learning society, nothing much changes so long as the society beyond formal training institutions teaches everyone that their futures are largely precast (Whitty, 1991). The maintenance of a civic welfare state is necessary to accommodate the restructuring of institutions whose life-cycle norms no longer prevail. The heart of a welfare society should be the civic covenant of life-time learning and education with multiple entry and exit points negotiated between family members, schools, universities and workplaces in accordance with a citizenship ideal of education. So, rather than yield knee-jerk training responses to a mindless market whose coherence is a necessary but not sufficient condition of social cohesion, we need to embrace a national myth of civic learning, mindful of all the pitfalls and blockages at work in our society (Hughes and Tight, 1995).

I do not mean to idealize schools. I do mean to love them. A school is not a training programme. The core of the difference is the civic curriculum which, even if it is administered with disciplinary intent, nevertheless introduces students to a world of history, language, nature and technology wider than anything in a training manual (Osborne, 1991). We know, of course, that the school curriculum is a carrier of national and class ideologies. We know that our schoolrooms are filled with the world's children and that their teachers have had to respond to the global classroom with little preparation and support. But it would be premature to resort to either the multicultural fragmentation of the global classroom or to realign its civic curriculum with the corporate agenda for numeracy and literacy (Barlow and Robertson, 1994). It would be quite unthinkable to make any such move at a time when the State's capacity to institute national standards is weakened by the breakdown in the social covenant that underwrites public education and its civic aspirations.

The reason that life itself is regarded as a great school is because human life is not a trivial machine, however much it amuses itself with their production. Life on our level is an organization that has learned to learn. To preserve its openness, human society has acquired a cultural memory that is itself open to endless refiguration through the arts and sciences. On the level of everyday life, society necessarily seeks trivialization in the sense that institutions count upon the repetition of successful behaviour so that social energy can be released for change and reformation. But as true learning organisms, human beings ought not to be trivialized through institutionally imposed ignorance and docility. Our children, therefore, must be given broad access to civic institutions whose open-endedness is both a global fact and a moral universal. Having said this, the open society is not open only for business. Indeed, the open society has as much to fear from closure by the market as by any other totalizing institution. Our schools and universities must be rededicated to the pursuit of learning to learn protected by a civic covenant that cannot be subcontracted or politically franchised.

Today, the educational covenant must be renewed at the bottom through universal pre-school care and at the top through a revision of our life cycle assumptions regarding school, work, family and community involvement. At each local point, accessibility should be understood as a citizen's right to learn that is translated into a teacher/student covenant through which a study path is taken that is at various points accountable to disciplinarity, skills and imagination (Fulton, 1989). What should be 'nationalized' is the civic determination to avoid loss of the value of human life in our schools starting from a child's first day at kindergarten and expanding endlessly through the life-time of anyone whose need to learn brings them to a teacher's door. It is essential to the ideal of civic education that its enjoyment is not enhanced by its uneven availability nor by its lack in anyone. From a civic perspective, then, it is intolerable that education, health, employment and personal security be treated as positional goods (Hirsch, 1977). Thus any notion that higher education is less valuable through its extension to the masses is completely immoral, let alone uncivil. It betrays an evil adoration of class division and a totally unacceptable fixation upon privilege and exclusivity.

General education has nothing to do with averaging or homogenizing students — a fear that merely expresses elite anxiety despite the fact that even modest educational expansion has served more to flexibilize themselves than the rest of society. Mill's fear that state education will homogenize students ignores intra-class homogenization that operates among the elites no less than others but whose total efficiency is reserved for fictional polities. No school, or church or factory or prison ever succeeds in matching Mill's vision which should therefore not stampede us into the marketization of education. Curiously enough, it is the neo-liberal government that has reduced the civil understanding between state and universities to one of inspection in order to guarantee their services to the market! Inasmuch as this directive is aimed at bringing schools and universities in line with an economy that economists themselves treat as unpredictable, neo-liberal statism is thoroughly contradictory. Even setting aside its ambition to deprofessionalize teachers, the market view of human capital is immoral because it promises students what cannot be delivered. To repeat, if there is one thing economists of education are agreed upon, it is that the ideal of flexibility is best achieved by leaving university education in the general mode rather than vocationalizing it in response to market trends whose prevalence no one can predict.

The quality/efficiency, elite/expansionist alternatives have always dogged the educational debate. What seems to make the difference is the national will to espouse universal higher education (Ramirez and Robinson, 1979). Here we put stress on *universal* rather than 'mass' education and on *higher*, meaning *continuing* education, rather than mass education. Government must play a role in the formation, funding and curriculum of the continuing educational system. But government cannot create an educational system that will fulfill the promise of universal education unless there is sufficient civic determination to set aside class and cultural exclusion in favour of citizenship and access in the principle and practice of both teaching and learning. Nor can industry push government further than society because the social values of industry itself are deeply divisionary and only secondarily expansionary according to its shaky projections of business prospects. It is almost certain that the business agenda will prematurely declare obsolete those very features of the educational system that it will later need to reinvent: witness the swings and roundabouts on general and vocational studies. By contrast, where society seeks to expand its civic welfare, as was the case in post-war UK, then the will to include education along with health and employment secures education's essential role in the increase of national well-being. The educational system, then, is always faced towards government, on one side, and towards business, on the other. In practice, government and the educational system may move in a civic alliance to deal with business, or else government and business may move in alliance to direct educational institutions. These shifting alliances are largely the source of the expansions, contractions and restructuring that we experience within educational institutions as threats to autonomy, reductions of standards, politicization of curriculum, commodification of values (Tapper and Salter, 1978: 145-167). But I think these are day-to-day problems whose ultimate significance can only be estimated by grasping the fundamental difference between the *civic covenant* in education and the business agenda for education.

It is no use fighting the government in the name of education if what we are really doing is defending an elitist curriculum that also belongs to the business agenda of binary education — unless we are defiantly mental amputees! Where the elite version of uniformity of standards prevails, as in UK secondary and university education, it effectively demoralizes the majority of young people who in turn join the wider constituency of a public that is shy of education. The result is that everyone loses — faculty, students, industry and the public. In such a climate, government and university relations are likely to be fitful and erratic unless a new educational covenant is brokered between the parties without prejudice to how accessibility and excellence are to be found in our schools and universities. Quality is not necessarily weakened by the diversity of programmes required by equity unless we confuse uniformity with equality. This is precisely the confusion built into the notion that we can only have 'further' or 'higher' education by 'massing' it. Such a view is determined by a wholly minimalist view of human talent.

The romance of continuing education created by primary schools open to universities and universities open to life-time learners is grounded in the belief that there is more human talent to be found than we know and that in the end we cannot be sure when, where, or in whom it will show. The true romance of civic education consists in its continuing surprises created by its continuing hopes. There are, of course, disappointments, failures and losses in the open education system — but they are not written in anyone's genes and they are to be admitted only once everyone at all levels of the education system has given it a go.

The civic ideal of open schooling is not visionary. If anything defeats its practice, it is the practice of excluding large numbers of young people from continuing education (Ainley, 1994). It is an uncivilized practice that not only involves a huge gift from the poor to the rich but also a terrible sacrifice by the ignorant on behalf of the educated. Nothing degrades our educational system so much as its collusion with the indifferent trashing of our youth. Only insult is added to this national injury, if the lost souls of our youth are merely shepherded into further education as consumers rather than citizens.

Educational consumerism will fragment the educational system. But it will not necessarily diversify it (Ball, 1993). Rather, consumerism is more likely to deepen the stratification of education in the name of 'public choice' — an expression that veils market results that are neither public nor chosen. The consumer model of education is a model for choices *between* institutions. It hides itself as a model of choices *within* educational systems. But a civic education system must be defended against such confusion. Paradoxically, our defence must be mounted around the modular curriculum (Berdahl et. al. , 1991) which elite theorists regard as the very practice whose avoidance justifies the call for a market choice between elite and mass education. The modular curriculum is easily despised. It may also be cynically indulged as the price academia must render to Caesar's wish that his army be disciplined in spirit as well as body. But the modular system may also be praised as a truly civic expression of our faith in the individual paths that students can be trusted to take towards their education. There are, of course, 'bird' paths in the modular curriculum. But there are also paths of imagination and independence, that are sufficiently taken to honour this curriculum and the administrative labour it entails. The more open the overall education system, the more the flexibility of the modular system permits both students and faculty to treat education as a self-imposed adventure, with ups and downs whose early effects are not absolutely binding on later outcomes. So long as the faculty itself continues to learn to teach and to do research, its alliance with the promise in students as unfinished as themselves is deepened through the necessary advisory functions imposed by the modular system. Somehow teacher and student wade through it all, rubbing seriousness against convenience, personality against anonymity, bending the rules, subverting administration in favour of classroom autonomy while sending professionalism to the needs of students with their own agenda.

The willingness to make the modular system work is only understandable if taken with the civic will to be of service in a public education system that continuously expands with a society that is, broadly speaking, open to its constituent groups of any age, color or creed. In Canada, this does not mean that our system is a perfectly open book, nor even that it is very good at explaining itself to the society it nevertheless serves more than it neglects. But the very heart of our school system is that it means to offer itself to its students; its joy is in receiving rather than withholding.

Beyond the class war

It is entirely unacceptable that we allow our schools and universities to be the killing fields of so many young people. The vice of secular societies is class privilege. Its practice is most pernicious when treating education as a privilege of the rich that is enhanced by the ignorance of the poor. Yet the ignorance of the poor does not diminish us nearly so much as the view of the rich that ignorance is necessary to the enjoyment of the educated. The class basis of education continues to hobble public education to this day (Kerckhoff, 1993). Industrialists continue to oppose and to demand the extension of secondary education. But if their mood has changed because of their understanding of the capital needs of industry, it has not altered nearly so much their conviction that on balance most people are not educable but merely serviceable to industry. Because of this conviction, we have still to embrace public education as a civic good or as an expression of public intelligence and solidarity without which society is enslaved by brute privilege. We cannot institute civic education so long as we continue to sacrifice the ideals of shared intelligence among the majority who remain working people to the lesser ideal of the competitive advantage of the educated individual seeking social mobility in a class society. What is needed, as R. H. Tawney taught so passionately, is the recognition that we must expand public education because the motive of the public that seeks education is not merely utilitarian but also spiritual. Of course, this position depends upon our civic understanding that we cannot separate our economic lives from our political and spiritual lives without eventually undermining even our material interests. This now requires that we reconnect industry with public service and accountability beyond the calculus of private profit but also beyond the indifferent autonomy of state bureaucracy.

Whatever their claims, the restorationist ideals of the marketeers do not represent a return to the original morality of unhampered capitalism. In fact, it can be argued that its current attack on the welfare state and the new theories of human capital formation arise from a split between public sector and corporate sector professionals (Perkin, 1989). Ironically, both parties enjoy a richer human capital investment than is proposed in any of the schemes for retraining the general populace for global competition. Both parties are the beneficiary of the rent of ability rather than the rent of property in land or in physical capital — a distinction that goes to the heart of liberal capitalism. But the great moral refusal that drove such Edwardian social reformers as Tawney, Titmuss and Marshall (see Dennis and Halsey, 1988) was their clear rejection of the waste of human ability — put so clearly by Alfred Marshall:

> In the world's history there has been one waste product so much more important than all the others, that it has a right to be called The Waste Product. It is the higher abilities of many of the working classes; the latent, the undeveloped, the choked-up and wasted faculties for higher work, that for lack of opportunity have come to nothing. (Pigou, 1925: 229)

To this day, Britain's education system has still to take up the moral imperative in the rejection of such waste of human potential. It is now clear that the appeal to social efficiency and competitiveness, whether voiced from the Right or from the Left, has not fully persuaded Britain to abandon its national vice of trashing the greater part of its children and youth. What violates the British welfare state is its acceptance of the elite prejudice that there are *minimal standards* of health, education and welfare rather than *civic levels of well being* whose sustainability should be a national priority. This minimalist concept of standards still hobbles today's expanded education system, which is curiously subject to an extraordinary national vetting whose closest agenda is to reproduce the old-order educational hierarchy. This time, however, the national state ratings will provide the rationale for state-sponsored marketization of educational success. What is missing is the lesson that a *civic education* is a universal good whatever the variations in teaching and research and whatever the variability of student ability. If this were not so, Britain's ruling elites would largely be thrown out of school, if not out of a job! The goal of civic education, however, cannot be realized without reconstructing the *tripartite complex* of the teaching profession Britain — a complex that internalizes the class divisions that education must resist. Current debates over comprehensive schooling, grammar schools, selectivity and streaming will remain stymied until their root in Platonic *three-soulism* is exposed once for all both on the level of the universities and the schools of Britain. It will not do to alter the ideology at one level of the education system without changing it on all other levels.

It is time to abandon the use of learning to winnow out the majority of children in favour of the intensive cultivation of a few (O'Neill, 1994). We must accord to the life of the mind more than an early but equal opportunity to blunt itself with failure. Our goal must be to let anyone learn at any time in life when there is need or desire to learn. To practice such an ideal of the civic mind we shall need open schools, open curricula and open universities. This prospect need not evoke fears of waste and inefficiency. It does not necessarily take more resources or more time to have a change of heart, to become a path for others who are looking for a road through our schools and universities that will extend their civic vision and understanding. We need to make it clear to the people in our country that our schools and universities are popular institutions because we are a people as determined to be educated as we are to be healthy, or to be occupied in the service of one another. We should therefore resist movements toward the marketization of our schools through voucher systems, parentocracy, religious or racial segmentation, even though parents, religious beliefs and ethnic cultures all have their place in a civic cultural mosaic. What must also be avoided is the removal of the state and municipality from educational decisions when what is really at issue are conflicting ideologies of national and common culture. Marketeers sacrifice civic culture in the name of anti-governance while fostering bureaucratic accountability in the name of populism. Much energy is consumed by these alternatives that should now be pulled toward a civic centre.

The civic mind is wholly an educative effect of the open institutions in which it is acquired. Civic learning is both a habit and an exercise of political will. It is a civic habit informed by the everyday assurances, provisions and reciprocal practices of the commonwealth through which we achieve personal aims. Our civic habits do not exaggerate our political life any more than they underestimate our economic interests or our religious interests. Our civic vision is determined by the linkages between our personal and public lives, between the comfortable and the needy, between the old and the new, between inviolable trusts and contingent contracts. Our civic habits are not exhausted by their practice. They cannot be depleted; nor can they be appropriated by any party, any more than a language can be reduced to its phrases, or family life be reduced to the isolated living of its individual members. Any such reduction or appropriation involves violation, misconception and injustice. Indeed, it is precisely the common good that gives perspective to our sense of justice, and to what we believe we owe to one another in the school of living together. The civic mind appears to us as not merely one more good but a good that 'makes sense' of all other goods in our life.

References

Ainley, P. (1994) *Degrees of Difference: Higher Education in the 1990s*. London: Lawrence and Wishart.

Apple, M. W. (1995) 'Cultural Capital and Official Knowledge', in M. Berube and C. Nelson (eds) *Higher Education Under Fire: Politics, Economics and the Crisis of the Humanities*. New York: Routledge, pp. 91-107.

Ball, S. J. (1993) 'Education markets, Choice and Social Class: the market as a class strategy in the UK and the USA', *British Journal of the Sociology of Education*, 14 (1): 3-19.

Barlow, M. and Robertson, H. J. (1994) *Class Wars*. Toronto: Key Porter Books.

Berdahl, R. O., Moodie, G. C. and Spitzberg, I. J., Jr. (1991) *Quality and Access in Higher Education: Comparing Britain and the United States*. Buckingham: Open University Press.

Blaug, M. (1970) *An Introduction to the Economics of Education*. London: Allen Lane /The Penguin Press.

Brown, P. and Lauder, H. (1992) 'Education, Economy and Society: An Introduction to a New Agenda', in P. Brown and H. Lauder (eds) *Education For Economic Survival: From Fordism to Post-Fordism?*. London: Routledge, pp. 1-44 .

Commission on Social Justice (1994) *Social Justice: Strategies For National Renewal*. London: Vintage.

Connell, R. W. (1993) *Schools And Social Justice*. Toronto: Our Schools/Our Selves Education Foundation.

Dale, R. (1989) *The State And Education Policy*. Toronto: OISE Press.

Dennis, N. and Halsey, A. J. (1988) *English Ethical Socialism*. Oxford: Oxford University Press.

Emberley, P. C. and Newell, W. R. (1994) *Bankrupt Education: The Decline of Liberal Education in Canada*. Toronto: University of Toronto Press.

Fulton, O. (ed) (1989) *Access and Institutional Change*. Milton Keynes: Open University Press.

Hirsch, F. (1977) *Social Limits to Growth*. London: Routledge.

Hughes, C. and Tight, M. (1995) 'The Myth of the Learning Society', *British Journal of Educational Studies*, 43 (3): 290-304.

Jones, G. (1993) *The Economics of Education*. London: Macmillan.

Jones, K. and Hatchet, R. (1994) 'Educational Progress And Economic Change: Notes On Some Recent Proposals', *British Journal of Educational Studies*, 42(3): 245-260.

Kerckhoff, A. C. (1993) *Diverging Pathways: Social structure and career deflections*. Cambridge: Cambridge University Press.

Kiker, B. F. (1971) 'The Historical Roots of the Concept of Human Capital', in B. F. Kiker (ed) *Investment in Human Capital*. Columbia: University of South Carolina Press.

McBride, S. (1992) *Not Working: State, Unemployment and Neo-conservatism in Canada*. Toronto: University of Toronto Press.

Miller, P. and Rose, N. (1990) 'Governing Economic Life', *Economy and Society* 19 (1): 1-31.

Oaks, J. (1986) *Educational Indicators: A Guide for Policymakers*. Madison: Center for Policy Research in Education.

O'Neill, J. (1994) *The Missing Child in Liberal Theory: Towards a Covenant Theory of Family, Community, Welfare and Civic State*. Toronto: University of Toronto Press.

Osborne, K. W. (1991) *Teaching for Democratic Citizenship*. Toronto: Our Schools/Our Selves.

Perkin, H. (1989) *The Rise of Professional Society: England since 1880*. London: Routledge.

Pierson, C. (1991) *Beyond The Welfare State? The New Political Economy of Welfare*. Oxford: Blackwell Publishers.

Pigou, A. C. (1925) (ed) *Memorials of Alfred Marshall*. London: Macmillan.

Ramirez, F. O. and Rubinson, R. (1979) 'Creating Members: The Political Incorporation and Expansion of Public Education', in J. W. Meyer and M. T. Hannan (eds) *National Development and the World System: Educational, Economic, and Political Change 1950-1970*. Chicago: The University of Chicago Press, pp. 72-82.

Schultz, T. W. (1971) *Human Investment in Capital: The Role of Education in Research*. New York: The Free Press.

Scott, P. (1984) *The Crisis of the University*. London: Croom Helm.

Sklar, M. (1988) *The Corporate Reconstruction of American Capitalism 1890-1916: The Market, The Law, and Politics*. Cambridge: Cambridge University Press.

Tapper, T. and B. Salter (1978) *Education and Political Order: Changing patterns of class control*. London: Macmillan Press.

Tawney, R. H. (1924) *Secondary Education For All: A Policy For Labour*. London: George Allen and Unwin Ltd.

—————— (1982) *The Acquisitive Society*. Brighton: Wheatsheaf Books Limited.

Whitty, G. (1991) 'The New Right and the National Curriculum', in R. Moore and J. Ozga (eds) *Curriculum Policy*. Oxford: Pergamon Press.

The Perverse Modernisation of British Universities

19

Michael Rustin

The difficulties which the British university system has been experiencing for the past decade need to be set in the context of the transformation of the entire public sector which was initiated under Margaret Thatcher, the momentum of which seems set to continue well into the epoch of New Labour.

The 'revolutionary' character of Thatcherism was of course most obvious in its decisive confrontations with the forces and institutions of the working class. Its legislative attack on trade unions, their defeats in decisive battles such as that of the 1984-85 miners' strike, the abandonment of full employment, and the weakening of the 'social guarantees' provided by the welfare state in its various aspects have all been clear enough in both their intention and effect.

But Thatcherism was no less radical in its strategy of dismantlement and transformation of almost the entire public sector of British institutional life — most obviously through the programmes of privatisation of hitherto nationalised industries and utilities, which have set a path-breaking example for other countries in different phases of economic development. Privatisation proved a highly exportable invention.

The Thatcherite project was radical no less significantly, though less obviously, in the transformation even of those large parts of the public sector which have remained publicly owned or funded. Among the key reform programmes here are the instituting of 'internal markets' in the National Health Service, the development of a 'contract culture' within local government, the hiving-off of many former civil service functions to independent agencies, and the imposition of contracting-out and of a managerialist culture and method in the BBC under the regime of John Birt.

The aim of this reform programme has been both to create private market involvement in the provision of public services, wherever this is feasible (e.g.

in the contracting out of local government services or the production of television programmes to private providers), and to create 'quasi-markets' even where 'full marketisation' was politically or for other reasons impossible. The 'purchaser-provider' split inside the NHS is one large example of this methodology, and it has many other analogues and equivalents. Another dimension has been the attempt to introduce an equivalent of 'consumer sovereignty' into public service provision. This has nearly always taken the individualist form of enlarged 'consumer choice' rather than the more collectivist form of greater consumer representation — in Hirschman's terms, enhancing 'exit' rather than 'voice'.

The explicit or implicit enemies, in this revolution in public provision, have been two overlapping systems and cultures. One of these is the forms of bureaucratically-organised provision mandated by the political process, funded by taxation, and implemented through state bureaucracies. These have been deemed to be inefficient, monopolistic, and inherently biased in their values against the free market. The second of these is the system and culture of professionalism, the provision of public services, on behalf of the state or the community, by largely self-regulating professional providers, such as the professions working within the NHS, or the schoolteachers. 'Professionalism', in this neo-conservative way of thinking, has been deemed to be inherently self-serving, little more than a trade unionism of the middle class.

So a national curriculum and external assessments have been imposed on the schools, devolved budgets (and the competitive mentality they unavoidably generate) on every public service provider from schools to GPs, and a managerialist form of both centralisation and hiving-off on to the BBC, supplanting a culture hitherto notable for its ethos of management by those with proven professional expertise in the various disciplines of programme-making.

It seems likely that this quasi-marketised public sector, in which auditors, accountants, and managers assume newly dominant roles over the specialist professionals of each sector, was intended to be merely an unstable transitional stage in the construction of a divided system, one part of which would operate in as near as possible to a full market environment (where it was not privatised entirely), and the other part of which would constitute a residual sector of public provision for those who could afford nothing better. This would be subject to authoritarian forms of control, legitimised in the name of 'standards' but also bearing a good deal of unconscious hostility to public provision and its indigent publics. We can see the spirit of this residual public sector to come in the 'tough' approach taken to failing schools and their teachers, even where the failure of some such schools is an unavoidable product of large-scale social neglect.

One reason, apart from the ideological agendas which underlie these developments, for inferring a full-market destination for public sector institutions is the climate of continuous defunding in which they have almost all been obliged to operate. If what is available on a universalistic, tax-funded basis fails to keep up with user expectations, or indeed with the improvements in standards continually experienced within the market sector, consumers will be progressively forced out of the public system, or at the least to supplement it with top-up private provision.

David Elstein remarked some months ago (he then worked for Sky TV) that the satellite companies had noticed that the terrestrial licence fee had been set 'too low': too low, that is, to fund the quality and range of services that audiences wanted. (This in spite of the dramatic economies of scale which are realised through a system of universal free access to broadcasting.) This gap between the optimal licence fee from the point of view of service provision and the actual licence fee charged is what has created the space for 'top-up' private provision by satellite and cable broadcasters. But of course, the BBC's licence-free is neither an accident, nor set by the BBC itself, but is decided by government. It is obvious that the inadequacy of the licence fee to meet the BBC audience's demand for services has been determined on purpose, both to necessitate Birt's internal market reforms, and to create space in which the subscription-based competition can flourish.

Very similar mechanisms have been set up in most other fields of provision. Under-funding of health, or dentistry practice, forces consumers into private provision. Under-funding of pensions requires investment in occupational or private schemes. Poor public transport increases the relative attractiveness of the car, and so on.

With remarkable boldness, and probably cynicism, the government that had created the conditions in which at least relative if not absolute standards were bound to fall, at the same time began to insist that standards were important, and that consumers must be given more power to insist on them. The era of the Citizens' Charters was born, for NHS patients, university students, school-children's parents, and even rail travellers. We were all given the right to say what was the matter with the services provided for us, and a new form of persecution of the professional providers of those services was invented. Whilst in principle there is much to be said for enhanced 'customer voice', its main function in this period was to give more power to higher level managers over the lower-level providers of services, and to give a new weapon to the ubiquitous inspectors and auditors. It also served to create impatience with the services themselves, in circumstances in which their general improvement was all but impossible. The effect was to visibly stratify them, the 'league tables' for schools and universities appearing as the visible register of these new competitive hierarchies.

The General Election of May 1, 1997 was in large part a plebiscite about whether this revolutionary dismantlement (or at least stratification prior to dismantlement) of the public sector should continue on its course or not. This was one reason why the health service and education were such central election issues, since these remain the largest nearly-universal public services. (They also remain, in autumn 1997, the main objects of public anxiety.) The Conservatives' falling-out with the professions had reached the point by the election when they were openly quarrelling not only with the BMA and the teachers' unions, which was only to be expected, or even with the clergy (now the main voices of the very poor in British society), but with the prison governors and with the judges, neither hitherto noted for their liberal sympathies.

The Conservatives, of course, lost, and lost badly. It should follow therefore that the crusade against the public sector, and against the professionalised forms of service-provision which flourish within it, should have been halted. Ideologically, this may be so, but the changes set in motion by Thatcherism have a momentum of their own, and it is by no means clear that a new direction has yet been, or will now be, set. The taxation and expenditure targets set by the previous government, and accepted by New Labour, impose impossible limits to doing anything really different, that is to the reconstruction of universally-acceptable public services. These limits enforce a regime of 'posthumous Thatcherism', and the resort to disciplinary measures (in 'welfare to work', toughness on crime, and no more than a month's tolerance of poor teachers) only displays a need for government to be doing *something* when it finds it impossible to do what is really necessary. 'Toughness', in other words, has the same displacement and diversionary function for New Labour as it had for its predecessor in office.

The universities

Where do the universities fit into all of this? The university sector is a branch of the public sector which had already, in its post-Robbins expansion, acquired many of the attributes of a well-functioning 'internal market'. Funding came largely through taxation, via grants administered by the University Grants Committee and its equivalents for the public sector, and via student grants and notional full-time fees paid in fact by the State. In this respect, it was and remains a public system. But students competed for places on the basis of their various merits and qualifications, and universities competed for students, offering their resources of quality, environment and prestige to attract the most valued student body. Universities competed also for research funding, in various public and private research markets. The severity of this competitive regime, in the period before 1979, was mitigated by the system of quinquennial grants, and by the fact that for many years priority was given to expansion rather than efficiency.

This 'quasi-market' system was the modernised legacy of the universities' original independence from central government. The universities have formed part of a substantial 'civil society', supported by endowments by aristocracy and later by the industrial bourgeoisie, and in the case of the great civic universities by municipal governments. The 'public sector' created by Crosland in 1976 was formally under the control of local authorities, even though virtually all of its funding came from central government). This 'devolved system' has protected norms of academic freedom, and has also been more supportive of innovation and differentiation than university systems such as those of France or Italy which are controlled by the central State.

From the late 1970s, the claims of the higher education system for ever more resources to fund the growth of student numbers became a problem for governments. The 'binary system' was established by the Labour Government ostensibly as a stimulus to 'useful knowledge', but in reality to facilitate the expansion of the higher education system at much lower unit costs than were then acceptable to the older universities. The polytechnics and colleges — after 1992 the 'new universities' — proved highly responsive to financial inducements to expand student numbers, enabling governments to meet the demands for places from students and parents which have remained the most potent driving force of the system throughout this period. The government devised other market disciplines for the university system. For example, the quinquennial funding round turned into an annual funding allocation, until it became decided to institute 'efficiency gains' on a three year rolling basis, returning to medium-term planning but without its advantages. The raising of overseas student fees to full-cost levels (at first controversial) forced universities into a new competitive market. The validation and quality-audit system of the Council for National Academic Awards (CNAA) was brought under pressure to impose more competitive and stratifying standards. When its academic membership proved reluctant to go along with this, it went the way of the HMI and was abolished for reason of its loyalty to its professional constituency. The regime of self-regulation which remained acceptable for the City was rejected by government for the professional sphere of higher education.

These pressures on the system, in the direction of internal marketisation and external control, were consolidated in the Education Reform Act of 1992. This Act offered the former polytechnics membership of a unified university sector (undoubted progress from the previous two-tier system). But it also strengthened the regime of audit and competition, with a universal system of 'teaching quality assessment' and 'research assessment' applying to the 'old' as well as the 'new' universities and colleges. These systems rapidly became digitalised, with a points and grades system making it easy to construct hierarchies of quality on each dimension. These were readily translated into more or less vulgarised 'league tables' of quality, exactly paralleling the outcomes of standard assessments for the school system.

At the same time as they were being made more publicly accountable through various regimes of audit and inspection, universities were also asked to become more accountable to their 'customers', the students, via Student Charters, formalised complaints procedures and the like. All these systems had costs attached to them, not least in diverting effort from the primary tasks of teaching, research, and the support of a learning environment, to the secondary tasks of meeting the requirements of the audit systems. I think it is likely that innovation has been inhibited in a climate in which nothing can now be done by academics without reference to audit procedures of one sort or another.

It is difficult to balance the costs and benefits of these changes. The unified UCAS system for undergraduate recruitment does seem to have reduced transaction costs in this huge internal market. The Research Assessment Exercise has plainly increased research outputs[1], especially in the new universities, though with the distortions of 'transfer markets' in researchers and with possibly a displacement of quality and originality by quantity and routine. The Teaching Quality Assessment system seems to have been introduced, however, without any built-in measures of its own consequences for standards, which may of course be negative, through the displacement of effort, as well as positive. On the whole, it seems that the harmful effects of these systems have been mitigated by the extent to which academics have been able to keep control of them. Both the TQA and RAE systems are based on forms of peer-review, and have therefore been responsive to norms generated within the universities themselves. Professional autonomy has been less undermined in the universities than it has, for example, in the school system, or even in the NHS, where the 'internal market' now sometimes resembles a bizarre form of Stalinist planning in its rigidity and arbitrariness. What is even worse than not being able treat patients because there are no resources is not being allowed to treat them when there are resources, as happens.

What has made the real difference, however, is that these changes have been introduced during a period when resources were being severely cut. In a pattern familiar across the rest of the public sector, the universities were made more accountable for 'standards', and to their 'customers', in a period when it was inevitable that standards would fall. It is not conceivable that standards of provision could *not* fall, when, according to Dearing[2], funding per student has declined by more than 40% since 1976, and is scheduled to decline by a further 10% by 1999-2000.

I will explore further what I mean by 'standards' later on. But it is interesting to see how ideologically determined the whole system of quality audit has been. By individualising the inspection of quality) to specified subjects and departments in universities, a general interest has been created in demonstrating that standards have *not* fallen, or that if by chance they have, it is the fault of some guilty or hapless local providers, and not a general problem. The system has no mechanism for detecting declines in general standards of higher education, even though 90% of academics would probably agree that they have been seriously affected especially by the problems of falling resources. Of course, everyone can remember what happens to watchdogs which actually bark, such as HMI.

The Dearing Report

Here then was the context for the Dearing Committee's work. All political parties acknowledged the existence of a serious funding crisis, within the constraints of taxation levels which the Conservative and Labour parties certainly accepted. All parties also agreed upon the need to expand the number and proportion of students in higher education, from its present capped level of 30% of 18 year olds, to something like 40% over the next ten years or so. This was both for reasons of keeping up with other countries (a major theme of Dearing), and of ensuring that parental and student demand for university places, a main vehicle for upward social aspiration, was met. There was virtually-universal agreement across the university sector, new and old, that continued reductions in funding would threaten the fundamental integrity of the British higher education system. Vice-Chancellors were saying, if the present 'unit of resource' is maintained, the present system may remain viable, but if it falls further, it will break. There was also a tacit and rather subtle consensus that the present system remained, in its essentials, a satisfactory design and that the various reforms of the past decade, teaching and quality audits included, should stay.

There were thus a variety of demands that had to be reconciled in some fashion. Dearing, established on a bipartisan political basis, was nothing more than a device for reconciling them. Its chosen instrument, long signified in advance, was a novel form of hypothecated taxation, the 'graduate tax'. By this magic device, money could be found, expansion could be resumed, and the status quo of the university system continued for a further period of years. In the event, the New Labour government found it hardly necessary even to allow debate on the report before adopting a version of its main recommendation which was more severe than Dearing's. Not only should students pay tuition fees, the government said, but the student grant should be replaced by a loan repayable through the tax system.

Only the NUS, and a few Old Labourites, seemed to object. It might be politically impossible to increase income or wealth taxes, but there seemed to be no problem in redefining the income derived from 'graduate jobs' as a kind of windfall, 'deserving' repayment in the cause of justice to fellow-citizens who had not been given this earning opportunity. David Blunkett referred to cleaners who would otherwise be paying taxes to support the children of the privileged in universities, failing to observe that under a more progressive tax system her children might be benefiting from free higher education and she paying nothing.

Here then is an example of the surreptitious (or not so surreptitious) continuity between the post-Thatcherite and New Labour regimes.

Dearing is a fitting monument to the managerial revolution in higher education. It has produced its predicted 'fix' (its members barely protesting when even this proved too fiscally demanding for the government), and has spent the rest of its hundreds of pages tinkering with the administration of the system that has evolved over the past two decades. (As part of its proposed medium-term concordat between the university system and the state, Dearing accepts the need for some further centralisation of surveillance and control, via the proposed Quality Standards agency, pools of licensed external examiners, required teacher training for university lecturers and the like. (Note, however, that universal teacher training has not saved the schoolteachers from being savaged.) The decline in innovativeness of a university system which has lost so much of its confidence and autonomy is reflected in the absence of challenging ideas or vision in this Report. The universities, like the rest of the public sector, are too weary and demoralised even to have noticed what is missing. A graduate tax may not be the ideal, but in these days who can quarrel with a lesser evil?

Radical choices for the British university system

Well, what broader dimensions of this problem should Dearing have taken note of? Where should a debate on the long-term future of the British higher education system start?

Perhaps what is most striking is the failure to make very much of the distinctive qualities of the British higher education system, in contrast to its comparators, though in fact a *sotto voce* view that it is this system that needs to be preserved pervades the Report. The virtues of the British system are quietly attested to in the Report's published annexes. Students, who were the subjects of a survey, profess high levels of satisfaction with their education, mitigated only by their concern at the lack of sufficient resources, books, small group teaching, and the like. Throughput rates (the proportion of students graduating in a three year period) are reported to be very high by comparison with most competitor countries (though there has been evidence elsewhere that wastage-rates have been rising). Staff are shown to be part of a remarkably uniform academic culture, in their commitment to teaching, scholarship and research, as all necessary elements of their professional role. Students, especially full-time students in the 'pre-1992 universities', value the opportunities for broad self-development which British university education, with its high proportion of students living away from home, and its rather generous infrastructure, provides.

Against this the high-drop out, open-access, and low-contact higher education cultures of many other countries present a considerable contrast. One could regard our system, on this evidence, as a remarkable comparative national success. The question that one might ask about it is whether it could not become *more* of a national competitive resource than it already is, since it appears to offer a better educational experience than most other higher education systems, and since there are considerable prospective economic benefits to be gained from educating students from other countries in Britain.

The question of whether the historically high investment in and intensivity of the British university system should be retained or dispensed with also needs now to be revisited in a radical way. The scale of investment in human capital is directly related to its outputs, including its marketable outputs. A large number of high-grade 'industries' in this country — for example, science, drama, medicine, the production of works of art and design, music — are largely based on the high-quality inputs and outputs of specialist university schools and departments. Without these, their vital reservoirs of new talent would soon dry up. The British economy should be in general becoming more skill- and knowledge-intensive. We should thus be looking to create more specialist centres of educational quality, not fewer. Britain happens historically to have a system which supports and sustains this quality, one whose 'traditional' virtues are (for once) advantages in 'modern' conditions. We should be seeking to maintain this as a source of comparative advantage, not diminish it, from a perverse disbelief in or even fear of the outcomes of mass education.

If one took the argument for creating a British higher education system of real excellence seriously, one would of course have to face up to a number of problems. It is clear that standards in the post-1992 universities and pre-1992 universities are not comparable, on many measures, including that of student satisfaction[3]. If there is to be a 'unified system', does it not have to become a more unified, and less stratified one, and the measures considered which might bring this about? It seems likely that the 40% reduction in the unit of resource over twenty years has been damaging to standards. The reason is that education is so labour-intensive. It is not possible to economise on the quality and continuity of contact between students and teachers without impoverishing the learning process. It is not enough now merely to consolidate the present resourcing level, which is the best that the Dearing Committee seemed to believe was possible. It would certainly be helpful if alternative desirable unit levels of funding had been explicitly discussed, as the basis for considering different policy-options.

If the resourcing levels do not prove sufficient to maintain the high uniform standards that the Report advocates, it seems likely that pressures further to stratify and divide the system will re-emerge. Any further degradation of resource levels will provoke fresh demands from elite universities to be able to charge in fees what their markets will bear. A system offering broadly equal levels of provision to all qualified students will come at a high price, and there is little evidence that the government is willing to ask the populace to pay it.

A worrying precedent for higher education is now being set in the secondary schools. Here the gap in achievement between private and State schools is growing. This is obviously the result of the huge resource discrepancies between them — in London some successful 'public' schools have five times the resources per pupil of State schools[4]. (This of course despite all the smokescreens of national curricula and standard assessments which are ostensibly intended to raise *all* standards.) With these visible differences in standards and outcomes, pressure for selectivity among State schools also grows. At this point we have a university system which is more universalistic, egalitarian, and fair, than the secondary system. (This despite the fact that half the Oxbridge entry comes from private education.) But not for long, if present trends continue, and as the differential aspirations nurtured by experience in the secondary schools impact on impoverished universities. Top-up fees and increasingly privatised elite universities cannot be long in coming if present trends continue.

Another key issue which is only addressed in the weakest terms in the Dearing Report is that of equity between those who enter the higher education system and those who do not. This is the justification for the idea that graduates should be expected to pay back some of the additional earnings which have been made possible by their higher education. (Why, incidentally, is there no demand that employers should pay an additional tax on their graduate employees, since they are presumably also gaining added value as a result of the taxpayer's investment in them?) This is presented as an argument against a 'middle class welfare state', though needless to say the more logical remedy for this, a more progressive tax system, is deemed to be beyond the limits of debate.

What is also out of the frame of discussion is the idea that support for post-school education might be widened, removing the relative privilege of university entrants *vis-à-vis* those engaged in other forms of education and training. At an earlier stage it was suggested that there should be a system of *comprehensive* support for post-18 education, to provide a learning entitlement not dependent on academic qualification at A-level. One advantage of a more universal system of educational support would be to encourage a greater diversity of provision, which could be more responsive to labour market needs than the present system. One gross distortion in higher education funding has certainly been its privileging of full-time undergraduate programmes over all others. There seem many advantages in giving transferable educational entitlements to students which they could then 'invest' in whatever programmes seem most beneficial them, and which are also able to meet appropriate requirements of quality. Such a system, if it were in place, could also support a reinvigorated adult education programme (one of the casualties of years of defunding), which would increase the diversity and the available starting-points of post-school educational opportunity for individuals of all ages.

Any extension of educational entitlements to young people presently excluded from them will involve an element of redistribution. To achieve this, funding might be provided for only two years of full time equivalent post-school education, with student loans and/or tuition fees being required for any longer period. Such limits could meet the claims of justice between members of the same educational generation whilst still embodying the principle of one generation investing in the development of the next.

This practice of large-scale inter-generational transfers is perhaps one of the deepest structuring principles of the British system, though it is rarely recognised as such. The funding of the university system until now has been based on the assumption that education is an investment by the parental generation for the benefit of their children. The significance of a tax-based system, providing student fees and grants, is that the investment has been a collective one, by a generation of parents (and non-parents) for a whole generation of children. In paying taxes, one funded not only one's own children but other people's, and tax-aversion, in this as in other domains, signifies increasing unwillingness to do this.

Of course, no-one seriously imagines that the majority of students can in future pay the full costs of their higher education, with or without parental support. The development and occupational placement of their children will go on being a principal concern of most families. What will change under the new arrangements is that students must depend increasingly on their own families (and on their own mortgaged future earnings). And families, through the holding-down of tax levels, will have proportionately more resources to invest in their own children. The likely consequences of these changes for equal opportunities are quite obvious, as the privilege-offsetting qualities of the free tuition and means-tested grant system are weakened. Those whose families cannot or will not give support are weakened as a result. The families least able to give support, in emotional as well as material was, will be those most battered by economic and social circumstances. Thus the higher education reforms of the New Labour government and the Dearing Committee make their own small contribution to possessive individualism, and to the idea that each generation must stand on its own feet.

The British system has historically been committed to a strong principle of 'social reproduction'. Originally, of course, this was an elite function, in which new generations were socialised into the norms and mores of the upper class through educational institutions (public schools, ancient universities, Inns of Court, etc.) which provided for intensive cultural transmission. Individuals selected on grounds of educational merit from lower social positions were strongly 'sponsored', as Ralph Turner's (1961) model put it, to ensure that they met the requirements of their new social location. This originally aristocratic system was then extended in a meritocratic direction, to much of the middle class (initially via grammar schools and redbrick universities), which retained the earlier model of strong socialisation and 'guaranteed' educational outcomes though in a diluted form. In effect, a norm of familial transmission through the family was collectivised, and its functions transferred to other strong institutions. This origin is what has given the British higher education system its unusual cultural density. (This quality is usually replicated in the elite but not in the 'mass' sectors of most other national systems, because of its functional value in reproducing educational quality.)

The issue now should be whether this model could become a truly universalistic system, as additional populations gain access to it. The tacit assumptions of 'modernisation' seem to be that it can't, that the resources previously accorded for the development of 30% of 18 year olds are unaffordable when we start to think of 40%, 50% or 60%. Of course the rejection of this possibility, like the critique of middle-class over-use of the NHS, takes a deceptively pseudo-egalitarian form. Graduates must be made to feel guilty about receiving a free education, in order to legitimise the denial of this opportunity to others! But why should this future of funded, post-school education for all, be summarily rejected? At earlier stages, the aspirations to universal primary and secondary education were also considered to be utopian, but are now taken for granted. Why, in a 'knowledge-based society', should universal tertiary education seem so utopian? And why, at this stage, should the students be expected to pay for it themselves?

The rejection of this British model, which is probably what is taking place despite the universities' and the Dearing Committee's rearguard action on its behalf, will not take the form of its open repudiation. Equality of aspiration will be abandoned in the ostensible name of more opportunity, and not less. What will be constructed is a system which ostensibly offers more consumer choice, higher standards ('guaranteed' by audit), and greater flexibility. It will however be more competitive, provide less support, have higher rates of failure, and become more steeply stratified. It will become more of a mirror of the market society.

The softly-softly, consensual approach of Dearing is unlikely to be enough to defend the university system we still have, let alone the one we might like to have. If the system is to become more universalist in its scope, then the advocates of a more democratic university system need to become bolder and more visionary about it. If fragmentation and stratification through market forces is to be avoided, then greater emphasis has to be placed on 'voice', on finding ways in which the various stakeholders in universities can make themselves heard.

Strong internal accountability, to students and staff, should be encouraged, even though to make this a reality requires resources. Students cannot be effectively empowered in universities without professional staffs to represent them with some continuity. Universities, whose resources are often under-used for many weeks in each year, could make more of a contribution to local cultural and educational life than they do. Not only should universities be represented, as Dearing proposes, on the new regional authorities, but regional authorities should become important stakeholders in the universities themselves. If this leads to a greater diversification in the mission and character of different universities, so much the better.

330

Only if universities can demonstrate a commitment to being open, accountable and democratic institutions in the public domain, with a variety of forms of partnership with other institutions, will they succeed in making the claims on resources on the scale that they need. Holding actions are not enough. A democratic and universalist public sector will only survive in Britain if it finds some radical advocates who have not been cowed by the supposedly 'modernising', but actually marketising, revolution of the past two decades.

One explanation of the attrition to which higher education has been subject for twenty years is a self-fulfilling fear that more really must mean worse. This is the unspoken belief that needs to be challenged.

Notes

[1]   The HEFCE's report of the 1996 Research Assessment Exercise described a significant increase in both the amount and assessed quality of research submitted.

[2]   The National Committee of Inquiry into Higher Education (Dearing Committee), 1997. (Main Report, p. 45).

[3]   Evidence of differences in the quality of experience of students and level of satisfaction from students in the old and new universities is given in the Dearing Committee's 'Report 2: Full and part-time students in higher education: their experiences and expectations'.

[4]   See the *Financial Times* annual schools survey for 1997, headed 'Independent schools take stranglehold', *Financial Times* , October 11/12, 1997.

VI

AN HERETICAL POSTSCRIPT

Universities or Nurseries? Education, Professionals and Taxpayers

20

Martin Parker and Jude Courtney

Introduction and explanations

This closing chapter, a short polemic, is intended to serve as an evaluation of certain common assumptions about the values and function of higher education in the UK, and hence also as a critical commentary on many of the arguments put forward in this book. To put it another way, we intend to challenge what we see as some rather self-serving arguments that academics often put forward to justify scarce public funding being spent on their institutions. Our central contention — a potentially unpopular one for the readers and authors of this volume — is that we should allocate no more money to universities and possibly think about spending a great deal less. This is because other forms of education, and nursery education is our main example, are both more needy and more justifiable in a context in which public sector funding is limited and hence hard choices are likely to be made. Rather than engaging in the sterile debate between elitist nostalgia and mass modernisation that characterises so much of this book, we suggest a rather different choice - - that of the title of the chapter.

Now, we are not saying that we have a generalised hostility to universities in themselves. This chapter is not simply an exercise in perversity. In fact, we have both done rather well out of universities: one of us enjoys working at one and we would hope that one day our children might enjoy some kind of higher education too — though what kind is not a matter we explore here. However, we also both have personal and very meaningful experience of seeing the development of young children whilst progressing through primary education. We have seen the fantastic achievements that can be, and regularly are, made by these youngsters. It is therefore difficult for us to accept that nurseries are any less deserving and rather easy to argue that increased resources are justifiable. At the time this paper was first delivered to the Dilemmas of Mass Higher

Education conference, our three year old daughter had her nursery education cut to two and a half hours a day whilst her father was asked to teach only slightly more than that in a week. This state of affairs is the result of policy choices that, to us, seem rather questionable — to say the least.

We will begin by critically assessing some common defences of universities, including those put forward by various authors in this book, and then briefly contrast these high-sounding arguments with the mundane reality of higher education in the UK which is the subject of many of the previous chapters. We then move on to considering the problems of contemporary nursery education in this country before making some arguments for nursery education as opposed to university education. We conclude by suggesting that disentangling professional self-interest from arguments in favour of universities leaves us with some rather good reasons to move funding to nurseries, but do not then make any detailed further proposals as to the shape and size of the higher education that would be left. This chapter is an exercise in thinking against academic received wisdom and not a fully worked out manifesto. If it manages to shake up a few complacent nostalgics or modernisers, and helps to encourage a genuinely self-critical post-Dearing debate about what universities are for, then it will have achieved something.

Some defences of universities

Academics like to defend universities. Doctors like to argue that the National Health Service should have more money. Admirals, prison officers and art therapists no doubt suggest that their particular institutional location is misunderstood, underpaid and unappreciated. Most members of 'professional' occupations will argue for the inherent value of what they do, and claim that the institutions in which they work need more money, better regulated qualifications, more public sympathy and so on. We state this as a general truth. But if you doubt it is true for professional academics, and a wide range of other higher education professionals too, then listen to them talking in the photocopying room, around the dinner table and in the pub, and most of all read what they have written about universities — in this book and elsewhere. What academics usually say is that universities are good things and need defending because they are places where high level teaching and learning takes place, because they help generate a productive economy, because they preserve the value of scholarship and because their very existence guarantees democratic freedoms.

We will take each of these four suggestions in turn, but note before we do that the latter two arguments find particular expression in this volume as the implicit or explicit rationale for the various critiques of present 'marketisation', 'managerialisation', 'bureaucratisation', 'commodification' and so on that are put forward here (see Shore and Selwyn, Clark et al, Ainley, Cotterill and Waterhouse, and Edwards). In our terms, these chapters largely rest upon a nostalgic hostility to modernisation, to the quantitative and qualitative massification of higher education. This seems similar to what Andrew Lawson (this volume) very neatly captures as the *agon* (or eternal dispute) of culture versus utility, and it seems to us that this volume is biased towards the former language game rather than the latter. In the chapters that precede this one it is really only John O'Neill's argument about 'civic capital' which attempts to conjoin culture and utility to any degree, and even then the agon continues within his chosen couplet and in the way in which he uses it to criticise forms of utilitarian capital(ist) theory. Whether this chapter could break the terms of this dualism we are unsure, but then perhaps being crudely utilitarian about some policy matters allows you to argue more strongly for elitism in other domains. We will return to these matters in the conclusion, but first examine some of the four main defences of universities in a little more detail.

Firstly, there is a functional argument about defending institutions that carry out a particular kind of work (see for example Court, this volume). The suggestion here is that no other organisations are specialised enough to do this work as efficiently as universities can, even if the way they do it at present might need some re-engineering via new management, audit or funding mechanisms. After all, HE institutions get most of their finances through carrying out various kinds of 'high level' teaching and research because it is conventionally deemed that they are the best institutions to do these jobs. Whilst it is certainly difficult to decide exactly what is 'high level' (and hence what is 'low level', and the relationship between the two), this argument usually relies on assumptions about specialisation and the importance of certain forms of knowledge in a complex society. All these various 'high level' knowledges are hence best collected in one kind of institution which specialises in teaching and research — knowledge transmission and generation — at a level of abstraction or difficulty which is somehow beyond everyday capacities.

The problem here, it seems to us, is deciding exactly what is the 'organising principle' behind the kinds of things that universities do and then asking whether or not some of these things could be done by other institutions. In other words, it is worth considering who decides what is 'high' and what is 'low'. The chapters by Watson and Ainley (this volume) rely on rather different approaches to this question — an essentialism of knowledge versus some form of contested social constructionism. We tend to favour the latter as an explanation because essentialisms of knowledge seem to be rather suspect when we examine the odd range of subjects and levels that are, and are not, taught in 'higher' education. Universities teach for qualifications in social work practice, astrophysics, ceramic design, medical technology and the history of art. They do not usually provide qualifications in bricklaying practice, knitting theory, garden design, hair technology and the history of football. In general, the pattern of things that universities do specialise in teaching does not simply reflect an abstract and a-historical essential principle like 'specialisation' or 'complexity' but follows shifting lines of legitimacy established by social class, gender, professional monopoly, work/leisure distinctions, patterns of state intervention and so on. In other words, it is quite possible to argue that many of the things that universities teach are historically contingent both in terms of 'level' and disciplinary area. It might be that there is no necessary (functional) reason why such things might not be taught in schools, Further Education colleges, adult education classes, commercial organisations, professional or occupational institutions, training agencies and so on. Indeed, many formal knowledges are already successfully transmitted this way.

As for research, it is fair to say that the same argument could apply. A great deal of 'research' is already conducted in the institutions listed above as well as in various arms of the state such as the Home Office or Department for Education. Most importantly however, research is also carried out by ordinary people in public libraries, newsagents, garages, betting shops and so on. It is not usually named 'research' proper because the topics are not 'high level' and the results are unpublished in the terms defined by academics, but it would, again, seem to underline that there is again no functional reason why academics in universities are the only ones capable of this form of activity. So, we would suggest that, in terms of specialisation, universities are not necessarily bad at teaching and research of very particular kinds (though this itself has been questioned by many), but that there are certainly other institutions that are involved in very similar practices. Indeed, it might be argued that spreading these practices more widely and not concentrating them within one form of institution would be a reasonable policy for anyone interested in sponsoring a more democratic and decentralised society.

On to the second defence of universities, which is really an economic extension of the first but, as we noted, one that does not find much support amongst liberal academics who are opposed to utilitarian 'marketisation' (see for example Shore and Selwyn, this volume). That is to suggest that universities are hothouses for the practical and conceptual innovations that are essential to a productive economy. This was the argument that was initially used by government, the Confederation of British Industry and right wing think tanks to reshape and expand universities in the UK but has more recently 'trickled down' to the research councils and even HE trade unions: "The country's economic prosperity depends on maintaining the excellence of our universities in both research and teaching" (AUT,1995: 2). In general terms this is an argument that is easier to use by those in the so called 'sciences' — whether natural or social — but one that has found particular expression in the huge expansion of business and management related teaching and research. The idea is often that human and material 'innovation' is a process that universities are good at fostering (though poor at exploiting) so pushing universities into a position where 'market forces' can shape these 'innovations' into 'entrepreneurial' practices will in turn lead to a more successful national economy (see Miller and Edwards, this volume). Universities will generate new ideas, technologies, computer programmes, qualifications and people and these will help the state move to a knowledge intensive, high skill, high wage economy. The 'white heat' of technology which modernisers of all political sympathies can call upon — as the Engineering and Physical Sciences Research Council titled its 1994 mission statement — 'Research and Training for Wealth Creation'.

Well, again this may be the case but, as Berg concluded almost a quarter of a century ago (1973) and the Confederation for British Industry conceded in 1994, there is little evidence of it. To put it crudely, the United States has more graduates and universities than anywhere else but it has not prevented severe economic downturn, chronic unemployment, wide social stratification and some of the worst urban dystopias to be found on the planet. In the UK, as Brown and Scase have argued, corporate recruitment is still largely based on cultural capital and the huge expansion of graduate numbers has done little to develop a knowledge based meritocracy (1994). In other words, the language of 'human capital', transferable skills, university science parks and technology transfer are certainly not the panacea that many optimists like to think they might be, and anyway, as any economist would remind us, there might be many other reasons why national economies succeed or fail (see O'Neill, this volume). So, national success could be the cause of HE expansion, not the result, and success will also be related to other factors such as technological change, natural resources, socio-cultural arrangements and so on. Even if these alternative cause arguments are not accepted the functional argument still applies. There are many other sites and institutions where 'innovation' is sponsored — the media, research and development labs, schools, colleges and public libraries. Universities have no very convincing monopoly over new ideas — and there are many historical and contemporary reasons to see them as reactive and conservative institutions in terms of innovation. Careers, politics, publications, research funding constraints, teaching and a form of disciplinary 'streaming' might all contribute to a cobwebbed lack of courage and not a hotbed of bubbling creativity (on conformity in research see Lee and Harley, this volume).

Far from this 'philistine' economic argument is the defence of universities based on their contribution to liberal culture, the 'civic mind', and this is a position which the majority of the chapters in this volume implicitly or explicitly wish to support. In this sense, humanities or human science academics often suggest that their institutions preserve the values of scholarship and inquiry that would otherwise be lost in an increasingly commercial world. The existence of universities allows some individuals to take on the task of protecting, annotating and discussing our shared cultural heritage. It allows someone the time to produce the definitive biography of Henry V, to catalogue and comment on the poems of T S Eliot or calculate the average number of floating voters in general elections in Stoke-on-Trent from 1945 to the present day. If universities were not properly funded then how would such things get done? Now, we are not going to suggest that these are bad things to do, merely that we wonder how intrinsically valuable they are. 'Scholarship' is a word that is usually held in awe by many academics since it refers to a kind of careful dullness about an obscure topic, or carefully synthesising the work of others into a review of writings on an obscure topic. The 'problems' identified by most academics are simply not problems for most people. Effectively, this means that most academics write a huge number of words that are unread, and if they are read it is by colleagues in the same circle. According to citations databases, the vast majority of pieces that get referenced at all are only referenced once — and usually in another piece by the same author. This has become even more true since the Research Assessment Exercises so decisively made publication a measure of academic worth. Now this might be a diverting way of keeping academics busy, but surely we should ask whether it has any more value than a parlour game. If this is the case, then why should this particular hobby — as opposed to pigeon racing for example — receive tax payers subsidy? After all, it is unlikely that the Department for Education would vote monks a large sum of money in order that they could spend time illuminating manuscripts and discussing the substance of angels. To emphasise the point, we are not suggesting that we want to discourage people from doing 'scholarship' if it makes them and others happy, but we see no necessary functional connection between this specialist practice, state funding and cultural transmission. As Illich seemed to suggest, well-funded public libraries, good adult education and co-ordinated 'skill exchanges' would probably achieve much the same result at considerably less cost (1973).

The final argument is the boldest claim of all, that the very existence of universities guarantees the democratic freedoms that we all hold so dear. Take for example David Triesman, one time general secretary of the Association of University Teachers. He described the 1995 settlement for HE as 'vandalism' — calling to mind a tribe of philistine barbarians smashing the statues in the groves of academe. Attacking the short term accountancy focus of the current government he suggests that:

> The pursuit of knowledge and its transmission, the creation of a sophisticated citizenry which understands the sciences, arts, democracy and mutual responsibilities in its society are themselves rich goals. (Triesman, 1996)

Universities are here articulated as the crowning glory of a state — a publicly funded public sphere in which reflection upon politics, economy, science, culture and so are seen to be good in themselves. The underpinning concept here is intellectual freedom — the capacity of academics and students to write, think and say what they like without fear of suppression or ridicule. As long as we defend the existence of free universities, the critical thinkers they protect and the critical citizens they educate then it is difficult for despotic regimes to rule comfortably.

Despite what we said in the last paragraph there are certainly some good points to this argument, but we wonder about the particular importance given to universities within it. A democratic society requires that freedoms be protected in a variety of different places — universities are central to this project but so are schools, newspapers, television stations, workplaces, political assemblies and so on. Again, it is not hard to suggest that there is no functional reason for asserting a particular priority to universities. It might well be said that the picture painted of universities by people like David Triesman is hopelessly romantic, or dangerously deceptive. For the general public, the actual freedoms they protect seem often to be the freedom for students to get drunk and academics to be funded for conferences in exotic locations at the same time that they cancel classes. In any case, in intellectual terms it is easy to see universities as narrow, conservative institutions — far more concerned with self-defence and self-aggrandisement than with protecting democratic freedoms and attempting to teach as if it were really a subversive activity. As an example, the conference version of this paper brought one of the authors a great deal of criticism from within his own institution. After a rather playful summary was published in *The Guardian* (Millar, 1996), he was discussed at the Vice Chancellor's committee, asked to put forward strategies for 'damage limitation' by the University's Head of Public Relations and advised (in a genuinely friendly way) by his Dean and Head of Department that further activities of this sort would be damaging for his career. It would seem that academic freedom becomes a matter for restraint when the public image of the institution is at stake.

In sum, and in the broadest of terms, we want to suggest that universities are moderately good at teaching and research but so are other institutions, that some of this research very occasionally does makes some people healthy, rich and/or happy and that they are one of the many places where intellectual freedom is and should be protected. All these are good things — that is to say, not usually in themselves bad things — but we also argue that these descriptions can apply, in some measure, to many other forms of public and private sector organisation — particularly other education and research institutions. Unfortunately, the corollary of this is that they actually don't apply to a great deal of existing higher education — a point which is commented on nostalgically throughout most of this volume. This is largely because existing higher education has widely-recognised problems that damage its ability to function in the idealised way that its defenders like to claim it can or should. Amongst these are increasing instrumentalism and credentialism amongst students, encouraged by modular degree systems and participation which now usually rests upon the economics of working and borrowing (see Walters and Baldwin, this volume). To this might be added larger class numbers, newly managerialist Vice Chancellors attempting to introduce innovations like Business Process Re-engineering and Total Quality Management, poor accommodation and equipment, underfunded libraries, academics who are often encouraged to regard teaching as an interference to research and local communities that are often hostile to the effect that large numbers of students are having on their neighbourhood. In sum, universities are getting worse at much of what they claim to do best.

In an earlier publication one of the authors put forward a diagnosis of the contemporary university which relied heavily on a condemnation of its present structural, managerial and subjective constitution (Parker and Jary, 1995; see also Hartley, 1995 for a similar account). Comparing new forms of university education to fast food, he suggested that it was necessary to rethink the aims and means of higher education in order to provide something more filling and wholesome. Well, rather than reforming the McUniversity towards liberal cultural ends — that guarantee his continued employment and protect his professional autonomy for 'principled' reasons — he now wants to suggest that it might be better to contract the system and use the money that has been saved to expand nursery education instead. This is not because the contemporary university couldn't be improved, perhaps by embracing a modernising McDonaldisation more fully (see Lucas and Webster, and Watson in this volume; also Parker, 1998). However, the professional, cultural and economic interests alluded to above suggest that it can't be improved that much without either becoming a mechanism for the generation of technicist kitsch (see Lilley, this volume) or being subject to massive institutionalised resistance. Nurseries, on the other hand, certainly can.

Some facts about nurseries

It is rather difficult for British higher education academics to complain about underfunding or policy chaos once they have discovered something about funded nursery education. Comparatively, the UK's provision is very poor, as noted by the National Commission on Education's 'Learning to Succeed' (1993; see also TES 1996: 3). The government's own figures consistently overstate provision because they include rising fives and charitable status pre-school playgroups so a more accurate figure is hard to come by. According to the British Association for Early Childhood Education, there were 580 state-funded nursery schools in England and Wales in 1990. If the average roll is generously estimated at 100, then that would give us 58,000 children receiving education in a nursery in a given year — though 90% of those would be part time, that is to say about twelve and a half hours per week. If we include a similar ratio for Scotland and conservatively assume there are about half a million children in the age group, that gives a figure of about 10% of three and four year old children nationally receiving some form of nursery-based state-funded education. This figure does not include pre-school playgroups, social services nurseries or nursery classes attached to schools. The local variation in provision is huge — ranging from 0% in Gloucestershire and 1% in Somerset to 56% in West Glamorgan and 69% in Hounslow. Staffordshire comes out at 22% but this again conceals patterns of variation. Though the county has 27 nurseries, 20 of them are located in the Stoke-on-Trent area which contains about a third of the county's population. This is because of the historically high number of working mothers in the pottery industry. In the mid 1990s, adjusting this imbalance by building new nurseries was simply beyond the means of the county council but making a decision to only fund half time places meant being able to double the numbers getting education and to look better on paper.

So, variation in provision is hence largely down to the historical vagaries and general underfunding of education authorities. After all, most of them would like to provide nursery education if it were possible. However, under the 1980 Education Act there is no legal requirement for education authorities to do anything for 3-4 year olds — it is a discretionary service. However, this is a stance that has been questioned in several subsequent documents. The DES White Paper 'Better Schools' (1985) recommended that particular attention should be given to the maturity of children entering schools at 4 or 5. The House of Commons Select Committee on Education Provision for the Under Fives (1988) suggested that:

> ... early education should be seen not as something separate and apart, but rather as the first step on the path into a relevant, coherent and integrated curriculum (para 2.5)

The report went on to suggest "steady expansion" of provision until it is available to all three and four year old children "whose parents desire it for them". Despite this, the 1989 Children Act offered some very contradictory messages to nursery educators and, in 1992, Government Training funds for Under Fives education were removed from LEAs. A year later the National Commission on Education's 'Learning to Succeed' (1993) re-emphasised the neglect of younger children in state education policy. Most recently, the 1995-96 nursery vouchers scheme merely suggested moving existing money into a new marketplace despite beginning with the Secretary of State endorsing the 'widespread recognition' that nursery education brought 'benefits' (1996a: 2). From 1997 education authorities have been given less money for nursery education but have to persuade parents to spend a voucher with a value of £1,100 with them, as opposed to private providers who would compete for the vouchers and attempt to make a profit. In Staffordshire, the voucher is currently worth less than county costings for a part time nursery place, so it is quite possible that parents will have to top up the vouchers themselves. A watered down version of the 'desirable' curriculum for nursery education issued at the same time attempted to quietly ensure that these new providers would not find the educational threshold too demanding (DfEE, 1996b). The effects of this new 'market' have yet to be worked through, but since it involved no new money, and required that providers invest in marketing to compete with each other and that both providers and the state invest in a validation process familiar to academics, it seems unlikely that the quality of nursery education will increase. In any case, the Labour government elected in 1997 has committed itself to reverse this policy, but has offered no new money or policy in its place.

These policy confusions and general underfunding lead to some severe problems within nursery schools themselves. Since they are often very small in size, and also a small interest group at local level compared to primary and secondary schools, there are problems with training and career structure that are rarely addressed as distinct. In fact, early childhood education has been removed from the initial teacher training curriculum. To add to these problems, the additional effects of compulsory competitive tendering and the local manage-ment of schools are very severe for small units like nurseries which need LEA support in a wide variety of areas. For example, in our daughter's school there was no more money to pay for a library van visit because the head teacher had spent over budget on books for the school library. Learning the language of accounting and unit costs and also dealing with newly marketised 'Quality Learning Services' organisations was both difficult and time consuming for this teacher. Add to this problems with clerical assistance, special needs support, co-ordinating parental involvement and a formula funding equation that is inade-quate and you have organisations that survive by continual recourse to charity and cost cutting. Weekly cash donations, frequent materials donations, permanent fund raising, voluntary activities from parents, abolishing meals and so on are necessary in order that many state nurseries continue to function at all.

Many of these difficulties are exacerbated by stereotypical assumptions about the gender of the nursery workers and the age of the children they educate. The overwhelming majority of nursery workers are female, yet they have to fight for resources at local government level from compulsory primary and secondary schools with more male head teachers, better co-ordination and larger budgets because their schools are larger. This is not to say that there is hostility to the needs of nurseries in education authorities or schools, simply that nursery education is not organised as an effective interest group. Further to that, a powerful set of assumptions about 3-4 year old children does not encourage nursery education (as opposed to a playschool or childminding model) to be taken professionally seriously. As our female nursery head told us, there is a hierarchy of status from nursery to primary to secondary that has a great effect on resource allocation. She simply can't play the games that other Head Teachers can.

So, the picture of nursery education in the UK is bleak. But need it be that way, or is it the result of particular policy choices that put universities at the top of the status hierarchy and nurseries at the bottom? Compared to nurseries, universities seem very well funded and until they have to hold jumble sales to pay for materials we will not be persuaded otherwise. The next section will put forward some arguments in favour of reversing, or at least flattening, the hierarchy.

What universities don't do

> If we don't find the funds now to pay the costs of education, what price shall we paylater for ignorance? (LSI, 1995: 8)

The most common justification for nursery education is in terms of its contribution to spectacular developmental changes in children. Though of course these arguments have often being deployed in a sexist and reactionary way, with regard to John Bowlby's 'maternal deprivation' thesis for example, it seems widely accepted that the impact of early experience on the child is much greater than that later in life and that learning (whether 'good' or 'bad') is far more effective in young children than it is in young adults. Patterns of sociability, eating habits, motor skills, IQ scores and a host of other features are supposedly related to early years experiences (Nutbrown, 1994). Even if the strong version of *tabula rasa* social imprinting is not accepted, it seems to make intuitive sense that experiences between the ages of 3 and 4 are likely to have more shaping influence than those between 18 and 21 or later (see Handy, 1995: 208). As the nursery school head teacher put it, children get self-esteem, confidence, basic skills and development of emotional, social, intellectual and physical skills "during their formative years". "Get the foundations right and the rest will follow". As John O'Neill's civic capital argument implies (Chapter 18), it is simply perverse to push forward an elitist credentialism in universities at the expense of a serious consideration of the general education of both the minority who go to university and the majority who do not.

Another justification of nursery education builds on the first but tends to stress the contribution of early years experiences to patterns of social inequality rather than child development *per se*. Central to the 1960s US Headstart and High/ Scope programmes was some sense that this was money invested in the future of deprived children. The Perry Preschool study in Michigan, comparing children who had experienced the High/Scope nursery curriculum with those who had not, seemed to demonstrate some very significant differences in offending and economic success twenty years after nursery school (High/Scope: no date, TES 1996: 2). To put it rather more brutally, a comment on another of these programmes suggested that through "every dollar spent on pre-school education, seven dollars were saved through increased tax contributions from those in employment and saving on special schooling, welfare payments and criminal damage" (Staffordshire LEA, 1994: 3-4). More recently, the State of Georgia has invested $210 million in offering a daily pre-school class to all four year olds in the hope that the eventual savings will be in the region of a factor of ten (*Newsweek*, 1997). Whether this is the case or not, it can be an added justification for concentrating on areas of social deprivation. In other words, a moral concern with social justice, remedying the 'unequal chances' of social class as our interviewee put it, can be justified in utilitarian terms as lowering the tax burden in twenty or thirty years time.

A further argument is a simple statistical one in terms of the present, not the future. At present about one third of the age cohort enter higher education. As many have argued, the majority who benefit from this burden on all taxpayers are the middle class, and this relation holds good even under conditions of continued expansion (see for example Berg, 1973, Brown and Scase 1994). Expanding state provision for 3-4 year olds from the current 10% might genuinely open doors to more education for greater numbers. This might be further increased if there were then also lower drop out rates at primary and secondary school. In other words, it might be a more economical way to spend money on education in particular because it is simply likely to reach more people, more cheaply, and is less likely to be 'hijacked' by dubious professional interests.

So, there we have three fairly robust arguments in favour of spending money on nurseries. It seems to be very beneficial for children, it might save us money in the long run and we can guarantee that we will be reaching more people. All these things might be true of universities as well — but the connections are less direct and the costs much greater. Of course it will cost money to provide state funded nursery education — one estimate of providing full time education for four year olds and half a day for three year olds is about a billion pounds (Kingston, 1995: 2). Whilst this is clearly not cheap, it is within the capacity of the higher education teaching and research budget to contribute a large amount, if not all, of this funding. As we have suggested, this would require a radical alteration in the size and/or practice of university education, but perhaps it is now time that this taboo should be discussed and not avoided in the name of either culture or utility.

Conclusions: universities or nurseries?

Well, ideally both. But the central assumption of this paper is that there is not enough money for both, and that there is not enough money for social services, legal aid, cheap housing, cycle lanes in cities, hip replacements, probation officers, pensions, community policing and open heart surgery. In other words, and as we said at the start of the paper, we are assuming that choices need to be made because late modern welfare democracies are simply unable to fulfill all the expectations of all their stakeholders (see some of the authors in Halpern, 1996). So, we propose cutting university budgets by as much as is necessary to meet the recommendations of the House of Commons Select Committee on Education Provision for the Under Fives (1988) — that it should be available to all three and four year old children "whose parents desire it for them". We believe this will be a better way to spend the money, not because we think universities should be closed down for some reason but simply because we do not believe that the voices of liberal academics should take precedence over those of nursery age children. It seems to us a sad irony that an old and powerful profession should defend its quadrangle with arguments that claim the economic, cultural and political high ground at the same time as they do so little to evaluate the value of their own practices.

The Committee of Vice Chancellors and Principles entitled its evidence to the Dearing committee 'Our Universities Our Future' but we wonder just who this 'our' is supposed to refer to. Berg quotes James W Kuhn comparing academics to robber barons along the Rhine who demand their toll before allowing travellers entrance to certain jobs, statuses, incomes and so on (1973: 188). Like Kuhn and Berg (and very like Illich) we are suspicious of professionals' claims to represent anyone but themselves and would rather sponsor a model of higher education that disaggregated its various institutions and functions in order to disempower its powerful professional monopoly. To borrow and twist Patrick Ainley's phrase — the self-defensive ideology of professionalism seems to be the problem. We would like to move away from the mediaeval undergraduate studying for credentials in the monolithic and expansionist university and towards life-long learning in a wider variety of sites (see Handy, 1995 for some similar ideas). We would like liberal or scientific education, funded research and professional training to be de-institutionalised and possibly separated in order to be more precise in the aiming of resources to particular domains of activity. Finally, we would like an end to the centralised audit of research productivity which has done so much to damage the 'education' which is intended to take place in higher education institutions. And yes, this de-monopolisation or de-institutionalisation might result in fewer students, fewer academics and fewer universities in the short run — and possibly none at all in the long run. But then we have dispensed with many other mediaeval institutions in the last eight hundred years — there may be no reason other than habit and the increasingly desperate rhetoric of academics to hang on to this one.

In saying this we are assuming that, ultimately, universities and nurseries are involved in similar educational projects — they are more similar than different and that moving money from one to the other may increase demand for some form of post-compulsory liberal education once the children are grown up. What form this will take is quite another matter, but, as we have argued, for reasons of both culture and utility it should ideally not look very much like the present system. Academic egos may not feel particularly comfortable with the comparison between the two types of institution, but maybe nursery teachers will finally feel that they are receiving long overdue recognition. This is not, of course, to argue that the compulsory and further education sectors are not also undervalued. They are. But the point of this essay was to highlight some dramatic contrasts in order that the debate about current university funding and future policy choices might be set in a less abstract context.

To conclude this chapter and bring us back to the title of the volume, let us continue with the polemical contrasts by putting one dilemma of mass higher education in quite brutal terms. A student writes another poor quality essay on something he is only vaguely interested in after being at the pub most of the evening. It is marked and sparsely annotated at two o'clock in the morning by a lecturer who has another sixty essays to go. They give it another 2.1 — just like 60% of the material marked in their institution. Somewhere else, a four year old writes her name for the first time, reads her first book, gains confidence in her ability to make friends and decides she wants to be a mountain climber when she grows up. Which would you like to spend your taxes on? Further to that, which do you think would be a better way of spending money?

> We need the vision to plan for whole human beings who have a clear and realistic personal identity whatever combination of religious background, racial origins, gender, ability or disability that may be. Children who know who they are will have the confidence to love, learn and communicate in a world of mathematical, scientific, aesthetic and technological experiences. Children who can collaborate and learn together in harmony with other people are likely to respect and value differences. Children who are able to have intimate responsive relationships with their significant adult will have better access to relevant early learning experiences. Children who play in inspirational, safe and challenging environments will take these values into adulthood and pass them onto future generations. An ethos of respect for and dignity in childhood may be set from the cradle. (Rouse and Griffin, 1992: 155-6)

Acknowledgement

Thanks to Ms J K Plant for being interviewed and for providing many of the references.

References

AUT (1995) *The Way Forward: Promoting Professionalism in University Salaries and Conditions*. Association of University Teachers.

BAECE (1990) *Nursery Schools: A View from Within*. London: British Association for Early Childhood Education.

Berg, I. (1973) *The Great Training Robbery*. Harmondsworth: Penguin.

Brown, P. and Scase, R. (1994) *Higher Education and Corporate Realities*. London: UCL Press.

DfEE (1996a) *Nursery Education Scheme: The Next Steps*. Department for Education and Employment.

DfEE (1996b) *Nursery Education: Desirable Outcomes for Children's Learning*. Department for Education and Employment.

Halpern, D. (ed) (1996) *Options for Britain: A Strategic Policy Review*. Aldershot: Gower.

Handy, C. (1995) *The Empty Raincoat*. London: Arrow.

Hartley, D. (1995) 'The McDonaldisation of Higher Education: Food for Thought', *Oxford Review of Education*, 21 (4): 409-423.

High/Scope (no date) *Significant Benefits*. London: High/Scope Institute (UK).

Illich, I. (1973) *Deschooling Society*. Harmondsworth: Penguin.

Kingston, P (1995) 'Steep Climb on the Nursery Slope', *Guardian Education*, June 27: 2-3.

LSI (1995) *What Price Ignorance? The Case for More School Funding*. London: Local Schools Information.

Millar, S. (1996) 'Off the Wall', *Guardian Education*, April 16: 8.

National Commission on Education (NCE) (1993) *Learning to Succeed?*.

Newsweek (1997) 'Some HOPE for College', 3rd February: 45.

Nutbrown, C. (1994) *Threads of Thinking: Young Children Learning and the Role of Early Education*. London: Paul Chapman.

Parker, M. (1997) 'The Middle Classes and Mass Culture: Cultural Elitism and McDonalds', in M. Alfino, J. Caputo and R. Wynyard (eds) *McDonaldisation Revisited: Essays on the Commodification of Culture*. Westport, CT: Greenwood.

Parker, M. and Jary, D. (1995) 'The McUniversity: Organisation, Management and Academic Subjectivity', *Organisation*, 2 (2): 319-338.

Rouse, D. and Griffin, S. (1992) 'Quality for the Under Threes', in G. Pugh (ed) *Contemporary Issues in the Early Years*. London: Paul Chapman.

Staffordshire LEA (1994) *Policy Framework: Under Fives*.

TES (1996) 'Extra: Early Years', *Times Education Supplement*, Feb 2.

Triesman, D. (1996) 'In Defence of Investment', *AUT Bulletin*, January.

Index

Hopfl, H. 212
House of Commons Select Committee on
     Education Provision for Under Fives
     (1988) 343, 347
Hughes, C. and Tight, M. 128
human capital theory 304-5, 309
humanities 19, 289-301, 339
Hutton, W. 48, 49, 154;
     atrogenesis 232-3
Illich, I. 340
Imperial College (London University) 118
imposition theory 259
Individual Learning Accounts 249
industry and HE links 53-4, 57
information technology 8
institutional stratification 94, 96-100
intellectual capital 8
intellectual freedom 340-1
intellectual prostitution 178, 182N
inter-disciplinarity 7
International Monetary Fund (IMF) 43J
Jack, D. and Jack, R. 215
Jameson, F. 254, 256
Jarratt Report (1985) 209-10
Jary, D.
     Gatley, D.A. and Broadbent, L. 83-101
     and Parker, M. 209-10
Jessop, B. *et al* 49
Joseph, Sir K. 282

K
kakistocracy 19, 290-1, 300
Karabel, J. 100 and Brint, S. 85, 95, 96
Keele University 101N
Kennedy, P.M. 41, 42
Kent University 134-5, 138-41
Kerman, L. 214
kindergarten 311
Kingham, Sir J. 128
Kitsch 173, 179-81
knowledge 33, 37, 50, 136;
     as a commodity 254-6;
     mode one/two production 38, 39
Kogan, M. and Becher, T. 258-9, 263, 264
Kolbert, J. 101N
Kuhn, J.W. 347

L
Landells, M. and Butler, A. 217, 218
language games 255
Lauder, H. and Brown, P. 271

lawyers, women 215
league tables 8, 321;
     learning in a civic society 309, 309-
     classical 274-5;
     communities 224-6;
     compact 156-8, 160;
     experiential 265, 267-8
lifelong 20, 52, 79, 265, 310
learning society 53, 134, 142
lecture scripts 175-6
Lee, F.A. and Harley, S. 202
legitimation principle 254, 256
Lewin, K. 259
life-styles 35
lifelong learning 20, 52, 79, 265, 310
line management 168
Linstead, S. 179-80;
     Sinclair, J. and Brewis, J. 183N
Local Enterprise Companies (LECs) 53
London University 275;
     Imperial College 118
Low, W. and Glennerster, H. 89
Lunneborg, P. 213
Lyon, K. and West, J. 213
Lyotard, J-F. 18, 33, 254, 255-6, 261, 273-4

M
McDonaldisation 15, 173-84, 342
Machiavelli, N. 210
MacIntyre, A. 283, 284
Mackay, L., Scott, P. and Smith, D. 66
McLaughlin, E., Clarke, J. and Cochrane, A. 2
Macmillan, H. 278
maintenance grant system 76, 239, 240
Malmberg, A. and Maskell, P. 52
management practice 15, 48, 57;
     total quality (TQM) 165, 166-7
managerialism 4, 6, 16;
     commercialism growth 290
masculine 212-15;
     public sector 210-12;
     women 16, 207-20
Mansbridge, J. 286
marketisation 4, 44-5, 47-8, 50, 58-9, 153-70,
     319-22
Marshall, A. 315
Marshall, J. 218
mass HE 3-5, 9-10, 29-40;
     dilemmas 4
maternal deprivation thesis 345
mature students 89, 142, 247